1992

JUSTICE UPON
PETITION

TITLES OF RELATED INTEREST

*Court patronage and corruption in early
Stuart England*
Linda Levy Peck

The first imperial age
Geoffrey Scammell

European society 1500–1700
Henry Kamen

JUSTICE UPON PETITION

The House of Lords and the
Reformation of Justice 1621–1675

JAMES S. HART

HarperCollins*Academic*
An imprint of HarperCollins*Publishers*

Published by
HarperCollins*Academic*
77–85 Fulham Palace Road
Hammersmith, London W6 8JB, UK

First published in 1991

British Library Cataloguing in Publication Data
Hart, James
Justice upon petition: The House of Lords and the
reformation of justice, 1621–1675.
I. Title
347.42

ISBN 0–04–942202–2

Library of Congress Cataloging in Publication Data
Hart, James S.
Justice upon petition: the House of Lords and the reformation of
justice, 1621–1675/James S. Hart.
Includes bibliographical references and index.
ISBN 0–04–942202–2 (hb)
1. Courts – Great Britain – History.   2. Justice, Administration of –
Great Britain – History.   3. Great Britain. Parliament House of
Lords – History.   I. Title.
KD6850.H355   1991
347.42'039 — dc20   91 – 19504
[344.20739]   CIP

Typeset in 10 on 12 point Garamond Light by
Falcoln Typographic Art Ltd., Edinburgh & London
and printed in Great Britain at the
University Press, Cambridge

*To the memory of
my parents*

Contents

Acknowledgements

I would like to thank all those who have contributed in various ways to the writing of this book. Since it began as a Cambridge University PhD thesis, first acknowledgements should go to the Master and Fellows of Sidney Sussex College, who elected me Junior Research Fellow and provided me with the very best possible conditions and company in which to pursue my research. My many friends and colleagues in the seminar in early modern British history, chaired by Drs Morrill and Cannadine, and Professor Pearl, and those in the seminar in Tudor history chaired by Professor Sir Geoffrey Elton, will know without my mentioning them by name how grateful I am for their continuing friendship and thoughtful advice.

I would also like to express my deep appreciation to the staff of the House of Lords Records Office, and in particular to David Johnson, Steve Ellison and Katherine Bligh, for their unfailing kindness, courtesy and efficiency. Their willingness to extend themselves on my behalf, in all manner of ways over many years, has made research in that office a constant pleasure. John Post of the Public Record Office and Janice Fairholm of the Cambridge University Library deserve special mention as well for their many acts of kindness. I am also very grateful for the continuing assistance and courtesy of the staff of the Institute for Historical Research in London.

I would like to thank the Southwestern Bell Corporation of Oklahoma and the University of Oklahoma Research Council for their generous grants which made possible essential research trips to London.

Over the years I have benefited greatly from conversations with and advice from many individuals. Sir Geoffrey Elton, Anthony Fletcher, Elizabeth Read Foster, Patrick Higgins, Derek Hirst, Mark Kishlansky, Sheila Lambert, Judith Maltby, Linda Levy Peck, Peter Salt, Jonathan Scott, Johann Sommerville and Anne Weikel have all been very generous with their ideas, their help and their honest criticism. I would also like to give special thanks to Guy and Cathy Gronquist who have done so much over the years to relieve the rigours and stress of research in London with their generous hospitality and their warm companionship.

My greatest debt of gratitude, however, is to John Morrill. As research supervisor, teacher, mentor and friend he has been an unfailing source of inspiration and support. Without his encouragement and enthusiasm, his knowing guidance, his seemingly infinite patience and his extraordinary kindness this book would never have been written.

Abbreviations

APC	*Acts of the Privy Council* ed. J. R. Dasent *et al* (32 vols; London, 1890–1907)
BIHR	*Bulletin of the Institute of Historical Research*
BL	British Library
CD 1621	*Commons Debates, 1621* ed. Notestein, Relf and Simpson (7 vols; New Haven, Conn., 1935)
CJ	*Commons Journals*
CSPD	*Calendar of State Papers, Domestic* (London 1856–97)
DNB	*Dictionary of National Biography*, ed. L. Stephan and S. Lee (63 vols; London 1885–1900)
EHR	*English Historical Review*
HJ	*Historical Journal*
HLRO	House of Lords Record Office, London
HMC	Historical Manuscript Commission
JBS	*Journal of British Studies*
LJ	*Lords Journals*
PC	Privy Council
PRO	Public Record Office, London
SP	State Papers

Introduction

Parliament in the seventeenth century was a bicameral institution. Contemporary Englishmen certainly recognized and appreciated that fact. Modern historical scholarship, by and large, has not. Until very recently studies of early modern English Parliaments have almost invariably focused on the political and procedural evolution of the House of Commons, while the parallel history of the House of Lords has been largely ignored. The reasons for the neglect are not hard to find. The modern fascination with – not to say reverence for – evolving democratic institutions has naturally made the House of Commons a more attractive field of study. Its membership – forged through the dynamics of electoral politics – has always seemed by nature more vocal, more volatile and more plainly representative of contemporary issues and concerns, both at the centre and in the localities. The House of Lords, by comparison, has appeared staid, traditional, self-absorbed. Its membership was not forged at all, but evolved instead through the combined accidents of inherited birthright and royal favour (and, occasionally, royal financial exigency) and to that extent it was not really representative at all. Lacking any popular mandate, it has always seemed (certainly in the traditional Whig view) almost an anachronism, its responsibilities and actions consequently of less immediate importance to the wider history of Parliament.

That view, however, is clearly based on a misconception. It assumes that Parliament was by design a political institution and that the contributions of its constituent parts must be assessed in those terms. It was not. Parliament, as Professor Elton has recently reminded us, was a court and however often it might have become a forum for important political debate, it was still primarily responsible for (and largely preoccupied with) the making of law.[1] By that definition the House of Lords must claim equal status and ought to command equal attention. It should do so not least because it served as a full partner with the House of Commons in the daily business of drafting, debating and amending legislation – a responsibility it undertook with great seriousness and, it should be said, with an equal commitment to improving the general good of the common weal.

But it should be given equal consideration for another reason. The House of Lords also served as a court in a conventional sense – as a judicial tribunal. In fact, over the course of the seventeenth century the

1

Lords were as often engaged in applying and enforcing the law as they were in making it. Historians have only acknowledged that in part – in so far as it involved the famous criminal proceedings on impeachments which punctuated parliamentary affairs at moments of political crisis. But ancient custom and statute law had actually conferred on the upper house a much broader legal authority. It could be called upon, for instance, to correct errors in lower court proceedings, to decide suits long delayed in other venues and, more generally, to offer remedy in cases where no extant law applied, or where the law itself remained unclear. It had authority in fact to act as the court of last resort for any party who had been victimized by failings in the legal system. For a variety of reasons, it had not been required to exercise that authority for almost 300 years. But it was required to do so in the seventeenth century on a scale that would surpass anything which had gone before and in ways that would altogether redefine the notional responsibilities of the High Court of Parliament.

This book sets out to tell that story: to trace the reemergence of the House of Lords as a court for private litigation and to examine its procedures, the scope of its powers and the nature of the legal remedies it provided. It is a story of singular importance to both constitutional and parliamentary history. The revival of private party judicature in 1621, though seemingly inconspicuous at the time, eventually transformed the internal dynamics of the house. The decision to settle a handful of cases in 1621 opened the door (no doubt inadvertently) to private suitors, and in every Parliament thereafter the Lords were inundated with petitions from individuals seeking some form of extraordinary legal remedy. The hearing and adjudication of these disputes commanded ever-increasing amounts of the Lords' time and attention and, as a consequence, the day-to-day operations of the house inevitably changed. The Lords now had to assume the responsibilities – and meet the demands – of a sitting court and that required new rules, new administrative procedures and new assignments for their personnel. In the process, the Lords also had to reintegrate their own judicial proceedings with those of the rest of the legal system. In practical terms, that meant establishing a close working relationship with every major court in the land, in part to secure their assistance, but mostly to ensure that their own orders and judgments were properly carried out. In real terms, it meant that the Lords had to reestablish the supremacy of their court and lay claim to their traditional place at the apex of the legal system. Their success in doing so represents one of the most important constitutional developments of the period.

The present study has two general aims. The first is, very simply, to explain why the House of Lords undertook this responsibility in the first place. The answer to that question really lies in a study of the litigation itself. The judicial authority of the upper house was revived almost entirely in response to the pressure of public discontent – a pressure which built up slowly but inexorably from Parliament to Parliament. In the Parliaments of the 1620s, petitions were counted in dozens; over four dozen in 1624, not quite seven dozen in 1626, another four dozen in 1628, with a total approaching nearly 200 for the decade. By the opening of the Long Parliament in 1640, however, public demand had increased dramatically. The Lords received over 200 cases in the first three months of the session. By the middle of 1641 the number had reached 500 and by the close of the year nearly 650. Only the outbreak of civil war in 1642 stemmed the tide, and even that did not interrupt the flow completely. Demand persisted until the house was abolished in early 1649. It was then renewed, on a scale comparable to 1640, when the house was restored *see note* in 1660. Indeed, over 850 petitions were presented to the comparatively brief Convention Parliament.[2] The numbers diminished in the Cavalier Parliament, but demand remained relatively steady with almost 300 cases *- shorter sessions* presented by its close.

However, the Lords were not convinced to revive their judicial authority so much by the number of complainants involved as by the nature of their complaints. Taken as a whole, the litigation demonstrates precious little uniformity. The petitioners represented all ranks of English society and all geographic areas of the country. Their complaints reflected a *type of complaint* broad range of problems from relatively mundane disputes over real property, debt, inheritance, wages, contracts and a variety of domestic matters, to more exceptional (and politically charged) appeals against unjust imprisonments, arbitrary taxation, judicial malfeasance, excommunication, deprivation of ecclesiastical livings and loss of public office. Some were brought originally as cases of first instance. Others requested review of proceedings and decrees in inferior courts. The only thing they seemingly had in common were insoluble legal problems which required extraordinary remedy.

Closer inspection, however, reveals that many of these cases can be traced to similar general causes. Each of them was, to some degree, the by-product of a broader contemporary crisis, either within the legal system or outside it and (as with most litigation) reflected nothing so much as the impact of major trends and great events on minor players.

The petitions presented to the Parliaments of the 1620s testify, above anything else, to Parliament's own failure to act in a legislative capacity to effect much needed statutory legal reform – this despite much talk and many concrete initiatives in those same sessions. That failure had left the legal system as a whole in a state of growing paralysis, increasingly unable to meet the demands and protect the interests of England's ever litigious population. Petitioners to the House of Lords sought relief from the chronic overcrowding which plagued common law and equity courts alike, from the myriad complexities and uncertainties of overlapping and ill-defined jurisdictions (and from the multiplicity of

3

lawsuits they engendered) and from a host of procedural irregularities in individual courts. They complained about the lack of appellate recourse from the court of Chancery and the equity courts generally, about the rigidity of common law procedure in cases of debt and contract, and about prohibitive legal costs – all notorious grievances which had been repeatedly identified and discussed in the context of earlier legislative proposals, but which had, in the event, been left unaddressed.

In 1640, those conditions therefore remained unchanged and in the absence of parliamentary remedy of any other kind in the intervening decade those same complaints were heard again, this time with greater intensity and in significantly greater numbers. However, the litigation presented to the Long Parliament was multidimensional. It also encompassed a number of petitioners who had fallen victim, not to built-in deficiencies in the legal system, but to the deliberate abuse of it by the Crown and its representatives in the course of enforcing public policy in the 1630s. In some cases these petitioners had suffered proscriptive penalties for their failure to subscribe to the religious innovations introduced by the Laudian bishops; in others from harassment, arrest, or imprisonment for their failure to enforce, or contribute to, the Crown's fiscal initiatives; and in still others from excessive fines levied for infringing trade monopolies or contravening royal proclamations. There were innumerable variations on the theme. But what these petitioners pointed to time and again was the Crown's failure to observe proper rules and safeguards – its tendency to sail on the windy side of due process – and its failure to protect the subject's sacred rights of private property and personal liberty.

Ironically, the Long Parliament's own early successes in legislating reform then generated another independent group of petitions. The pell-mell rush to outlaw Ship Money, Coat and Conduct Money, Forest Fines and Knighthood distraint had led legislators to overlook the legal interests of Crown officials who had enforced those programmes in good conscience and according to duty. The failure to indemnify them led those officials to seek the protection of the upper house. Similarly, the abolition of the courts of High Commission and Star Chamber and the legal restraints placed on the Privy Council's judicial activity left litigants who had used those courts by choice without an alternative forum. They too would be forced to turn to the upper house. In due course the Lords would hear as well from petitioners whose legal proceedings had been interrupted (or stalled altogether) by the growing disorder in the court system on the eve of civil war and, subsequently, from those who had been caught in the crossfire of the war itself, as judicial authority divided between Oxford and London.

Not surprisingly, the petitions presented to the Convention Parliament in 1660 again reflected the residual effects of broad religious and political change. Rather like those who had first appealed to the Long Parliament 20 years earlier, the majority of petitioners here were those who had suffered for their religious and political convictions, in this case during the late 1640s and 1650s. They included ministers who had been deprived or sequestered from their ecclesiastical benefices, Crown officers who had been removed from their administrative posts, royal patentees deprived of their monopolies and university presidents and dons removed from their academic livings. They included as well those seeking reparation of war debts, restoration of sequestered property and revocation of the sentences of the Cromwellian high courts of justice. A small contingent of petitioners with more or less conventional legal problems – the Lords' traditional clientele – also requested assistance, but the primary challenge of this Parliament would be to repair the damage done by civil war and revolution. Indeed, it would only be in the subsequent sessions of the Cavalier Parliament that the Lords would be able to return to the kind of problems with which they had begun 50 years earlier – the simpler complaints arising from a legal system still awaiting reform.

Private party judicature was revived in the House of Lords because it was needed; because the problems and issues raised by petitioners were so serious and compelling. What mattered in the long run, of course, was how the Lords actually responded to them. And that is the other general aim of the study: to offer an inside view of the workings of the institution itself; to explain the underlying assumptions which led the Lords to take up this responsibility – at a time when their resources and energies were already overcommitted – and to demonstrate precisely how they met the enormously varied and complex challenges posed by this litigation.

In fact, much of the Lords' response was conditioned by history, or more accurately, by a common understanding and appreciation of the historical role and function of their institution. Parliament, after all, had begun life as a court. The earliest Parliaments had been designed as opportunities for the subject to present his particular grievances to the king and his council and, as F.W. Maitland demonstrated many years ago, those grievances had, more often than not, been legal in nature. The business of Parliaments became the business of rendering decisions in private disputes between party and party.[3]

The King has his court in his council in his parliaments, in the presence of prelates, earls, barons, nobles, and other learned men, where judicial doubts are determined, and new remedies are established for new wrongs, and justice is done to every man according to his deserts.[4]

That description remained essentially accurate throughout the Middle Ages. Indeed, Professor Sayles has recently suggested that 'if we were

5

to subtract the record of judicial business from the parliament rolls of Edward I's reign, we should be left with little else'.[5] By the early fourteenth century, the process had become so popular that special procedures had to be established to manage the business. Proclamations had to be issued before each Parliament to explain when and how petitions should be presented, and officers called Receivers and Auditors eventually had to be appointed in each Parliament to sort through the petitions and select those most worthy of hearing by the king and his council. The opportunity to present petitions and receive royal justice came to be seen as a customary right and on at least one occasion, in 1322, the failure to appoint receivers elicited a protest from the Commons.[6] So important were the services offered by the parliamentary receivers and triers that Parliament elected in 1341 to create a special court by statute – composed of a bishop, two earls and two barons, assisted by the chancellor and the common law judges – to hear and decide complaints about judicial proceedings in the intervals between Parliaments. This body was to be appointed in each Parliament, and was to have 'the power and commission of the King'. Cases which they found too difficult or too important to decide themselves were to be presented to the full parliament at its next meeting.[7]

With the gradual separation of the King's Council in Parliament from the King's Council proper (the smaller body of administrative officials) the task of hearing and judging private suits fell to the emergent House of Lords. The Lords assumed the role of the king's judges, while the Commons took the role of petitioners. By the close of the fourteenth century those functions were well established and clearly understood: 'the judgments of parliament pertained solely to the king and the lords and not to the commons. . . . The Commons are petitioners and demandants, and the king and the lords have for all time had and shall have by right judgments in parliament.'[8]

Over time, of course, public demand for the hearing and settlement of private legal disputes in Parliament had gradually waned. This was largely due to improvements in the legal system which made available more efficient and dependable remedies – the development of bill procedure in King's Bench and, more importantly perhaps, the evolution of equitable relief in Chancery being notable examples. Indeed, by the sixteenth century Parliament had all but ceased to function as a conventional court of law. It had 'no bench of judges, no counsel pleading at its bar, no litigant parties, no established law to administer'.[9] Its status as the High Court now rested almost entirely on its role as the sovereign law-making body of the realm.

That was in practice. In theory Parliament still retained a broad legal jurisdiction which could be employed in a variety of ways. Its power to offer particular remedy had not been abrogated by neglect or the passage of time. Indeed, the great sixteenth-century legal antiquarian Sir Thomas Smith still maintained in 1583 that parliamentary judgment was available in all causes 'betwixte private and private man, and betwixte the prince and any private man, be it in matters criminal or civil, for land or heritage'. Smith assumed that in his day such cases were rare 'because that great counsell being enough occupyed with publique affaires of the realme, will not gladly intermeddle it selfe with private quarels and questions'.[10] That was only partially true. As suggested above, the disappearance of such cases in the fifteenth and sixteenth centuries probably reflected, more than anything else, the lack of public demand, rather than an unwillingness on the part of the upper house to entertain them. Parliamentary judicial remedy had always been made available in response to public pressure and in answer to public need. The jurisdiction had simply fallen into abeyance in their absence.

When demand revived in the 1620s, the Lords acknowledged their responsibility and took the necessary steps to accommodate it to the ordinary routine of their house. The management of business was gradually reorganized to ensure that sufficient time was made available for judicial matters. Internal procedural mechanisms were devised to monitor the flow of petitions and ensure proper record keeping. Standing committees were appointed to hear the cases and report their findings and the judicial personnel of the house was reassigned to provide them with expertise and assistance. All of this was done more or less automatically with little question or comment. The Lords certainly did not need, as one historian has suggested, encouragement or instruction from Sir Edward Coke or his fellow lawyers in the House of Commons to undertake these proceedings.[11] Nor were they unduly influenced or indeed, misdirected, as Sir Matthew Hale once claimed, by Sir John Selden's report on their privileges, which the house had commissioned in 1621.[12] By the time Selden delivered his report, the famous *Privileges of the Baronage of England*, the Lords had been hearing cases for months.[13] Their authority to do so had simply been taken for granted.

What really motivated the Lords to revive these judicial proceedings, apart from the historical imperatives involved, was a genuine sense of commitment to the public welfare. As members of the King's Council in Parliament – and they clearly continued to see themselves in those terms – they had a sacred duty to maintain the good government of the realm. Certainly, they were moved by the predicaments of individual complainants, but their decision to assist them reflected a more general concern: a wish to protect the integrity of the law itself. Failings in the law, regardless of the cause or form they took, were always a threat to social order and stability. They had to be prevented at all costs. In the 1620s the threat was perhaps less immediately apparent because the complaints were so disparate in nature and were presented in such piecemeal fashion.

But the evidence of a crisis was real enough. The progressive breakdown of the legal system had allowed too many conflicts between 'private man and private man' to go unresolved. That was unhealthy and it needed to be addressed, if not by legislation then by adjudication.

In the Long Parliament the threat was more palpable – and the responsibilities more complex. The conflicts here were not just between private man and private man, but between private men and the prince. Public faith in the rule of law had been seriously undermined by the king and his government in the 1630s (if not before) and that had deeply disturbing implications. There was an immediate and compelling need to restore that faith, for the sake of subject and sovereign alike. That meant applying the law, retroactively, against the Crown, by reversing – and awarding compensation for – decisions made by the ecclesiastical courts, by High Commission and Star Chamber and by the Privy Council itself. It meant offering protection and remedy to those unduly compromised by Parliament's own reform legislation. And, after the collapse of the king's government in 1640, it meant exercising the powers of general law enforcement in an effort to maintain public order. In all of this, the Lords were attempting to minimize division and restore harmony. The powers they assumed were not designed to 'win the initiative'. They were designed to preserve the very fabric of government.

Even during the years of civil war that followed the now divided and much reduced House of Lords maintained that pretence. They continued to insist (albeit, with increasing difficulty) that they were acting to protect the fundamentals of English law and government. As part of that commitment they continued to hear and redress the complaints of private litigants and to enforce the law against the disorderly and against those who appeared to threaten both church and state. Indeed, those responsibilities now seemed more important than ever. Inevitably, given the demands of war, compromises were made and their powers were sometimes abused for political ends, but the broader objectives remained the same. They continued to see their judicial authority as essential to the security and stability of the realm. Others, of course, would see the matter differently.

The abolition of the house in 1649, however, did little permanent damage. The Lords' view of their role and responsibilities remained unchanged (or, if anything, enhanced) at the Restoration and they responded to the multifarious demands for judicial remedy made by litigants in 1660 with as much alacrity and sure-footedness as ever. The situation in 1660 was every bit as compelling as that which faced the Lords at the opening of the Long Parliament. The legal rights and interests of the subject had, once again, been sacrificed to political expediency, this time by Parliament itself during the Civil War and by the Cromwellian governments in the wake of revolution. Those transgressions had to be corrected, both to protect essential principles of law and, perhaps more importantly, to speed the process of national reconciliation.

In the Cavalier Parliament that followed the Lords would find themselves reengaged with more mundane matters – standard appeals and complaints against conventional legal proceedings. By that stage hearing private litigation had become a routine, inescapable part of the business of the house. In 1668 and 1675 the Lords would be forced to defend their judicial prerogatives against strong attacks from the House of Commons. But they would survive both challenges (and the constitutional crises they provoked) with their authority (if not all of their jurisdiction) intact. They would do so, not just because historical precedent convincingly supported their claims, but because their proceedings had been proven to be in the best interests of the litigating public.

What follows does not pretend to be a comprehensive study of all judicial functions of the House of Lords. Such a study would have to include, among other things, criminal proceedings on impeachment, the trial of peers and disputes over aristocratic title and privilege – subjects which would have demanded far more space than is available here. Those matters have been thoroughly documented and discussed elsewhere, and as a consequence will be treated here only peripherally.[14] What this study does offer is an in-depth view of the Lords' proceedings in civil litigation – in the belief that they were crucial to the history of the High Court of Parliament. It was really this undertaking, rather (or more) than the conduct of state trials which determined the evolution of the court, the nature of its jurisdiction and its relationship to the rest of the legal system.

The records of the court are in fact extensive. During the seventeenth century the House of Lords was blessed with a particularly distinguished set of clerks, men who were well trained and conscientious archivists. For all practical purposes, there were only two clerks in charge of the records of the upper house for the entire period in question. Henry Elsyng acquired the office in 1621 and served until 1635. It was Elsyng who established the procedures that would be used to manage the business of the house (judicial and otherwise) throughout the Parliaments of the 1620s, assuring through his exemplary organizational skills and constant supervision a high degree of continuity.[15] The office changed hands twice in the 1630s, but both of Elsyng's immediate successors, Thomas Knyvett and Daniel Beddingfield, served only very briefly. In 1638 the office passed to John Browne, who held it until the house was abolished in 1649 and then (having served the Cromwellian Council of State in a variety of capacities) returned to serve until 1691.[16] Browne appears to have adhered closely to Elsyng's procedures, even if he rarely matched Elsyng's reverent interest in parliamentary procedure or his scrupulous eye for detail.[17] The fact that both men served for inordinately long periods (and one effectively succeeded the other) guaranteed a high level of consistency in the way the records were kept. Both men were also trained lawyers and Elsyng at least had an avid interest in House of Lords' judicature.[18] That interest may well have assured that those records were properly preserved.

Drawing on a variety of sources, the proceedings can, for the most part, be reconstructed from the ground up.[19] The most important documents are, of course, the original petitions of the plaintiffs, housed in the Main Papers Collection of the House of Lords Record Office. In their basic outline these petitions differed little from the standard English bill of complaint in Chancery, containing (after a suitably deferential opening address) a lengthy history of the dispute between the parties and where appropriate an account of any previous litigation in other courts. The recital was carefully designed to demonstrate precisely how justice had been denied and, more importantly, why the special jurisdiction of the upper house was being sought. In some cases (notably where the guiding hand of an attorney is evident) the petition itself was kept to a minimum and served only as conveying document for a more extensive and detailed outline of the dispute contained in accompanying 'articles of grievance'.

Since there were no established rules about what had to be (or could be) included in the petition, the complainants often exercised considerable freedom in their choice of relevant facts and information. Their petitions need to be read therefore, as the Lords read them, with a cautious eye and in conjunction with the other documents, most particularly the responding petitions of the defendants. These too are preserved in the same collection. Interrogatories and depositions of witnesses survive in some cases (usually where it had been necessary to take testimony locally) and they often provide additional insight. In cases on appeal, of course, the general history of the dispute can frequently be reconstructed from the records of inferior courts. The Lords often subpoenaed records of proceedings in other tribunals, but did not (except in writs of error) retain copies on a consistent basis. Recourse to the court of origin is usually necessary. Beyond that, the substance of the cases can often be gleaned from the reports of the Lords' own judicial personnel. Very often, in particularly difficult or complex litigation, the Lords referred the dispute, or some specific point of law, to the Lord Chancellor or one or more of the common law judges for their review. Many of their resulting certificates survive and they make essential reading. In many cases it is possible to gain additional information on the participants from sources outside the archives of the House of Lords, for instance from the State Papers Collection and the Privy Council registers.

The Lords' response to these cases is also generally well documented. The most important source here is obviously the journal of the house itself in one or another of its compositional stages.[20] It was entirely up to the discretion of the clerk (subject to later review by the members of the Committee for Privileges) as to what would be included in the journal. Though there were apparently no hard and fast rules (and therefore no great degree of consistency) with regard to judicial proceedings, the general pattern was to include notations on the receipt and reading of petitions in the house – and in some cases the full text of the petition itself, notes on scheduled hearings and interim reports of the committee or the judges to whom it was referred. The final order and judgment reached by the committee, and subsequently approved by the house, was almost always entered in full.

In many cases, however, a dispute might be settled at an intermediate stage, through arbitration in committee, or through interlocutory orders issued to a lower court, for example to remove some particular obstruction to proceedings there. Because they did not constitute a formal judgment of the house, they were not always considered important enough to be entered in the journal. Instead, John Browne kept a separate book of orders and judgments which contained all of the recorded decisions of the house and its committees.[21] Actions not recorded in the journal can usually be found here. There are also a great many draft orders scattered throughout the Main Papers collection.

Unfortunately, what we do not have is a full record of committee deliberations on individual cases. The clerk's assistants who attended the judicial committees appear to have been instructed to record only the final decision; that is, whatever orders or judgments were to be recommended by the committee to the house. Given the amount of business which might be under consideration on any given day, that is not surprising. The clerk's assistant would have been hard pressed to keep up with recording even the final orders of the committee. Nonetheless, at least for the first half of the century there are no accounts of the discussions or debates which led to those decisions. In some cases the Lords did include the specific reasons for their decision in the final declaration and that often makes clear the path of their deliberations. So too, of course, do the judges' certificates; the Lords relied heavily on the judges' expertise and tended to adopt whatever recommendations they made as a matter of course. The situation improves somewhat after the Restoration. At least by the Cavalier Parliament the pressure of business had eased somewhat and better records were kept of judicial business. More or less continuous notes on the proceedings of the Committee for Petitions were now kept in separate minute books. They do not always provide details about the committee's deliberations, but they invariably contain some information not available elsewhere. Also, after 1660 the manuscript minutes of the journal frequently contain the arguments of counsel in appeal cases. Both are of great value.

Obviously, it is not possible to reconstruct in detail all of the cases brought before the House of Lords during the period. Given the disparate nature of the litigation, the amount of source material (over and above the initiating petition and answer) differs to a considerable degree in each case, depending on the particular circumstances of the dispute. But the history of the vast majority of cases can be recreated and the result is an archive of exceptional importance. Though this study has been organized chronologically – in order to trace the progressive development of the court itself – it will focus considerable attention on the litigation, simply because individual cases and groups of cases have so much to say about contemporary conditions and problems. These cases reveal a great deal about the nature and operations of the early modern legal system and about the limitations (and idiosyncrasies) of seventeenth-century law. More tellingly perhaps, they offer important evidence about the way that law was – or was not – applied, both ordinarily and in times of political crisis.

From a broader perspective, the litigation also reveals something important about public perception of the House of Lords. The litigants who appealed to the upper house did so without much hesitation and without any apparent sense that they were doing something inappropriate or out of the ordinary. There were, of course, those who would come to see the availability of remedy in the high court as only one more opportunity to attempt the proverbial 'try-on', to circumvent normal channels in order to achieve a quick and definitive resolution from a court whose decrees were beyond appeal or simply to harass their opponents with vexatious litigation. The relative ease and lack of expense involved in initiating proceedings in the upper house would prove irresistible to those so inclined. But the vast majority appealed to the house out of genuine need and with every confidence that their requests would be answered with appropriate remedy. In their view at least, the House of Lords remained critically important to their security and wellbeing.

The Lords' response to their demands clearly confirmed those expectations. These proceedings in fact offer an entirely new and important perspective on the upper house during this critical period. They make clear that its responsibilities were much broader, more central and of considerably greater impact than has usually been assumed. Too often, the seventeenth-century House of Lords has been portrayed (when it has been considered at all) as somehow disengaged from the public concerns and preoccupations which defined a Parliament. That was never really true, though admittedly in matters legislative and political the running was often with the House of Commons. But as these proceedings make clear, the business of seventeenth-century Parliaments was not all politics and legislation. It was also adjudication. That responsibility fell to the House of Lords, and it required that they remain constantly aware of and responsive to all of the contemporary problems and crises which shaped the lives of ordinary Englishmen over the course of the century. It was a challenge the Lords were both willing and able to meet.

NOTES

1 G.R. Elton, 'Parliament in the Sixteenth Century: Functions and Fortunes,' *Studies in Tudor and Stuart Politics and Government*, vol. 3, Cambridge (1983) p. 159.

2 Of these petitions 632 concerned restoration of ecclesiatical benefices.

3 F.W. Maitland (ed.), *Records of the Parliament holden at Westminster in the thirty-third year of King Edward the First* (Rolls series, 1893). Maitland's introduction is reprinted in Maitland, *Historical Essays* (Cambridge, 1893).

4 H.G. Richardson and G.O. Sayles (eds), *Fleta*, Selden Society Publications (London, 1973), Vol 2, p. 109.

5 G.O. Sayles, *The King's Parliament of England* (New York, 1974), p. 79.

6 ibid., pp. 109–110.

7 14 Edward III, stat. 1, cap. 5.

8 Rot. Parl., 1.371 (cited in Sayles, *King's Parliament*, p. 107).

9 G.R. Elton, *The Parliament of England 1559–1581* (Cambridge, 1986), p. 17.

10 Sir Thomas Smith, *De Republica Anglorum*, ed. Mary Dewar (Cambridge, 1982), p. 89.

11 Frances Helen Relf (ed.), *Notes of the Debates in the House of Lords, 1621 ... 1628*, Camden Society, 3rd series, vol. 42 (1929). Professor Relf argued that the seventeenth century House of Lords remained essentially ignorant of its medieval inheritance as a court – an assertion rather difficult to support given that the Lords' appellate authority over common law decrees had been confirmed by statute as recently as the 1580s. She claimed that common lawyers and 'opposition' members in the House of Commons worked to reeducate the upper House about its judicial authority (initially through the impeachment of Sir Giles Mompesson) and then manipulated the Lords into accepting petitions for judicial remedy. According to Relf, this was done to regain supremacy over courts of equity, notably Chancery, and to establish Parliament as 'the apex of the judicial system', thereby enhancing its power to protect the subject against the increasingly arbitrary behaviour of the sovereign. The thesis is simply not supported by the evidence.

12 Sir Matthew Hale, *The Jurisdiction of the Lords' House*, ed. Francis Hargrave (London, 1796). Hale claimed that Selden's work had given 'the lords occasion of looking into the *Placita Parliamenti* tempore Ed. I which they applied singly to the house of lords'. That convinced the Lords to

> enlarge their jurisdiction not only to causes of appeal, but almost to all kinds of jurisdiction in the first instance, so that ... they had gotten it to be a settled court by petitions to themselves in all causes civil as well as criminal ibid., (p. 194).

13 For the original manuscript of Selden's report (subsequently published in 1642) see HLRO, Main Papers, H.L., 15 December 1621. In fact, Selden's assertions regarding judicature were very modest. He claimed that 'the Power of Judicature belonging to the Lords of Parliament is chiefly seen in their Jurisdiction upon Writs of Error, and their Judgments of Offences, as well capitall as not capitall, which they give to any publicke mischiefe in the State' (ch. 4). He also made reference to the above mentioned statute of 1341 by listing, as one of the privileges of the house, 'their appointing Judges out of themselves for examination of Judgments and delayes of other courts' (ch. 6).

14 On impeachment see Clayton Roberts, *The Growth of Responsible Government* (Cambridge, 1966); C.G.C. Tite, *Impeachment and Parliamentary Judicature in Early Stuart England*, (London, 1974); and J.H. Timmis, *Thine is the Kingdom: The Trial For Treason of Thomas Wentworth Earl of Strafford* (University, Alabama, 1974). For a good general discussion of the Lords' proceedings in judicature, see E. R. Foster, *The House of Lords 1603–1649* (Chapel Hill, NC, 1983).

15 For a detailed discussion of Elsyng's contributions, see E.R. Foster, 'The painful labor of Mr. Elsyng', *Transactions of the American Philosophical Society*, vol. 62 (1972), pt 8.

16 Foster, *House of Lords*, p. 46.

17 There are two rather glaring exceptions to Browne's careful record. On one occasion he loaned a large body of parliamentary papers to Dr John Nalson, canon of Ely, so that he could prepare an 'antidote to Rushworth'. Nalson never returned the papers, but the collection was later recovered in the estate of the duke of Portland, and is now on deposit in the Bodleian Library, Oxford. Browne also had a large collection of records at his home at the time of his death. Those papers were kept by his descendants and were later sold. They too have been recovered and are housed in the House of Lords Record Office, as the Braye MSS. Maurice F. Bond, *Guide to the Records of Parliament* (London, 1971) pp. 268, 278. For an extended discussion of Browne's recordkeeping, see E.R. Foster, 'The journals of the House of Lords for the Long Parliament' in Barbara C. Malament (ed.), *After the Reformation* (Philadelphia, Pa, 1980), pp. 129–145.

18 Elsyng actually wrote a short treatise on the subject, called 'Of judicature', in the early 1630s. For a discussion of the treatise and its authorship, see Foster, 'The painful labor of Mr. Elsyng', pp. 42–45.

19 It needs to be said that the materials in the Main Papers collection discussed below have never been identified as a separate class of papers relating to judicial business and were never catalogued as such. The collection is organized chronologically, with all papers listed according to the date of receipt (or according to the date of the nearest journal entry which seems to relate to the subject at hand). The papers relating to any given case are therefore scattered about the collection and have to be reassembled document by document.

20 During Elsyng's tenure the composition of the journal took place in three stages. It began with the clerk's so-called 'scribbled book', a collection of rough notes on debates and proceedings on bills, petitions and so forth. Those notes were then fashioned, in the second stage, into a draft journal and that, in due course, was reviewed by a subcommittee of the Lords Committee for Privileges to ensure its accuracy. Once corrections and additions were made, the final version was engrossed on parchment in the so-called 'fair written book'. Browne appears to have followed much the same routine, except that the extraordinary press of business in the Long Parliament defeated his efforts to complete the final stage. The printed journal of today is in fact only his draft journal, with his marginal notes and instructions to his assistants on how the final version ought to be composed. For a discussion of this procedure, see Foster, *House of Lords*, pp. 53–55. The manuscript minutes and the draft journals are housed in the Braye MSS in the House of Lords Record Office.

21 There are in fact two separate collections here. They are HLRO, Parchment Collection, B9 (Book of Orders and Warrants) and B1 (Book of Orders and Ordinances). Although it is not entirely clear, the former appears to have been a collection of draft orders and the latter the clerk's fair copy book.

1

The 1620s:
the remaking of a court

The revival of House of Lords judicature in the Parliament of 1621 began quietly and unobtrusively. Strictly speaking, the revival got underway on 3 March. The cause was a private one and the request for judicial assistance came, not from the Commons, but from the king. On that day James I forwarded to the Lords the petition of Edward Ewer asking that the record of Ewer's case in King's Bench be removed into the upper house for their review. The case signalled the revival of the Lords' appellate authority over the court of King's Bench – a jurisdiction long established but unused since 1589.[1] The proceedings went entirely unnoticed. What seemed far more important at the time was the request made five days later by Sir Edward Coke on behalf of the House of Commons. Admonishing the Lords to 'tread in the steps of your noble progenitors', Coke pressed them to assume once again the role of judges and take responsibility for the trial and punishment of the notorious patentee, Sir Giles Mompesson.[2] The very public proceedings which followed Coke's demand – the trial of Mompesson and the subsequent impeachment proceedings against Sir Francis Michell, Sir John Bennett and Lord Chancellor Bacon – entirely overshadowed the private proceedings effectively initiated by the king. But in fact Ewer's appeal (however inconspicuous) was every bit as important as Coke's. Intentionally or not, it opened the door to the resumption of private party litigation in the upper chamber. His was the first of more than a dozen such petitions which the Lords would receive and accept in the 1621 Parliament, and those petitions would establish an all important foundation for a dramatic expansion of the Lords' judicial responsibilities over the decade. Though their number was small, these cases still required that the Lords reallocate time and personnel to their hearing. Committees had to be appointed, administrative procedures put in place and new rules devised to govern the process. It was all done in a very business-like manner – efficiently, purposefully and, notably, without comment, but a major step had been taken all the same.[3]

Table 1.1 Number of cases accepted by upper house for each Parliament, 1621–9

Parliament	Number of cases
30 January 1621 to 6 January 1622	14
18 February 1624 to 27 March 1625	57
18 June 1625 to 12 August 1625 (Oxford)	3
6 February 1626 to 15 June 1626	86
17 March 1628 to 10 March 1629	47
Total	207

LITIGANTS AND LITIGATION

By the close of the second session of 1621 the machinery was in place to handle any petitions which might be presented. Few members involved in those proceedings, however, could have anticipated the impact which their actions would have in subsequent Parliaments. No doubt at the time the Lords assumed they were administering special remedies to special cases. Each of the petitions accepted in 1621 appeared to be an isolated complaint reflecting a unique set of conditions and circumstances. There was little evidence to suggest that the problems they presented were more widespread. But they were and other litigants with similar complaints would soon follow the example set by the pioneering petitioners of 1621. The scale of the public response was perhaps surprising – more than a four-fold increase in the number of petitions presented from 1621 to 1624 – but the legal community in Westminster was not a large one, and however small scale and seemingly inconsequential the private judicial proceedings of 1621 may have been (certainly in comparison to the rest of the parliamentary agenda), the renewed availability of parliamentary remedy would not have remained a secret for long.

As a consequence the number of petitions presented to each of the subsequent Parliaments (excepting the sessions of 1625) multiplied dramatically. Table 1.1 indicates the number of cases accepted by the house in each of the five Parliaments of the 1620s. It needs to be stressed that these totals represent only those cases which were accepted by the house after preliminary consideration and on which there were subsequent proceedings. They do not represent the number of cases actually submitted for review. Records kept by the Clerk of Parliament of the petitions delivered into the house suggest that the number actually presented was a good deal larger. The clerk's 'Catalogue of petitions received this Parliament' for 1621 lists an additional 16 names for which there are no original petitions or records of further proceedings.[4] A similar 'Register of petitions' for 1624 lists an additional 15 names unsupported by documentation, those for 1626 an additional 47 and that for 1628 another

9.[5] During 1626, the clerk also kept a separate list of 'petitions rejected' which contains the names of another 48 petitioners who appear on none of the above lists for that year.[6] As this last list suggests, the majority of these causes were in all likelihood rejected outright on a first reading of the initiating petition, in which case the petition was redelivered to the plaintiff. Alternatively, some of these disputes may have been resolved between the parties themselves before further action was taken in the house. The plaintiff would then have asked to withdraw his petition and no further record would have been made. There is clear evidence that this happened in at least two cases in 1624 and 1626 and it no doubt happened in others.[7] As will be seen, litigants soon learned that the prospect of judicial proceedings in the House of Lords could have an intimidating effect on adversaries. It is also possible, though somewhat less likely, that some of these petitions were informally referred to outside arbitration without proper notation being made of the fact through carelessness or oversight on the part of the clerk. In any event, it is clear that the house received many more petitions than it accepted. The total number presented appears to have been well over 300.

The cases which were accepted included both first instance causes and those in which there had been prior proceedings in other courts. The litigation in fact divides almost equally between the two. The latter designation has been chosen with some care. Not all of the cases with prehistories in other courts can be fairly described as conventional appeals against lower court decrees. In some instances the petitioners were asking the house to review the conduct of court officials, in others to intercede with lower courts to remove some technical obstruction to further proceedings, and in still others to stay lower court proceedings altogether to prevent a potential injustice. There were, in fact, a few requests that the Lords confirm and enforce lower court decrees. The majority were, however, appeals against earlier decrees or judgments. Table 1.2 indicates the origin of these complaints and the number of cases from each court. To these number might be added a half dozen more appeals from prisoners in the King's Bench prison who had been imprisoned by the court for debt. They have not been included in Table 1.2 because their petitions did not, strictly speaking, ask for review of their conviction, but for redress against the strict interpretation of the laws of debt. An argument might also have been made to include some 16 cases which had previously been heard before the King's Privy Council. Some of these did in fact come to the Lords as appeals against council proceedings, but many more of them were requests for a new hearing of a dispute which the council had failed to act on or resolve. They have something important to say about the special relationship between the two bodies and will be treated on their own.

Table 1.2 contains few surprises. At first glance it may seem curious that there are not more appeals from the central courts of common

Table 1.2 Courts of origin

Court	Number of cases
Chancery	38
Star Chamber	12
Requests	7
King's Bench (via Writ of Error)	4
High Commission	4
Exchequer	3
Wards	3
Admiralty	3
Prerogative Court of Canterbury	2
Court of Audience	1
Assizes	2
London Court of Orphans	1
Unspecified	3
Total	83

law (King's Bench and Common Pleas) given the disproportionately large amount of business which those two courts normally attracted.[8] However, appeals to the House of Lords from the common law courts were regulated by statute and had to conform to strictly defined writ of error procedure. Appeal was only possible for errors in law, not in fact, and the procedure was long, complicated and expensive. On the other hand, appeals from the prerogative and equity courts were not governed by any known procedures: there was simply no established appellate recourse available, save by petition to the king for a specially appointed royal commission of review, or for direct intervention by the king himself – a time-consuming and unpredictable process at best. Given the high level of business normally handled by these courts, most particularly that of Chancery, that had become increasingly impractical, and the lack of effective recourse from their decrees had become a serious grievance. These appeals were a product of that discontent. (In the case of Chancery, they reflect as well growing concern over the court's procedure and practice.) In all events, appeals from these courts represented an important innovation and quickly laid the foundation for the Lords' claim to a comprehensive appellate jurisdiction.

The nature of the litigation itself becomes clear when the cases are identified by subject matter. The classifications are listed in Table 1.3. The most striking thing about Table 1.3 is the extraordinary diversity of the litigation covered. At this very early stage of development the jurisdiction of the House of Lords was (and would remain for some time) rather imprecisely defined, if, indeed, it was clearly understood at all. Without predetermined rules or limitations, prospective litigants understandably defined its authority to their advantage. Nor were they discouraged from

Table 1.3 Classification of litigation

Subject in dispute	Number of cases
Real property	74
Debt	51
Disputed wills and trusts	21
Wardship	2
Domestic disputes	2
Trade disputes	9
Disputed office	1
Maritime disputes	5
Complaints against judicial personnel	7
Complaints against attorneys	4
Complaints against local magistrates	2
Fraud	2
Riot	2
Miscellaneous[1]	7
Unspecified	18
Total	207

1 These cases include a dispute over the use of a highway, a complaint against King's College, Cambridge, over its failure to admit a prospective candidate; an appeal against the deprivation of an ecclesiastical living; an attempted prosecution for recusancy; a dispute over the disafforestation of Leicester Forest; a complaint against vexatious proceedings at law, and an appeal of a prisoner committed by the Privy Council in 1624 for refusing to serve in the wars in the Low Countries.

doing so. Lords and litigants alike were loath to impose restrictions on the High Court of Parliament. The result, however, was that the litigation as a whole remained remarkably eclectic. The disproportionate number of cases involving real property and debt does in fact reflect the general pattern of litigation in early modern England,[9] but even within these classifications the cases do not conform to any recognizable patterns or prescribed forms of action. They include, in the former class, an infinite variety of disputes over copyhold rights, leases, mortgages and titles to property, and in the latter, an almost incomprehensible array of failed financial agreements. Petitions requesting administration of the massive debts of the Muscovy Company took their place along side those requesting collection of a £10 obligation.

As such variety suggests, petitioners to the House of Lords also appear to have represented a broad cross section of English society. Unfortunately, it is not possible to offer a comprehensive breakdown of the litigants according to social class. The records simply do not provide sufficient information. Unlike the common law courts where procedure required both plaintiffs and defendants to designate their social status at an early stage of proceedings,[10] petitions to the House of Lords remained relatively informal and social class designation was left to personal discretion. Litigants did not follow any consistent practice.

Indeed, a significant majority failed altogether to identify either their rank or occupation. One can be certain only about the 3 peers who were plaintiffs and whose status was obvious, and about the 21 petitioners who identified themselves as knights or baronets. Another 6 plaintiffs described themselves as 'esquires' and a further 8 as 'gentlemen'.[11] However, it is clear that members of the so-called gentry represented a greater proportion of these litigants than those numbers might suggest. There are, for example, litigants whose social rank is not specified, but who appear to be substantial property owners, or at the very least, to have a vested interest in large land holdings and would in all likelihood have styled themselves gentlemen or better.[12] But without more detailed information it is not possible to be any more specific.

Information regarding those whose livelihood derived from sources other than land is, again, somewhat sporadic because only a handful of petitioners identified themselves by occupation. As the large proportion of debt cases might suggest, these litigants included a number of prominent London merchants, such as Aldermen Richard Deane and Cuthbert Hackett. There are, in fact, a dozen or more petitioners who identify themselves as 'creditors' of joint stock companies and whose investments were substantial enough (between £50 and £1,000) to suggest a fair measure of affluence. But there are also a half-dozen small-scale purveyors (grocers, vintners, clothiers) and an equal number of local artisans. The sample also includes minor office holders (constables, JPs, and two town heralds), members of the lower clergy, poor widows and prisoners for debt. But it remains just a sample. The best that can be said in the absence of any thorough statistical analysis is that the House of Lords attracted petitioners from all ranks of English society.

It clearly attracted litigants from all geographic areas of the country as well. Again, complete information is not available in all cases, but documentation in roughly half of the cases makes it possible to identify the county in which the dispute originated. The distribution is indicated in Table 1.4. Again, these figures do not suggest anything unusual and in fact, some minor variations aside, they reflect a similar pattern of case distribution to that recently described by Professor Brooks for the courts of Common Pleas and King's Bench.[13] The one rather curious feature is the absence of any cases from the East Anglian counties of Norfolk and Suffolk whose population and prospering economies traditionally gave rise to inordinate levels of litigation.[14] In all, 25 of the 40 English counties are represented in the sample, reaching as far north as Cumberland and as far west as Devon. The very high percentage of cases originating in London was to be expected, given London's already large (and growing) population and its role as the major centre of trade and commerce. Beyond that, the sample would seem to reflect little more than the general distribution of the population, with more cases originating in the

Table 1.4 Geographic distribution by county and assize circuit

---

Home (12):
Kent (4); Essex (4); Sussex (1); Hertfordshire (2); Surrey (1)

Midlands (13):
Derby (1); Lincolnshire (3); Nottinghamshire (0); Rutland (0);
Northamptonshire (5); Warwickshire (0); Leicester (4)

Norfolk (7):
Norfolk (0); Suffolk (0); Cambridgeshire (3); Huntingdonshire (1); Bedfordshire (0); Buckinghamshire (3)

Northern (7):
Yorkshire (6); Durham (0); Northumberland (0); Westmorland Cumberland (1)

Oxford (11):
Oxfordshire (4); Berkshire (2); Gloucestershire (3); Monmouthshire (0);
Herefordshire (2); Worcestershire (0); Shropshire (0); Staffordshire (0)

Western (11):
Hampshire (4); Wiltshire (1); Somerset (1); Dorset (1); Devon (4); Cornwall (0);

Lancashire and Cheshire (4)

London and Middlesex (36)

---

midlands, south and west than in the north and east, and in those counties,
such as York, Devon, or Kent which housed major urban centres (and as
a consequence, a higher concentration of knowledgeable attorneys). The
numbers involved are really too small to suggest any substantive conclusions about problems in particular regions or counties. What they do
suggest, however, is that even at this early stage interest in (and knowledge
of) the judicial proceedings of the House of Lords was widespread.

THE CAUSES OF PUBLIC DISCONTENT

None of this, of course, explains why litigants turned to the House of
Lords in the first place. There are no simple answers to the question.
Petitioners addressed themselves to the upper house at different times for
different reasons. Indeed, one would not expect such a large and disparate
body of litigation to have emerged from a common cause. As a whole, the
cases themselves can be seen (like all litigation) as the product of changing
social and economic conditions. But their appearance in the House of
Lords in the 1620s can be traced more directly to changing conditions
within the legal system. The complaints reflect, above anything else, public
frustration with the failure of the system to provide fast and effective remedy. These litigants had been defeated by (and were seeking relief from)

21

a variety of obstacles which were, in large measure, built into the system itself and which had plagued English judicial proceedings for generations.

The primary problem was one of chronic congestion. The legal system, for all its noted expansion in the sixteenth century, had simply been unable to cope with the volume of business being brought before the central courts. In the century before 1640 England had experienced an unprecedented rise in litigation. The rate of increase differed from one court to the next and fluctuated from one period to the next, but the overall pattern from the mid-sixteenth century to the mid-seventeenth is pretty well unmistakable.[15] The most recent study of the problem in the central common law courts of King's Bench and Common Pleas suggests that there was as much as a six-fold increase in cases presented in the period from 1560 to 1640.[16] Under the reforming hand of Lord Keeper (later Lord Chancellor) Ellesmere the court of Chancery experienced a similarly notable increase. Litigation rose nearly 50 per cent in the brief period from 1603 to 1610 and almost 25 per cent over the period from 1596.[17] Statistics are not available for the whole of the first half of the seventeenth century, but there seems to be little question that the pattern continued, especially after Ellesmere's successful defence of the court's prerogatives in 1616. Indeed, J.H. Baker has described the Lord Chancellor's famous victory in 1616 as a near disaster for the court because of the resulting increase in litigation. Chancery was already seriously overburdened and was simply not equipped to accommodate an increase in its caseload. He cites the claim of one contemporary barrister, Timothy Tourneur, that there were some 8,000 cases pending in Chancery by Hilary term 1617.[18]

The evidence for the other London courts is less dramatic, but conforms to the general trend. Professor Barnes's research on the early seventeenth-century court of Star Chamber identified some 8,228 actions brought by bill or information in the period between 1603 and 1625, amounting to an average of 357 cases per annum.[19] This compares to the yearly average of 120 cases for a comparable period a century earlier during the administration of Cardinal Wolsey.[20] Though there are no published figures available, the courts of Wards and Requests both appear to have experienced appreciable increases in the volume of their business in the early Stuart period.[21] So too did the equity side of the Exchequer. Professor Bryson's study of the court indicates that there was a four-fold increase in the number of bills filed in the court from the beginning of Queen Elizabeth's reign to 1625, though the most dramatic increase took place in the latter years of the sixteenth century.[22]

Such a sharp increase in litigation across the board could hardly have gone unnoticed and, indeed, seventeenth-century commentators complained bitterly about the matter, attributing it to a wide variety of causes from a general decline in civility to the increase in the number of attorneys. But the explanation was more complex. The rise in litigation was really a product of large-scale economic and demographic change. It can be attributed first to the inordinate growth in population in England from the mid-sixteenth century to the mid-seventeenth – roughly a two-fold increase – and even more directly to steadily improving economic conditions.[23] The dramatic rise in population at a time of stagnant agricultural production pushed prices for agricultural products and land itself continually upward, thereby improving the economic position of both those who possessed land (and could benefit from increased rents or potential profits from resale) and those who were able to produce surplus food.[24] These inflationary pressures created a far more fluid land market (especially after 1540) and a great deal of land changed hands.[25] The principal beneficiaries were the landowning gentry and the upper yeomanry, but successful merchants, lawyers and public office holders took advantage of the conditions and entered the market as well.[26] Those able to purchase property were also able to spend lavishly on building homes and on furnishing them with imported luxury goods.[27] These activities all involved complicated transactions. Property transfers were almost invariably complex; titles were not always clear and were often encumbered with intricate mortgages, trusts and leasehold or rental agreements. Moreover, purchases of both property and goods and services were usually financed through multilayered and interconnected credit arrangements, involving numerous loans made by separate individuals, for differing amounts, at different rates, secured by different penal bonds. The complexity of all these transactions invited litigation when disagreements arose and the resulting suits often multiplied in proportion to the number of interested parties involved.[28]

Nor were these complications restricted to the land market or the agricultural economy. Economic activity had accelerated across the board (albeit at different rates in different sectors). Despite intervals of depression, the export market for wool had shown consistent growth from 1450 to the mid-seventeenth century and the continuing success had led to greater expansion and diversification of the industry.[29] The growth in population had made possible a greater division of labour through the putting-out system, thereby decentralizing the process of production and involving larger numbers of people, and as a consequence larger numbers of financial transactions, any of which might lead to litigation. Conversely, the development of industries such as mining, smelting, glass-making, ship building and paper manufacture was, by the nature of production, more centralized in that they required the construction of a fixed plant which inevitably had to be financed through large scale capital investment.[30] In some cases this was done through the formation of joint stock companies, in others through unincorporated partnerships among wealthy business-men and landowners. But in either case, the complications involved in such relationships, especially the more informal partnerships, were the breeding ground of litigation when disputes arose over the distribution of profits, or more often, over the distribution of liability for losses. That was true as well of the numerous chartered trading companies which had proliferated from the middle of the sixteenth century. The expansion of overseas trade from the mid-1550s could be (and had been) enormously profitable. But economic depression and a decline in trade, as for instance occurred in the 1620s, could bring serious hardship or financial collapse leading to a succession of law suits by company creditors and investors alike – a fate that befell even the venerable East India and Muscovy Companies in this period.[31] In the end, all of this economic activity, while undoubtedly good for the country as a whole, had the unfortunate side-effect of producing inordinate levels of litigation – a fact duly noted by astute contemporary observers such as Sir Edward Coke and Sir John Davies.[32]

The problems of congestion associated with the growth of litigation were then compounded by the increasing centralization of the legal process in London. Professor Brooks has recently demonstrated that there was a growing inclination among litigants in the late sixteenth and early seventeenth centuries to initiate their suits in the central courts of King's Bench and Common Pleas, rather than in their local county or borough courts.[33] There is also considerable evidence to suggest that suitors were attempting with increasing frequency to have cases already initiated locally removed to London, thereby speeding the decline of local court jurisdictions. This phenomenon was also of great concern to contemporaries. Sir Edward Coke considered it to be one of the most serious problems confronting the legal system, contributing as it did to the chronic overcrowding in the central courts, and he drafted no less than three separate bills to address the issue in the Parliaments of 1621 and 1624.[34] Coke ascribed the problem to the behaviour of unscrupulous litigants who used the procedures to engender delay and avoid prosecution. There was certainly some truth in his assertions. The prospect of a long and costly suit in Westminster was often enough, in itself, to compel an out-of-court settlement. But there were other broader causes which fostered the growth of litigation in London. One of the most serious was inflation. The central courts had traditionally been limited to hearing suits which involved amounts in excess of 40s, but inflationary pressures had effectively rendered that rule meaningless. Even the most ordinary disputes now involved amounts in excess of 40s, and the parties therefore had the option of pursuing their cause at Westminster. In many rural areas litigants were in fact forced to go to London because the manorial courts only had statutory authority to hear cases up to a value of 40s.[35] Many local jurisdictions were also ill-equipped to deal with the changing patterns of litigation. The expansion and diversification of trade and industry, and the network of commercial relationships across the country which developed as a result, made reliance on local court jurisdictions increasingly impractical and led litigants to seek help from the central courts whose authority transcended regional boundaries. For all sorts of reasons (not least monetary advantage) the legal profession, including the central court judges, often encouraged them to do so.[36]

The increasing centralization of judicial activity reflected another, perhaps more troubling, problem – the failure of local intervention and arbitration to resolve disputes before they went to litigation. Local magistrates had been increasingly overburdened by administrative duties mandated by Tudor reform legislation and were, as a consequence, less able to devote the necessary time and attention to the mediation of disputes among neighbours.[37] Nor (for many of the same reasons) had the justices on assize been able to act in this capacity as frequently as might have been hoped. It was not really their responsibility to do so, but the opportunity existed all the same. Lord Chancellor Ellesmere, who was clearly aware of the problem, on one occasion admonished the justices to make a special effort to intervene in the interests of forestalling litigation at Westminster:

> I have noted one thing, that your ancestors though they had no authority, were so painful and careful as soon as they heard of any differences or suits between any of their neighbours, that they would interpose themselves and mediate an end, by which means the expense of time and much money was saved, and the courts of Westminster nothing near so filled and pestered with causes as they now are.[38]

Ellesmere's admonitions could not, in themselves, have altered the situation significantly and, not surprisingly, the matter was still of central concern to Interregnum law reformers. The Hale Commission's proposals for a revived and expanded county judicial apparatus were motivated, at least in part, by a wish to strengthen the traditions of local justice,[39] as were the similar reforms proposed by William Sheppard.[40]

All of these forces then combined to place inordinate strain on the central courts in London, leading to intolerable levels of congestion. And the inevitable consequence of congestion was delay. The weight of numbers was in fact the primary cause of slow process, but it was not the only contributing factor. The problem lay equally in the increasing complexity (and uncertainty) of judicial procedure. Law courts across the system were continually modifying and adapting their procedures during the early modern period, in part to provide better regulation of existing business and, in part, to make their procedures more attractive to potential clients. Competition for business had forced all courts to remain, to a certain degree, flexible and accommodating to the demands of litigants. To some extent the courts of common law had led the way by allowing the growth of new actions based on legal fictions, as, for example, with bill of Middlesex and *latitat* procedure in King's Bench, or with the many 'special case' variations on traditional trespass writs – the so-called 'actions on the case' such as *assumpsit* (to enforce parol agreements) and *ejectment* (to recover leasehold property). These innovations, while offering greater freedom of action for litigants, also introduced a greater degree of uncertainty about how and where to proceed to remedy.[41]

> The classical world of the common law where the King's Bench heard criminal causes and the Common Pleas civil ones, where wrongs were distinguished from rights, and where there was a meaningful distinction between personal and real actions (if that world ever existed) had become a world of the past.[42]

The new forms of action were also accompanied by changes in common law procedure, most notably with regard to pleadings. Tentative oral pleadings before trial had gradually given way over the sixteenth century to increasingly formalized and binding written pleadings. As a consequence pleading became increasingly complex and intricate and subject to challenge on the basis of technicalities of form. Challenges proliferated (lodged by way of formal demurrers) and as Coke lamented in 1628, 'more jangling and questions grow upon the manner of pleading, and exceptions to form, than upon the matter itself, and infinite causes [are] lost or delayed for want of good pleading'.[43] The growing procedural sophistication was a natural part of the process of expansion, but it inevitably made the outcome of litigation less clear-cut and predictable.

A similar process had taken place in the court of Chancery with similar results. Chancery procedure, notably during the administration of Lord Keeper Ellesmere had become increasingly rigorous and detailed. Ellesmere believed strongly that Chancery procedure needed to be clearly established and understood so as to reflect a level of judicial integrity coequal with the central courts of common law. Indeed, its relations with those courts depended on its own internal procedures being clearly defined.[44] But as procedure in Chancery became more formalized it also became more complex. Here too rules and regulations regarding pleading and proofs were repeatedly tightened to ensure more uniform procedure. In doing so, however, the court inadvertently created innumerable grounds on which parties might register objections to their opponents' conduct. Chancery proceedings were increasingly plagued by the placing of motions before the court (which could be entered at any time before hearing) alleging insufficient pleadings, acts of contempt, improper examinations, or corruption of commissioned referees.[45] These motions inevitably led to references, delayed proceedings and increased costs. Litigation could likewise be frustrated almost indefinitely by a host of more conventional motions for injunctions to stay suits at common law, to settle possession, or to stay the committing of waste. George Norburie, the seventeenth-century chronicler of the court, claimed that ten to twelve separate orders and a half a dozen referees' reports might ensue before a case came to hearing.[46] In such cases final resolution and determination must have seemed (and usually was) an illusive prospect.[47]

Similar problems had developed in the court of Star Chamber, again most noticeably under the reforming hand of Lord Keeper Ellesmere, who served as presiding officer of the court from 1596 to 1617. Star Chamber litigation was inherently complicated because it so often involved multiple charges and multiple defendants and 'this meant multiple answers, multiple replications and rejoinders, and multiple procedural skirmishes between groups of defendants and the plaintiff'.[48] But, as in Chancery, even straightforward cases could be compromised by procedural complexity. The initiating bill had, like its counterpart in Chancery, become increasingly formalized and subject to exacting standards of specificity and detail with regard to the charges being made. Challenges to the sufficiency of the bill were equally commonplace here and were all too often accepted on grounds which must have seemed at times superficial or downright bewildering.[49]

The growing complexity affected the proof stage as well. Interrogatories, and the examinations and depositions which ensued, necessarily became more intricate and precise. As Professor Barnes has suggested, they became in the process proportionately less concise and consequently 'more time was demanded for drafting them, acting on them and perusing them'. In the end the material presented at the trial was often so cumbersome and unmanageable that there was a real danger of a miscarriage of that justice through the court's inadvertent failure to discern issues of central importance.[50] And, perhaps even more than in Chancery, judicial speed in Star Chamber was defeated by the proliferation of pre-trial motions. Aside from those which claimed exceptions to plaintiff's bill (which were increasingly allowed after pleadings and which always required time-consuming references to the judges), motions could be lodged to secure a wide variety of requests – from simple demands that the plaintiff put in sureties to ensure payment of costs to requests for injunctions to quiet or restore possession of property.[51] In some cases the requests were entirely legitimate, in others they were simply used to delay and complicate proceedings. But, inevitably, they slowed the judicial process and increased costs.

The growing complexity of procedure in each of these courts clearly impaired their ability to provide fair and speedy justice – in spite of the best intentions of reformers and often because of deliberate misuse of those procedures by unscrupulous litigants. But the real problems affecting the operation of the system lay in the confused relations between courts. As suggested above, jurisdictions remained somewhat fluid and unpredictable throughout the late sixteenth and early seventeenth centuries. In large measure the problem was structural. The various components of the legal system had evolved at different times and in response to particular needs and there was, therefore, bound to be some degree of duplication and confusion with regard to jurisdictions. The court of Star Chamber, for example, laid claim to a special jurisdiction over crimes against justice – matters such as perjury, forgery of deeds or documents, fraud, and embracery of juries. It was not altogether clear, however, just how Star Chamber was to proceed when those crimes had been perpetrated in the course of a case proceeding at common law. To what extent could the court impede or suspend common law proceedings or, indeed, impeach a judgment already obtained? The uncertainty led to frequent conflicts which were often difficult to resolve.[52] Much the same could be said of the court of Chancery because its jurisdiction was designed in large measure to correct the failings of common law procedure. Common injunctions staying proceedings at law could be issued by Chancery for any number of equitable considerations including breach of confidence, fraud, forgery, accident and mistake.[53] More seriously perhaps, Chancery claimed the right to rehear cases, on similar grounds, after judgment at common law. This was the most contentious jurisdictional issue in early modern English law.[54] Objections had been raised to the practice throughout the sixteenth century (beginning with the chancellorship of Thomas Wolsey) and increased dramatically during the tenure of Ellesmere. Despite an Exchequer Chamber ruling in 1598 in the case of *Finch* v. *Throgmorton* that Chancery was prohibited from reexamining matters after judgment at law, Ellesmere had pursued the practice with single-minded determination.[55] His policy deeply disturbed common lawyers and judges alike and ultimately provoked a monumental clash with Chief Justice Coke in 1616. The result was a victory for Ellesmere (both personal and professional) and for his court. The royal decree of 18 July 1616 conferred on the chancellor full power to review all matters at common law both before and after judgment.[56] In the short-term the decision appeared markedly to broaden Chancery's jurisdiction and led to a dramatic (and ultimately debilitating) increase in its business. But the long-term consequences were actually more serious. The decision effectively diminished the value and finality of judgments at law. As the judges had argued in 1598, allowing litigants to proceed to Chancery after verdict at law would mean that 'suits would be infinite and no one could be in peace for anything that the law had given him by judgement'.[57]

The process could, of course, work the other way. The clash between Chancery and the common law was perhaps the most notable jurisdictional dispute of the age, but it certainly was not the only one. From the time of his elevation as Chief Justice of Common Pleas, Coke had been involved in a protracted struggle with the civil lawyers and the officials of the ecclesiastical courts over their respective jurisdictions. Here again, the expansion of the common law had left matters uncertain. Increasingly, the common law had found ways of assuming jurisdiction over a variety of matters which by tradition had been handled by the ecclesiastical courts or by High Commission – cases of slander and defamation, suits over tithes, presentation to benefices, even wills (usually where payment of the testator's debts was concerned).[58] In order to protect their turf (and ostensibly to offer the protection of due process to litigants before ecclesiastical commissions), Coke and his colleagues were increasingly given to issuing writs of prohibition against church court proceedings. The prohibitions could be used either to halt further action in a cause, or to prevent execution of judgment and, unlike the common injunction in Chancery, were directed to the court in question rather than to the plaintiff. Since the writ did not require the court to explain its decision, the litigant was usually left in the dark as to why his proceedings had been suspended.[59] In any event, since they had been, he was forced to begin anew elsewhere.

Nor were prohibitions directed only at ecclesiastical courts. They were issued repeatedly against the courts of Admiralty and Requests and against both the provincial conciliar courts in the north and in Wales. Here again the common law courts (most notably during the tenure of Chief Justice Coke) were attempting to exercise a broad supervisory authority over the rest of the legal system to ensure conformity with the notional rules of procedure and jurisdiction. Prohibitions were issued against the court of Admiralty to challenge its jurisdiction over commercial contracts made abroad – common lawyers and judges argued that all contracts made on land, whether in England or abroad, were the concern of the common law and that Admiralty could only adjudicate those contracts (or other matters) which had actually arisen on the high seas – or to restrict its powers of arrest and imprisonment.[60] Conflicts arose with the court of Requests, as they had with Chancery, over the court's use of injunctions and its practice of hearing suits in equity after judgment at law, and with the Council in the North and the Council of the Marches of Wales over their summary procedures and their perceived invasions of common law jurisdiction.

Common law judges liked to insist that it was their responsibility to ensure that all court jurisdictions be clearly defined and scrupulously enforced. But their pretensions to supremacy over all other courts and forms of legal administration could no longer be seriously maintained in the early seventeenth century (especially after 1616) and their attempts to circumscribe other jurisdictions had less force and carried less conviction because they lacked consistent or wholehearted support from the Crown. James I's active interest in the law, and his own self-image as a kind of latter day Solomon made him more sympathetic toward the prerogative and equity courts, where his own role as a participant in the legal process was, at least in theory, more direct and immediate. But in undermining the supremacy of the common law on this issue he only added to the chaos.[61]

There were, of course other forces at work. Competition between the courts for business worked against establishing clear lines of demarcation – and in this the common law courts had been as guilty as any – and attorneys worked the system in whatever way would bring advantage to their clients and greater fees to themselves. But the real cause of the problems was the litigant. In theory, a more flexible system created greater opportunities for effective resolution of law suits, but in fact greater opportunities bred greater opportunism. Litigants were now increasingly able (and increasingly inclined) to manipulate the system to their advantage by engaging in multiple suits in multiple courts on the same or collateral issues. Professor Barnes's recent research on Jacobean Star Chamber litigation suggests that a significant majority of that court's cases (55 per cent) were initiated as some form of collateral action.[62] And the practice was by no means confined to Star Chamber litigants. Litigation all too frequently became a game of tactics and strategies designed, not to test the law, but to test the patience and perseverance of opponents. Forcing an adversary to maintain a variety of related suits in the central courts inevitably cost him a good deal of time and money. Multiple suits multiplied court charges, attorney's fees and living expenses in London. But the most serious consequence of this sort of behaviour – quite apart from exacerbating the already critical problem of congestion – was that it delayed or, indeed, precluded final resolution of the conflict. Suits became interminable (or as John Chamberlain once put it, 'immortal')[63] and the honest litigant gradually lost faith in the ability of the system to guarantee lasting remedy to those who genuinely needed it.

In a variety of ways, all of these problems contributed to the rise of litigation in the House of Lords. Certainly, in practical terms, petitioners saw in the upper house a refuge from congestion and delay and in its straightforward procedure by petition and hearing an escape from the technical complexities of legal process in other courts (and from their costs). Moreover, they saw in the High Court of Parliament an authority able to override jurisdictional conflict and provide final, definitive resolution of their disputes. At the heart of their complaints, however, was a broader and more fundamental (if largely unspoken) concern – a need to be reassured of certainty in the law. During this period there was a pervasive sense, not just among litigants, but among lawyers and judges alike, that all of the recent innovations in the law had actually undermined legal certainty. The law was now not only immensely complicated, it was also unpredictable. The refrain in fact runs through almost every major commentary on early seventeenth-century law. Leading figures such as

Coke, Ellesmere and Sir Francis Bacon all had something important to say on the subject and, though their differing backgrounds and professional biases led them to lay blame on different doorsteps, the general point was made time and again.[64] Bacon in fact claimed that uncertainty of law was 'the principal and most just challenge that is made to the laws of our nation at this time.'[65]

The responsibility for reestablishing certainty and order clearly lay with Parliament – as the sovereign law-making body in the land – and to these petitioners at least it mattered not whether they did so by legislation or judicial fiat. Seventeenth-century Englishmen did not, on the whole, view legislation and adjudication as separate and distinct parliamentary functions. Private concerns notwithstanding, it was all part of the same process. In that context it is possible to suggest (though difficult to prove) that some of these petitioners may have been motivated by the fact that Parliament had already embarked, early in 1621, on what appeared to be a comprehensive programme of law reform. The connection is based on more than just common sense. There is a direct correlation between the issues discussed in the long and very public legislative debates in the House of Commons in 1621 and 1624 and the concerns, both specific and general, raised by petitioners to the House of Lords. MPs considered proposals to relieve congestion and delay, to regulate procedure, to limit court fees and to control the spread (and centralization) of litigation.[66] Considerable attention was also paid to problems in particular courts. Chancery came in for a great deal of criticism (generated as much by its overall reputation as by the pervasive enmity toward Bacon) and a variety of proposals were put forward to reorder its procedure, to limit its fees, to control its personnel (notably the Masters of Chancery) and to define – and reduce – its jurisdiction. Bills were in fact put forward to impose time limits on Chancery actions, and even to regulate its administration of debt cases.[67] Similar attention was focused on specific abuses in the court of Wards (principally regarding its procedures in inquisitions post-mortem) and in the court of Exchequer (concerning the so-called *quominus* procedure). Throughout the debates in both Parliaments there was a strong feeling that the system as a whole needed to be 'rectified', as Sir Lionel Cranfield once put it. In that way all courts could be 'kept within their bounds' and the subject might not be 'tossed to and fro'.[68] That general concern was no doubt transmitted to the public. That is not to say that these petitioners would not have looked to the House of Lords without the lead provided by discussions in the House of Commons. Given the critical predicaments which many of them faced, they would surely have done so on their own initiative. But, at the very least, the debates on law reform may have suggested that the High Court of Parliament would now be more receptive to private demonstrations of public grievances. What is clear is that the failure of Parliament to enact more than a handful of these reform measures guaranteed that there would be a continuous flow of petitions to the upper house throughout the 1620s and beyond.

There may have been another practical consideration which led litigants to look to parliamentary remedy; their inability to obtain a hearing in the only other forum which customarily handled special appeals, the King's Privy Council. Defining the council's role in the legal system is difficult. It was not in any conventional sense (and certainly not in the view of seventeenth-century common lawyers) a court of law. It had no particular body of law to administer and did not, as a rule, try individual cases, or attempt on its own to resolve technical legal issues. Its only clearly defined jurisdiction was as a court of appeal from the Isle of Man and the Channel Islands. And yet, the council had always played an important role in private litigation. It served in a kind of supervisory capacity, offering assistance to private suitors whose ability to proceed to law through customary channels had in some way been compromised. It might, for example, order a change of venue, where judicial corruption or undue influence on a prospective jury threatened fair proceedings. It might prevail upon a given court to speed up proceedings or to give consideration to special circumstances in a case, or it might act to resolve a jurisdictional dispute which had left both parties without remedy. More often, however, the council was asked to facilitate arbitration of disputes which had not yet gone to law. For this it would customarily appoint special committees, either from within the council itself, or more often, from among prominent gentry in the local community where the dispute had originated. These committees were then empowered to settle the conflict in whatever manner seemed most appropriate and equitable, with the proviso that they eventually report back to the council on their findings. This method was used in the overwhelming majority of cases, in part because it saved the council considerable time and trouble, and in part because local arbitration fostered social stability and cohesion.

The council had always handled a wide variety of cases in this capacity. It received petitions from debtors seeking relief from the unreasonable penalties of penal bonds under the common law of contract and from creditors unable to collect outstanding obligations from imprisoned debtors. It attracted the complaints of foreign merchants, who felt ill equipped to handle the vagaries of English law, and from domestic merchants unable to settle commercial accounts. Poor petitioners looked to the council for relief from costs (and often for protection against powerful adversaries). Deserted wives sought orders for financial assistance from wayward husbands, and children orders for support from negligent parents. It handled disputes over marriage contracts, property, public offices and ecclesiastical livings. There was no predetermined jurisdiction – any more than there would be in the House of Lords – which defined the type of case which might be presented. The council represented 'a royal reservoir for the redressing of grievances' and, as such, was willing to act in all cases where there had been (or might be) inequitable proceedings or outright denial of justice.[69]

Its willingness to do so had made it immensely popular, and certainly under the Tudors the administration of private law remained a major component of council business.[70] Indeed, the board frequently found itself overwhelmed by private petitions. On a number of occasions it attempted to halt the flow of cases altogether because they had begun to distract the council from important affairs of state. The orders accomplished next to nothing – other than drawing further attention to the fact that the council was in the business of hearing private suits – and the numbers tended to grow rather than diminish.[71]

Under the Stuarts the practice of hearing private suits in council continued, but because the Privy Council registers for the first decade of James I's reign were destroyed in the fire at Whitehall in 1619, it is impossible to determine the degree to which private business remained an integral part of conciliar responsibilities. In May 1603 James I issued regulations specifying that the council should devote Tuesday afternoons to the hearing of private causes, but he was gradually forced to revise his thinking.[72] In November 1608 he appointed a special group of commissioners (effectively a subcommittee of the council) to consider the private suits presented to the king and report their findings to the council. This was done expressly to relieve the full council '(who in regard of their place and neerness to our person are often tymes so occupied in the affaires of the greatest moment of our estate) as they cannot attend the care of private suites'.[73] It is also clear that the King assumed much of the burden directly, at least for the first half of his reign. A surviving register of the king's answers to private petitions indicates that James I himself entertained and processed large numbers of appeals for legal redress of various kinds from 1603 to 1616.[74] Such activity was entirely consistent with James's self-image as the primary source of all justice. It reflects as well his interest in the law and perhaps his sense of responsibility toward his new subjects. Predictably, the public responded with enthusiasm. In the first year alone, James appears to have handled some 466 private disputes.[75] Again, in the vast majority of these cases the matter was referred to other courts or to outside arbitration, but the task of processing the petitions and choosing referees was formidable all the same.[76] In subsequent years the number of cases handled declined steadily – perhaps because of the work of the new commissioners for suits – to a low of 26 in 1616 (the final year of the surviving register), but until then they rarely dropped below a level of 100 petitions per year. Precisely what effect this had on the council's business is difficult to assess without the evidence provided by its own register, but it seems likely that the impact was substantial. During the latter part of Elizabeth's reign the

Privy Council handled on average 125–50 cases a year.[77] If the number of petitioners seeking redress remained relatively constant into the 1600s, it would suggest that James was in fact relieving the council of a great deal of troublesome business. Just how long he remained willing and able to do so after 1616, however, is not clear. Advancing age and his notoriously short attention span and lack of interest in administrative detail may well have gradually reduced his enthusiasm for the task. Increasingly during the later years James can be found referring petitions addressed to him to the council or directly to the subcommissioners for suits.[78]

What is clear is that by the 1620s the council itself was growing increasingly impatient with the job of hearing private quarrels. Administering to these petitioners was tedious and time-consuming. The council was not equipped with a staff of legal advisers (apart perhaps from the ever-present Lord Chancellor) nor did it have a supporting bureaucracy to assist in processing the complaints. And invariably private litigation proved to be a distraction from other more important matters of state. This was especially true in the 1620s (as it had been in the 1580s) as England prepared for war and undertook projects to finance overseas campaigns and the defence of the realm. Quite apart from the daily business of government, these matters required almost constant attention and afforded little spare time for what must have seemed wholly inconsequential private disputes. The council register for the 1620s is replete with protestations from the board denying a hearing to private suitors on those grounds – 'Their Lopps havinge noe time in respect of manie important affaires for his Majesties service.'[79] Almost every reference to outside arbitration which followed carried the plea that the council 'be no more troubled'. By this stage that phraseology had become standard, but there is little reason to doubt its sincerity. Indeed, in one notable case the council sent a petitioner to the House of Correction as a reward for his incessant appeals to the board.[80]

Even so, without more evidence from earlier decades and from other sources, it is difficult to demonstrate in concrete terms that the Privy Council was actively reducing its workload in this area. It remains only a strong impression. Clearly, it continued to handle private disputes of various kinds throughout the 1620s and beyond. But, if the registers can be trusted, it heard an average of only 35 to 50 cases per year, a not inconsiderable number but still a marked reduction from the levels maintained during the Elizabethan period.[81] There is also the evidence provided by the cases brought to the House of Lords in the early 1620s. At least 18 of them had been heard, often repeatedly, by the Privy Council in previous years without successful resolution. Most had abandoned the council in frustration after long delays and inattention. In some cases, of course, there may have been strategic reasons for turning to Parliament. The long list of creditors of the Muscovy (or Russia Company), for example, may have felt that the upper house would be more diligent in assisting them in the collection of their debts, since the council, in its concern over the company's crisis in 1621 and the wider effect on trade, repeatedly had issued protections for the company against its creditors.[82] In the main, however, there were few cases in the 1620s in which the plaintiff would have (or could have) anticipated contrary responses from the two institutions.[83] Indeed, a half-dozen complainants moved their cases back and forth between the two bodies during the 1620s, when circumstances – such as the dissolution of Parliament – dictated.[84] Their primary motivation in turning from the council was to achieve a speedier and perhaps more effective remedy in the House of Lords, an established court which was, after all, composed of many of the same powerful individuals who made up the council. And there was every reason for the council to encourage them to do so. Privy councillors would have recognized that the House of Lords was equipped with the powers – for instance, the ability to administer oaths – and the personnel to carry out the task more effectively. They would no doubt have welcomed any relief the upper house might have been able to offer.[85]

THE LORDS' RESPONSE: PROCEDURE AND PRACTICE

Whatever the varied forces may have been which drove petitioners into Parliament, their increasing presence gradually transformed the daily operations of the House of Lords. Initially, when the first petitions began to arrive in the winter of 1621, the house appointed *ad hoc* committees to handle each suit separately and report their findings to the house.[86] By the end of May, as the number of petitions increased, that solution had become impractical and the house elected to appoint a standing Committee for Petitions. Composed of eight members, led by the earl of Bridgewater, it was authorized to 'consider of all Petitions . . . exhibited to the House and unanswered; and to report to the House what answers are fit to be made unto them'.[87] The composition of the committee suggests that, at least at this stage, it was not considered very important. Seven of the eight members were sitting in the house for the first time, having been elevated to the peerage only in the latter half of the preceding decade, and only two – the earl of Bridgewater (son of Lord Chancellor Ellesmere) and the earl of March, had any legal training or experience.[88] Very quickly, this committee became the centre of operations for all civil litigation in the house. Its responsibilities and authority were enhanced with each Parliament in the 1620s and its membership continually increased in size and prestige. The second session of 1621 saw three new members added to its roster.[89] In 1624 the committee was appointed rather late – three weeks into the session – but it now included a dozen members, 9 of whom had sat on the original committee of 1621.[90] It was instructed to meet every Friday afternoon to conduct business. No committee was appointed at either meeting of Parliament in 1625, no doubt due to the brevity of the sessions, but the Parliament of 1626 saw the committee double in size. Twenty-four members were appointed at the opening of the session. The roster now included the Lord President of the Council as well as 10 'holdovers' from 1624.[91] A little over a month later the earl of Clare was coopted and two months after that, on his motion, the house appointed an additional 12 members, bringing the total to 37.[92] This expanded committee was now instructed to meet every Tuesday and Thursday afternoon. In 1628 a slightly smaller committee of 29 was appointed (of whom 18 had served previously), including not only the Lord President of the Council, but the Lord Admiral (the duke of Buckingham) the Lord Chamberlain (the earl of Pembroke) and the Lord Great Chamberlain (Lord Willoughby of Erseby).[93] For reasons that are not entirely clear, the house appointed a separate committee for the second session in 1629. This committee was larger, increasing from 29 to 39, but its personnel remained much the same, with 22 members held over from 1628. The Lord Admiral (assassinated the previous July) and the Lord President of the Council (appointed Lord Privy Seal in July) were replaced by the archbishop of York and Lord Treasurer Weston.[94]

All of these committees were supported by the legal assistants of the house – a large group of professional personnel summoned to attend the House of Lords by writs of assistance. These writs were issued to all of the justices of the King's Bench and Common Pleas, the barons of the Exchequer, the Master of the Rolls, the Attorney General, the Solicitor General and four king's sergeants.[95] They were summoned to give expert legal advice on all legislative and judicial matters of interest to the house and their responsibilities were taken very seriously. The command to attend the Lords, 'all other things laid aside', was seen as a binding commitment and the provisions of the writ were rigorously enforced.[96] Their role in offering legal advice to the Committee for Petitions was obviously crucial, though their attendance at the committee was not regularized until the Long Parliament. In 1621 assistants were not assigned to the committee until the second session. Then, at the request of the earl of Bridgewater, three king's sergeants and the Attorney General were appointed and the committee was given discretion to call any of the judges to attend as proved necessary.[97] There is no record of assistants being formally appointed to the Committee for Petitions in 1624, but they were clearly consulted on a regular basis.

In the beginning each petition was supposed to be delivered to the Clerk of Parliament who would then bring it before the whole house, where it would be read and (if accepted) referred to the Committee for Petitions.[98] By 1624, however, this procedure had been abandoned under pressure of new business. There was no longer time to have every petition read in the house and it was therefore decided that petitions should be sent directly to the committee.[99] Practical considerations also forced the house to broaden the committee's mandate. Initially, each committee was simply directed to consider petitions and offer recommendations to the house as a whole as to their disposition before any action was taken. But in each of the Parliaments of the 1620s the procedure proved to be too cumbersome and the committee was eventually given power to retain or reject petitions without prior consultation with the whole house.[100] Its decisions, however, were to be reported to the house once a week.

There were in fact no well-defined ground rules for accepting or rejecting petitions. The basic presumption was that cases would be accepted only where the parties had been entirely without remedy elsewhere; that is, where parliamentary remedy was a matter of last resort. But that claim could be (and was) made in a variety of ways, not all of which were strictly legitimate. It was therefore left up to the committee to exercise its own judgement. The lack of specific guidelines was probably intentional. It reflected the Lords' belief that their ability to offer remedy could not be (and ought not to be) constrained by preconceived notions about their jurisdiction. Nonetheless, rejections were numerous. In most cases the underlying reason was that the Lords felt that remedy was available elsewhere. In 1624, for example, Francis Chapman petitioned the Lords seeking redress against a relative who had withheld documents and evidence of his title to property in Lincolnshire. He had made no effort, over 22 years, to prosecute his claim in any court, as for instance, by way of discovery in Chancery. So, despite his claim to be a 'simple poore man' who was 'not able to wage lawe with soe powerful an adversarie' (an assertion all too commonly made) the Lords recommended that he 'take his course, as others of the King's subjects doe, in other courts of equity'. They declared it 'not a fitt busines for the parliament'.[101] Other cases were dismissed because the claims made against defendants were too vague and obscure, or because the matter itself was frivolous or inconsequential. Rank opportunism was also treated with contempt, as in the case of John Johnson. Johnson had been sued in the King's Bench by Sir Giles Mompesson for selling 200 bushels of oats at a rate well above the standard market price, and had had judgment passed against him for £38. Taking advantage of the Lords' proceedings against Mompesson, Johnson requested that the judgment against him not be enrolled and the proceedings in King's Bench be dismissed. However, the Lord Chief Justice of King's Bench informed the house that Johnson had in fact sold oats at 2s above the market price and the Lords summarily returned his petition without answer.[102]

The Lords were also protected against this sort of abuse by rules adopted early in 1621 which imposed penalties against those who made false accusations. The original suggestion had come, perhaps not surprisingly, from Lord Keeper Williams, who had just been exonerated by the house in the case of Sir John Bouchier.[103] The Lord Keeper actually proposed that in future no party complained of should be summoned to appear until the complainant had put in security to pay costs, in the event that his allegation proved untrue. The notion was adopted, but not the specific practice. The Lords did not demand security of all plaintiffs – the complications would have been enormous – but freely levied costs against those making unjust accusations or unduly troubling adversaries.[104]

If the plaintiff was successful and his case was accepted for review, the petition would normally be returned to the clerk's office, copied and then forwarded to any named defendants. The defendant was then ordered to appear, within a specified period to answer the complainants', charges, or to show 'good cause' why the plaintiff's requests should not be granted. The summons carried the force of a formal subpoena and the defendant ignored it at his peril. Failure to appear rendered the defendant 'in contempt of court' for which he could be fined and/or imprisoned.[105] Very few failed to present their case.

It was clearly in their interests to do so, and in timely fashion, because of actions which the Lords might take on the plaintiff's behalf prior to a hearing. In many cases, in fact, the Lords were required to act just to facilitate a hearing in the house itself. The most compelling request of this kind, and one often made by plaintiffs, was for an order securing their release from imprisonment. The request could be made for a variety of reasons. In some cases the plea was an end in itself; that is, the petitioner claimed that he had originally been arrested without just cause and he requested release on grounds that his imprisonment had been unreasonable or unwarranted.[106] In other cases the imprisonment had occurred according to due process, but had been a result of the very case which the plaintiff wished to reargue before the Lords. Here release was a matter of practical necessity: the petitioner required his freedom in order to prepare and present his appeal.[107]

Providing that the evidence appeared to justify it, the Lords could respond to these requests in one of two ways. They could either instruct the Clerk of the Crown (who was always present) to issue, through the Crown Office in Chancery, a standard writ of habeas corpus, returnable to the house itself, or they could issue their own order directly to the keeper in question, commanding him to release the plaintiff into Parliament's custody.[108] In most cases, release was provisional and the Lords were careful to provide security for the individual's continued appearance, either in the form of bail (provided prior to release), or in the form of a personal recognizance to the house. The Lords were also careful to specify the particular pretext on which the order was issued. This was vitally important because a number of plaintiffs had been imprisoned on a judgment of debt, or in consequence of suits wholly unrelated to that over which the House had taken cognizance. If the plaintiff ultimately failed to make his case, or to justify his continued liberty, the order would be revoked and the individual returned to the custody of the original warden.

Another common request made by plaintiffs was for an order staying proceedings in an inferior court. The request was usually made in order to allow the house to consider some major issue, not pleadable in that particular court, which was central to the petitioner's interests in the suit. In other cases the plaintiff might question the appropriateness of that court to hear the suit, or might claim that its proceedings were inherently prejudicial to the plaintiff's cause. In responding to these requests, the Lords issued what amounted to a 'common injunction', such as was often used in similar circumstances in the court of Chancery but with one important difference. In Chancery, common injunctions bound the individual litigant and prohibited him from pursuing his case. Alternatively, injunctions issued by the House of Lords were, almost without exception, directed to the court in question.[109]

Again, in most cases, the stay was provisional and might be removed once the house had completed its investigation, though orders allowing the court to resume proceedings might, in consequence, include new instructions as to how the case should be disposed.[110] In some disputes, of course, the house was able to bring about a settlement between the parties through in-house arbitration, in which case the original proceedings might be suspended altogether.[111] Whatever the outcome, the House remained adamant that its own proceedings in a case superseded all others. In one instance the Lords had ordered the parties to a suit to join in a new commission designed to settle differences between them. In an attempt to scuttle the commission the defendant resumed proceedings against the plaintiff in the King's Bench for debt, an action which resulted in the plaintiff's arrest and imprisonment. The house immediately ordered the plaintiff released and then summoned both the defendants and the arresting office to answer for their contempt.[112]

The house was also called upon to issue a number of 'special injunctions' (similar to those used in Chancery) designed to protect the material interests of plaintiffs during litigation in the house. This could involve issuing orders to secure possession of property (under threat of unlawful entry) or to prohibit specific actions being taken, such as laying waste to woods or crops.[113] In most cases, however, the injunction was an order for sequestration of assets or profits from property in dispute, typically into the hands of a third party – 'some indifferent hands' – until right had been established, either in the house or elsewhere.[114] In all cases the action was taken only after the defendant had been given the opportunity to 'show cause' why it should not be done.

Two other preliminary expedients were often needed by plaintiffs. The first was the removal into the house of records and documentation from other courts. The request was usually acted upon when removal was clearly necessary for the plaintiff to make his case, or if the Lords wished to have a comprehensive 'brief' of the case at hand. In most cases, the request was usually limited to specific items – court orders, articles of evidence, or depositions of witnesses – but the committee was empowered to summon any and all records which it might feel were necessary to make an informed decision.[115] The other expedient was the appointment of legal counsel for impoverished litigants. This might be done when it appeared that the plaintiff was genuinely too poor to afford representation. In one case, for instance, the house called on two members of Gray's Inn to represent a plaintiff *'in forma pauperis'*.[116]

The final step in the preliminary proceedings before hearing was the summoning of witnesses. This was normally handled in one of three ways. For the most common method, the parties would simply be granted a warrant, directed to the witnesses named, commanding them to attend the house and appear at the hearing to testify viva voce. The warrant was usually worded along the following lines:

> Ordered ... that AB etc. shall forthwith, and without any delaye, by virtue of this order, attend the most Honorable and High Court of Parliament, there to make answers to all such questions and interrogatories as shall be administered unto them, either by that High Court, or by any person or persons authorized by the same, Whereof they and every one of them are not to fail, or they will answer the contrary to their uttermost perrilles.[117]

Once the witnesses were assembled, they were sworn by the clerk at the bar of the house and then waited to be called to testify. The wait could be a long one. Increasingly over the decade, as cases began to back up in the house, prescheduled hearings had to be postponed, often repeatedly. The delays could place an inordinate burden on the plaintiff, who not only incurred the cost of bringing witnesses to London, but was also responsible for their maintenance while there. The house was aware of the problem and in cases where the plaintiff could demonstrate hardship (or where the witnesses were old and in danger of dying before they could testify) the second option was exercised. Here the witnesses would be examined by specially appointed Masters in Chancery on the basis of interrogatories submitted by both parties and approved by the house. In all cases the defendant and his counsel were allowed to cross-examine. The resulting depositions would then be sealed and returned to the clerk to be kept until the hearing.[118] The third option was identical to the second, except that the process was conducted locally; that is, the house would order that a special commission be granted, under the Great Seal, to a body of local magistrates or dignitaries (most often JPs) and would give them authority to conduct the examinations on previously approved interrogatories. The sealed depositions would then be returned to the house on or before a specified date well in advance of the hearing.

The scheduling of hearings was generally based on the principle that cases were to be heard in the order in which they were brought into the house. This made it imperative that each petition be presented first to the clerk, so that he could keep an accurate record. In the early 1620s Henry Elsyng kept a running list of cases presented. Later, his successor, John Browne, would number each petition as it came in. (Neither system appears to have been terribly successful.) Inevitably, complications arose as cases developed more slowly in the prehearing stage than expected and the order of precedence would have to be manipulated for greater efficiency. But on the whole the house adhered to the general rule. Indeed, at the close of the 1624 Parliament it was agreed that cases which had not been resolved at the end of the session would maintain their standing into the next Parliament.[119]

Once the case had been scheduled (with some degree of certainty) the plaintiff was required to give adequate notice of the forthcoming hearing to the defendant. There were no rules governing the amount of time required for adequate notice, but first hearings were rarely scheduled less than a week in advance, so it is safe to assume the defendants were given at least that much warning. By 1628 the house had begun to specify the period of warning in its orders. One plaintiff was ordered to provide written notice 'within these seven days' of a hearing scheduled three weeks later.[120] Complaints from defendants that they had not had proper notification were taken seriously and, if the complaint proved genuine, the house would willingly reschedule the hearing to give the defendant adequate time to prepare his case.

As in any court, the length and number of hearings required in any given case depended entirely on the nature of the request being made and on the complexity of the legal issues involved. Often the hearings were brief and of limited purpose because the house was only asked to remove obstacles which had prevented the plaintiff from initiating or completing proceedings elsewhere. These requests were usually quite straightforward, but they depended on the house being willing and able to exercise its authority externally. They reflected, in fact, many of the same problems that traditionally arose in cases before the Privy Council and in dealing with them the house was exercising much the same function. One of the most common applications of this kind came from indigent petitioners who had been prevented from initiating normal proceedings because of their poverty. Typically, they would ask the house to intercede on their behalf with a lower court, to gain permission to sue *in forma pauperis*.[121]

Like the council, the house was more than willing to do so, and the request was usually granted *pro forma* (though the house would eventually require that the petitioner offer evidence that he or she was worth less than £10 per annum). In most cases, the house simply moved the court in question to waive its customary fees and admit the petitioner to writ process and representation free of charge.[122]

Another common request of this kind was for the house to override claims of privilege which had protected defendants from legal action. Where the defendant was a member of the house, as often happened, the house normally informed the individual of the complaint and solicited his response. Almost invariably the member agreed to waive privilege and allow the matter to be heard.[123] There was a sense in all of these cases that the Lords expected as much from fellow members. Where the member was not forthcoming, as occurred in one case, the house could override privilege on its own initiative. In this instance, Lord Deyncourt had left his 94-year-old father destitute by refusing to pay rents on properties divested to him in trust, forcing his father to sue in Chancery to collect the arrears. Lord Deyncourt's subsequent claim of privilege had stayed the suit and his father therefore petitioned the house for relief. The Lords summarily ordered the suit to proceed, notwithstanding the claim of privilege, unless the arrears of rent were paid before the beginning of the next legal term.[124] Not all claims, however, involved members of Parliament. In one notable case, the house was asked to override a general protection issued by the Privy Council in favour of the Muscovy Company against suits initiated by its creditors. It did so without hesitation.[125]

The Lords were also asked on occasion to intercede directly in lower court proceedings. In one case they did so to protect a plaintiff against what appeared to be prejudicial actions taken by the staff of the court of Wards.[126] In another, they were asked to prevail upon the court of Requests to expedite a case which had been inadvertently suspended by the departure of the then Master, Sir John Suckling, who had conducted the initial hearings.[127] More often, however, the problems encountered by litigants were recurring ones which arose because of procedural or structural defects in the system. Frequently cited as problematic were the rules governing Bill of Review procedure in the court of Chancery. In the absence of any outside appellate recourse from the court, disgruntled litigants wishing to challenge a Chancery decree were forced to secure a rehearing in that court through a Bill of Review. However, the procedure was inherently prejudicial to the applicant. In order to be granted a review, the appellant had to demonstrate his 'good faith' by first fulfilling all of the conditions of the original decree; that is, the judgment had to be obeyed in all points before a bill to reverse it would even be entertained.[128] This imposed undue hardship in many cases, especially where, as often happened, the decree involved a major financial settlement between the parties. In addition, the complainant was forced to provide bonds and securities to guarantee the payment of costs and damages should the case go against him.[129] Perhaps more importantly, the bill would only be granted if the petitioner could demonstrate some error or errors in the law in the body of the decree. Only those errors could be discussed, and then 'without averment or further examination of matter of fact'.[130] It was, as Sir Matthew Hale later described it, a 'somewhat straight-laced' procedure.[131] In special cases a bill might be allowed if new matter were discovered which could not have been made available for the original hearing, but this was much more the exception than the rule. In short, the procedure was not designed to accommodate a rehearing on the general merits of the cause or on the basis that the proceedings had been arbitrary or corrupt.[132] And yet that was very often what was needed. In the case of Richard Wright, for example, the masters of the court had issued a decree awarding possession of a piece of property to Wright's adversaries, contrary to a report issued by referees and without a hearing by the Lord Chancellor. As he explained to the House of Lords ('his last refuge') he was required to turn over the property in question before he could be admitted to a Bill of Review. He requested that they prevail on the Lord Keeper to waive that condition. The Lords agreed and recommended that the case be reheard on a Bill of Review, with the sole proviso that Wright put in sufficient security to defray any costs or damages that might be awarded.[133] A similar situation had occurred in the case of a London merchant. George Morgan had actually obtained a decree in Chancery from Lord Chancellor Bacon awarding him £22,600 in settlement of some long-standing commercial accounts. Unfortunately, Bacon's decree was abruptly voided by Lord Keeper Williams, solely on the basis of a petition from the seven defendants. His decision – that Morgan should settle instead for £879 – was made out of term and without a proper hearing. Again, by the rules of the court once the decree had been enrolled Morgan would have had to accept the lesser amount and presumably discharge the defendants of their obligation before he could be admitted to a Bill of Review. That was clearly unreasonable and the Lords ordered instead that the case be reheard in its entirety (this time by Lord Keeper Coventry) and that neither party was to 'take any benefit of any former decree or order.' The Lord Keeper was additionally requested to proceed with 'all convenient expedition'.[134]

Perhaps not surprisingly, the Lords were also called upon to intercede in a variety of jurisdictional disputes, typically in the context of a complaint made by a petitioner that his or her legitimate proceedings in one court had been stayed by an injunction issued out of another – the usual result of collateral actions frequently undertaken by defendants. The petitioner would then request that the house overrule the injunction or, alternatively, make a clear determination on where the suit ought best to be tried. Ralph Starkey, for example, petitioned the house in 1626 asking for a determination on the proper jurisdiction for a case involving a disputed will and property in Cheshire. Starkey had initiated proceedings in Chancery, but the defendant (his younger brother) had then secured a reference to the judges to determine whether the Chancery proceedings did not in fact infringe on the jurisdiction of the County Palatine of Chester. The judges ruled that they did and the Chancery proceedings were stayed. In reviewing the case the Lords determined that the suit ought to proceed in Chancery, notwithstanding the Chester jurisdiction. Their decision was based on the fact that the northern jurisdiction would not accept the depositions of witnesses taken in the earlier Chancery proceedings and, since most of Ralph Starkey's witnesses were now dead, his case would have been wholly and unfairly compromised.[135] Equitable considerations, rather than a strict ruling on jurisdiction, carried the day. In another case in 1628 Sir Humphrey Ferrers petitioned the house protesting an injunction issued out of the court of Wards which had stayed proceedings in the Prerogative Court of Canterbury touching the estate of his father-in-law, Sir John Packington. The injunction had ostensibly been issued to protect the interests of Sir John's grandson, a ward of the Crown, but had actually been granted on a minor technicality at the behest of his widow, to prevent the ecclesiastical court from awarding administration of the estate to Ferrers. The Lords reviewed the case in full and determined that the Ward's injunction amounted to unwarranted and unnecessary interference. They not only ordered that the proceedings should continue in the Prerogative Court (taking the concerns of the court of Wards into account), but, in a rather unusual departure, went on to issue their own recommendations as to how the case should actually be settled.[136] As a rule, injunctions were seen as a nuisance and an impediment to judicial celerity and the courts which had granted them were expected to offer clear and reasonable justification for their issue or withdraw them.[137]

Most of these actions were designed to facilitate proceedings elsewhere and did not constitute a formal appeal, at least in a conventional sense. Clearly, however, the Lords were required to consider the substance of many of these cases in order to make an informed decision on how best to resolve them elsewhere. And they could (and did) choose in a number of instances simply to void all prior proceedings and former decrees in a case in favour of an entirely new trial of the central matters in dispute.[138] That was not the same as reversing the substance of an earlier decree in favour of one party over another, but for the aggrieved plaintiff, it amounted to a successful appeal all the same.

The house was, of course, willing and able to hear appeals fully itself. In the case of complaints from the courts of common law it generally did so, according to statutory authority, by way of writ of error.[139] Its appellate jurisdiction over courts of equity was perhaps less clearly defined, but evolved rapidly (largely out of necessity) through the Parliaments of the 1620s. As suggested above, the absence of appellate recourse from the courts of equity, and most particularly from the court of Chancery, was one of the central complaints against the early modern legal system. But it was also a difficult problem to resolve. On the face of it the limitation made sense. In theory the provision of equitable remedy was the responsibility of the king, who acted through 'intermediaries' appointed from his council. As James I reminded his Star Chamber audience in 1616, the Lord Keeper was nothing so much as 'the dispenser of the king's conscience', and the principle undoubtedly applied relative to the responsibilities of the Lord Privy Seal in the court of Requests.[140] To suggest that an appeal was possible, in any conventional sense, from either court, was to imply that royal justice was fallible or that it could be (or ought to be) subject to independent review. Contemporary political theory would not easily accommodate that sort of assertion.

However, the theory itself bore little relation to practical reality. None of these courts was any longer an adjunct assembly of the king's council. They were completely independent and thoroughly institutionalized courts with highly sophisticated procedures and professional staffs and, in truth, they operated far more frequently with reference to principles of common law than to any 'divinely ordained' system of natural law.[141] Moreover, as suggested above, the powers exercised by these courts had steadily expanded during the early seventeenth century and their actions – particularly in real property disputes – could have a considerable and often decisive impact. In view of the increasing delegation of real judicial authority within the courts themselves (notably to the masters in both Chancery and Requests) and the increasing participation of the common law judges in equity proceedings, the immunity of those decisions from subsequent review or reversal must have seemed both anachronistic and unfair.

As it was, once a Chancery decree had been enrolled the disgruntled litigant had few options. He or she could proceed by Bill of Review, with all of the limitations which that involved, or he could petition the king, requesting an entirely new hearing by a special commission of review appointed under the Great Seal. The latter procedure was inevitably slow and expensive and remained singularly unpopular.[142] The only other avenue of redress was to proceed by private bill and attempt to reverse the decree by act of Parliament. Again, this method involved great cost and delay, requiring as it did extensive hearings by both houses. It was, however, tried repeatedly in the 1620s, notably without success. Of the seven bills presented to reverse decrees in the court of Chancery, five never made it past a first reading in the House of Commons. The remaining two passed the lower house and were read and committed in the upper, but one was lost at the dissolution of the

1624 Parliament, and the other was withdrawn when both parties agreed to have the Lord Keeper rehear the entire case on its merits.[143] Similarly, the one bill presented to reverse a decree in the court of Requests was laid aside in favour of a special commission, appointed by the Lords, which was given authority to rehear and settle the original dispute.[144]

The logical solution to this difficulty (or so it obviously seemed to litigants) was a straightforward appeal by way of petition to the upper house. Technically, this was probably not correct practice. Towards the end of the century, Sir Matthew Hale would contend that the upper house could only legitimately review a Chancery decree with the express permission of the king, granted, by way of special commissions, on a case by case basis.[145] But that was not altogether clear to (or accepted by) members of the house in the 1620s. In fact, their response to the first petitions presented in 1621 was somewhat ambiguous. Four petitions requesting review of Chancery proceedings were presented in the first session of the Parliament. No action appears to have been taken on any of them, though this may have simply reflected the Lords' preoccupation with the proceedings against Lord Chancellor Bacon. Significantly perhaps, one of these petitions was endorsed by the earl of Leicester, with a note which read 'the petitioners must accuse some particular of bribery or corruption, else reiected'.[146] That might suggest either that the Lords were not interested, at this stage, in complaints which did not pertain directly to Bacon's case, or that they were genuinely reluctant to hear a straightforward appeal on the merits of a cause.[147] The issue then arose more directly, in second session, when the Lords began proceedings on the case of Sir John Bouchier.[148] Bouchier's petition was not actually an appeal on the substance of a Chancery decree, but instead a complaint that Lord Keeper Williams had decreed his case peremptorily, without hearing his witnesses. The debates which followed the reading of Bouchier's petition reflect some notable uncertainty among the members about this type of litigation. In the first place, there was considerable confusion as to whether his complaint represented a formal appeal. Some insisted it was, others claimed it was a simple petition of complaint. The question was then raised as to whether appeals from Chancery lay to the house and, if so, what form they ought to take.[149] Lord Say, for one, argued that this was an appeal and it ought to be heard because there was 'noe appeall from the Chauncery but hither'.[150] The Lord Keeper himself agreed, but claimed that appeals lay to the house only indirectly. The proper course was 'firste to the Kinge and then hither', presumably by way of a specific commission to the house.[151]

In the event, the petition was referred to the Committee for Privileges, which was asked to determine 'whether it be a formal appeal for matter of justice or no'.[152] The committee's report, made a week later, did little to clarify matters. They claimed that they could not find 'that the word "appeal" is usual in any petition for any matter to be brought in hither, but they find that all matters complained of here were by petition only'. Therefore, they seem to have concluded, since matters were only brought before the house by way of petition, and the word appeal was not used in any of them, this must not be an appeal. They suggested that 'the ancient accostomed form' of appeal was 'to the King and his Great Council' – wording which could have been construed to mean, in a medieval context, the king in Parliament. They went on to say that the only available precedent was a complaint of corruption brought before Parliament by petition against the late fourteenth-century Lord Chancellor, Michael de la Pole.[153]

Notwithstanding, the committee left the 'form' of Bouchier's petition to the house and recommended that they hear his accusation against Lord Keeper Williams. Bouchier failed to support his charges, and the house agreed (with three dissenting votes) that Lord Keeper Williams had in fact offered Bouchier a fair hearing.[154] Bouchier then asked that the house review the case on its merits. The request was not rejected out of hand, as has sometimes been suggested.[155] During the hearing a number of members expressed a willingness to consider the substance of the case, as an appeal, once the Lord Keeper's reputation had been cleared. Indeed, even the Lord Keeper claimed that he was 'wylling that the merittes of the cause might be herde here'.[156] The idea was endorsed by the earls of Cambridge, Dorset, and (by implication) Sheffield, as well as by Archbishop Abbot and the Lord Chamberlain. The only voice in outright opposition was that of Prince Charles, who claimed that Bouchier had based his appeal on a claim that he had not been properly heard in Chancery and, since that had now been disproved, the house ought not to proceed with him further. That perhaps prompted the suggestion from the Lord Chamberlain that a new petition might later be submitted by the plaintiff.[157] In the end Bouchier was censured and forced to make a public submission both at the bar of the house and in Chancery and no further word was heard from him.[158] But the willingness of at least some of the Lords to entertain his case, notwithstanding his reckless accusation, signalled the emergence of a new appellate jurisdiction.

During the Parliament of 1624 the house received a handful of petitions requesting review of Chancery proceedings and took action on at least four of them. One petitioner complained that his case in 1621 had never been heard by Lord Chancellor Bacon. The decree had been issued instead by the Masters in Chancery, without notice and during the long vacation on the basis of a petition from his adversaries.[159] Another complainant asserted that the meaning of the Lord Keeper's decree had been improperly understood by the clerk and wrongly entered on the records.[160] In both of these cases, the Lords took what seemed to be the most expedient and reasonable path. They simply referred the petitions back to the Lord Keeper to review and give relief, if he saw just cause, with the proviso that the complainants were to pay their opponents' costs if their claims proved unfounded.[161] Their response to the other two cases more nearly resembled a formal appellate review, and embroiled the house in minor controversy. In the first Timothy Pinkeny appealed against a decree issued by Lord Keeper Williams in 1623.[162] Pinkeny had been involved in a protracted series of suits to recover debts owed him by Sir John Kennedy. His case had first been heard in Chancery under Lord Chancellor Bacon. Referees had been appointed to settle accounts and had certified that Pinkeny was owed some £700. Unfortunately, the case lapsed with Bacon's dismissal and had to be initiated anew under Lord Keeper Williams. The new Lord Keeper decreed in favour of Kennedy, but did so without proper hearing. At that point Sir John Kennedy died and, in desperation, Pinkeny petitioned the king. James I referred his petition to two Privy Council referees, Lords Sheffield and Russell, who subsequently recommended that Pinkeny be relieved. The case was then reheard by the Lord Keeper, who ordered that Sir John Kennedy's principal estate, the manor of Barne Elmes, should be sold to pay his debts, but again he refused to admit Pinkeny as a creditor.

At that point Pinkeny and other creditors appealed to the upper house, alleging that the property was being sold at well under its real value (to a friend of Kennedy's) and that the Lord Keeper's distribution of the assets gave everything to Kennedy's heirs, leaving only £1,000 for his creditors. The Lords reviewed the case and ordered that the manor should be sold 'at the best value'. They then directed that a new commission be issued out of Chancery to audit and sequester the profits of Kennedy's estate and control distribution of the assets. This order was issued on the last day of the 1624 Parliament.[163] It was not carried out. In 1626 Pinkeny petitioned the house again, alleging that the Lord Keeper had flatly refused to issue the new commission.[164] After witnesses verified Pinkeny's charge, Bishop Williams was summoned to answer his 'contempt'. The former Lord Keeper, while claiming that he had never behaved with anything but 'awe, duty, and reverence', towards the authority of the house, argued that the Lords' order of 1624 had been 'misconceived'. He claimed that the house had been ignorant of the fact that he had already been directed by the king to sell the manor and distribute the profits. Having done so, he saw no need for a new commission and accordingly ignored their order.[165] The explanation was not well received by the house, nor should it have been. Their order had not been 'misconceived' – they had been fully aware of his earlier proceedings and had clearly found them wanting. Indeed, they had been the very basis of Pinkeny's appeal. Williams was ordered to acknowledge his mistake and apologize to the house.[166] In the meantime the present Lord Keeper was instructed, once again, to review the proceeds from the sale of the property and relieve the petitioner, Pinkeny, according to justice and equity.[167]

The other important Chancery appeal in 1624 was brought by William Matthews. Matthews had purchased the manor of Llandaffe, in Glamorganshire, from Sir Henry Billingsley, who had in turn acquired the property through a forfeiture, when the original owner, one Edmund Matthews, failed to make good his debts. After the sale Edmund Matthews sued both Billingsley and William Matthews in Chancery to recover the property, alleging that they had conspired to defraud him. The then Lord Chancellor Ellesmere dismissed the claim, but a subsequent suit in Chancery under Lord Chancellor Bacon resulted in a decree for Edmund Matthews. Bacon decreed that the manor should be reconveyed to Edmund Matthews, for which he was to reimburse William Matthews a mere £2,000, some £3,000 less than the property was then worth.

Matthews had actually appealed the decision to the Lords in June 1621, but had not been heard. By the time he petitioned in 1624, Edmund Matthews had died and the property had passed to his son, George Matthews. In the event, his appeal was heard by Committee for Petitions, who reviewed the Chancery proceedings in full and elected to set aside Bacon's decree. They ordered George Matthews to pay William Matthews £5,260, in compensation for the loss of the manor of Llandaffe, and even devised the schedule by which payments were to be made over the next three years. In the meantime, the property itself was to stand encumbered, until the debt was fully paid. Their recommendation was then approved by the house.

The same afternoon, however, the Lords received a petition from the defendant, George Matthews, protesting the order. He claimed that Bacon's decree had already been appealed to the king, and had been duly confirmed, and he argued that the house did not, as he understood it, reverse decrees, except by bill. In any event, he argued, he had not been party to the original suit, and should not be penalized by this reversal. His petition was referred to a committee of three lords who on the following day recommended that the entire dispute be reviewed in Chancery by the Lord Keeper, and 'by such Lords of Parliament, as shall be nominated by the House . . .'. Toward that end, the Lord Keeper was to 'be an humble suitor to his Majesty, from the House, for a commission unto himself and the Lords that shall be named by the House for the said review and final determination of the cause . . .'. The recommendation was promptly adopted, eight lords were appointed to sit on the commission and the house then ordered that the case should be heard in Chancery the following Michaelmas term.'[168]

Sir Matthew Hale made much of this order (as have other historians since) in his discussion of the Lords' appellate jurisdiction. He argued that the house, having reversed Bacon's decree, suddenly thought better of the idea, and decided to pursue the 'true and regular way of reviewing a decree; namely by commission'.[169] The evidence really does not support that view. The committee which drew the order – none of whom had sat on the Committee for Petitions – may have concluded on their own that the Committee for Petitions had acted hastily or unfairly toward George Matthews, and that another hearing was in order. But the decision to solicit a commission from the king was, in all probability, not a reflection of uncertainty over their jurisdiction, but instead a matter of practical necessity. The petition was received and considered on 28 May, and ordered on the 29th, the very day on which Parliament was prorogued until 2 November. If a rehearing of the dispute was to take place, it would have to be done elsewhere. It was for that reason that they ordered the case to be heard in Chancery at the beginning of Michaelmas term, before Parliament was scheduled to reconvene. What is important is their insistence on continuing participation in the case during a recess – something for which a special commission would have been entirely appropriate.[170] They could just as easily have referred the dispute to a rehearing and determination by the Lord Keeper on his own, as they had done in earlier cases. But instead they delegated members of the house to assist in the hearing, to demonstrate their continuing interest in (and responsibility for) the outcome of the suit.

Thereafter, in the Parliaments of the 1626 and 1628/9, the Lords continued to review Chancery proceedings and decrees on a regular basis. In at least two cases, decrees were set aside;[171] in two others, the decree was referred back to the Lord Keeper for his review,[172] and in another, a Chancery suit was stayed in favour of a complete hearing and settlement in the house.[173] They did, it should be said, find as well for the court and acted on a number of occasions to confirm or enforce Chancery judgments and orders.[174] In either case, at no time were their proceedings challenged, either by the Lord Keeper, or by the king. Nor were objections raised about the Lords' decisions in appeals from other courts. In one case, for example, the house overturned a decision of a court of Delegates, which had unfairly annulled a grant of administration awarded in the Prerogative Court of Canterbury.[175] In this case, however, the Lords instructed the plaintiffs to petition the king for the appointment of a new Commission of Delegates to review the prior proceedings. The Lord Keeper volunteered to 'further the matter with the King' and a new commission was duly granted six weeks later.[176] In another case, in early 1629, the Committee for Petitions reviewed a decision in the consistory court of Carlisle, and on the recommendation of the archbishop of York, annulled an order of excommunication which had been issued by the chancellor of the diocese against the plaintiffs. Then, on the further recommendation of the bishop of Norwich, they summoned the chancellor of the diocese to answer in the house for his vexatious proceedings.[177]

Had the king or officers of any of these courts felt their judicial prerogatives threatened by these proceedings, there clearly would have been protests from all quarters. But there were none. This was very much a cooperative effort, made possible, in part, by the fact that many of the officers involved (not least the Lord Keeper) were present in the house and privy to its deliberations. The Lords were not (and were not seen to be) deliberately expanding their jurisdiction at the expense of other tribunals. They were merely attempting to carry out their responsibilities as the High Court of the realm – responsibilities which had been expressly conveyed to them by the Crown.

Much of the work done by the house did not, of course, involve conventional appeals. Far more of their time was given over to the simple process of arbitration, either in first instance suits or in cases where previous litigation had failed to resolve differences. Most often these cases involved disputes over property or outstanding debts. A long-standing argument, for instance, between the widow Rogers and Sir Arthur Ingram, over boundaries and property rights belonging to two adjoining manors in Somerset, found its way into the house in 1624, and was conclusively settled after arbitration by the earl of Bridgewater and Lord Russell.[178] A similar conflict between Sir John Savage and Thomas Taylor, over title and possession of the manor of Wooton in Hampshire, was brought to the house in 1624 and again in 1626 and was heard extensively by the Committee for Petitions.[179] Documents were summoned, accounts of the profits were audited and witnesses were heard, but the case could not be concluded by the end of the latter Parliament. Savage then took the case to the Privy Council in 1627, where it was heard by a committee of three. But they too were unable to resolve differences,[180] and the case came back to the House of Lords in 1628. It was finally settled through a compromise agreement offered by one of the parties and endorsed by the committee in late June.[181]

By far the most time-consuming and complex process of arbitration undertaken by the Lords in the 1620s involved the financial affairs of the Muscovy Company. Over the course of the decade the Lords heard more than a dozen claims against the company for outstanding debts. The company had, in fact, fallen on hard times in the previous decade and matters had reached a critical stage in 1620.[182] Two years before the company had entered into a joint venture with the East India Company to undertake whaling expeditions. The Muscovy Company did not have the capital to finance its share, so borrowed heavily from outside individuals. The venture was a total failure, resulting in losses of £11,000. At the same time the Russian trade was in a state of severe decline. The combined effects of these losses convinced the governor of the company, Sir Thomas Smythe, that it ought to be wound up. This was done in 1620. But almost immediately a new joint stock company was formed, under the same name, which purchased the remaining assets and privileges of the old company for £12,000. Under the agreement, however, the new company also undertook to pay all of the outstanding debts and liabilities of the old. Unfortunately, the new company's finances were badly managed –

all of the capital raised was put into new trading ventures and nothing was put in reserve to pay the interest due on its inherited loans.

By early 1621 the loans were coming due and creditors began to appeal for assistance to the Privy Council. The council's position, however, was difficult. In order to convince the prospective adventurers of the new company to invest in the first place, they had promised them protection against suits for the old company's debts. This was clearly done to prevent the further decay of trade, but it was grossly unfair to the creditors because the new company had in fact assumed responsibility for paying the loans as part of its purchase agreement. The council may have been misled, but they fulfilled their promise and protected the goods of the new company from seizure in October 1621.[183] By November, however, the creditors had petitioned the king, and James attempted to mitigate the crisis by appointing a special commission to investigate the company's debts and devise a method of repayment.[184] The commission reported its findings in mid-December – that the company had debts of £24,000 – and recommended that the debts of the old company should be paid by those who incurred them and those of the new by means of a new assessment levied on the stockholders. The matter could not be so easily settled, however, largely because the membership of the new company included members of the old and because the liabilities of the respective companies were then in litigation in the court of Exchequer. The company was effectively able to ignore the commission's directive and, by 1624, the creditors remained unpaid and turned to the House of Lords for relief.

The Lords had already taken responsibility for one such complaint, in early 1621, when the house was asked to enforce the Privy Council's previous award to Sir James Cunningham.[185] Cunningham's claim had been reviewed by a committee of Lords, who resolved, after examining the company's accounts and the testimony of Sir Thomas Smythe, that the debt ought to be paid.[186] (In doing so, of course, they invited all of Sir James's many creditors to petition the house for relief against *his* debts.)[187] However, the company managed, once again, to evade its obligations and the debt remained unpaid when the next set of creditors approached the house in 1624.

This group was led by two ladies, Mary Brocas and Mary Overton, both of whom had lent the company over £1,000. Brocas had appealed to the council in 1621 asking permission to sue for recovery of her debt. The council had refused, but did write a letter to the company demanding that the debt be paid. It had no effect and Brocas had petitioned the council again in 1622. This time they gave her liberty to proceed at law, but the company continued to plead the original council protection and had successfully evaded all process.[188] In response to Brocas's petition, the Lords immediately summoned the governor of the company to answer. He admitted the debt, but claimed that it remained unpaid because it was among those in dispute between the old company and the new in the continuing suit in the Exchequer. The Lords, no doubt annoyed at the company's non-performance of its earlier order in Cunningham's case, this time ordered the company immediately to collect in full the assessment made on its stockholders the previous year (many of whom had not yet paid in their contribution) and to pay Mrs Brocas out of the proceeds, before any other creditors, together with a 5 per cent interest penalty. Those involved in the old company were directed to pay in their assessments to the court of Exchequer, pending outcome of the suit. If they were found not liable, their deposits were to be refunded; if they lost, their deposits were to be used to satisfy all remaining creditors.[189]

This order appears to have had some effect. Mary Brocas was eventually paid a significant portion of what was owed her (£700), but was back in Parliament in August 1625 (at Oxford) and again in 1626 seeking the remainder. So too was another group of unpaid creditors, led by John Manning.[190] They alleged that the Lords' order of 1624 had not been obeyed and that they had not been able to collect their debts. The company was cited for its contempt and made to offer a formal submission to the house. Again, the Lords ordered that all of the creditors holding bonds under the company's seal were to be paid out of the 1623 assessment, with interest at 5 per cent. The payments were to be completed by 1 May 1626.[191]

This order too was subsequently disobeyed. The creditors, this time led by Richard Cole, appealed to the house in February 1628 complaining yet again that the Lords' directions had been willfully ignored.[192] Their cause was referred to the Committee for Petitions, who then reported to the house in mid-June 1628. The committee informed the house that the petitioners' allegations were indeed true. The company had made no attempt to meet its obligations and, in fact, a subsequent audit (conducted by referees appointed by both sides) had revealed 'gross juggling' of the company's accounts 'to defraud the creditors'. The Lords declared again that the Company deserved to be punished for its 'contempts', but in the event drew a new order which provided that all stockholders who failed to bring in the money adjudged against them by St James's Day would be committed to prison. The company was then to perform the Lords' previous order and, if they failed, all creditors would be free to prosecute them to the full extent of the law, for which the company was to be assessed the resulting costs.[193] To that end (and with the pending prorogation in view) the Lord Keeper was instructed to pursue any complaint of non-performance and, if proved, was to commit the guilty parties to prison, where they were to remain until they had submitted and performed the order as directed. The Lords heard nothing more from the creditors in 1629.

To some extent the saga of the Muscovy Company creditors illustrates both the strengths and the weaknesses of the Lords' proceedings. Clearly, in the beginning the Muscovy Company had felt free to defy the Lords' orders (as, indeed, they defied those of the king's commission) with impunity. They did so in part because the Lords' authority could only be exercised while Parliament was sitting, and the intermittent and unpredictable sessions of the 1620s allowed them time to gamble. But over the course of the 1620s, the Lords themselves recognized that fact and took measures to compensate for it, both by issuing more forceful directives and by using the machinery of the legal system to ensure that their orders were carried out after the close of the session.

This decade was, for the most part, a period of learning and rediscovery for the Lords. The status and authority of their house as the High Court was (and had always been) taken for granted, but until 1621 the term had had little practical meaning. There had been precious few occasions over the previous two hundred years when they had been called upon to exercise judicial responsibilities and it was only natural that the resumption of those activities would be marked by some measure of uncertainty and experimentation. This was true both with regard to the internal mechanisms of the court and to its developing relation to the rest of the legal system. The provisions made to handle a dozen petitions in 1621 quickly proved inadequate to handle four times that many in 1624 and so adjustments had to be made – committees were expanded, more staff assigned, new rules developed to govern the judicial process. The transition was not a complete success. This court, like all others, had its flaws. In particular, the press of other business often made the scheduling of hearings an uncertain business. A number of complaints were never heard at all (though in some cases this may have been because the parties came to a settlement on their own) and those cases which required extensive hearings were often postponed repeatedly – as, for example, Robert Lane's appeal against an Elizabethan Chancery decree, which was initially heard in 1626 and was still being heard by the house in the Long Parliament.[194] That was an exceptional case, but other litigants often grew impatient with delays and requested reference to outside arbitration in lieu of an in-house hearing.[195]

The greatest handicap to the court's proceedings was, of course, the ever-present threat of prorogation, or worse, dissolution, which suspended hearings altogether. But, as suggested above, where there was adequate foreknowledge, provision could be made to have important cases heard and decided elsewhere. That, however, depended largely on the cooperation of other courts and their personnel (and on the availability of qualified referees). Throughout these proceedings the Lords' success was dependent on reestablishing a working relationship with the rest of the legal system, something which they discovered could not always be accomplished through a simple declaration of authority. The mechanics had to be worked out. They had to determine how references were to be made, to whom they could be made and under what terms and conditions. They had to establish rules of accountability and procedures for follow up. For the most part, they had to feel their way into the process through trial and error, and mistakes were no doubt made. Orders had to be reissued and/or clarified and tighter controls imposed on referees and outside commissions. But by the end of the decade they had convincingly reasserted their authority and reintegrated their own proceedings into the maelstrom of the legal system.

Their success and growing reputation would eventually lead them into other areas of the law. In 1628, when conflicts arose over the billeting of soldiers, both the Privy Council and the public looked to the House of Lords to mediate disputes. On 16 March the duke of Buckingham informed the house of a riot in the town of Witham, Essex, in which 'great outrages' had been committed by the inhabitants against the soldiers. He asked the house to 'take notice' of the dispute and call the inhabitants to account – this despite the fact that they had already been called to appear before the council.[196] The same day George Phillips, a constable of the town of Banbury, Oxfordshire, petitioned the house complaining of 'divers outrages' committed by the soldiers against the inhabitants – including setting fire to the town – and of their refusal to acknowledge civilian legal authority. He too asked that they be summoned to answer for their behaviour.[197] Both of these informants saw in the upper house a paramount authority willing and able to enforce the law for the safety and good of the realm. Their complaints were an ominous sign of the challenges to come.

NOTES

1   HLRO, Main Papers, H.L., 3 March 1620/1. There were two ways that appeals could be brought from the court of King's Bench. First, an individual could petition the king requesting that the record be removed into Parliament. If the king endorsed the petition that justice should be done, the Chief Justice was commanded to bring the record into the upper house and the king's endorsement served as a special commission for the Lords to proceed. Second, the king could be petitioned to direct the Chancery to issue a formal writ of error, returnable in Parliament, which then required the Chief Justice to deliver the record into the upper house. E.R. Foster, *The House of Lords, 1603–49* (Chapel Hill, NC, 1983), p. 180. Ewer's petition actually requested that a writ of error be issued, but the king appears to have proceeded by the former method. The case had already had a long history of proceedings in other courts, notably Star Chamber, and Ewer appears to have been something of a professional litigant whose hard-earned legal expertise might well have led him to initiate new parliamentary remedies. On Ewer see Thomas G. Barnes, 'Star Chamber litigants and their counsel, 1596–1641', in J.H. Baker (ed.), *Legal Records and the Historian*, (London, 1978), p. 15.
2   *CD 1621*, 2:197.

3　On one occasion, in late April, a group of Kentish fishermen presented a petition against Lord Teynham disputing his claim to title over their sea commons. The duke of Buckingham remarked that 'The Courtes of Justice are open', implying that the plaintiffs ought to proceed first to common law. However, his objections were overridden when Lord Sheffield explained that they were too poor to undertake a suit at law. S.R. Gardiner (ed.), *Notes of the Debates in the House of Lords . . . 1621*, Vol. 103 (Camden Society, 1st series; London, 1870). Buckingham was then appointed to the committee to hear the case (LJ, iii, pp. 101–2).

4　HLRO, Main Papers, H.L., 12 December 1621.

5　ibid., 22 and 26 May 1624; 6, 23 and 28 February 1626; and 17 March 1628 (Book of Orders) and 20 and 15 April 1628. There does not appear to have been a surviving record for the Parliament of 1625.

6　ibid., '1626'.

7　ibid., 26 May 1624; '1626' (Sir Gilbert Houghton); 'List of petitions rejected' (Edmond Warner).

8　For a discussion of the distribution of litigation among the central courts in the late sixteenth and early seventeenth centuries, see C.W. Brooks, *Pettyfoggers and Vipers of the Commonwealth, The 'Lower' Branch of the Legal Profession in Early Modern England* (Cambridge, 1986), ch. 4.

9　Brooks, *Pettyfoggers and Vipers*, pp. 66–71.

10　ibid., p. 57.

11　The latter designation needs to be qualified. By the early seventeenth century the term 'gentleman' had lost the specific meaning it had once had. It was increasingly being used by many men of wealth who were not members of the traditional landed elite. Keith Wrightson, *English Society 1580–1680* (London, 1982), p. 24.

12　See, for example, the case of *Robert Lane* v. *Ferdinando Baud*, a dispute over the manor of Walgrave in Northamptonshire. Lane was the grandson of Sir Edward Montague, Lord Chief Justice of the Common Pleas.

13　Brooks, *Pettyfoggers and Vipers*, p. 64.

14　ibid., p. 63.

15　As yet, there has not been a systematic or comprehensive study of the increase in litigation in the central courts. The pattern emerges from the information provided by individual studies of particular institutions. Naturally, these studies employ different methods of assessment and are concerned with differing periods within the early modern era.

16　Brooks, *Pettyfoggers and Vipers*, p. 53.

17　L.A. Knafla, *Law and Politics in Jacobean England, The Tracts of Lord Chancellor Ellesmere* (Cambridge, 1977), p. 163.

18　J.H. Baker, 'The common lawyers and the Chancery: 1616', in *The Legal Profession and the Common Law* (London, 1986), p. 223. By 1621 it was claimed that the number and complexity of suits being brought to Chancery simply could not be handled by the chancellor and Master of the Rolls alone. A bill was put forward in the House of Commons to provide for the appointment of two judge's assistants in the court. HLRO Main Papers, H.L., 30 April 1620/1. The bill was read once but was not proceeded with any further. (*CJ*, i, 596).

19　Barnes, 'Star Chamber litigants and their counsel', p. 8.

20　J.A. Guy, *The Cardinal's Court, The Impact of Thomas Wolsey on Star Chamber* (Totowa, NJ, 1977), p. 51.

21　Brooks, *Pettyfoggers and Vipers*, p. 55, n. 24. Professor Brooks cites research by Professor Wilfred Prest which indicates a significant rise in the number of entries in the decree and order books of both courts between 1616 and 1636. Those in the court of Requests increased from 183 in 1616 to 862 in 1636, and those in the court of Wards from 583 to 862. As he points out, these are not numbers of cases, only orders and decrees, but the increase suggests a notable one in business generally.

22　W.H. Bryson, *The Equity Side of the Exchequer* (Cambridge, 1975), p. 16. The annual average for the period from 1558 to 1587 was 84 bills, that from 1587 to 1603 was 334, and that from 1603 to 1625 was 331.

23　Much of what follows draws heavily on the recent research conducted by Professor

Brooks on the legal profession. Brooks, *Pettyfoggers and Vipers*, ch. 4 and 5.
24 D.C. Coleman, *The Economy of England, 1450–1750* (Oxford, 1977), p. 29.
25 ibid., p. 43.
26 ibid., p. 45.
27 ibid., p. 46.
28 Brooks, *Pettyfoggers and Vipers*, p. 96.
29 Coleman, *Economy of England*, pp. 76–77.
30 ibid., p. 87.
31 W.R. Scott, *The Constitution and Finance of English, Scottish and Irish Joint-Stock Companies to 1720* (3 vols; Cambridge, 1912), Vol. 1, pp. 166-8.
32 Brooks, *Pettyfoggers and Vipers*, pp. 94–5.
33 ibid., p. 66.
34 S.D. White, *Sir Edward Coke and the Grievances of the Commonwealth, 1621-1628* (Chapel Hill, NC, 1979), pp. 65–6.
35 Brooks, *Pettyfoggers and Vipers*, p. 97.
36 ibid., pp. 98-100.
37 J.S. Cockburn, *The History of the English Assizes, 1558–1714* (Cambridge, 1972), pp. 155–6. For a fuller discussion of the role of local magistrates, see Anthony Fletcher, *The Reform of the Provinces* (New Haven, Conn., 1986), esp. ch. 8.
38 'Divers cases, speeches, and presidentes in the High Court of Starre Chamber', Folger MS X.d 337, f. 16v, cited in Knafla, *Law and Politics*, pp. 108–9.
39 Mary Cotterell, 'Interregnum law reform: the Hale Commission of 1652', *English Historical Review*, no. 38 (1968), p. 697.
40 Nancy L. Matthews, *William Sheppard, Cromwell's Law Reformer* (Cambridge, 1984), p. 149.
41 For a discussion of these changes, see J. H. Baker, *An Introduction to English Legal History*, 2nd edn (London, 1979), pp. 56–61, and S.F.C. Milsom, *Historical Foundations of the Common Law*, 2nd edn (London, 1981), pp. 60–81.
42 Knafla, *Law And Politics*, p. 106.
43 Sir Edward Coke, *Institutes of the Laws of England* (London, 1628-44), Vol. 1, p. 303. Professor Baker points out that Coke's answer to the problem was not a return to more informal, less technically exact forms of pleading. He wanted lawyers to learn to be more precise. Baker, *Introduction to English Legal History*, p. 75.
44 W.J. Jones, *The Elizabethan Court of Chancery* (Oxford, 1967), p. 9.
45 ibid., p. 310.
46 George Norburie, *The Abuses and Remedies of the High Court of Chancery*, in Francis Hargrave (ed.), *A Collection of Tracts Relative to the Law of England* (London, 1787), pp. 437–41.
47 Professor Jones has estimated that a typical Chancery case took two to five years to reach determination; Jones, *The Elizabethan Court of Chancery*, p. 306.
48 Thomas G. Barnes, 'Due process and slow process in the late Elizabethan and early Stuart Star Chamber', *American Journal of Legal History*, Vol. 6 (1962), pp. 231–49.
49 ibid., p. 234. Professor Barnes cites a case in Hilary term 1608 which was dismissed because the plaintiff used the words 'this instant September' instead of the actual year in which the crime had taken place.
50 ibid., p. 235.
51 ibid., p. 240.
52 Barnes, 'Star Chamber litigants and their counsel', pp. 20–2.
53 Jones, *The Elizabethan Court of Chancery*, pp. 462–73. W.H. Holdsworth, *A History of English Law* (London, 1969), Vol. 1, p. 457. The injunction was directed to the parties involved and their counsel, rather than to the court.
54 For a full discussion of the conflict and its background, see Baker, '*The common lawyers and the Chancery: 1616*,' pp. 205–29.
55 ibid., p. 210.
56 ibid., p. 222.
57 ibid., p. 209. The reference is to Coke's report of *Finch* v. *Throgmorton* in BL Harleian MSS 6686, f. 228.

58 Ronald A. Marchant, *The Church under the Law* (Cambridge, 1969), pp. 9–10. For an extensive discussion of the jurisdictional dispute see Knafla, *Law and Politics*, pp. 123–44.

59 ibid., p. 136.

60 W.J. Jones, 'The Crown and the courts', in Alan G.R. Smith (ed.), *The Reign of James I and VI* (London, 1973), pp. 186–7. The claims of the common law courts had begun with the use of a fiction which described all contracts as having been sealed in the London parish of 'St. Mary le Bow in the ward of the Cheap'.

61 King James, of course, assumed quite the opposite. He intervened in the dispute between Chancery and Chief Justice Coke in 1616 with the express purpose of ending the conflict between his courts. He claimed that he alone had the right and the responsibility to determine jurisdictional disputes, and he was acting to ensure certainty in the law. In practical terms, however, this simply was not possible. The problem was much too great and arose far too frequently and in far too many contexts to be left to the sole determination of the king. It required controls built into the system itself.

62 Barnes, 'Star Chamber litigants and their counsel', p. 12.

63 Chamberlain to Carelton, 14 November 1616; *Letters of Chamberlain*, Vol. 2, p. 36. Cited in Baker, *Legal Profession*, p. 223.

64 Ellesmere, a judicial conservative, felt the problem was the result of the new fictional actions at common law (Knafla, *Law and Politics*, pp. 118–19). Bacon saw the problem as developing from too many laws, too much procedure and uncertainty of title (Donald Veall, *The Popular Movement for Law Reform, 1640–1660* (Oxford, 1970), pp. 68–70). Coke thought the problem lay with the proliferation of common informers and in absence of statutes of limitations and proposed legislation to extend the statute of limitations to personal (not just real) actions (White, *Sir Edward Coke*, pp. 68–72).

65 Sir Francis Bacon, 'Maxims of the law', in James Spedding *et al.* (eds), *The Works of Sir Francis Bacon*, 7 vols (London 1870–6), Vol 7, p. 319.

66 For a full and thoughtful discussion of the various proposals for legal reform in the 1620s, see White, *Sir Edward Coke*, ch. 3. One of the most important, and controversial bills was that proposed by Coke, which would have imposed a statute of limitations on all personal actions at common law. Coke also sponsored a bill to control common informers, seen by many as the cause of much vexatious litigation.

67 ibid., pp. 59–63.

68 *CD 1621*, 2:89. Cranfield listed problems with the administration of justice as the first of three great grievances then troubling the subject.

69 G.R. Elton, *The Tudor Constitution*, 2nd edn (Cambridge, 1982), p. 103.

70 ibid., p. 105. See John Herbert's 'Memorandum on Council business', 26 April 1600.

71 J.P. Dawson, 'The Privy Council and private law in the Tudor and Stuart periods', *Michigan Law Review*, Vol. 48, no. 4 (1950) pp. 393–428, 627–56, 629.

72 APC, Vol. 32, p. 499.

73 PRO SP 14 /37 fol. 72–3.

74 The register is in BL Landsdowne MSS 266. It contains some 290 folios written in a number of hands, two of which belonged to Masters of Requests, Roger Wibraham and Sir Christopher Parkins. It covers the period from May 1603 to June 1616. For a full discussion of the document and its contents see Dawson, 'Privy Council and private law', pp. 629–36.

75 ibid., p. 631.

76 James I was assisted by the Masters of Requests, who served both as the conduit for private petitions to the king and as his administrative agents. See Dawson, 'Privy Council and private law', p. 630 and n. 127.

77 This figure is based on a representative sampling of the Privy Council registers for the years 1581, 1586, 1587, 1588 and 1591. The number of petitions handled by the council may have been higher. It is clear from other evidence that the registers do not always record every item of business transacted in any given meeting.

78 There are numerous examples of this. See, for instance, *APC* 1621–3, p. 13 (*Condon v. Fleetwood*); p. 145 (*Perrin v. Le Hardy*); 1623–5, pp. 78–9 (*Allen v. Meysey*); p. 170 (Alexander Stevenson); p. 433 (Richard Bellamy). [*C]alendar of [S]tate [P]apers [D]omestic*, 1619–23, pp. 148, 179, 184.

79 *APC*, 1619–23, p. 368.

80 ibid., 1630–1, p. 29.

81 In the ten years between 1621 and 1630 the council handled approximately 374 private causes. Of those, 78 were petitions from Ireland – usually referred back to the Lord Deputy and council – and 55 were appeals from the Channel Islands. There are, of course, a number of unknown variables at work here. There is no way to tell whether the number of petitions seeking relief from king and council remained at the levels of the Elizabethan period though, given previous patterns, it seems rather unlikely that they would have diminished significantly. Nor is it certain that the registers recorded every action taken by the council in a private matter – some petitions may have been handled informally by individual members and not recorded. The number of petitions received and acted upon may, therefore, have been slightly higher. The same, however, would have been true of the Elizabethan council.

82 CSPD, 1619–23, pp. 300, 301; *APC*, 1621–3, p. 327. See Scott, *Joint-Stock Companies*, Vol. 1, pp. 179–80; Vol 2, pp. 57–65. The council later began to apply pressure on the company to meet its obligations (CSPD, 1619–23, p. 469). See discussion pages 51–3 above.

83 One notable exception may have been the appeal of Robert Yeo, imprisoned in the Fleet by the Privy Council in 1624 for refusing its warrant to serve in the Low Countries under Sir Edward Conway. During his four years in the Fleet actions of debt had been brought against him and he looked to the House of Lords to stay the suits and for a writ of habeas corpus (HLRO, Main Papers, H.L., 30 May 1628).

84 See, for instance, HLRO, Main Papers, H.L., 29 April 1624; *APC*, 1627, p. 285, 338, 366; HLRO, Main Papers, H.L., 20 May 1628 (*Savage v. Taylor*). CSPD, 1619–23, p. 17; *APC*, 1623–5, p. 45; HLRO, Main Papers, H.L., 2 May 1626; *APC*, 1626, p. 125 (*Greene v Greene*).

85 The impact of House of Lords' proceedings on the workload of the council in this area is not as dramatic as might be expected. Overall, the number of cases handled by the council during the 1620s remained relatively constant from year to year, despite the frequency of parliamentary meetings. However, the immediate pressure on the council does appear to have been relieved somewhat when Parliament was in session. For example, in 1624 the council dealt with 37 separate cases; 8 of those were presented in the period from 12 February to 29 May, when Parliament was sitting, and the remaining 29 in the subsequent six months after Parliament had been dissolved. Similarly, in 1626 the council handled 12 cases in the first six months of the year when Parliament was sitting (6 February to 15 June) and 31 in the latter half of the year.

86 See, for example, *LJ*, iii, p. 101 (*Fishermen of Kent v. Lord Teynham*) and p. 131 (Sir James Cunningham).

87 *LJ*, iii, p. 141. The other members of the committee were the earl of March, the bishops of Bath and Wells and Bristol, and Lords Hunsden, St John, Russell and Denny.

88 The exception, Lord Denny, had succeeded to his barony in 1604. The earl of Bridgewater had served as baron of the Exchequer in Chester (1599–1605) and the earl of March had been a member of Gray's Inn.

89 *LJ*, iii, p. 165.

90 ibid., p. 258.

91 ibid., p. 500.

92 ibid., pp. 540, 630.

93 ibid., p. 694.

94 ibid., iv, p. 6.

95 The writ of assistance read as follows:

Whereas by the advice and assent of our Council, for certain arduous affairs concerning us ... we have ordered a certain parliament to be holden at our city of Westminster on the XX day of XX month next ensuing, we strictly enjoining, command you (waving all excuses) to be at the said day and place personally present with us and the rest of our Council to treat and give advice upon the affaires aforesaid; this in no wise do you omit. (J.F. MacQueen, *A Practical Treatise on the Appellate Jurisdiction of the House of Lords and the Privy Council* (London, 1842, p. 36).

96 Early in 1621 two of the judges attending the Committee for Privileges refused to give their advice with regard to the Lords' protestation upon honour, claiming that it 'touched the King's Prerogative'. Their 'forbearance' was reported to be 'much disliking [sic] and distasteful to the Lords' Committees'. Lord Houghton reported to the house that their irritation with the judges 'did not proceed from Curiosity, but instead from a perusal of the writs of summons directed to the Lords the Judges which found that they are thereby called consillium impensuri'. The matter was eventually settled, in conference with the king, in the Lords' favour (*LJ*, iii, pp. 21, 43, 41. HLRO, Main Papers, H.L., 12 March 1621). For a full discussion of the role of the legal assistants, see Foster, *House of Lords*, ch. 5.

97 *LJ*, iii, p. 179.

98 The house appears to have been very sensitive about proper procedure. In one case in April 1621 a petition was brought in by a member of the house who was delivering it for a member of the Commons, to whom it had originally been addressed. The Lords rejected the petition outright and ordered that the house would 'receive no petition except that it be exhibited to this House by the party himself, or commended by the House of Commons' (*LJ*, iii, p. 88).

99 ibid., p. 296

100 ibid., pp. 174, 296, 540. In 1621, the committee delegated the Clerk of Parliament to deal with petitions during the upcoming recess between sessions. The earl of Bridgewater reported to the house on 4 June that time had not permitted them to answer all petitions presented. They had therefore instructed the clerk to work in consultation with the judges, who were to review the cases only if they found sufficient cause. If not, they were to certify to the house what should be done with the petitioners. However, they warned that no suits were to be stayed on pretence of a petition in Parliament which had not been answered, and that no decrees were to be reversed without a hearing of counsel on both sides. In all cases, the clerk was to retain the petition, and (together with the judge's resolution) present them to the house when it reconvened (*LJ*, iii, p. 157).

101 HLRO, Main Papers, H.L., 14 May 1624.

102 LJ, iii, p. 157

103 See below, pp. 46–7.

104 See, for example, *LJ*, iii, p. 547 (*Johnson* v. *Johnson*); p. 680 (*Galthorpe* v. *Reynolds*); p. 872 (Thomas Grey).

105 See, for example, *LJ*, iii, p. 785 (Ferdinando Baud).

106 See, for example, HLRO, Main Papers, H.L., 30 May 1628 (Robert Yeo).

107 See, for example, *LJ*, iii, p. 587 (*Horsley* v. *Rogers*).

108 The former method was usually used. See, for example, *LJ*, iii, p. 170. The Lords' authority to release a prisoner by virtue of its own order was questioned on one occasion in 1641 by the keeper of Ludgate prison. He had been ordered to release a prisoner on what was, in effect, a claim of privilege. Having released the prisoner, the keeper subsequently petitioned the house, asking to be indemnified, because the individual had originally been imprisoned on a judgment for debt. The Lords recognized that he was, in essence, questioning the legal authority of their order, and referred his petition to two of the common law justices, requesting their opinion as to whether 'the order of this House only, without any writ of *Habeas Corpus* was sufficient warrant in law' (*LJ*, iv, p. 462). The judges declared that

While it would have been more formal and warrantable if a writ of *Habeas* v *Corpus* had issued directing the sheriffs to bring the prisoner before your Lordships, yet seeing that your Lordships are not tied to such regularity of proceedings as inferior courts are, and must be, and that the Court of King's

Bench doth many times, by rule of court, without any writ, bring prisoners in execution before them, we are of the opinion that your Lordships' order is sufficient warrant in this case. (HLRO, Main papers, H.L., 3 December 1641).

109 See, for example, LJ, iii, p. 303 (*Rogers* v. *Ingram*); p. 833 (*Conningsby* v. *Blount*); iv, p. 24 (*Briscoe* v. *Singleton*).
110 See, for example, ibid., iii, p. 833 (*Conningsby* v. *Blount*).
111 See, for example, ibid., p. 303 (*Rogers* v. *Ingram*).
112 ibid., p. 171 (*Crokey* v. *Smith and Hunt*).
113 See, for example, ibid., p. 487 (*Haines* v. *Parnham*).
114 See, for example, HLRO, Main Papers, H.L., 24 May 1624, Register of Petitions (Timothy Pinkeny).
115 *LJ*, iii, p. 509.
116 ibid., p. 780 and iv, p. 36 (*Lane* v. *Baud*).
117 HLRO, B2, Book of Orders and Ordinances, p. 662.
118 *LJ*, iii, pp. 511–13 (Timothy Pinkeny).
119 ibid., p. 417.
120 ibid., iv, p. 20 (*Lane* v. *Baud*)
121 ibid., iii, p. 416 (Henry Williams); iv, p. 32 (Margaret Dyer).
122 HLRO, Main Papers, H.L., 17 March 1627–8, Minute Book of Proceedings of the House of Lords (John Horsley; Ralph Lynskell). This practice had in fact been customary since at least 1495. The statute of 11 Henry VII, c. 12 enshrined the policy by directing that legal aid to the poor be made available wherever possible (*Statutes of the Realm*, ii, p. 578). The Lords do appear to have been somewhat less generous than other courts in this regard. The £10 limit later imposed in 1641 was substantially higher than the universally accepted standard of £5 used in most other courts (G.I.O. Duncan, *The High Court of Delegates* (Cambridge, 1971), p. 92, n.4).
123 *LJ*, iii, pp. 774–6 (*Rodier* v. *earl of Warwick*); p. 553 (*Lazenby* v. *Lord Scroop*).
124 ibid., p. 609. The original dispute had also been heard numerous times in the Privy Council in the early 1620s (*CSPD*, 1619–23, pp. 476, 601, 616, 624; 1623–5, pp. 339, 344, 372, 508; 1625–6, pp. 168–9). The Lords appear to have been less than impressed with Lord Deyncourt's treatment of his father and, like the Privy Council, no doubt found the whole affair something of an embarrassment. The case did in fact proceed in Chancery and was decreed in favour of the father, Sir Francis Leeke, in October 1627. Lord Deyncourt refused to comply with the decree and was arrested for his contempt in December 1628 – technically during Parliament. Deyncourt protested his arrest and attempted to appeal the decree (and impugn the Lord Keeper) in the house in 1628, but his appeal was rejected and he was ordered to apologize to the Lord Keeper and submit to his decree (*LJ*, iv, p. 29). Ever persistent, he raised the matter of his arrest in the Privy Council in 1629 (*APC*, 1628–9, pp. 7, 101–2).
125 *LJ*, iii, p. 412 (Mary Brocas).
126 ibid., p. 569. HLRO, Main Papers, H.L., 6 February 1625–6, Book of Answers to Petitions (John Moygne) 23 February 1625–6.
127 HLRO, Main Papers, H.L., 20 April 1626 (*Ap Evan* v. *Vaughan*).
128 Jones, *Elizabethan Court of Chancery*, p. 283.
129 *Lord Nottingham's Manual of Chancery Practice and Prolegomena of Chancery and Equity*, ed. D.E.C. Yale (Cambridge, 1965), p. 97.
130 ibid., p. 96
131 Sir M. Hale, *The Jurisdiction of the Lords' House*, ed. Francis Hargrave (London, 1796), p. 185.
132 *Lord Nottingham's Chancery Cases*, ed. D.E.C Yale, Selden Society, Vol. 72 (1954), p. lxv. In the context of one case later in the century, Lord Nottingham declared that 'injustice be not in itself cause to review and reverse, for that would be alleged in every case'.
133 HLRO, Main Papers, H.L., 28 May 1624, 2 May 1626; *LJ*, iii, p. 591.
134 HLRO, Main Papers, H.L., 24 March 1625–6; *LJ*, iii, p. 540.
135 HLRO, Main Papers, H.L., 3 April, 1628; *LJ*, iii, pp. 557, 831.
136 HLRO, Main Papers H.L., 28 May, 1628; *LJ*, iii, pp. 827, 862. The Lords

recommended that the administration of the estate should be granted to Ferrers and his co-plaintiff, Sir Richard Brooke, under certain conditions. The court complied, but the defendant, Lady Packington, refused to accept the ruling and appealed the decision to a court of Delegates. Informed of this, the Lords summarily quashed the appeal. It was declared 'void' because 'it doth directly cross and avoid the said order of Parliament'. (*LJ*, iv, pp. 23–4).

137 In April 1628, Anthony Lamplaugh petitioned the house complaining of an injunction, issued by Lord Keeper Williams three years earlier, which had stayed his proceedings at common law against the warden of the Fleet for an escape. The petition cast 'scandalous aspersions' against both Bishop Williams and the then Lord Keeper Coventry and the house promptly censured Lamplaugh and committed him to the Fleet. At the same time, however, the House referred his complaint to the Lord Keeper and asked that he rehear the case on its merits (*LJ*, iii, p. 741).

138 The above cited case of George Morgan is an example (*LJ*, iii, p. 540). See also HLRO, Main Papers, H.L., 3 April, 1628. *LJ*, iii, pp. 736–7 (*Richard Hill and the Bailiffs and Burgesses of Stow on the Wold* v. *Edmund Chamberlain*).

139 27 Elizabeth I, c. 8. This statute actually created the court of Exchequer Chamber and confirmed the right of appeal from there to the House of Lords. The house heard only four writs of error during the 1620s. See HLRO, Main Papers, H.L., 2 March 1620–1; *LJ*, iii. p. 152 (*Ewre* v. *Moyle*). HLRO, Main Papers, H.L., 14 May 1621; *LJ* iii, p. 121 (*Stafford* v. *Stafford*). HLRO Main Papers, H.L., 8 July 1625; *LJ*, iii, p. 457 (*Haines* v. *Crouch*). *LJ*, iii, p. 646 (*Martine* v. *Blakiston*).

140 *The Political Works of James I*, ed. C.H. McIlwain (Cambridge, Mass., 1918), p. 331.

141 For a discussion of this issue, see Knafla, *Law and Politics*, p. 157.

142 The procedure appears only to have been used once before 1640, in Moyle Finch's case in 1598. See Coke, *Institutes*, iv, p. 85.

143 *LJ*, iii, p. 418 (Feltmakers of London); p. 525 (*Wrenham* v. *Fisher*).

144 HLRO, Main Papers, H.L., 9 July 1625, and 16 May 1626. *LJ*, iii, pp. 402, 408, 414, 463 (*Edwards* v. *Edwards*). The Lords appear to have appointed the commission in late May 1624 in anticipation of the dissolution of Parliament. They realized that the bill would be lost, in any event, and saw this as a viable alternative. The parties to the dispute were father and son and as a rule the house preferred to settle such conflicts through arbitration. The commission was required to end the dispute or certify otherwise at the next meeting of Parliament.

145 Hale, *Jurisdiction of the Lords' House*, pp. 191–2.

146 HLRO, Main Papers, H.L., 19 April 1621 (creditors of Thomas Frith).

147 As far as it is possible to tell, only one of the cases was actually an appeal against a decree made by Bacon. It was not taken up, and was refiled in 1624 (HLRO, Main Papers, H.L., 4 June 1621 (William Matthew)).

148 *LJ*, iii, p. 179.

149 Gardiner, *Notes of the Debates in the House of Lords*, pp. 107–8.

150 ibid., p. 107.

151 ibid., p. 108.

152 *LJ*, iii, p. 179.

153 HLRO, Main Papers, H.L., 10 December 1621. *LJ*, iii, p. 189; Gardiner, *Notes of the Debates in the House of Lords*, p. 114.

154 ibid., p. 117

155 Hale, *Jurisdiction of the Lord's House*, p. 195. Foster, *House of Lords*, p. 105.

156 Gardiner, *Notes of the Debates in the House of Lords*, p. 114.

157 ibid., p. 117.

158 ibid., pp. 119–20; *LJ*, iii, pp. 190–2. Bouchier was also sentenced to be imprisoned at the pleasure of the house, but the sentence was remitted through the generous intervention of Lord Keeper Williams, who claimed Bouchier had no malice in him and had only made the accusation to 'induce the House to heare his cause'.

159 HLRO, Main Papers, H.L., 28 May 1624 (*Wright* v. *Archibold*).

160 ibid., 28 May 1624 (*Underwood* v. *Pennyman*).

161 *LJ*, iii, p. 416.

162 HLRO, Main Papers, H.L., 28 May 1624.

163 *LJ*, iii, p. 416.
164 HLRO, Main Papers, H.L., 23 February 1626.
165 *LJ*, iii, pp. 529–31. Williams also claimed that the king had refused to grant the commission, something which flatly contradicted his earlier statement that he had ignored the Lords' order.
166 *LJ*, iii, pp. 532, 538.
167 ibid., p. 532.
168 ibid., p. 421.
169 Hale, *Jurisdiction of the Lords' House*, pp. 195–6.
170 The statute of 14 Edward III, c. 3 had provided for just such an eventuality.
171 HLRO, Main Papers, H.L., 24 March 1625–6; *LJ*, iii, p. 540 (*Morgan v. Bowdler*). HLRO, Main Papers, H.L., 28 May 1624; *LJ*, iii, p. 591 (*Wright v. Archibold*).
172 ibid., p. 416 (*Underwood v. Pennyman*); p. 546 (*Cope v. Ewer*).
173 ibid., p. 833 (*Conningsby v. Blount et al*). Though there is no evidence to suggest it, the Lords may have taken a special interest in this case because the plaintiff was the brother-in-law of Lord North.
174 See, for example, HLRO, Main Papers, H.L., 20 May 1624; *LJ*, iii, p. 533 (*Waterhouse v. Ingram*); HLRO, Main Papers, H.L., 14 March 1625–6 (*Tyrwhyt v. Hicks*).
175 HLRO, Main Papers, H.L., 27 March 1628 (*Vaughan v. Colmer*).
176 *LJ*, iii, p. 831; *CSPD*, 1628–9, p. 208.
177 HLRO, Main Papers, H.L., 7 February 1628–9; *LJ*, iv, pp. 23–4 (*Briscoe v. Singleton*).
178 HLRO, Main Papers, H.L., 14 April 1624; *LJ*, iii, pp. 303, 415.
179 HLRO, Main Papers, H.L., 13 June 1626, 26 June 1628; *LJ*, iii, pp. 413, 422, 804.
180 *APC*, 1627, pp. 285, 338.
181 HLRO, Main Papers H.L., 26 June 1628.
182 For a thorough and detailed account of the company's fortunes, see Scott, *Joint Stock Companies*, Vol. 2, pp. 36–75.
183 *CSPD*, 1619–23, pp. 300–1.
184 Ibid., p. 322.
185 HLRO, Main Papers, H.L., 25 May 1621. *LJ*, iii, pp. 131, 152, 199; *APC*, 1621–3, pp. 59, 68.
186 HLRO, Main Papers, H.L., 25 May 1621. The House ordered the company to pay immediately £124 in lost wages to the mariners whom Cunningham had hired. The remaining £800 was to be negotiated at a further meeting between the parties in the second session of the Parliament (*LJ*, iii, p. 152).
187 See, for instance, HLRO, Main Papers, H.L., 18 March 1624, 16 April 1624, 23 April 1624, 21 March 1625–6, 28 March 1626, 18 April 1626. There were well over a dozen claims against Sir James's award.
188 HLRO, Main Papers, H.L., 27 May 1624.
189 *LJ*, iii, p. 412.
190 HLRO, Main Papers, H.L., 9 March 1625.
191 *LJ*, iii, p. 569.
192 HLRO, Main Papers, H.L., 3 February 1628.
193 *LJ*, iii, p. 864.
194 HLRO, Main Papers, H.L., 24 May 1626; *LJ*, iii, pp. 539, 650, 778, 780, 785, 794, 798, 825, 829, 833; iv, pp. 20, 36, 39.
195 See, for example, HLRO, Main Papers, H.L., 4 April 1626 (*Chambers v. Leigh*); 16 May 1626 (*Bynsted v. Langridge*).
196 *LJ*, iii, p. 700. The riot was a very serious affair. The soldiers, an Irish company, appear to have provoked outrage in the town by celebrating St Patrick's Day rather too publicly. The quarrel quickly got out of hand and the town rose in arms. At least 30 inhabitants and a number of soldiers were wounded and the Deputy Lieutenants had great difficulty in pacifying the town, 'notwithstanding proclamations in the King's name' (*CSPD*, 1628–9, p. 24). The council may have felt that, under the circumstances, a punishment handed down by Parliament would carry more weight in the town. In the event, the Lords summoned both the chief inhabitants and the soldiers involved to appear and make their cases.
197 HLRO, Main Papers, H.L., 26 March 1628; *LJ*, iii, p. 700.

2

The Long Parliament (i): looking back

> And the Lords, being trusted with a judicatory power, are an excellent screen and bank between the prince and people, to assist each against the encroachment of the other, and by just judgments to preserve that law which ought to be the rule of every one of the three . . .
>
> The king's answer to the Nineteen Propositions (1642)

House of Lords judicature came of age in the early 1640s. The accomplishments of the 1620s, however important and impressive, had been largely developmental. The High Court of Parliament had been successfully revived, but the evolution had proceeded in piecemeal fashion, from Parliament to Parliament, from session to session and, indeed, from case to case, as the Lords responded, essentially on an *ad hoc* basis, to the multifarious demands of their clientele. By the close of the decade their jurisdiction had been firmly established and the procedural mechanisms were in place to ensure the provision of effective remedy. What was missing was a clearer sense of direction and purpose.

The demands placed on the house in the early 1640s would bring its role more sharply into focus. The end of Charles I's personal rule and the wholesale collapse of his government in 1640 created major new responsibilities for both Houses of Parliament. Apart from the immediate practical need to resolve the near-catastrophic financial crisis and to reestablish peaceful relations with the Scots, Parliament's first essential task was to provide a sense of cooperative leadership – and in so doing restore public confidence in the future security of the English church and state. First, it meant taking steps to remove the perceived threats to parliamentary government, to English religion and to the liberties of the subject which had developed during the previous decade or more. It meant impeaching the earl of Strafford and Archbishop Laud, as well as the Laudian bishops and the errant judges of the 1630s, passing the Triennial Act and the act against Dissolution, abolishing the courts of High Commission and Star Chamber (together with the judicial authority of the Privy Council) and outlawing the innovative fiscal measures of the Personal Rule.

But that was not all that was required. The constructive reforms undertaken in 1640 and 1641 were, for the most part, preventative (or, in the case of impeachments, punitive) in nature. They were principally designed to ensure that the abuses of the 1630s would never recur. In that sense they looked forward rather than backward and did not, except in the most general sense, provide real redress of grievances. There was no retroactive remedy offered to those who had already suffered at the hands of Archbishop Laud or the earl of Strafford, before the courts of Star Chamber and High Commission, or at the hands of the Privy Council. And yet providing that remedy was as important to restoring public faith in the fundamentals of English government as anything Parliament could do. The programmes and policies imposed by the Crown in the 1630s were, in the long run, less troubling to the average Englishman than the severe and seemingly arbitrary penalties imposed for resisting them. For many they, rather than the policies themselves, represented the real threat to the rule of law. Impeaching or removing the officials who had devised the policies and directed the enforcement was no doubt consoling, but did not really provide the necessary assurances that the subject's legal rights and interests remained secure under the law. That could only be done – convincingly – by offering true remedy on a case by case basis. That responsibility would fall to the House of Lords.

When Parliament was recalled in spring 1640 the upper house immediately set about making the usual preparations to handle private litigation. Three days after the opening of the Short Parliament the Lords appointed a new Committee for Petitions, numbering 41 members (the largest committee to date) and, as before, directed that it meet every Tuesday and Thursday (or as often as necessary) to consider answers to new petitions.[1] The composition of the committee reflected, in the first place, the need for some measure of continuity and, not surprisingly, the new body included a dozen members of the committee of 1629. However, it appears that political considerations affected the selection process as well. In a clear break with recent tradition the Lords failed to appoint any Crown officers to the committee, such as the Lord Treasurer, the Lord Chamberlain or the Lord Privy Seal, all of whom had been mainstays of the committees of the 1620s. Privy councillors were also noticeably thin on the ground – only the earls of Dorset, Berkshire, Salisbury, Bridgewater and Holland, and Lords Goring and Cottington, none of whom could be counted as strongly supportive of the policies and practices of 'Thorough' which had marked the previous decade.[2] Instead, the committee was dominated by noted critics of the Crown and would-be reformers – Essex, Bedford, Bristol, Warwick, Saye, Mandeville, Brooke and the like – and in sufficient numbers to suggest a deliberate attempt to pack the committee. Only the clerical contingent (customarily selected by the Bishops themselves) did not fit the mould. Six of the eight bishops appointed to the committee were well-known Laudians.[3] The Committee for Privileges, the only other standing committee appointed during the session, showed none of the same signs and, indeed, included eight senior officers of state, among them Archbishop Laud and Lord Treasurer Juxon. However, the Committee for Petitions traditionally had a more important and functional role and, given both past experience and presumed levels of discontent, the emergent opposition peers may have felt it necessary to secure control over a committee which would clearly be deciding important matters of law.

In the event, the committee was given little work. During the three week session the house received only a dozen petitions for judicial remedy. The litigation reflected much the same pattern as had been evident in the 1620s and, indeed, included one case – the ubiquitous Chancery appeal of Robert Lane – which was carried over from the session of 1628. There were two appeals from decisions in the Admiralty Court, and one each from the Marshal's Court, Common Pleas, Star Chamber and the Commission for Sewers. The remaining cases had been brought in the first instance and involved a testamentary dispute, a case of debt, a domestic conflict over alimony and a property case involving a disputed lease. The house began work on at least five of these cases, and reported one of them to the house, before the session was abruptly terminated on 5 May.[4]

This was very much a case of business as usual – in itself a testament to the enduring accomplishments of the 1620s, but a somewhat surprising result all the same. Given the long intermission of Parliaments during the 1630s and the considerable advance warning given of the new session in 1640, more petitions might have been expected. The absence of any complaints regarding the administration and enforcement of Crown policies in the 1630s is also curious, in view of the plethora of county petitions of grievance presented to Parliament as a whole. It is possible that some prospective litigants held back to see how Parliament responded to those petitions – to judge the level of parliamentary commitment to general reform – before applying for personal relief. It is also possible that, like everyone else, they simply expected this Parliament to be in session far longer than it turned out to be, and therefore felt no immediate pressure to present their case. If so, the sudden dissolution of the Short Parliament quickly brought them to their senses.

The response to the opening of the Long Parliament was altogether more emphatic. Where only a dozen petitions were presented during the three weeks of the Short Parliament, almost four times that many were brought in the corresponding period in November. The pace continued to escalate in the ensuing months, with December bringing another 83 petitions, January 125, and February a further 83. Cases were being presented at a rate of a dozen or more a day and the house was simply unable to keep pace. On 10 February they ordered that 'no more private petitions whatsoever' were to be presented until those already accepted had been dispatched.[5] The order took some time to have an effect, but the flow of petitions slowed noticeably in March, when only 31 new cases were presented, and dropped again in April when the house received a mere dozen. No doubt the clerk would, in any event, have discouraged litigants from pressing the house during those months because of the Lords' preoccupation with the trial of the earl of Strafford. Once that obstacle had been removed, however, the numbers began to climb again rapidly and over five dozen new suits were brought to the house in May. By this stage the Lords had accepted responsibility for well over 400 cases and, in desperation, at the end of the month they issued another in a long series of orders designed for public consumption:

> Upon information this Day of the Multitude of Petitions that remain in this House unanswered, and the Great Concourse of Petitioners daily resorting hither, and their earnest pressings for a Dispatch of the said Petitions; it is thought fit and so ordered, for the speedier Dispatch of the said Petitioners, that no Petition whatsoever shall be received into this House, until the Pleasure of the same be declared by Order.[6]

The pronouncement was not particularly effective. June's intake of 84 new petitions substantially exceeded May's. July produced half as many again (47), and August roughly half of that (22). The house was under siege. All of the attempts to regulate or halt altogether in-house judicial proceedings in July – to allow concentrated effort on political and legislative concerns, and in August – in anticipation of the king's departure for Scotland, proved ineffective. Only the parliamentary recess in early September brought some relief. That, and the Lords' decision in late October to begin printing and publishing its orders putting off private business, substantially reduced the intake of new cases in the autumn session. Only a dozen more would be presented before the end of 1641, by which point the total had reached nearly 650. Cases would, of course, continue to be brought to the house up to and beyond the outbreak of the Civil War, but the major challenge had already been laid.

The primary responsibility for handling these complaints rested, as before, with the Committee for Petitions. The committee appointed on 6 November was, for all practical purposes, identical to that selected the previous spring. It initially included 41 members, 35 of whom had served in the Short Parliament.[7] New members were added at various stages during the first few months of the Parliament ultimately bringing the total membership to 53. Political considerations clearly affected the selection process here, as it had in the Short Parliament. Only 8 members of the king's Privy Council (as it stood in 1640) were included – the same 7 from the Short Parliament, plus the earl of Newcastle –

and there were no senior officers of state. Only 3 other members, Lords Digby, Coventry and Howard of Charlton, could be counted as government loyalists. The remainder of the committee, aside from 8 or 9 politically inactive peers, were either well-known critics of the government or men who were tied to them through friendship, family, or business connections.[8] The committee included, for instance, 11 of 12 signatories of the petition for a new parliament presented to the king in August 1640.[9] Again, Laudian bishops were in the majority among the clerics appointed – five of the six selected in April were reappointed here – Wren of Ely, Curle of Winchester, Bancroft of Oxford, Warner of Rochester, and Duppa of Chichester.[10] All the same, the committee was overwhelmingly weighted in favour of the nominal opposition. There was nothing unusual about that. As Dr Crummett had demonstrated, there was considerable and apparently deliberate 'underemployment' of the membership in terms of committee appointments and his conclusion that most committees in the Lords were 'dominated by a small group of Court and government critics' appears to be well founded.[11] The Committee for Petitions simply conformed to that general pattern.

So too did the special judicial committee appointed by the house on 26 November. Despite the conspicuous absence of such cases in the Short Parliament, the Lords apparently anticipated an influx of complaints regarding the enforcement of Crown policies in the 1630s and elected to create a new committee, composed of 32 members, which would 'examine Abuses in Matters of Imprisonment and all other Abuses in Courts of Justice'. The house seemingly intended that this new committee should handle primarily charges of false imprisonment, judicial malfeasance, or allegations of official misconduct, leaving the more straightforward litigation, which turned on substantive legal matters, to the Committee for Petitions. In fact, however, the division of labour between the two bodies was not particularly well defined – the term 'Abuses' could be variously construed – and consequently it did not always hold fast. Both committees set to work immediately, hearing cases which could hardly be distinguished by their content. The clerk was certainly left confused. Cases clearly referred to one committee were subsequently said to have been reported to the house by the other. That was hardly surprising since, in terms of its membership, this second committee was little more than a subcommittee of the first. Fully two-thirds of its members (20 of 32) served at the same time on the Committee for Petitions.[12] In mid-March 1641 the Lords appear to have recognized that the two committees represented an unnecessary duplication of effort. The committee for 'Abuses' was laid down, and its responsibilities and pending litigation were referred to the Committee for Petitions.[13]

Table 2.1 Complaints originating in the 1630s

Complaint	Number
(1) Appeals against prosecutions for alleged religious non-conformity	41
(2) Appeals against deprivation of ecclesiastical livings or income	29
(3) Appeals against deprivation of ecclesiastical offices	6
(4) Appeals against interference with impropriated livings	15
(5) Complaints about Ship Money and Coat and Conduct Money administration	15
(6) Appeals against prosecutions for violations of Patents and Royal Proclamations	12
(7) Complaints arising from the sale of administrative and judicial offices	17
(8) Complaints of arbitrary imprisonment or other improper judicial procedure	85
(9) Miscellaneous complaints against Crown officers	21
Total	241

THE GENERAL PROBLEM

From the opening of the session, the house was inundated with petitions seeking redress from a wide variety of legal proceedings and arbitrary practices which had been used to enforce public policy in the 1630s. Table 2.1 indicates the nature and distribution of these complaints. The cases have been classified according to what appeared to be the primary and most serious issue in dispute. Many of these petitioners voiced more than one complaint and it is clear that, whatever the specific charge, some of them had been prosecuted for more than one reason.

There is nothing particularly surprising about the list in Table 2.1. The complaints point to most of the major concerns about government programmes in the 1630s voiced more generally in county petitions and in subsequent parliamentary debates. But for the petitioners here, those concerns had been played out on a very personal level. All of them had fallen foul of the king's government at some point during the 1630s: by standing out against the Laudian innovations in the church, or by refusing to pay or collect Ship Money or Coat and Conduct Money, by challenging the king's right to make law by proclamation and regulate trade by patent, or simply by acting to protect their rights of private property and personal liberty. No doubt some had done so for self-serving reasons, but just as clearly, others had acted from deeply held convictions – for what were often called 'matters of conscience'. Those who did so resisted the Crown's programmes in the 1630s, in part because they brought abrupt change, challenged traditions and upset local and personal relations, but also because they genuinely felt that the king's authority to impose change of this kind and on this scale was suspect. Whether or not they were able to articulate their objections in precise legal language (and some clearly were), they sensed that the king was acting arbitrarily, or at the very least, contrary to the traditions of consensual government. On those grounds they had felt compelled to resist.

As the list in Table 2.1 suggests, resistance had carried a heavy price – deprivation, excommunication, inordinate fines, imprisonment, loss of income and property. But the petitioners in these cases appealed to the House of Lords not just because the penalties had been excessive and debilitating. Most failed to understand why they had been prosecuted at all. As they saw it, the law had been on their side. It was they who had stood by the true doctrine of the church of England. It was they who had acted to uphold Parliament's right to make laws and levy financial exactions on the subject. They had been the conformists. It was the king who had changed the rules. Therefore, what they needed from the House of Lords was more than just redress for their immediate suffering. They needed (and rather more urgently) a broader statement on the law – a determination, within the context of these cases, on the Crown's right arbitrarily to redefine the law on its own terms and for its own purposes.

CONFLICTS OVER RELIGION

Perhaps predictably, the most urgent appeals for redress came from those petitioners who had been charged with, or prosecuted for, alleged religious nonconformity. For these individuals, whether Puritans or adherents of the Elizabethan 'middle ground', the implication of nonconformity was deeply disturbing. In their view they had always been entirely 'conformable' to the doctrine and practices of the church of England. Not all of them, certainly, would have been able to articulate precisely what that doctrine was – the specific tenets of orthodox Calvinism – but they clearly knew what the established forms of worship were and had been and were deeply committed to them. The fact that they may not have been fully conversant with the doctrinal implications of Arminian theology did not make the controversy any less real for them. The suppression of preaching, the demands for strict compliance with the rubrics of the *Book of Common Prayer*, the renewed emphasis on the liturgy, on ceremony and on the administration of the sacraments, and – most emphatically – the transformation of communion tables into altars, were all outward, tangible signs of change which suggested that *some* form of doctrinal revolution was underway. Whatever their level of comprehension, that was a deeply disturbing prospect – even more so, perhaps, the less it was understood. Whether out of fear or conviction, these petitioners had felt compelled to resist the change. What really troubled them, quite apart from the penalties they had incurred as a result, was the fact that they had become outlaws from the church of England (at least in the eyes of its present governors) and in an age of intense Protestant piety, that meant a great deal – spiritually, emotionally and practically. Appeal to the House of Lords was therefore a matter of real necessity. In the short term what these petitioners wanted was immediate relief, either in the form of restitution or compensation for their suffering. But in the long run they were also attempting to question both the Crown's right abruptly and dramatically to alter the definitions and parameters of religious conformity and its right summarily to punish those who had inadvertently fallen outside those new boundaries.

The issue of nonconformity had in fact arisen in a number of different contexts, but the most frequent source of conflict involved the disputed position of the communion table.[14] Its proper placement had never been clearly established. The Elizabethan injunctions of 1559 had instructed that the table should reside at the east end of the church – 'where the altar stood' – when not in use, but should be placed during the divine service 'in good sort within the chancel, as thereby the minister may be more conveniently heard by the communicants in his prayer and ministrations and the communicants also more conveniently, and in more numbers, communicate with the said minister'. The canons of 1604 had reiterated that direction, but, importantly, had failed to indicate where the table should rest when not in use.[15] In any event, the phrasing was broad enough to allow individual parishes to proceed as they deemed appropriate. Most appear to have refrained from moving the table at all and simply allowed it to stand, more or less permanently, in the middle of the chancel.[16] Problems began to develop in the early 1630s when the king and his two archbishops, Laud of Canterbury and Neile of York, embarked on a concerted programme to convert communion tables into altars. There is evidence that both Neile and Laud had undertaken the programme on their own initiative, before their appointments to their respective archbishoprics, but the policy was officially sanctioned in 1633, in the case of the parish of St Gregory's in London, when the king lent his support to the change and to the notion that parish churches should follow the example of their mother cathedrals.[17] Thereafter individual parishes, certainly in the dioceses of Laudian bishops, came under increasing pressure to move the table and rail it in 'altar-wise' at the east end of the church.

This was a very important and very visible sign of change to the interior structure of parish churches and to patterns of worship and, judging by the petitions to the upper house, it met with no little resistance. The chief victims had been the parish churchwardens who, as the primary contact between the parish and the national church, were in a particularly vulnerable position. They were caught between the demands of their ordinaries and the wishes of their parishioners. In these cases the wardens had opted to support the interests of the former over the latter and had paid the penalty. In *Farren* v. *Clarke*, for instance, the churchwardens of the church of All Saints, Northampton, had been directed to move the table to the east end on three separate occasions in 1638 by Dr Samuel Clarke, chief surrogate of the bishop's court. They had refused, or in their words had 'delayed execution thereof' because 'they could not justify the same, either by Rubric or Canons'. They insisted that the table had stood in the middle of the chancel 'ever since the Reformacion', and that moving it meant that 'a third part of the congregation can neither see nor hear' the officiating minister – a clear reference to the admonitions of the canons. On their third refusal, however, Dr Clarke had excommunicated them. They then appealed to the court of Arches, seeking absolution and an inhibition against Dr Clarke, but found Sir John Lambe, the principal of the court, unwilling to hear their cause. Lambe, in fact, entered a caveat into the court records permanently suspending their appeal. Undeterred, the wardens then appealed to the court of Delegates, where 'after great charges and long attendance' they were awarded a decree of absolution. Ignoring that decision, Clarke then exhibited articles against them in High Commission and, under threat of those proceedings, the wardens had finally complied.[18] According to Clarke, writing to Sir John Lambe, the wardens had eventually conformed 'in requital of my love and pains.'[19] The wardens, however, had seen the situation rather differently. They petitioned the House of Lords in early February 1641 (now two years after the fact) requesting to be freed from the still pending proceedings in High Commission and asking to be awarded damages for their expenses in pursuing appeal.

The churchwardens of the parish of Upton, also in Northamptonshire, had likewise fallen foul of Dr Clarke. In this case, however, Clarke had 'of his own authority, and without the consent of the churchwardens or any of the parishioners' commissioned a local joiner to make the alterations and then demanded that the wardens pay him for the work. They had refused, having, they said, 'given neither their directions nor their consent', and as a reward had been summarily excommunicated. They too had appealed to the court of Arches and subsequently to the court of Audience seeking an absolution and an inhibition against the bishop's surrogate, but on both occasions they had come up against the ubiquitous Sir John Lambe. Lambe had finally explained to them that he was powerless to help them because 'the Archbishop had given orders that no inhibitions should go into Northamptonshire, Bedfordshire, or Buckinghamshire without his special knowledge'. Having by then suffered under the penalties of excommunication for six months, the wardens finally gave in and paid the carpenter. Two years later they too appealed to the House of Lords requesting, first, an order allowing them to restore the communion table to 'where it ancientlie stood according to the rubricke in the Book of Common Prayer', and, second, 'satisfaction for costs and damages unjustly susteyned'.[20]

Similar complaints were presented from parishes in Bedford, Suffolk and Essex. In the latter case the excessive diligence of clerical officials had had serious repercussions. In 1635 the churchwardens in the parish of St Botolph's in Colchester, James Wheeler and John Hocker, had refused to move the communion table to the east end, on orders of Dr Robert Aylett, the commissary of the London diocese. Wheeler had protested that to do so was 'againste his Maties lawes' and 'contrary to ye Rubricke in ye booke of common praier', and he felt he could not comply until he had 'some lawe and sufficient authority for it'. He suggested that Aylett give him 'an acte of yor Courte under yor hand and seale to bear me out to do it' so that he could 'ye better justifie ye doinge of it' to his parishioners. Aylett responded that he 'would make no bargaines' and excommunicated the wardens for their intransigence.[21] Sometime later Aylett obtained a warrant to bring the two wardens before High Commission. Hocker fled the kingdom. The High Commission messenger then attempted to apprehend Wheeler, but finding that he too had escaped, attached two of his children instead and carried them before Robert Buxton, then Mayor of Colchester, who imprisoned them for three days, releasing them only after they had undertaken to appear at the next quarter sessions. Wheeler himself was eventually apprehended and imprisoned for three years. Thereafter, still 'deprived of his calling' and unable 'to practice commerce or trade', he too left for 'foreign parts' where he died, leaving his wife and children without support. In February 1641 his wife petitioned the House of Lords asking recompense for 'the great loss and damages susteyned.'[22]

The Lords also received a number of petitions from individual parishioners who claimed to have been prosecuted for their refusal to receive communion at the newly constructed altars – in those parishes where the change had in fact been successfully implemented. Thomas Woolrick, of the parish of Kowling in Suffolk, for example, had been excommunicated by Dr Thomas Eden in 1638 for his refusal to take communion at the rails. Woolrick claimed that he had refused because he was unwilling 'to consent to the alteration of the old custome'. He asked that the Lords call Eden to account and that they award him reparation for his troubles. In his view, the penalty he had suffered had been 'contrary to ye Ecclesiastical Government of this Kingdome, and not agreeable to the Word of God, and not according to Christian Charity'.[23] Robert Prior of Cambridge had also refused to take communion at the rails 'lately made' in the parish church of St Michael. He had instead 'received the blessed sacrament in the chancel of the said church, as formerly and anciently it had been used to be administered', and for that had been cited into the consistory court of the bishop of Ely. He asked that he be discharged from the still pending proceedings in the bishop's court and given satisfaction for his charges, because, as he protested, he 'was and is conformable in all things to the Canons of the Church, and hath committed no offence'.[24]

Some of these petitioners had been willing to go to inordinate lengths to protest the change. Samuel Burroughs, of the parish of St Reynolds in Colchester, had presented himself to take communion on four separate occasions in 1636, but had been denied the sacrament by his parson, Thomas Newcomen, because he refused to come up to the altar and kneel at the rails. He had then been convented before the diocesan court for neglecting to receive communion and, despite his protests that he had been entirely diligent and willing to participate in the sacrament 'in such manner as had bene formerly accustomed', Dr Aylett, the ever-diligent commissary of the diocese, had pronounced two sentences of excommunication against him – one excluding him from 'divine ordinance' and the other 'from all consort and commerce whatsoever'. The decrees had stood for two years, but in the meantime, Burroughs had taken matters into his own hands. He had preferred a bill of indictment against Newcomen at the assizes for 'innovacon in Ecclesiastical ceremonies', citing the provisions of the Elizabethan Act of Uniformity as the basis of his charge.[25] According to Burroughs, the indictment had been 'contemptuously rejected' by the foreman and others of the jury because it was 'contrary to the directions of the Bishop'. Undeterred, Burroughs preferred a second identical indictment at the next sessions and this time the jury found for the bill. Unfortunately, before Newcomen could be brought to plead, the indictment was removed by writ of *certiorari* into the court of King's Bench where it remained dormant. Newcomen then preferred articles in High Commission against Burroughs and the members of the jury who had found for his bill and Burroughs was eventually imprisoned for five months. Like the others, Burroughs protested to the Lords that he was 'and allwayes hath been a man conformable to the doctrine and discipline approved and declared by the Lawes of the Kingdome'. He asked that the Lords examine the illegal and malicious persecutions of Newcomen and his 'confederates' and award him compensation for the 'damages, miseries, and oppression' which he had undergone.[26]

The Lords' response to all of these cases appears to have been dictated by their conviction that the order to remove and rail in the communion table had been issued and enforced without proper authority. However adamantly the king and his archbishops may have wanted the change, simply declaring the policy had not made it law.[27] The canons of 1604 remained in force and provided the only legitimate legal definition of acceptable practice.[28] There was nothing in those canons which either suggested or required that the table be permanently stationed at the east end and railed in. Indeed, as many petitioners pointed out, the new policy violated both the spirit and the letter of the canons by making it more difficult for the communicants to see and hear the minister. Presumably, it was those considerations which moved the house to declare, in February 1641, that 'there is no ground in law to warrant or compel the railing in of the communion table'.[29] The declaration was careful to emphasize that there had been no grounds to *compel* conformity and therefore ministers, churchwardens and parishioners alike had, in their view, been legally blameless in defying the authority of their ordinary or his surrogate.

Given that assumption, the Lords did not hesitate to offer appropriate remedy to these petitioners. Where necessary they gave directions to church courts to grant absolution to parishioners who remained excommunicate,[30] or in other cases to discharge the plaintiffs from still pending proceedings.[31] But the Lords were also concerned to offer appropriate compensation to those who had clearly suffered (and in so doing register their disapproval of over-zealous and misguided clerical officials). Punitive damages were therefore awarded in a number of appeals. In the case of the parish of Upton in Northamptonshire, for example, the Lords not only ordered that the churchwardens should be granted costs for their expenses in pursuing appeal, but went on to order that Dr Clarke, the offending surrogate, make a new communion table for the church at his own cost. They directed that it should be 'set in the ancient place where it hath formerly stood'.[32] Other awards ranged from £8 levied against the promoter who had cited Robert Prior in the bishop's court at Ely, to £300 levied against the mayor of Colchester and the High Commissioners who had prosecuted James Wheeler and his fellow churchwarden John Hocker.[33] There was nothing ambiguous about these decisions. The Lords clearly felt that the Laudian bishops had misread and misapplied (deliberately or otherwise) the canonical instructions of 1604, and with these cases recently in view, they moved to correct any remaining misapprehension about the matter. On 1 March, they issued a general order

> that every Bishop in his particular diocese shall give order and take care that the communion table in every church in his diocese shall stand decently in the ancient place where it ought to do *by law*, and as it hath done for the greater part of these three score years last past.[34]

The other prosecutions for nonconformity appealed to the house attest to Archbishop Laud's broader attempts to impose order and liturgical uniformity on the church – his efforts to enjoin strict compliance with the rubrics of the prayer book regarding church ceremony, with injunctions governing clerical dress and conduct, and with rules about lay attendance and comportment. For the most part the petitioners here were Puritans, or indeed, dedicated nonconformists, who had objected to the rigorous enforcement of the ecclesiastical injunctions and who had been prosecuted, sometimes repeatedly, for their intransigence. Strictly speaking, these petitioners were in a far less defensible position, simply because the law was on the side of the archbishop and his subordinates. Laud was in fact applying existing regulations. But the sense of injustice was no less keenly felt. Practices which had been generally tolerated under the Jacobean policy of occasional conformity (or simply overlooked in the interests of establishing broad-based support for the national church) had suddenly become subject to punitive legal proceedings. The generally accommodating policies of the Jacobean church had led many of these petitioners to believe, in a curious way, that they had earned the right to practice their religion according to their consciences. Now that right had been abruptly revoked.

George Daniel, vicar of Steventon in Bedfordshire, for example, petitioned the house, together with two other local clergymen, complaining of the 'cruelties' and 'oppression' of Walter Walker, sometime 'treacherous' secretary to the bishop of Lincoln and commissary for the jurisdiction of Bedford.[35] Daniel claimed that he and other clergy of Bedford had been suspended by Walker for failing to wear the surplice during the divine service, for neglecting to bow at the name of Jesus and for refusing to stand within the rails during the communion service. He claimed as well that his parishioners had been harassed in the ecclesiastical courts for likewise failing to bow at the name of Jesus, for failing to stand at the Creed and the 'Gloria Patria', and for leaving their heads covered in church. All of these were, according to Daniel, 'illegal demands and injunctions', which had been enforced 'only to the end that the commissarie might ingratiate himself with the Archbishop of Canterbury'.[36] He asked that the Lords examine the articles of grievance and award him and his fellow Bedfordshire clergymen damages for their troubles. A similar complaint was presented by Miles Burkitt, the vicar of Pattishal, a notoriously Puritan parish in Northamptonshire. Burkitt claimed that he had been continually persecuted over the previous six years by Nicholas Gare, the chief apparitor for the diocese of Lincoln. Gare had promoted six separate suits against Burkitt in the ecclesiastical courts and in 1637 had initiated proceedings in High Commission. There he had been charged with exhorting his parishioners to 'contribute to the necessities of the Sayntes in want' – meaning Henry Burton and William Prynne. He had also been charged with being at a fast in the parish church of Marston, Northamptonshire, with preaching on Sunday afternoons until six o'clock, and with preaching without the prayer book in his visitations to the sick. Burkitt claimed that these proceedings had cost him upwards of £500 and he asked that Gare, Sir John Lambe and Dr Robert Sibthorpe be brought to account for their part in the prosecutions.

John James, Thomas Wells and John Ponder, all of Rothwell, North-amptonshire, also complained to the house of sustained harassment by clerical officials.[37] All three had at different times been cited in the consistory court of the bishop of Peterborough for nonconformity. In 1634 they were convented together before High Commission, where they were initially accused of participating in a conventicle – where they did 'conceive and utter openly among them a praier' – and with gadding to sermons. They were charged as well with speaking out against the 'ceremonies, rites, and orders of the church of England, as namely against the ministers wearing of the surplysse, ye use of the cross in Baptism, the ring in marriage, and the like', and with repeatedly refusing to bow at the name of Jesus and to stand at the reading of the Creed.[38] In the event, they were found to be 'refractory and unconformable' and all of them had been fined and excommunicated. Wells objected that these matters were 'trivial and illegal' and protested that 'out of conscience' he could not comply. All three objected to having to take the oath *ex officio* and to the inconvenience and the excessive cost of pursuing their defence over a three-year period. Wells and James also complained that their attempts to appeal earlier convictions to the court of Arches had been blocked by Sir John Lambe. In frustration James had eventually moved to Buckinghamshire, but by the time he petitioned the House of Lords, he had been prosecuted twice more by Sir John Lambe for gadding to sermons in that county.

The house in fact heard a number of complaints about prosecutions for gadding to sermons. Again, the law was fairly clear on this point. Both the Elizabethan Act of Uniformity and the Injunctions of 1559 required regular attendance by parishioners at their own parish churches (though they did not prohibit travelling to sermons on days other than the sabbath). But as Professor Collinson has recently demonstrated, in Puritan circles at least, the admonitions on attendance were increasingly considered 'a matter of conscience rather than of positive law'.[39] Indeed, legislation had actually been proposed in the 1628 Parliament which would have prevented prosecutions for nonattendance, providing the individuals had been present at proper Anglican services elsewhere. The bill drew support from no less a figure than Sir Henry Marten, then dean of the court of Arches, who argued before the Commons that to prosecute in such cases was 'against law'. He claimed in fact that as dean of the Arches, he had awarded costs against prosecuting ordinaries and 'would ever do it'.[40] By 1633, of course, Marten was out of office and his views on this and other matters were distinctly out of fashion. Hence the complaint of John Cushie of Caddington in Bedfordshire, that he had been prosecuted by his minister in the bishop's court, in 1636, for attending a church nearer his home, a proceeding which eventually led to his excommunication and subsequent imprisonment by High Commission.[41] Francis Gurnett, of

Mitford, Northamptonshire, made a similar complaint, claiming that he had been repeatedly threatened and twice excommunicated by the ever-diligent Dr Samuel Clarke for 'going out of his parish to hear sermons'. On the second occasion, Clarke had actually imprisoned him for refusing the oath *ex officio*, holding him until Gurnett paid him £3.15s in fees. The hapless Gurnett, finally 'worn out' by Clarke's violence and prosecutions, had abandoned his wife and five children and settled in another diocese, hoping, as he rather charmingly put it, that 'either the Doctor would have forgotten your petr or would have grown more moderate in the execution of his office'. Neither happened. When Gurnett returned to Mitford he resumed his travels and was cited again and fined.[42]

The Lords were in something of a difficult position with regard to these cases. Their obligation to uphold the law left them little room to offer redress to petitioners who were, strictly speaking, operating outside it. Nor could they really afford to be seen undermining discipline in the church of England (especially in 1641) by openly sanctioning blatant nonconformity, however sympathetic some of the Lords may have been with the views (and the plight) of their clients. While most of these cases proceeded to hearing, few of them appear to have been concluded – though that may well be an accident of record keeping rather than a telling coincidence. Where they were concluded, the Lords stepped rather gingerly around the issues, focusing as closely as possible on allegations of judicial impropriety. In the case of John James, cited above, the Lords were clearly outraged by what they saw as a 'criminal' misuse of the ecclesiastical court to harass a subject.[43] James, however, was unable to produce more than one witness to substantiate his charges and the Lords, holding fast to evidentiary rules, regretfully declined to award him the damages they plainly thought he deserved.[44] They did, however, take direct action in the case of *Rodways et al.* v. *Baber*, which concerned a prosecution for gadding to sermons. Here the plaintiffs John Rodways, Walter Coles and William Newarke had been cited in the consistory court of the bishop of Gloucester for going out of their parish to hear sermons. When called before the court the men had refused the oath *ex officio* – 'knowing no crime by them committed' – and had been excommunicated. They repeatedly petitioned the court to revoke the sentence or to provide a copy of the articles exhibited against them, but were denied both requests. They were then arrested on pretence that a writ of *significavit* had issued out against them.[45] They remained in prison for 11 days, after which they were taken to London, ostensibly to answer the charge. Once there, however, they discovered that no such writ had ever been requested or issued. They had in fact been illegally detained, and on those grounds, and in light of the unnecessary costs incurred they had petitioned the house to recover damages. The Lords awarded them

£60 'in consideration of the said Imprisonment, and Losses, and Trouble sustained herein', which they assessed against both Dr Baber, the official who had promoted the case in the bishop's court, and the undersheriff who had imprisoned them on the basis of a 'pretended' writ.

In two other cases the Lords acted to correct what appeared to be arbitrary and unwarranted judicial proceedings. The first was the case of Thomas Foxley. Foxley was a well known and influential Puritan lecturer in London. In 1631 he had been interrogated before Archbishop Laud and forced to promise that he would 'conform' to the views of the ecclesiastical authorities. He failed to do so, and in 1636 was cited in High Commission and suspended from his lectures in the parish of St Martin's in the Field. Three years later, he was again brought before High Commission and charged with 'schismatical preaching'. It was alleged that he had attempted to 'bring his auditors into dislike with the present government of the Church' by suggesting that the bishops 'were inclining themselves and others into popery'. However, before High Commission could proceed with the articles, Foxley was summoned before the Privy Council and without formal hearing, was committed close prisoner in the Gatehouse.[46] He remained there until the opening of the Long Parliament, when his wife petitioned the House of Commons for his release. The Commons declared that he ought to have his liberty, but failed to transmit the case to the upper house for an order for his release. The parishioners of St Martin's in the Field then petitioned the upper house requesting that he be freed to continue his lectureship.[47] The Lords reviewed the case and declared that Foxley had been committed 'without cause shown' and on 25 February ordered that he be freed and granted full liberty to preach as before.[48]

The other case involved a Northamptonshire yeoman named John Eckins. Eckins had been prosecuted in High Commission in 1634 on the basis of three charges. It was alleged that he had sat with his hat on during the divine service, that he had caused £100 to be counted on the communion table and that he had openly declared that 'a plowman was as good as a priest'.[49] The High Commission heard the charges and ultimately determined that Eckins was

> guilty and deserving punishment for his irreverent and profane behavior, which now grows so frequent and common among lay people of all sorts, that unless some present course be taken for the repressing and reforming of the same, according to his Majestie's instructions, there will be a gapp open to all manner of profaners.[50]

No doubt keeping that in mind the commissioners, with the archbishop in the chair, elected to make an example of Eckins. They fined him £100, plus £20 costs, and commanded that he make a public submission of his errors in the parish church of Isham.

Eckins appealed to the house in August 1641 claiming that he had spent some £800 in the cause and asking for compensation. The Lords reviewed the case and found in his favour. Their judgment reflects to some degree the conclusions which had already been reached in legislating the court's abolition. They declared that the High Commission had had no jurisdiction over the case in the first place and no power to impose a fine of any sort on Eckins. Their conclusion followed the basic argument, repeatedly advanced by Sir Edward Coke and others in earlier debates, that the court's jurisdiction had always been limited to the review of 'enormities and heinous crimes' – of which this was clearly not one, despite the archbishop's manic obsession with order and reverence – and that it had never had explicit authority to impose punitive fines.[51] They therefore declared that the commission's proceedings in this case had been 'contrary to the laws of this land and the liberty of the subject' and awarded Eckins damages of £120, which they assessed proportionately against the 15 commissioners who had endorsed the decree.[52]

In many ways the most serious complaints arising from the Crown's religious programme in the 1630s were those in which individuals had been arbitrarily deprived of their church livings for their suspected disaffection with the new Laudian orthodoxy. In fact none of the defendants in these cases had been charged with doctrinal offences. Nor could they have been. All of them had been entirely orthodox Calvinists and had clearly subscribed to the Thirty-nine Articles, and so were protected by the law. But they had been targetted as critics of the Laudian innovations and church officials had simply found other ways to proceed against them. In most cases they had been brought before High Commission on a manufactured charge of simony, usually in a collusive action brought by an avowed Laudian cleric. Almost invariably the accused had been deprived and the accuser awarded the newly vacated living. What was disturbing about these cases, certainly in the Lords' view, was the court's crass and deliberate disregard for the law and its blatant abuse of proper judicial procedure.

The case of John Ward provides a useful introduction to the problem.[53] Ward had been minister of the parish of Dennington in Suffolk for 12 years when, in 1637, he was suspended by Ezekial Wright, chancellor for the bishop of Norwich, for refusing to read the second service at the communion table, which had only recently been moved 'altar-wise' to the east end of the church. Not content with suspension Wright had then presented articles in High Commission charging Ward with simony. Ward had in fact acquired the living a dozen years earlier through an arrangement that was by any definition simoniacal.[54] The crucial factor, which Ward subsequently insisted upon in court, was that he had already been prosecuted for the offence and pardoned in the Coronation Pardon of 1625. The commissioners, however, chose to ignore the matter of the pardon. Ward was convicted of the charge, deprived of his living and permanently prevented from holding any ecclesiastical preferment.

The Lords reviewed Ward's case in early July 1641. They initially solicited a formal opinion from justices Reeve and Heath as to 'whether the Pardon ought not to have freed the Petr from all suits in the Ecclesiastical Courts and High Commission for simony . . . supposed to have been done before the date thereof'. When the judges reported, not surprisingly, that the pardon had indeed constituted a valid protection, the Lords declared the High Commission decree to be 'void' and summoned the nine commissioners who had delivered the sentence to appear and show cause why appropriate damages should not be awarded to the complainant.[55]

The proceedings in the case of Ezekial Johnson had been altogether different.[56] In 1631 Johnson had himself initiated a prosecution in High Commission against the incumbent minister of Paulesbury in Northamptonshire on a charge of simony. The incumbent's transgression had been, according to Johnson, 'publiquely and notoriously known'. It was easily proved and he was accordingly deprived. In the meantime Johnson had applied to the Crown to be presented to the living. He was successful and subsequently received the king's grant and took possession. In 1637, however, unspecified articles were exhibited against Johnson himself in High Commission, questioning the validity of his own presentation to the living. After a single hearing, in which no proofs were offered to the general charge, Johnson was summarily excluded from the living through the issue of a superinstitution. In theory a superinstitution was granted in those cases where the incumbent's presentation was suspected of being invalid for want of a proper title in his patron. It was issued to another party and allowed the grantee to supersede the incumbent's presentation and possession, on the assumption that he would then try the title to the living at common law through an action of ejectment. In Johnson's case the use of the device was singularly inappropriate. His predecessor's lawful conviction for simony had meant that the right of presentation had automatically reverted to the Crown – from whom Johnson had directly obtained the living. His patron's title had been unassailable. As Johnson argued in the course of the proceedings, his presentation had been entirely legal and according to the letter of statute law.[57] The court ignored his argument and, under direct orders from Archbishop Laud, granted the superinstitution to Dr William Beale, sometime chancellor of Cambridge University and master of St John's College and a noted Arminian divine whose outspoken support for the Laudian innovations would draw a stinging rebuke from John Pym on the opening day of the Long Parliament.[58]

The Lords were noticeably unimpressed with the court's reasoning and its subsequent proceedings on the case. In early March, they ordered Johnson reinstated to the living, and summoned the errant commissioners to explain their decision, and to show cause why the complainant should not be awarded compensatory damages.[59] They did so for two reasons: first, because of 'the many falsehoods stuffed into that sentence', and, second, because in their view 'the High Commission hath no power to dispose of the freehold of any man without trial at law'.[60] The latter statement referred to the fact that the superinstitution had amounted to a *de facto* judgment on title, a decision which the court had no authority to make. However, the declaratory nature of the judgment was not accidental and was meant to have a wide and lasting application.

The principle inherent in the judgment in Johnson's case had in fact been clearly articulated less than a month before in the case of *Bloxam* v. *Sandiland*.[61] The petitioner, Nicholas Bloxam, complained to the Lords in February that he had been deprived of the living of Great Waldingfield in Suffolk, in 1637, as a result of a suit brought in High Commission by one Andrew Sandiland. He too had been accused of simony. The basis of the charge (brought some three years after his institution) had been a supposed agreement between Bloxam's uncle, Thomas Brooke, and two other parties, Duncombe and Clare. Under the pretended agreement, Duncombe and Clare were to be paid £500 for securing the King's permission to sue out a writ of *quare impedit* in his name in order to remove the incumbent (who by all accounts had himself been simoniacally presented). It was also alleged in High Commission that Bloxam had entered into a prior agreement with the patron of the living, promising to increase the existing rent on the rectory and parsonage house, in exchange for the patron's testimony against the incumbent at the upcoming trial.[62]

Technically, neither of the charges, even if they had been proved, would have amounted to simony under the statute. The supposedly agreed payment to the agents Duncombe and Clare was only for their efforts in securing the king's permission to sue (and presumably his promise to present Bloxam in the event of a successful outcome). No payment was made to the king who was, or would have been, the patron. Bloxam's agreement to pay an increased rent was in fact a necessity. The existing arrangement between the patron and the incumbent minister had been declared simoniacal precisely because the rent had been conspicuously lower than what the properties appeared to warrant. Bloxam's advocates insisted that neither of the supposed agreements was simoniacal, but the court took another view, declaring that 'both were simonies, though under other names and titles'.[63] Bloxam was deprived of his benefice and imprisoned for the offence and Sandiland, the promoter, was immediately instituted and inducted in his place, much to the evident dismay of the parishioners who later petitioned the house complaining of his 'popish' and superstitious conduct.[64]

In his petition to the house Bloxam insisted that he had committed no offence and after an extended hearing of the original arguments, the Lords concluded that, indeed, there had not been sufficient evidence to prove the charge of simony.[65] Their final declaration went much further, however. As in Johnson's case, the Lords declared first that the Commission's proceedings had been 'illegal' because 'they conceive the ecclesiastical courts cannot remove the possession of a Freehold' without trial at law.[66] In the context of this particular case, that declaration represented a dramatically narrowed view of the court's authority. The deprivation of clerics for serious offences such as simony had long been an accepted part of the commission's jurisdiction and responsibility. Nor had the court ever been compelled to defer to a prior determination at law on the facts of any given case before executing an eviction. The notion that it ought to do so had been vigorously asserted in the famous Cawdry's case in 1592, but the idea had ultimately been rejected by the assembled judges of Queen's Bench in favour of a wider and less restricted definition of the court's jurisdiction.[67] The Lords, however, clearly felt that the law ought now to be redefined, or perhaps reinterpreted, in the light of the abuses which had arisen in these and other cases.

Their judgment in these two appeals essentially reflects a decidedly secular point of view: that ecclesiastical livings were, above anything else, freehold property, and as such were (or certainly ought to have been) protected by the safeguards inherent in common law procedure. The final actions taken in Bloxam's case developed logically from that position. The Lords directed that the case was to proceed to a trial at law on the question of fact – whether Bloxam had been guilty of simony – and they requested that Justices Reeve and Berkeley devise an appropriate means for bringing the matter to trial.[68] Interestingly, the procedure recommended by the judges was precisely that tried unsuccessfully by Robert Cawdry 50 years earlier. Bloxam was directed to bring an action of trespass in the King's Bench and the issue was then to be tried by *nisi prius* at the next Suffolk assizes. Sandiland was directed to plead not guilty and the jury was to be instructed that the only issue before them was the question of whether or not Bloxam had been simoniacally presented.[69] Accordingly, on 5 March Baron Hendon reported to the house that a trial had been concluded as directed and that a verdict had passed on behalf of the plaintiff, Nicholas Bloxam.[70] On the basis of that report the Lords then declared the High Commission sentence which had originally deprived Bloxam to be 'annulled, frustrate, and made void' and ordered him restored to the living immediately.[71]

Not all of these plaintiffs had been prosecuted on charges of simony.[72] Lambert Osbaldiston, the headmaster of Westminster School, had been undone, as it were, by his own hand. Osbaldiston had succeeded to a series of clerical posts from the beginning of the 1620s largely as a result of the patronage of John Williams, bishop of Lincoln. Like Williams,

Osbaldiston was a man of moderate religious and political views, who frequently found himself at odds with the prevailing ecclesiastical policy of the 1630s. Unfortunately, he was also inclined to commit his feelings to paper. In 1638 certain of his letters to Williams found their way into the hands of Archbishop Laud. One of those letters contained an only vaguely enigmatic reference to the archbishop himself. Osbaldiston had referred to Laud at one point as 'the little urchin' and at another as 'that meddling little hocus pocus'. The letters in fact became the basis for the second Star Chamber prosecution against Williams later that year, where Osbaldiston found himself an unwitting co-defendant.[73] The eventual success of the case against Williams did little to temper the court's hostility toward the headmaster. He was fined £5,000 to the king, an additional £5,000 to the archbishop, deprived of all of his ecclesiastical preferments – and thereby his means of paying the fines – and sentenced to be pilloried in the Dean's Yard at Westminster, before, as he would later lament, 'the very schollers he had so painfully and successfullie bred up and taught'.[74] However, before the court had the chance to execute the sentence in full, Osbaldiston had, according to Thomas Smith, 'shown them a light pair of heels.'[75] He disappeared and remained in hiding until the opening of the Long Parliament 18 months later.

When Osbaldiston petitioned the house in January 1641, he claimed, as he had in Star Chamber, that the letters had been deliberately misconstrued.[76] He also claimed, somewhat more credibly, that the court's proceedings had been improper and that the sentence had been wholly unjust. He maintained that he had been denied the opportunity to examine the prosecution's two central witnesses, whom he claimed were notoriously unreliable, having been sentenced in that court less than 12 months before for subornation.[77] He also argued that his deprivation had been illegal, because Star Chamber itself 'hath no Power to sentence any subject from his Freehold,' and because High Commission had carried out the sentence summarily, at the direction of Star Chamber, without its own independent hearings and determination.

It was in fact those two specific points which the Lords focused on in their review. They subsequently declared that 'in Truth, neither the one Court nor the other had or hath the Power to sentence any subject of this Realme out of his Freehold and Inheritance'. They then went on to say that 'neither the High Commission, nor any other Ecclesiastical Court hath Power to execute a sentence or decree of Star Chamber ministerially'.[78] Accordingly, they directed that Osbaldiston be fully restored to all of his livings and to their profits. The Star Chamber decree was ordered to be vacated, and the petitioner was to be 'freed from all fines, damages, costs of suit, and corporeal punishments given by that sentence'.[79]

The issue of freehold property was perhaps even more directly at stake in cases which involved lay impropriations. Archbishop Laud's hostile attitude toward lay patronage is well known. The large proportion of church livings in lay hands – estimated at one third of all benefices in England – had, in his view, sharply reduced his ability to establish uniform control over the church and over the quality and conformity of its clergy.[80] In theory, however, there was little he could do about it. He might harass lay impropriators in High Commission, and he could (and did) forcibly disband the Feoffees for Impropriations in 1633 in Star Chamber, but lay advowsons were private property and were ostensibly protected by the rules of common law. Or so it seemed. In practice, judging by the subsequent appeals to the House of Lords, ways were found to tackle the problem, albeit on a case by case basis. Time and again lay patrons complained to the house that their right of presentation had been abrogated, either through improper procedures on the part of the bishop of their diocese, or (more alarmingly) because of irregular proceedings in the court of Common Pleas. The case of Sir Peter Vanlors was fairly typical. In 1637 Vanlors had presented Andrew Blackwell to the Bishop of Salisbury as his candidate for the vicarage of Tylehurst in Buckinghamshire. Bishop Davenant refused to admit Blackwell, however, because he claimed he had received 'a countermand from the Archbishop of Canterbury' alleging that the title to the living lay with the king.[81] The king's candidate, a Dr Littleton, was presented to the living instead. Vanlors then followed established common law procedures and sued out a writ of *quare impedit* against the Bishop and Littleton to recover his right of presentation. He also obtained two writs of *ne admittas*, one out of Common Pleas and one out of Chancery, which were duly served on the bishop to prevent him from encumbering the living during the forthcoming litigation. Unfortunately, the court of Common Pleas abruptly reversed itself the following term and superseded the writ of *ne admittas*, and despite the second writ from Chancery, Dr Littleton was then instituted and inducted into the living. Vanlors meanwhile pursued his *quare impedit* and obtained a verdict in his behalf, but when the verdict was returned to Common Pleas, instead of issuing judgment, Chief Justice Finch issued an order staying all further proceedings on the writ. There the matter rested until Vanlors appealed to the upper house.

Jeremy Powell and his wife had faced similar obstacles. They had presented their candidate to the bishop of Hereford to fill a recent vacancy in the vicarage of Bucknill, Shropshire. Bishop Coke, however, had refused to admit their candidate, claiming that 'the Archbishop of Canterbury had taken special notice of the King's title and right of presenting to that vicarage'. They too had prosecuted a *quare impedit* and had secured a writ of *ne admittas* to prevent the vacancy being filled in the meantime, but the Bishop had simply ignored the court's injunctions and, on the basis of the king's 'pretended' title, had instituted and inducted another candidate, one Richard Edwards. The Powells appealed to the house requesting that Edwards be evicted and that the bishop be called to account for his 'contempt'.[82]

In a number of cases the house heard from clerics who petitioned for assistance on behalf of their patrons. John Sharedlow, for instance, had been presented to the parsonage of Beckles, Suffolk, by 'the true undoubted patrons' of the living in 1637. But he too had been denied institution by the then bishop of Norwich, Richard Montague. 'Upon some pretended right from the Archbishop of Canterbury', Bishop Montague had then instituted his own chaplain in the living. In due course, Sharedlow and his patrons had ('to his great charge') brought a *quare impedit* in Common Pleas, but their case was dismissed when it was discovered that they had misspelled the name of Montague's chaplain, one of the named defendants. By that stage more than six months had passed since Sharedlow's presentation and his patron's rights had therefore lapsed, leaving him without recourse.[83] Hence his petition to the House of Lords.

The Lords' response to these appeals was fairly predictable. Since an advowson was considered freehold property, the right of presentation was determinable at common law and the Lords insisted (in part to protect the long-term interests of their clients) that the matter be tried at law. Where, as in Sharedlow's case, common law proceedings had been initiated only to fail, the Lords normally ordered a retrial (notwithstanding the relevant six-month statute of limitations which applied to a patron's right of presentation). The profits of the livings were then sequestered in the hands of a third party during the legal proceedings.[84] In at least one case, *Powell* v. *Edwards* cited above, the Lords also elected to award damages to the plaintiff. In view of his blatant disregard of proper legal process, the bishop of Hereford was ordered to pay Jeremy Powell £30 as partial compensation for the year's income lost from the vicarage of Bucknill.[85]

In general, it is fair to say that decisions made in these cases sprang from a careful consideration of legal rather than religious or political issues. No doubt many of the members of the house were favourably predisposed toward these petitioners and there may well have been some internal pressure, from certain quarters of the house, to use these judgments as a platform for criticism of the ecclesiastical establishment (and from the clerical contingent of the house to do otherwise). But it was essential that that be avoided at all costs if the integrity of the court were to survive. The Lords had to judge (and be seen to judge) these cases on purely legal grounds. Even had it been possible, within the context of these cases – and it was not – it would have been singularly inappropriate (not to say reckless in the volatile climate of 1641) to make sweeping statements about religious policy.[86] The Lords' responsibility, when functioning as a court, was to uphold the law and their primary concern here was to correct and offer compensation for violations of established legal rules and procedures.

RAISING REVENUE:
SHIP MONEY AND COAT AND CONDUCT MONEY

The administration of the Crown's fiscal measures during the 1630s generated considerable discord as well. The cases here were far more heterogeneous and notably fewer, but they raised just as many important issues. Predictably perhaps, the Ship Money and Coat and Conduct levies were the cause of a number of appeals. Again, for the most part the petitioners here did not raise questions (except by implication) regarding the legality of either levy. They were concerned instead about the means and methods used by the Crown to enforce payment. Significantly, all of the disputes regarding Ship Money originated either during or in the aftermath of Hampden's case, which was heard in Exchequer Chamber between November 1637 and June 1638. This may simply reflect the fact that the Crown encountered greater resistance from local officials, who either anticipated a favourable verdict for Hampden, or were disturbed by the evident lack of consensus among the judges in their final decision. It probably reflects as well the fact that the Crown enforced its demand with greater rigour in anticipation of (and after) its success in the courts.

That would seem to explain the council's behaviour in the case of Francis Freeman and the inhabitants of Wilby, Northamptonshire.[87] In late December 1639 the Privy Council dispatched its pursuivant, one Davenport, to apprehend Constable Freeman for his alleged failure to collect Ship Money. Freeman refused to accompany Davenport unless and until Davenport produced a warrant from the council. Davenport had none and instead produced his sword, threatening to take Freeman by force. Freeman's neighbours then intervened, holding the messenger while Freeman disappeared to his home. The incident was duly reported to the council and three weeks later Freeman and his fellow constable, Thomas Pentloe, as well as a number of other townsfolk were apprehended and brought before the Board by Matthew Francis, the Serjeant at Arms. Freeman and Pentloe were eventually committed to the Fleet. Pentloe was able to secure his release through the payment of substantial fees, but Freeman had been forced to remain in prison for 15 weeks. He was finally released by the council on 23 May 1640.[88] Importantly, during his imprisonment, Freeman had applied for a writ of habeas corpus, but the judges of King's Bench (with the apparent exception of Justice Croke) had denied him bail, despite the absence of a stated cause for his imprisonment. At the same time, 13 of Freeman's neighbours had been cited in the King's Bench by the Attorney General, for an alleged rescue – this stemming from the original confrontation with the messenger Davenport. The prosecution was still pending against all of them when Freeman petitioned the House of Lords in early December 1640.

In reviewing the case the Lords' Committee for Petitions focused initially on the issue of Freeman's imprisonment. Justices Berkeley and Croke were summoned to explain the court's refusal to grant bail. The judges claimed that 'the return, as it appeared before them, had stood in generals, and so [they] did not know to the contrary but that it might have been for treason'.[89] They also maintained that they had been influenced by the information that the Attorney General had a suit still pending against Freeman and the others in the court. The committee was not convinced by the explanation. They concluded that Freeman had in fact been imprisoned for an unreasonable period on the basis of a warrant which failed to show proper or justifiable cause. They therefore reported to the whole house that it had been 'unanimously resolved . . . that both the Warrants from the Lords of the Council, and also the proceedings of the Judges, were directly against the Petition of Right', and so illegal.[90] The house accepted the committee's judgment, and granted Freeman's requests that he and the others be freed from the pending King's Bench prosecution, and that they be recompensed. The Attorney General was ordered to suspend further proceedings on the information in King's Bench and Matthew Francis, the Serjeant at Arms, was ordered to repay the £10 he had demanded of the complainants without proper authority.[91]

The same day, the Committee for Petitions began to consider another case which involved the Ship Money levy. Brought by William Waters and the inhabitants of Patishall, Northamptonshire, it provides an interesting glimpse of the way in which the Crown's programmes, religious and fiscal, could combine seriously to disrupt the harmony of local communities. In December 1637 the Arminian cleric Richard Powell had preached a sermon exhorting his parishioners to pay Ship Money, using as his text the biblical admonition from the gospel of Mark, 'Render unto Caesar the things that are Caesar's'.[92] Powell admitted that the levy might seem 'cruel and unjust', but went on to suggest that 'such Kings were often given to a Nation by God in his wrath for the people's sins . . . and that if we had such a king we ought notwithstanding to submit to him'.[93] Conceiving that the sermon had been 'dangerous to His Majestie's honor', William Waters and other parishioners reported it to one of the local JPs, Sir Richard Samuel, who in turn reported it to Justice Hutton, then on assize.[94] Hutton duly reported Powell's remarks to the council and in response the council commissioned Samuel and two other local JPs, the notorious Drs Clarke and Sibthorpe, to investigate Powell and his sermon. (In the meantime, the vicar had sensed impending danger and had hurriedly amended his subsequent sermons, adding the words, 'But blessed be God, he hath given us a gracious King, such as no age can parallel'.) Having excluded Samuels from the commission, Clarke and Sibthorpe perused the (newly altered) sermon and some of Powell's other writings and reported to the council that, contrary to the opinion of his informants, Powell was 'a very orthodox man, fully conformable to the Doctrine and Discipline of the Church of England, perfectly obedient in cases ecclesiastical and temporal, heartily affected to His Maties gratious government, and one who endeavors to persuade others to the like'.[95] As evidence the JPs claimed that Powell had voluntarily paid his portion of Ship Money, while all of his parishioners had refused and had been distrained. They also claimed to have found 'by sundry testimonies' and 'by our own experiences' that those who informed against Powell were 'schismatically affected in not obeying the Rites and Ceremonies of the Church of England, and also refractory agst his Maties proceedings in civil government'. Three weeks later, on 18 April, all of the parties were summoned before the Privy Council and on the basis of the JPs' certificate Powell was officially exonerated. His accusers, on the other hand, were condemned, ordered to compensate Powell for his expenses (including his fees to the clerk of the council) and commanded to give bond of £100 to ensure the payment of 'all such sums for Shipping' as were required by the writ.[96] As Waters was later to complain, 'the petitioners, being produced as witnesses, were punished, and the party accused acquitted'.[97]

The Lords' Committee for Imprisonments and Courts of Justice conducted hearings on Water's petition intermittently over a six-week period and on 21 January 1640/1 reported their findings to the house. The committee had concluded that the JPs Clarke and Sibthorpe had seriously abused the authority given to them by the council's original directives, specifically by returning 'a Certificate of matter no way concerning the Business, nor their commission'. Their certificate had, in addition, seriously misrepresented the facts. Far from being orthodox, Powell was, in the committee's view, 'Popish and Superstitious in divers particulars'.[98] More to the point, none of the petitioners, save Waters, had in fact refused to pay Ship Money, and only he had been distrained. The committee felt that the complainants had been 'unjustly and unduly troubled and informed against' and recommended that they receive appropriate recompense. The house concurred and ordered Clarke and Sibthorpe to repay £134 expended by the petitioners 'by way of damages'. They then directed that both men should be 'put out of the Commission of the Peace, and never to be Surrogates to any Bishop hereafter'. Sir Richard Samuel – who had since been put out of the commission at Clarke's behest – and John Crew were then appointed as replacement JPs.[99]

Again, the Lords were careful here to limit the scope of their response to the specific issues raised by the petitioners. There is, significantly, no discussion of the legality of the Ship Money writ or even of the council's right to summon the petitioners to demand payment – this despite the fact that the Lords had joined with the Commons only the day before in declaring the levy illegal.[100] Indeed, the order implies (if only by omission) that the council itself was entirely blameless in the affair. There may have been a degree of self-interest in that conclusion, since the committee who drafted the judgment included three members of the Privy Council, two of whom – the earls of Manchester and Arundel – had actually signed the Council's decree in Waters's case in 1638.[101] But it was still legally correct. The council's actions, however unjust, had been entirely predicated on the dishonest certificate of the two errant JPs. It was they who were responsible for the miscarriage of justice and it was they who were made to pay. What is rather striking is the Lords' order – and it was an order rather than a recommendation – removing the JPs from the Commission of the Peace and from their ecclesiastical posts as bishop's surrogates. It was certainly understandable under the circumstances and in light of the fact that the two men had, by this stage, been cited in four other complaints (with one more to come). But the House of Lords did not, in theory anyway, have the legal authority to remove or appoint JPs. Whether recognized as such or not, this was clearly an invasion of the king's prerogative. At this critical juncture, however, that appears to have been less important than the need to reestablish faith in the propriety of local government officials. The Lords would take similar action in at least two other cases.[102]

By the third week of January 1640/1 the Long Parliament had made its views on Ship Money clear. The joint declaration of the two houses, issued on the 21st, resolved

> that the Ship Writs, the extra-judicial Opinion of the Judges thereon, both first and last, and the Judgement given in Mr Hamden's case, and the proceedings thereon in the Exchequer Chamber, are all illegal, and contrary to the Laws and Statutes of the Realm, contrary to the Rights and Properties of the Subjects of this Realm, contrary to former judgments of Parliament, and contrary to the Petition of Right. Likewise . . . that the extra-judicial opinions inrolled in the Exchequer Chamber and in other courts concerning Ship Money and all of the proceedings thereupon are illegal, in part and in whole . . .[103]

On 9 February the Lords ordered that 'by judgement of Parliament' a *vacat* was to be issued against the judgment in Hampden's case in the Exchequer and enrolled on the record, to which the resolutions of Parliament were to be annexed. The same procedure was to be applied to the enrollments of the judges' decision in all other courts. The house then appointed a committee to expedite the matter.[104] The committee made its report on 26 February, recommending that all of the relevant records from the courts of King's Bench, Common Pleas, Exchequer, Star Chamber and

Chancery be brought into the house by senior members of each bench. There the clerk could formally enter the *vacat* against them and annex the appropriate resolutions. The report was unanimously adopted and the procedure was carried out the following day.[105] Six months later the entire process was enshrined in statute.[106]

Those actions effectively answered the complaints of three other petitioners to the house, the sheriffs of Essex, Berkshire and Northamptonshire, who had sought protection in early December 1640 from pending prosecutions in Star Chamber, initiated for their 'Great and Supine Negligence' in collecting Ship Money in their respective counties.[107] But the declarations had only exacerbated the problems of another petitioner, William Lawrence, constable of the parish of St Nicholas in Colchester. Lawrence had seemingly had the worst of all possible worlds. In 1638 he had been given responsibility for collecting the £18 in Ship Money assessed against the parish. He had only been partially successful because a number of parishioners had refused to pay their portion. He duly returned the money he had been able to collect, together with a list of refusers, to the then mayor of Colchester, Henry Harrington. Harrington, however, reported to the council that the constable had been deliberately remiss in his duties and had failed to collect the required sums out of disaffection. Lawrence was then attached, brought before the council and forced to provide a bond of £100 to guarantee the eventual payment of the outstanding amount – said to be £3 or £4. Under that threat Lawrence had returned to the parish and, 'by way of distress or otherwise', managed to collect the remaining sums. As a result he was promptly sued by one of the parishioners for illegal distraint of goods. He claimed that a number of other parishioners now threatened to do likewise and he asked for the protection of the house.[108] Unfortunately, there is no record of the Lords' response to his petition, but it is possible to suggest, on the basis of other evidence, that he was granted the request. Thomas Insley, another constable imprisoned by the council for refusing to distrain in the collection of Ship Money, had responded to Parliament's declaration by suing the Warden of the Fleet for false imprisonment. The warden in turn applied to the upper house to be indemnified against this and all future prosecutions. His request was immediately granted on grounds that he was 'but a minister to obey what was enjoined him'.[109] Other extenuating circumstances notwithstanding, there is little reason to believe that Constable Lawrence would not have been awarded the same protection.

The cases which had developed from the administration of the Coat and Conduct Money levy raised many of the same issues as the Ship Money levy, but were, on the whole, somewhat less complicated. Three of the complainants here had been, like William Waters *et al.*, 'unjustly informed against' to the Privy Council. Richard Cooke, Robert Harris and Thomas

Chater had all been accused by Thomas Marrat, the constable of Harpole, in Northamptonshire, of refusing to pay the levy. Marrat had given their names to the Deputy Lieutenant of the county, who in turn reported them to the Privy Council. Each of them had been summoned before the board, but each had been released when it was discovered that they had in fact never been rated – that the constable had never even demanded payment from them. The petitioners complained that they had expended upwards of £10 in the proceedings and they asked for compensation.[110] The Lords reviewed the case, declared the entire proceedings 'illegal', ordered Marrat discharged from his office and summoned the Deputy Lieutenant to the house to explain his own spurious report to the council.[111]

A far more serious complaint was brought in early February 1641 by Robert Cooke and William Hanman of Gloucestershire. Their petition accused the Deputy Lieutenant of the county, Sir Ralph Dutton, of gross misconduct and corruption in the administration of the levy and in the impressment of soldiers for the Scottish campaigns. They claimed that the previous April Dutton had sent out over 100 individual warrants summoning men for impressment. The majority of those men were then released, but only after they had been forced to pay 'divers good somes of money' to Dutton and additional fees to his clerk. They maintained as well that Dutton had arbitrarily raised the agreed rate of assessment for the hundred of Bisley from £25 to £30, and had taken the residue for his own use. In particular, the petitioners complained that Dutton had repeatedly detained certain individuals ('Officers, Constables, Tything Men') who had already collected and contributed to the levy and refused to release them until they had paid all manner of fees – often as much as £2 and £3 – to his messenger. For his part, Cooke had refused to pay those fees and had found himself before the Privy Council, while Hanman had found himself in prison for the same offence. The two petitioners asked that the house appoint a commission to investigate the charges, with a view to awarding them damages for their troubles.[112]

Their request was granted on 16 February and the commission was directed to submit its report, together with the accompanying examinations and depositions, by 29 March.[113] The report was actually submitted, along with Dutton's reply to the charges, on 12 April, after which the Committee for Petitions held hearings on the case intermittently over the next two months. The committee then reported to the house on 11 June. They concluded that Dutton and three of his associates had 'unjustly taxed and received Divers Sums of Money, contrary to all Law and Justice . . . and converted the same, or the most part thereof, to their own use'. The committee felt that their conduct had 'left the County much oppressed, and the King's service much dishonored'.[114] Dutton, a member of the House of Commons, appears to have been fully chastened.[115] He agreed to make a formal submission to the house and to offer whatever appropriate satisfaction to the county the Lords might recommend. The Lords then appointed a committee to devise a final order to meet those ends. In the event, the committee undertook an audit of the Coat and Conduct Money accounts for the county and reported to the house that a surplus of £400 remained in the hands of the treasurers.[116] The Lords then directed that Robert Cooke should be paid £30 and William Hanman £20 from that residue. The remainder of the surplus was to be used to 'relieve such poor men as the commission shall judge have suffered most in the carriage of this business'.[117]

PRIVATE PROPERTY AND PERSONAL LIBERTY

The Ship Money and Coat and Conduct Money levies were clearly the most visible and openly contentious of the fiscal programmes undertaken by the Crown in the 1630s, but they were not the only government programmes to provoke serious complaint in the House of Lords. The continuing trade in government offices under Charles I – though less pronounced (at least at higher administrative levels) than in the reign of James I – remained an important bone of contention.[118] The sale of patents granting reversions to administrative posts, often held under other long-standing arrangements, inevitably generated conflict between resident office holders (or their patrons) and the Crown's new patentees. The scenario had been played out repeatedly during the 1630s with regard to a wide variety of administrative and judicial offices. The conflicts brought before the House of Lords involved disputes over, among others, the offices of registrar in both the court of High Commission and the court of Arches,[119] the office of senior judge in the Prerogative Court of Canterbury,[120] the offices of senior and deputy Clerk of Deliveries in the Tower,[121] the offices of Customs Searchers at both Gravesend and Sandwich,[122] the office of Clerk of the Hanaper,[123] and even the governorship of Virginia.[124] All of these petitioners appealed to the House of Lords because they resented the loss of income from their own initial investment, but also because they felt that the grants to new patentees interfered directly with their rights of private property.

In many ways, the most serious complaints here involved disputes over the sale of judicial offices in the central courts. In fact, the sale of judicial offices had been specifically prohibited by statute as early as 1552, but the provisions of the statute had been conveniently, indeed studiously, overlooked thereafter.[125] The corrupt sale of offices during the reign of James I perhaps reawakened concern over the matter, and the issue was in fact raised generally in the 1625 Parliament, and again in 1626 in connection with the Commons' attack on the duke of Buckingham.[126] However, as in so many other areas, parliamentary protests had seemingly little impact on this king. The Crown appears to have made special efforts during the 1630s to regain direct control over rights of appointment to lucrative offices in both Chancery and Common Pleas (and perhaps elsewhere) and it did so not (or not always) to increase administrative efficiency, but rather in order to regrant the offices for a price. Perhaps the classic example here is the case of the Six Clerks offices in Chancery. In 1635 the Six Clerks were forced to strike a bargain with the Crown to avoid prosecution for taking excessive fees. The clerks were required (over the strenuous protests of the then Master of the Rolls, Sir Julius Caesar) to surrender their patents to the king. Each of them then received a new grant from the king – thereby leaving their places perpetually in his gift – which confirmed them in their offices and regranted them the same fees and privileges. The new grant, however, came at a heavy price – between £2,500 and £3,000.[127] Unfortunately, the agreement of 1635 was left ambiguous (perhaps deliberately) with regard to the right of reversion to the offices and, since the Crown had already granted reversions to future vacancies to other parties in other unrelated agreements, there was bound to be future conflict and ultimately proceedings in the House of Lords.[128]

The complaint brought to the house by the clerks of Common Pleas indicated that a similar problem had existed in their court. They petitioned the Lords in January 1641, protesting that the Crown had issued letters patent granting reversions to no less than ten separate offices in their court between 1635 and 1639.[129] These grants appear to have been the by-product of an agreement signed between the king and Sir John Finch in 1635, in which Finch agreed, as a condition of his appointment as Chief Justice, not to appoint any officers of the court without the king's approval and command.[130] The clerks complained that the patentees had 'exposed them [the offices] to Sale at unreasonable and excessive Prices, against law and contrary to ancient Usage'. The basis of their appeal, however, was not so much the subsequent abuse of the grants, as the illegality of the patents themselves. They argued that the offices were not, and had never been, in the King's gift. Instead, they claimed, 'the Disposition of the same hath, time out of mind, appertained to the Chief Justice of that Court, to dispose of them, for the Common good, to such skilful and experienced Clerks, as are most fit and able for the execution of such places'.[131]

The Lords responded to this complaint by initially ordering all of the grantees to appear and produce their patents. Hearings, however, were repeatedly delayed, due to other business, and it was not until late June that the matter was taken up again. The issue was then referred to the justices of King's Bench and the barons of the Exchequer, who were asked to determine whether the king's grants to the offices in Common Pleas were 'good in law'.[132] The judges reported their findings on 21 July. Having carefully considered the arguments of counsel on both sides, as well as precedents, they had concluded that all the disputed offices had 'by Prescription, belonged to the Chief Justices for the time being, and that he hath always granted the same for the lives of the grantees, who have held them by his admittance only'. Therefore, in their view, none of the grants made by the king was 'good in law'.[133] The house accepted their opinion, and unanimously resolved that 'the Rights and Privileges truly Incident to that Place ... should be restored and continued'.[134] The patents in question were declared 'illegal and void in law' and were ordered to be brought 'forthwith' into the house.

The patents issued to grant corporate monopolies during the 1630s produced a small number of complaints as well. The Monopolies Act of 1624 had left the Crown all sorts of room to manoeuvre, because it exempted from its provisions patents granted by the Crown to 'first and true' inventors of new products, Crown officers and corporate entities.[135] That allowed Charles I to evade the spirit of the act, either by declaring a proposed commodity an innovation or by simply incorporating a group of merchants wishing to monopolize a particular trade. The complaints in the House of Lords reflect the range of patents granted as a result. Petitioners protested against the authority given the blanketmakers of Whitney, in Oxfordshire,[136] the tobacco sellers of Clink and Montagu Close in Surrey,[137] the Corporation of Woodmongers of London,[138] and even a corporation of London parish clerks.[139] Patents granted to Sir William Middleton to collect taxes on silk and to Sir Robert Rich to do the same for gold and silver thread likewise generated petitions from the silkmen of London.[140] So too did London Alderman William Abel's monopoly on the sale of wine, in this case, from a wineseller (also a patentee) from Exeter.[141] In only one case, however, did the petitions elicit any response from the house. In the case of the blanketmakers of Whitney, the Lords did summon the patentees and their patents to the house and stayed any further impositions they might levy until the complaint had been heard. But no further action was taken. The neglect of these cases may simply have reflected the fact that there was little immediate remedy which the Lords could offer. The patents issued by the Crown in these cases were perfectly legal and unless the petitioners could prove some undue or unwarranted actions taken to enforce them, there was little the Lords could do. It is, on the other hand, entirely possible that the complaints were settled through some unrecorded arbitration.

That was the path ultimately pursued in the case of the notorious soap monopoly, the only one of its kind to receive any direct action by the Lords. In late 1640 a group of London soapboilers petitioned the house protesting the patent which had been granted in 1632 to a syndicate known as Westminster Corporation of Soapmakers and complaining of the grievous prosecutions initiated by the company in 1633 in Star Chamber for violations of their monopoly.[142] No action appears to have been taken on the petition, and a similar petition was then presented to the House of Commons. The lower house heard the complaint and resoundingly condemned the original patents, the patentees and the prosecutions of 1633, declaring them illegal and suggesting that the offending Star Chamber decree 'ought' to be vacated. But that was as far as they could go.[143]

The case then returned to the upper house in August 1642, this time by way of a writ of error, brought by two of the original complainants, John Overman and Thomas Doughty.[144] In a subsequent petition the two men recited the injustices of the Star Chamber proceedings and reiterated the Commons condemnation of them, which they complained had not gone far enough. But they then 'humbly confessed' that there was more to the story than they had first made known. In fact, in 1637, the original syndicate of Westminster Soapmakers had been wound up (on the death of the earl of Portland) and the independent soapmakers, headed by Doughty and Overman, had themselves formed a corporation and had bought out the privileges of the older company, agreeing to pay the king £8 a ton return. To protect their investment, they had followed the lead of the Westminster corporation and had, as they put it, 'taken such course as was necessary to debarre those that had never served the trade', a euphemism for what had been a campaign of sustained harassment and abuse of the remaining independent soapmakers of London. They admitted those actions 'not to be convenient or justifiable' and acknowledged their mistake.

Their contrition, however, was somewhat disingenuous. It had been forced on them by the fact that a group of independent soapmakers had brought an action of trespass in King's Bench for the illegal seizure of their goods and equipment and had had a judgment awarding them treble damages. It was that judgment which had prompted Overman and Doughty to bring a writ of error. They acknowledged to the Lords that there was no error in the record to warrant the writ; they were only asking for time and a chance to negotiate a more equitable settlement. They declared themselves 'willing, according to their abilities, to give satisfaction to everyone complaining against them, in such manner as your Lordships shall appoint'.[145] The Lords were, at least temporarily, unmoved and held to the letter of the law. The writ of error was declared 'insufficient in law' and was ordered to be 'quashed and abated'. The transcript and record of the case were ordered to be returned to the court of King's Bench.[146] Having done that, however, the Lords then reconsidered the petitioners' case on its merits and ten days later appointed a committee of five to reexamine 'the equity of the business', to see if they might effect a settlement appropriate to the interests of all parties.[147]

Not all the complaints heard by the upper house can be directly related to specific policies or programmes. Some of these petitioners had simply found themselves on the wrong side of powerful political figures during the previous decade, or had been penalized for their alleged association with government critics. Many of them had been imprisoned – some for long periods – without, as they saw it, justifiable cause, and they looked to the House of Lords to reaffirm the protections supposedly guaranteed in the Petition of Right. Henry Darley, for example, petitioned the house at the end of November 1640 complaining that he had been imprisoned in the castle of York the previous September by the earl of Strafford.[148] Questioned about the matter, Strafford claimed that Darley had been imprisoned because he (Strafford) had been 'very credibly informed' that Darley had harboured some Scotsmen and had 'concealed them in such manner as gave Great Occasion of Suspicion and Apprehension'. He had examined Darley and had found 'his discourse full of Ambiguity and Improbability' and as a consequence had decided (with the advice of Sir Henry Vane and the earl of Manchester) to keep him close prisoner until advised to do otherwise by the king. In his petition Darley insisted that Strafford's warrant had shown no cause for committal and produced the warrant to prove his point. He requested to be released on those grounds. The Lords examined the warrant, obtained Strafford's verification of its authenticity and ordered Darley released 'forthwith'.[149]

Katherine Hadley's problems, on the other hand, had stemmed from her association with John Lilburne.[150] A servant of Lilburne's, Hadley had been arrested without warrant and imprisoned for seven months by the Lord Mayor of London, Sir Morris Abbot, 'upon mere suspicion' of having distributed Lilburne's pamphlet, *A Cry for Justice*, in Moor Fields. She had then applied to the Privy Council to hear her case, asking that they either punish her or set her at liberty. But the council responded instead by transferring her, without examination, to Bridewell prison, where, as Hadley described it, she was 'put among common sluts whose society is Hell upon earth for one who fears the Lord'. She had remained in prison for two years when she appealed to the upper house for her release. The Committee for Imprisonments and Courts of Justice reviewed her case and recommended to the house that she be promptly released 'in regard that the warrant by which she was committed mentioned no cause for her commitment'.[151] The house immediately ordered her freed.[152]

Sir Robert Howard petitioned the house in late December 1640, claiming that he had been committed close prisoner 'without cause shewd' by the court of High Commission.[153] A younger son of the earl of Suffolk, Howard had been ordered to produce the person of Lady Viscountess Purbeck – his alleged mistress – who had escaped from her confinement in the Gatehouse after being convicted of adultery.[154] He had been unable to comply because she had apparently 'fled beyond the seas', and his imprisonment followed as a consequence. He had remained in prison for three months and was only released after entering into bonds with £3,500 sureties to guarantee his further appearances before the court. He complained to the house that the proceedings had been 'contrary to Lawe, Equity, and the Petition of Right, wherein every subject hath his interest', accordingly requesting reparation and redelivery of his bonds. His case was also considered by the Committee for Imprisonments and Courts of Justice and they again reported their opinion that the imprisonment had been 'unlawful'. The house endorsed their report and promptly awarded Howard damages of £1,000, which they assessed against Archbishop Laud, Sir Henry Marten, and Sir John Lambe.[155]

The decision in Howard's case was made at the outset of the Long Parliament and was undoubtedly meant to serve as something of an example. The damages levied against the High Commissioners were severe – and perhaps reflected the penalties due those who had toyed with the sons of peers of the realm. But they were clearly meant to convey as well the Lords' impatience with and contempt for their flagrant abuse of the law. Fines of this nature (if rarely of this scale) continued to be imposed throughout these proceedings as a reminder to those who had erred that the law could not be violated with impunity. All of the remedies provided by the house, however different in kind, were designed to make that point – emphatically.

The Lords had clearly been moved by the plight of these petitioners and even more by their very evident determination to secure redress. The overwhelming majority of these petitioners were, after all, people of very limited means for whom a journey to London (and a long stay) represented a major undertaking. Many of them were also initiating appeals as long as five years after the fact – an indication both of the depth of their discontent and of their enduring belief in the redemptive powers of Parliament. The Lords were understandably compelled to repay that confidence with effective and meaningful responses. That meant not simply providing for the immediate needs of these petitioners – be it absolution, restoration, or appropriate compensation for wrongs done – but explaining those actions with clear reference to established legal rules and principles. These appeals had in fact been generated by a very real crisis of confidence. The actions of Crown officials, from councillors, to commissioners to common law judges, had seriously undermined the public's faith in the rule of law. These petitioners were looking to the High Court of Parliament to restore it and the Lords were clearly determined to meet that obligation.

NOTES

1 *LJ*, iv, p. 56.
2 See G.E. Aylmer, *The King's Servants, The Civil Service of Charles I* (New York, 1961). pp. 350–1.

3 The bishops were Wren of Ely, Curle of Winchester, Bancroft of Oxford, Warner of Rochester, Towers of Peterborough and Duppa of Chichester.

4 Four of the litigants presented new petitions to the Long Parliament in the autumn and claimed that their cases had either been heard at least once, or were scheduled for hearing when the Short Parliament was dissolved. The case reported was the Admiralty appeal of Archibald Nichols (*LJ*, iv, p. 78).

5 ibid., p. 158. The Lords made exceptions for two petitions expected to be brought the following day by Lord Mowbray, and for a petition to be presented by Lord Willoughby of Erseby concerning Ship Money.

6 *LJ*, iv, p. 260.

7 The members not reappointed were the earls of Cleveland and Newport, Barons Clifford, Dunesmore and Lovelace, and the bishop of Peterborough.

8 The presumed political affiliations (always somewhat precarious) are largely based on the classifications provided by J.B. Crummett's 'The lay peers in parliament; 1640–4', PhD thesis, Manchester University (1970). Using a slightly modified version of Dr Crummett's categories, the committee divides into the following groups:

(a) *Court peers* (office holders, appointees and clients of the Crown):

Berkshire, Bridgewater, Dorset, Holland, Newcastle, Salisbury, Coventry, Digby, Goring, Cottington, Howard of Charlton (11)

(b) *Primary country peers* (signatories of the petition for a new Parliament in August 1640 and others associated with the petition):

Bristol, Bedford, Bolingbroke, Essex, Exeter, Hertford, Lincoln, Rutland, Warwick, Say, Brooke, Kimbolton, Paget, North, Saville, St John, Wharton, Howard of Escrick (18)

(c) *Associate country peers* (relatives and associates of the above group, and peers with personal grievances with the Crown):

Bath, Southampton, Montague of Boughton, Robartes, Herbert (5)

(d) *Neutral country peers* (those demonstrating little or no evidence of political views):

Huntington, Monmouth, Nottingham, Stamford, Grey, Maynard, Paulet, Dover, Devonshire (9)

9 The signatories were Bedford, Essex, Brooke, Warwick, Say, Mandeville (Kimbolton), Exeter, Hertford, Rutland, Mulgrave, Bolingbrooke and Howard of Escrick.

10 The other three bishops appointed were Hall of Exeter, Morton of Durham and Davenant of Salisbury. John Williams, bishop of Lincoln was added to the committee in early December (*LJ*, iv, p. 106).

11 Crummett, 'Lay peers in Parliament,' p. 267. Dr Crummett's survey indicates that this group of opposition peers controlled 80 per cent (31 of 39) of committees established in the first five months of the Parliament. The eight committees on which the 'court' peers had a majority representation were all singularly unimportant, as for instance, the committee appointed to draft the Queen's jointure bill, or that for a bill for river navigation (LJ, iv, pp. 88, 169).

12 The 12 members who did not sit on the Committee for Petitions were the earls of Manchester, Arundel, Pembroke and Portland; the bishop of Carlisle; and Lords Mowbray, Clifford, Strange, Willoughby of Eresby, Dacre, Wentworth and Dunesmore. This committee therefore differed from the Committee for Petitions in that it included three important Crown officers in Manchester (Lord Privy Seal), Arundel (Earl Marshall) and Pembroke (Lord Chamberlain). This may have been done to rectify the glaring omission of such officers from the Committee for Petitions, though the inclusion of Manchester may well have been thought appropriate because of his long and distinguished legal career. Their presence did little, however, to alter

the political profile of the committee, which was decidedly weighted in favour of those critical of the government's programmes.

13 *LJ*, iv, p. 188.

14 For a full and illuminating discussion of this issue see Nicholas Tyacke, *The Anti-Calvinists: The Rise of English Arminianism c.1590–1640* (Oxford, 1987), pp.199–216.

15 ibid., pp. 200–1. The applicable canon was number 82.

16 ibid., p. 201.

17 ibid., p. 200.

18 HLRO, Main Papers, H.L., 6 February 1641.

19 *CSPD*, 1637–8, p. 157.

20 HLRO, Main Papers, H.L., 22 December 1640.

21 PRO, SP16/314/fol. 130. This document is a long and detailed legal defence subsequently made by Wheeler before the High Commission.

22 HLRO, Main Papers, H.L., 9 February 1641.

23 ibid., HLRO, Main Papers, H.L., '1640'.

24 ibid., 11 December 1640.

25 The practice of indicting ministers at the assizes on this charge was becoming frequent in Essex. In December 1639 the king asked the judges to determine whether such indictments were permissible under statute law. Esther Cope, *Politics Without Parliament 1629–1640* (London, 1987), p. 181.

26 HLRO, Main Papers, H.L., 18 January 1641.

27 The evidence provided here, while by no means definitive, would seem to belie Archbishop Laud's claim, in 1637, that he viewed the position of the table as 'a thing indifferent'. It also casts more than a little suspicion on his assertion that nothing had been done to enforce the policy 'by violence or command' (*The Works of William Laud*, ed. W. Scott and J. Bliss (7 vols.; Oxford, 1847–60), Vol. 4, pp. 59–60; cited in Tyacke, *The Anti-Calvinists*, p. 201).

28 Convocation's formal sanction of the policy in the new canons of May 1640 was clearly seen as irrelevant, not least because it could not bind retroactively, but also because the canons had not (and would not) receive parliamentary confirmation. The theory that canons required parliamentary confirmation to be legally binding was first articulated in a bill passed by the House of Commons in 1607. The bill was designed to 'restrain the executions of Canons Ecclesiastical not confirmed by Parliament'. It was rejected by the Lords, but was instrumental in formulating subsequent legal opinion (J.R. Tanner, *English Constitutional Conflicts of the Seventeenth Century* (Cambridge, 1960), p. 34).

29 *LJ*, iv, p. 157.

30 See, for example, the case of *Keats* v. *Eden*. HLRO, Braye MSS 2, fol. 167.

31 HLRO, Main Papers, H.L., 22 December 1640 (*Garfield and Wolfe* v. *Clarke*), 23 December 1640, Orders on Private Petitions (*Prior* v. *Parret*).

32 ibid.

33 HLRO, Main Papers, H.L., 23 December 1640, Orders on Private Petitions; *LJ*, iv, p. 157. The damages were originally assessed against Mayor Buxton, Dr Robert Aylett, Dr Arthur Duck and Sir John Lambe. Lambe and Duck later appealed the award, claiming that they had not been party to the hearing and decision in the court, but had only signed the final decree in accordance with 'the Course and Custom of the Court' (HLRO, Main Papers, H.L., 11 February 1640–1). The Lords accepted their argument and relieved them of their portion of the award (*LJ*, iv, p. 186). This was in fact Mayor Buxton's second visit to the house in as many weeks. On 23 February the Lords had heard the case of Abraham Hill, whom Buxton had imprisoned for four months in 1636 for refusing to take communion at the rails. They awarded Hill £16 in damages (*LJ*, iv, p. 171).

34 ibid., p. 174.

35 HLRO, Main Papers, H.L., 5 August 1641. Daniel's reference to the 'treachery' of Walker refers to the fact that Walker provided evidence against his former employer in the Star Chamber proceedings against Bishop John Williams in 1638. See n. 73 below.

36 ibid. Daniel also accused Walker of extorting excessive rates of Coat and Conduct Money for the Scottish campaign, in order to impress Laud. He had apparently demanded £5 from Daniel, who was in fact only rated for 46s.

37 HLRO Main Papers, H.L., 30 November 1640, 18 December 1640, 9 February 1640–1. The house also received a more general petition from the inhabitants of Rothwell, outlining a long list of complaints against Sir John Lambe, which involved both his activities as a local landlord, and his active support for 'superstitious innovacons in religion' (HLRO, Main Papers, H.L., 5 January 1640–1).

38 PRO, SP/16/ 280/ fol. 33.

39 Patrick Collinson, *The Religion of Protestants* (Oxford, 1982), p.246.

40 ibid,. p. 249.

41 HLRO, Main Papers, H.L., 23 February 1640–1.

42 ibid., 18 January 1641.

43 ibid., 26 January 1640–1.

44 *LJ*, iv, p. 156.

45 The writ of *significavit* was normally issued out of Chancery on the basis of a certificate provided by the ordinary, which claimed that the individual had stood excommunicate for a period exceeding 40 days. It allowed the person to be imprisoned until he had submitted to the authority of the church.

46 *CSPD*, 1639–40, pp. 97, 115, 120, 263, 406, 409. Foxley was eventually fined £100 by High Commission (*CSPD*, 1640, p. 229).

47 HLRO, Main Papers, H.L., '1640'.

48 HLRO, Parchment Collection, B1 Book of Orders and Ordinances, p. 117.

49 HLRO, Main Papers, H.L., 17 August 1641. Eckins would later establish something of a reputation as a troublemaker in the parish. In April 1637 Charles Cockayne reported to the council that Eckins was 'ill-affected to his Majesty's service' and had had a 'nag' distrained for Ship Money (*CSPD*, 1636–7, p. 552).

50 ibid., 17 August 1641 (annexed copy of the High Commission sentence).

51 Roland G.Usher, *The Rise and Fall of High Commission* (Oxford, 1968), pp. 170 ff.

52 *LJ*, iv, p. 367.

53 HLRO, Main Papers, H.L., 19 May 1641; *CSPD*, 1637–8, p. 248.

54 Ward's agents had paid the incumbent £650 to give up his presentation to Ward. Ward then redelivered it to the patron and had a new presentation made out in his own name. He had then made arrangements to repay the agents the £650 (*CSPD*, 1637–8, pp. 497, 519).

55 HLRO, Main Papers, H.L., 23 December 1640, Orders on Private Petitions.

56 ibid., 8 February 1640–1. See also, *CSPD*, 1634–5, pp. 325, 329, 333, 539.

57 Johnson in fact cited the statute of 31 Elizabeth, c.6 which governed simony offences.

58 *CSPD*, 1637, p. 508; *The Journal of Sir Simonds Dewes*, ed. Wallace Notestein (New Haven, Conn., 1923), pp. 7–8. On Beale, see Tyacke, *The Anti-Calvinists*, p.194. Laud was in fact confronted with Johnson's case at his trial. He claimed that 'if I had not looked into the superinstitution, there would have been blood shed about the bringing in of the Tythe', suggesting that Johnson's presence in the parish had been the cause of considerable discord. The evidence does not support his claim. Johnson appears to have been well liked during his six years in the parish (HLRO, Braye MSS 8).

59 *LJ*, iv, p. 181.

60 ibid.

61 HLRO, Main Papers, 5 January, 10 March 1640/1. *CSPD*, 1631–3, p. 349.

62 S.R. Gardiner, *Reports of Cases in the Star Chamber and High Commission* (Camden Society, new series 39, 1876), p. 298.

63 ibid.

64 HLRO, Main Papers, H.L., 9 February 1640/1.

65 Bloxam had claimed that the case against him had rested on the testimony of a single witness, his uncle Thomas Brooke. Brooke claimed as well that his statement had been unfairly altered by the notary. In reviewing the case, the Lords requested that

Dr Eden, an officer in High Commission, certify to the house whether Bloxam had in fact been convicted on the testimony of a single witness and whether Brooke's statement itself had been the principal proof of simony. Eden reported in the affirmative on both points (HLRO, Main Papers, H.L., 10 March 1640/1).

66 *LJ*, iv, p. 155.

67 Usher, *High Commission*, pp. 136–40. Another view of the matter had been presented in *The Appellation of John Penri unto the Highe Court of Parliament from the bad and injurious dealing of the Archb. of Canterb. and his other colleagues of the High Commission* (London, 1598). Penri had been subjected to lengthy proceedings before High Commission, leading ultimately to his imprisonment for contempt. In this treatise he argued that the most appropriate course of action was appeal to Parliament. He insisted that the commission was bound by the judgment of Parliament 'whereunto all courts in the land are and ought to be subject'.

68 *LJ*, iv, p. 155.

69 HLRO, Main Papers, H.L., 10 March 1640–1.

70 ibid.

71 *LJ*, iv, p. 181.

72 For other examples of High Commission's singularly flexible interpretation of the laws governing simony offences, see HLRO, Main Papers, H.L. 16 January 1640–1; *LJ*, iv, p. 273 (*Halke* v. *Denn*) and 9 February 1640–1 (*Sedgewick* v. *Layford*).

73 Osbaldiston maintained that the letters had been obtained from two of Williams's secretaries, Walter Walker and Cadwalader Powell. Both secretaries had been cited in the earlier Star Chamber case against Williams, and Osbaldiston claimed that they had provided the letters in exchange for clemency.

74 HLRO, Main Papers, H.L., 23 January 1640–1.

75 *CSPD*, 1638–9, p. 491.

76 Both Osbaldiston and Williams had attempted to convince the court that the offending passages referred to one Dr Spicer (Hugh Trevor-Roper, *Archbishop Laud* (Oxford, 1940), pp. 357–8).

77 The two witnesses were the aforementioned secretaries, Walker and Powell. See n. 73 above.

78 *LJ*, iv, p. 205.

79 ibid. The Lords had in fact sequestered the profits of Osbaldiston's offices when he presented his petition two months earlier.

80 See Derek Hirst, *Authority and Conflict, England 1603–58* (London, 1986), p. 166.

81 HLRO, Main Papers, H.L., 25 May 1641.

82 ibid., 5 February 1640–1.

83 ibid., 22 January 1641. Sharedlow claimed that he had 'often tymes waited upon the said Bpp of Norwich for institution, but instead thereof he hath received evill termes, and vowes, that whosoever had the said parsonage, your petr shall not have itt'.

84 HLRO, Main Papers, H.L., 23 December 1640, Orders on Private Petitions (*Riddington* v. *Croft*); *LJ*, iv, pp. 152, 163 (*Powell* v. *Edwards*).

85 *LJ*, iv, p. 152.

86 The Lord's declaration, issued in Wheeler's case in February 1641, regarding the legality of railing the communion table, was as close as the house would come to doing so and that was carefully worded to reflect the Lords' own reading of existing law.

87 HLRO, Main Papers, H.L., 1 December 1640.

88 *CSPD*, 1640, p. 210.

89 *LJ*, iv, p. 101. The manuscript journal of the House reads 'and yet afterwards confest it was against the Petition of Right', but this addition is lined out (HLRO, manuscript Journals, v. 15, p. 99).

90 ibid.

91 HLRO, Parchment Collection, B1 Book of Orders and Ordinances, pp. 15–16. In an addendum to this order the Lords made a note to take up the matter

of fees, mentioned in the case, at a later date. There was some concern that the fees taken by the council's messengers needed to be regulated. The council itself had already recognized the problem. The previous May the board ordered that no one brought before the council by warrant was to remain in the custody of the messenger for any longer than was strictly necessary because his fees were so high. Two subsequent petitioners to the house, both constables in Freeman's situation, would complain about excessive fees taken by the messenger, £4 in one case, and £3 10s in another (HLRO, Main Papers, H.L., 8 January 1640–1 (Robert Beeton) and 25 January 1640–1 (William Lawrence)).

92 Mark 12:17.
93 HLRO, Main Papers, H.L., 21 January 1641.
94 Waters claimed in his petition to the house that he and the others had been summoned by warrant to appear before Samuel, 'the petitioners not knowing to what purpose they were called'. Given the other evidence, this appears doubtful. It seems far more likely that the information was reported to Samuels beforehand and the warrant issued as a consequence.
95 HLRO, Main Papers, H.L., 21 January 1640–1 (JP's certificate).
96 ibid. (copy of the Privy Council's decree).
97 For a strikingly similar example of the intrusive and unsettling effects of political and religious conflict on local communities in Northamptonshire, see Victor L. Stater, 'The lord lieutenancy on the eve of the civil wars: the impressment case of George Plowright,' *HJ*, Vol. 29, no. 2 (1986) pp. 279–96.
98 This conclusion was drawn from the testimony of many witnesses. The 'particulars' included 'crossing the bread and wine at the sacrament, and bowing to it afterwards, and crossing himself a Mornings, before he drank, and such like' (*LJ*, iv, pp. 136–7).
99 ibid.
100 ibid., p. 136.
101 There is, unfortunately, no way to determine from the records whether or not Manchester and Arundel actually participated in the Lords' proceedings on the case.
102 See *LJ*, iv, p. 146 (*Arnold* v. *Jay*) and p. 390 (William Lockton's case).
103 *LJ*, iv, p. 136. The manuscript journal reads 'proprieties' rather than 'Properties' (HLRO, Manuscript Journals, v. 15, p. 314).
104 ibid., p. 156.
105 ibid., p. 173. The vacat and the resolutions were also ordered to be published at the assizes by the judges on each circuit.
106 17 Charles I, c. 14.
107 *CSPD* 1640, p. 127. On 7 May 1640 the king had ordered the Attorney General to proceed 'with all convenient expedition' against the three sheriffs, as well as against the sheriffs of London and Middlesex, York, Leicester and Surrey.
108 HLRO, Main Papers, H.L., 25 January 1640–1.
109 *LJ*, iv, p. 345.
110 HLRO, Main Papers, H.L., 8 January 1640–1.
111 *LJ*, iv, p. 130.
112 HLRO, Main Papers, H.L., 9 February 1640–1.
113 *LJ*, iv, p. 163.
114 ibid., p. 272.
115 Dutton had already been cited as a defendant in a domestic suit brought by his sister-in-law, Frances Dutton (HLRO, Main Papers, H.L., 4 March 1640–1).
116 HLRO, Main Papers, H.L., 23 June and 5 July 1641.
117 *LJ*, iv, p. 300.
118 For a full discussion of this problem see Aylmer, *The King's Servants*, pp. 225–239.
119 HLRO, Main Papers, H.L., 27 May 1641 (*Boucher* v. *Roulston*) and 18 December 1640 and 5 February 1640–1; Braye MSS 2, fol. 162 (*Paule* v. *Lambe*).
120 ibid., 26 October 1641; *LJ*, iv, pp. 406, 409, 429. (*Duck* v. *Merrick*).
121 ibid., 27 May, 2 July and 13 August 1641; *LJ*, iv, p. 361 (*Kniveton* v. *Freeman*); 23 December 1640, Orders on Private Petitions, 20 May 1641 (*Farmer* v. *Johnson*).

122 ibid., 27 July and 18 December 1641 (*Morgan* v. *Rookes*). 15 and 24 February, 21 March and 28 June 1642; *LJ*, iv, p. 168 (*Watkins* v. *Ward*).

123 ibid., 6 and 21 December 1642; *LJ*, iv, pp. 519, 523, v, pp. 476, 508 (*Minne* v. *Young*).

124 ibid., 4 September, 30 October and 3 November 1641; *LJ*, iv, pp. 411, 419, 424 (*Panton* v. *Berkeley*).

125 5 & 6 Edward VI, c.16.

126 Aylmer, *The King's Servants*, p. 229.

127 ibid., pp. 71–3.

128 See, for example, the case of Edward Burgh; HLRO, Main Papers, H.L., 8 February 1640–1; *LJ*, iv, pp. 155, 259, 305. In 1628 Burgh had forgiven a substantial debt (£1,245) owed to him by the king in exchange for a reversion to the first of the Six Clerks' places in Chancery to become vacant after the death of Sir Julius Caesar. The king had in fact granted the same reversion to two other men. When the agreement was sealed with the clerks in 1635, Charles demanded that Burgh surrender his reversion, without any compensation.

129 HLRO, Main Papers, H.L., 21 January, 1640/1. The offices included six Filazers places, two prothonotaries (court chief clerks), an Exigenter and the clerk of the Treasuries.

130 HLRO, Main Papers, H.L., 13 October 1635.

131 *LJ*, iv, p. 139.

132 ibid., p. 291.

133 ibid., p. 322.

134 ibid., p. 323.

135 21 & 22 James I, c.3.

136 HLRO, Main Papers, H.L., 12 August 1641; *LJ*, iv, p. 361.

137 ibid., 25 January, 4 February 1640–1 (*George* v. *Colton*).

138 ibid., 10 June 1641 (petition of Phillipa Turner *et al.*).

139 ibid., 24 February 1640–1 (*Speckard* v. *Weoly*).

140 ibid., 17 February 1640–1.

141 ibid., 8 March 1641–2 (*Baron* v. *Abel*).

142 HLRO, Main Papers, H.L., '1640'. The patent had been granted to a syndicate of mainly Catholic businessmen headed by the earl of Portland and was based on their rather dubious claim to have invented a new method for making soap. The patent was highly contentious, not simply because of the religious persuasion of the patentees – their product came to be known as popish soap – but because they had been granted the rights to inspect all other soap not made by their methods and to prohibit its sale if it did not meet their standards. This was effectively a license to run their competitors out of business. For a full and detailed discussion of the case, see Samuel Rawson Gardiner, *History of England*, Vol. 8 (10 vols; London, 1883), pp. 71–6, 284.

143 *CJ*, ii, p. 260.

144 *LJ*, v, p. 297.

145 HLRO, Main Papers, H.L., 27 May 1643.

146 *LJ*, vi, p. 171–2.

147 ibid., p. 181. A settlement was not in fact achieved between the parties until 1656.

148 HLRO, Main Papers, H.L., 30 November 1640.

149 *LJ*, iv, pp. 101–2.

150 HLRO, Main Papers, H.L., 20 December 1640.

151 ibid.

152 *LJ*, iv, p. 113.

153 HLRO, Main Papers, H.L., 21 December 1640.

154 The affair between Sir Robert and Lady Purbeck had been something of a public scandal since the mid-1620s. When Lady Purbeck gave birth to a son in 1625, it was widely rumoured to have been fathered by Howard. The duke of Buckingham had been outraged by the conduct of his sister-in-law and had wanted her imprisoned and her marriage annulled. The couple was first brought before High Commission to answer the charges of adultery in 1625 (no doubt with Buckingham's influence)

and Lady Purbeck was convicted in late November 1627. (The case is discussed at length in Roger Lockyer, *Buckingham* (London, 1981) pp. 185–6, 408.)

Lady Purbeck herself applied to the House of Lords for relief in 1628, claiming privilege against the proceedings in High Commission. Her husband protested to the house, but the matter was considered nonetheless. It was not concluded, however, and Lady Purbeck again petitioned the house in February 1641, this time seeking assistance in gaining financial support. Her title to lands and annuities had been voided by the High Commission sentence and she requested that the matter be reviewed. The Lords accepted the case and ordered the archbishop of Canterbury, Sir Henry Marten and Dr Reeves, the king's advocate, to appear and 'make their defence touching the legality of the said sentence'. No further proceedings were recorded, however (HLRO, Main Papers, H.L., 31 March, 3, 8, 16, 18 and 24 April 1628 and 19 June 1641).

155 *LJ*, iv, pp. 106, 114.

3

The Long Parliament (ii): old problems in new cases

'Their House is not an extraordinary remedy, but an ordinary remedy in extraordinary causes'.[1]

The House of Lords faced a multitude of responsibilities at the opening of the Long Parliament. Resolving the crisis engendered by the administration of Crown programmes and policies in the 1630s no doubt seemed (and clearly was) of paramount importance and, given the highly charged atmosphere of political reform which characterized the first session, the Lords could have been expected to devote considerable time and attention to that task. But that was not the only crisis at hand. The prospect of a new Parliament had generated interest from all quarters, and, predictably, the Lords also came under heavy pressure in the opening weeks of the session to return to the continuing (and by now increasingly serious) problems which plagued conventional legal proceedings. The passage of time had done little to rectify the inherent defects of the English legal system. Indeed, in the natural course of things – given consistently high levels of litigation in the central courts – they had grown steadily worse. Chronic congestion and delay, procedural complexity, jurisdictional confusion and conflict and escalating costs remained the by-words of contemporary litigation just as they had in the 1620s. Litigants could still complain that there was no effective appellate recourse from the courts of equity, nor redress for the multiplicity of special problems (and corrupt practices) indigenous to particular courts. These defects had continued to generate widespread public discontent during the 1630s and that discontent ultimately found expression, as it had in the 1620s, in scores of petitions to the House of Lords.

This litigation was, in fact, very much a product of the 1620s and, more specifically, of Parliament's rather conspicuous failure to enact much needed law reform during those earlier sessions. All of the problems raised by these petitioners, both the general grievances about the system as a whole and the specific complaints about individual courts, had been clearly outlined in discussions on law reform in the Parliaments of 1621, 1624 and 1626. Bills had been proposed (sometimes more than once) to provide appellate remedy from equity courts, to clarify and refine court jurisdictions, to regulate legal fees and to reform procedural irregularities in Chancery, in the court of Wards and in the court of the Exchequer. Many of them were drafted, some were even read and committed, but few of any consequence ever passed into law.[2] Parliament's inability or unwillingness to follow through with these remedial measures had effectively guaranteed that these grievances would have to be raised by individual litigants on a case by case basis. They had already done so in the parliaments of the 1620s and with those precedents clearly in view they did so again in the Long Parliament.

This 'crisis' was admittedly less dramatic and indeed less immediately apparent than that engendered by the Crown's aberrant judicial practices in the 1630s, but in a sense it was more serious. The scale and diversity of complaint suggested, at the very least, that public dissatisfaction with the legal system was reaching disturbing levels; that there was, in fact, an increasingly widespread loss of confidence in the ability of the central courts to perform basic services and meet basic needs. Even in the best of times, such a loss of faith in the operation of the law had disturbing implications. In the uncertain political climate of the early 1640s, given the other factors at work, it no doubt represented – for those who fully understood the problem – a particularly ominous threat to future order and stability.

But this loss of faith in legal competence was also less easy to address. These problems still required comprehensive legislative remedy, the prospect for which was now even less promising than it had been in the 1620s. The Long Parliament simply had too many other pressing matters crowding its legislative agenda to undertake a carefully considered programme of legal reform. So the problems had to be tackled one case at a time. And that had to be done with some care. Even more than in the 1620s, the Lords needed to work (and to be seen to be working) cooperatively with common law and equity courts and their personnel – that is, within the system rather than outside it. They had to be especially careful to follow as far as possible the established rules and procedures of those courts and to punish those who attempted to use their house to evade ordinary legal process for strategic advantage. They could ill afford at this stage, either practically or politically, to suggest, by acting unilaterally, that their house represented an all-purpose alternative to (or an escape from) a judicial system in disrepair. That would only have further undermined faith in the system (and no doubt would have led to an even more debilitating increase in business in the house). Their job was to restore a measure of confidence in the legal system, by making it work with appropriate corrections and assistance.

The proceedings of the 1620s had clearly laid the necessary groundwork for the task. The Lords' extensive experience in dealing with many of these problems in those earlier sessions allowed them to identify them more readily and apply tested solutions. Their own internal

Table 3.1 Litigation by subject matter

Primary issue	Cases
Property	138
Debt	101
Testamentary disputes	47
Domestic disputes	24
Trade disputes	21
Complaints of judicial malfeasance	18
Disputes over wardship	5
Maritime disputes	9
Criminal proceedings	3
Miscellaneous	21
Total	387

procedural mechanisms were well established (and had survived the long intermission of Parliaments intact) and their previous working relationship with other courts and judicial officers was by now taken for granted. They could therefore hit the ground running, as it were. As a consequence, their responses to these cases were, by and large, more forthright, more knowing, more direct than they had been earlier. They reflect a clearer understanding of legal issues and a greater sense of consistency and purpose. They reflect the fact that the High Court of Parliament was coming into its own.

The patterns of complaint presented to the Long Parliament differed very little from those in earlier Parliaments. Table 3.1 indicates the distribution of cases according to primary issue in dispute between the parties. Again, as in the 1620s, the most notable fact about the litigation is its diversity. The broadly defined jurisdiction of the house continued to attract a correspondingly wide variety of complaints. The list does not reveal any special problems regarding the particular subject matter of cases which would necessarily explain their appearance in the House of Lords. It simply reflects the general patterns of litigation at work in the system. The disproportionate number of cases involving property was to be expected, because that was the most common litigation in the period. As suggested earlier, the fluidity of the land market and the growing complexity of property transactions normally generated inordinate levels of litigation in the central courts and, leaving aside all other secondary problems, the resulting congestion alone would have led litigants to look elsewhere. Similarly, the large number of debt cases (and those involving trade) reflects the increasing frequency with which parties went to law to enforce contractual obligations in the seventeenth century – a natural by-product of an emerging credit economy – and more directly perhaps, the failure of equity courts to provide consistent and effective relief from the often drastic penalties associated with the use of penal bonds. Nor is

Table 3.2 Courts of origin with a number of cases

Chancery	62
Wards	21
King's Bench (by writ of error)	17
Requests	11
Exchequer (equity side)	11
Exchequer (plea side)	5
Common Pleas	9
Admiralty	10
Total	146

the relatively high number of cases dealing with inheritance surprising. Wills were often subject to lawsuits among disgruntled beneficiaries and these were particularly susceptible to jurisdictional conflicts, as litigants found ways to bring them before the secular (notably Chancery) rather than the church courts.

The one class of cases which does appear to have represented something of a new development were the domestic disputes. The vast majority of these cases involved private marital quarrels, and were invariably brought by women (largely of the aristocracy and gentry) who demanded that the Lords intervene to ensure them proper maintenance. To some extent, they appear to have been the product of changing legal doctrine; specifically, of the notion – only just evolving in Chancery – that a woman had the right to sue in equity to establish certain proprietary rights in marriage. No doubt, they were also the product of a growing impatience on the part of divorced or abandoned women with the lack of protection afforded them under the law.

Many of these cases were, of course, brought on appeal from inferior courts. These appeals represent roughly half of the total and originated in the courts listed in Table 3.2. Again, there is nothing surprising about this list. As in the 1620s, the primary source of complaint was the court of Chancery. Normally Chancery handled a disproportionate amount of equity litigation and the court was also beset with more than its share of internal procedural problems. The number of appeals from the court of Wards is somewhat unusual, at least in comparison with the 1620s. The evidence seems to suggest that the increase can be ascribed largely to the more forceful application of the court's authority (as well as to a greater level of corruption) under the administration of Francis, Lord Cottington (1635–40). No doubt, some litigants were also encouraged to appeal in 1640 because of the very vocal criticisms levelled at Cottington in the early weeks of the session. Beyond that, the numbers involved from any one court are too small to suggest any significant patterns of change.

THE LEGAL SYSTEM AT LARGE

The complaints made by these petitioners can be divided into two general groups: those which had developed from the continuing problems affecting the system at large; and those which had developed from irregularities in particular courts. Apart from the pervasive problem of congestion, the most serious complaints in the former group concerned the absence of effective appellate remedy from courts of equity, the lack of clear jurisdictional boundaries between courts (or, more precisely, the problem of jurisdictional conflict) and the matter of cost – all prevalent issues in the 1620s. As the numbers in Table 3.2 perhaps suggest, the largest group of complaints once again concerned the first of these. Chapter 1 illustrated in detail why litigants felt aggrieved by the absence of appellate remedy from Chancery and the other courts of equity. The complaint had been made time and again in the 1620s and had generated considerable discussion in the House of Commons in 1621 and 1624 (to say nothing of the appeals to the House of Lords during the same period). A bill had in fact been drafted in 1621 to remedy the situation – the so-called 'Act for the Reversing of Decrees in Equity Courts upon Just Cause'.[3] It would have allowed equity decrees to be challenged and subsequently reexamined up to a year after their issue by a board of review consisting of the two Chief Justices, the Chief Baron and the Lord Keeper. The bill was actually read twice and committed in the lower house in April 1621, but disappeared for the remainder of the session, presumably because James I had expressed serious opposition to it.[4] The bill was revived, however, in 1624 and was reported by the Committee for Courts of Justice. Opposition on this occasion came, curiously enough, from none other than Sir Edward Coke, who argued that the bill was flawed because it stated that there was no recourse from equity decrees except in Parliament. He pointed out that this was untrue; appeal was always available in the form of royal commissions of review. He requested that the bill be recommitted, and it never resurfaced.[5] The measure was undoubtedly flawed in some respects – the one-year allowance for appeal would almost certainly have compounded the problems of congestion and delay – but the absence of any follow up, either in the form of amendments, or alternative proposals, is curious, given the notoriety of the complaint and the general parliamentary concern with Chancery reform. What is clear is that the ultimate failure of the effort left a major problem unresolved. The petitions to the upper house in the 1640s demonstrate that repeatedly. While the appeals themselves differ considerably in substance, all of them focus on a single problem: the inadequacy of Bill of Review procedure in equity courts. Bill of Review procedure was the only method by which decrees could be reconsidered after they had been enrolled, but the procedure was conducted internally and was inherently prejudicial to the interests of the complainant. It would be granted only if there were demonstrable errors in law in the body of the decree, and only after the complainant had performed the provisions of the decree in their entirety. Petitioners to the House of Lords either complained that they had been unable to perform the terms of the original decree as it stood and were therefore disqualified from appeal by Bill of Review, or they argued that the form of pleading required by the bill itself was too restrictive to encompass their 'just' complaint.

The appeal of Sir Conyers Darcy was an example of the former.[6] He petitioned the upper house in June 1641 complaining of a decree issued by Lord Keeper Coventry two years earlier, in June 1639. On that occasion, Coventry (with justices Bramston, Jones and Berkeley assisting) had abrogated a property agreement between Darcy and his cousin, Ann Savile, under which Darcy had held possession of a family property, Rothwell Haigh Park. In the original agreement, Savile had released all claims to the property in exchange for the provision of two annuities for her and her children. She subsequently challenged the settlement in Chancery, alleging that she had been deliberately deceived about her rightful title to the estate. The court upheld her claim, awarded her possession and ordered Darcy to repay her the mean profits from the land for the preceding three years during which the agreement had been in effect. On the advice of his counsel, Darcy had then attempted to bring a Bill of Review, but had had to abandon the project because he had been unable to satisfy that first necessary precondition. He complained to the Lords that 'by the strict rules of that Court, yor petr cannot be admitted to any reversal of the said decree upon a bill of review without payment first made of the sum decreed, which yor petr can no ways perform'.[7] The award amounted to just under £1500.[8]

Sir William Russell complained, alternatively, about the limited scope of the Bill of Review.[9] Russell and a number of others had been unsuccessful co-defendants in a suit before Lord Keeper Finch in 1640. The original dispute had involved a contested enclosure in the parish of Eckington, Worcestershire. Russell, Richard George and others had broken open an enclosure maintained by Francis Hanford, claiming right of common pasture. In response, Hanford brought a bill of complaint in Chancery, and obtained a temporary injunction awarding him 'quiet possession'. He then 'disturbed' certain enclosures maintained by the defendants on a similar claim of common pasturage. Following his example, they proceeded in Chancery and obtained a corresponding injunction. The suits were eventually joined, and the case was heard in Michaelmas 1634. The court (in the person of Mr Justice Vernon of Common Pleas) directed both parties to proceed to a trial at law on their respective claims, and reserved consideration of the 'equitable' issues until after the basic question of right had been determined. Russell and his fellow complainants duly brought three separate actions at common law and had successful verdicts in each. Hanford did not proceed at all. After repeated delays, the case was finally returned to Chancery in Michaelmas 1640, when the new Lord Keeper, John Finch, declared that his court's earlier reference to trial at common law had been wholly unnecessary and 'vexatious'. He then stayed the execution of judgment on those verdicts and awarded Hanford permanent 'quiet possession' of the enclosure, 'free from all claymes of Common by the defendants'.[10]

For the defendants the obstacles to a rehearing lay not in the difficulties in performing the decree prior to appeal, but in the fact that the decree itself contained no specific, identifiable error or technical irregularities on which to base a complaint. The defendants could only plead that the decree had been unjust and arbitrary and contrary to verdicts at common law, but the court would not have accepted those claims since they did not fit within the strict definition of error required by the Bill of Review.[11] The procedure, as Russell well recognized, was of no use to them. He complained to the Lords that

> the defendants have no remedy in Chancery but by Bill of Review, which in the formalities thereof will spend too much time and charge, and yet the merits of the cause at the end of that way, will be no riper for a determinant hearing than now.

Unsuccessful plaintiffs in Chancery were similarly handicapped by the court's restrictive appellate procedures. When a plaintiff's original bill had been dismissed from the court, and the dismissal signed and enrolled, the litigant was barred from bringing the matter before the court again, except by Bill of Review on the basis of specific errors in the decree. No new bill on the matter would be considered.[12] Assigning errors was not always easy, particularly if the case had been dismissed on general grounds that the plaintiff's bill had been 'insufficient'. This was, on balance, unlikely to happen after hearing unless, as happened occasionally, the case was accepted by one Lord Keeper and subsequently rejected by another. Lady Elizabeth Cope, for example, had brought a bill in Chancery to enforce the terms of a rental agreement with a tenant, one Edmund Fisher.[13] Her husband had originally agreed, in late 1637, to lease Fisher 500 acres of marshland in Essex for a rent of £200 per annum. Fisher had tentatively agreed to accept a lease in writing, according to the specified terms, and provided 20s surety. Cope then instructed his bailiff to deliver possession of the property. Once in possession, however, Fisher declined to accept the prearranged lease and then refused to pay rent. Lady Cope's husband died shortly afterwards and she was forced to proceed in Chancery. Her case initially came before Lord Keeper Coventry, who accepted her bill of complaint and ordered the defendant to deposit the arrears of rent with the court pending trial. The case proceeded to examination and publication, but was eventually heard, after Coventry's death, before Lord Keeper Finch. Contrary to the expressly stated opinion of his predecessor, the new Lord Keeper declared that the plaintiff's original bill did not contain 'sufficient matter in equity' to be retained. He refused to examine the proofs, or to hear testimony of witnesses, and instead summarily dismissed her suit from the court. Not surprisingly, she turned to the House of Lords for another opinion.[14]

The Lords' response to these complaints varied according to the particular circumstances in each case. In Darcy's case, they ordered that the decree be entirely set aside and directed the Lord Keeper to rehear the case 'upon the whole matter and merits of the cause' on the basis of a new bill to be brought by the complainant. Darcy was then ordered to put in sufficient security with the court to make good the earlier award in case the cause was later decreed against him.[15] The decision to order an entirely new trial went further than was usual in these cases, but in fact Darcy's complaint had raised another sensitive issue about Chancery's proceedings. In the course of their investigation of Ann Savile's allegation of fraud, Chancery had summoned all of the relevant documentation regarding ownership of the property. Their investigation led them to conclude that title was vested in Ann Savile and that Darcy, having been fully aware of that interest from the start, had deliberately misled her in order to execute a binding release agreement, effectively 'upon a surprizal'. They then went on to declare that Darcy himself 'had no title either in Lawe or Equity' to the property and on that basis awarded Ann Savile possession.[16] Practically speaking, their decision made sense. Having determined to their satisfaction where title lay, they felt justified in securing Ann Savile possession. But in Darcy's view, the court had no right to make that determination at all. He argued that the 'assistance' of the three common law justices was not an adequate or appropriate alternative to a separate trial by judge and jury at common law – the only forum in which his title and the validity of his deeds could be properly and fairly established. He claimed that the court had not only superseded that process, but had effectively barred him from proceeding to that remedy in the future. It was really on those grounds that he appealed to the upper house, and it was for those reasons that the decree was set aside.

In Sir William Russell's case the problem had not been so much Chancery's efforts to forestall common law proceedings, as its decision to ignore them after the fact (and in direct contradiction to its own earlier recommendation). For that reason the decree that resulted appeared to be faulty and the Lords felt that it ought to be reviewed, despite the absence of clear errors which the Bill of Review required. They directed that the decree be 'recommended to the Lord Keeper to reverse if he thinks good upon hearing, without a bill of review, as is desired'.[17] Lady Cope's case, on the other hand, was retained for settlement in the house itself. It is not clear exactly why, but since the case had actually been dismissed from Chancery, the Lords would not necessarily have felt compelled to return it there for review. They may have been motivated as well by Lady Cope's precarious finances and by the feeling that more direct and immediate action was required. In the event, they ordered the defendant, Fisher, to appear and answer the petitioner's complaint and, when he failed to do so on three separate occasions, they awarded possession of the property to Lady Cope and ordered that Fisher be handed over to the custody of the Gentleman Usher until he paid her £700 in outstanding arrears.[18]

However, this sort of response was exceptional. The great majority of these cases were referred or 'recommended' back to the Lord Keeper, or, where appropriate, to the Lord Privy Seal.[19] The form of reference, the recommendation, reflects the care which the house exercised in addressing these officers in their own courts. The Lords did not attempt, in any of these cases, to direct the future actions of the court or to pre-empt any final decision which the Lord Keeper might make. They were concerned to make a rehearing available where it appeared warranted and therefore requested only that the Lord Keeper temporarily suspend the rules of the court – in what were clearly exceptional cases – to allow that to happen. At the same time, the fact that a 'recommendation' (as opposed to a direct order from the house) was sufficient to guarantee a rehearing testifies to the existence of a close and effective working relationship between the respective courts. The Lords' directions were consistently executed in Chancery with exemplary speed and efficiency.[20] Admittedly, the situation in 1641 may have been made somewhat easier by the fact that this particular Lord Keeper was being asked, more often than not, to review his predecessors' decisions rather than his own, but there is no reason to assume that Lord Keeper Littleton would have been any less diligent than his predecessors in protecting the rights and prerogatives of the court, had he felt they were being endangered by these proceedings. He clearly did not feel that way, and cooperated fully with the house during the first 18 months of the Parliament.[21]

The complaints about jurisdictional conflict presented the house with a more complex set of problems. The absence of clearly delineated jurisdictional boundaries between the various courts in the legal system had led to growing competition for business and in turn to increasing abuse of the system by opportunistic litigants and their counsel seeking to play one court off against another for temporary strategic advantage. In the long term, of course, the war of injunctions and prohibitions which inevitably followed from this sort of gamesmanship served no one's interests. It ultimately slowed judicial process across the board and created a pervasive lack of finality in all kinds of litigation. The issue had, again, been raised repeatedly in the Commons' debates on law reform in the 1620s. The lower house had in fact been offered a classic demonstration of jurisdictional conflict in the case of *Hall* v. *Fuller* in 1621.[22] The parties in this case had contested the title to an ecclesiastical benefice. Hall had turned to the court of Chancery for relief, Fuller to the court of Wards. Both had obtained successful decrees from their respective courts, but understandably neither was willing to acknowledge the authority of the other's judgment, and both had eventually been imprisoned by contrary injunctions from either court. Significantly, when the case was brought to the lower house for settlement, the Commons deliberately tried to ignore the question of jurisdiction and attempted instead to effect some kind of workable compromise. The Committee for Courts of Justice which was assigned to hear the dispute eventually reported to the house that 'neither court did injustice'. Neither the parties nor the judges involved were satisfied with that response and the matter was immediately raised again. After further debate, the house reversed itself and declared that 'both courtes had done wronge'. They then directed that both the litigants be freed. The settlement conspicuously avoided the central issue, but to their credit the Commons did suggest that 'some course be taken for the reformation of abuses in both Courtes'.[23]

That was hardly a novel suggestion, but Fuller's case did provoke a considerable amount of discussion in the ensuing debates. Sir Edward Coke, for one, felt strongly that the case had clearly illustrated the need to redefine the jurisdictional boundaries between all courts. He spoke of the danger of courts 'clashing' and 'interfering' with one another (not without some irony, given that he was a past master at this sort of thing) and he moved that a bill be drafted which would establish proper and recognizable limits for each jurisdiction.[24] The bill never materialized. Nor, for that matter, did Coke's own bill which he proposed to check the expansion of Chancery jurisdiction. This proposal was discussed on numerous occasions and the house eventually appointed a special committee headed by Coke to draft a bill 'to regulate' the court of Chancery. But the committee never reported back to the house and the plan came to nothing.[25] The special interests involved were presumably too strong for even the most reform-minded legislators and the general problem was left unresolved.

Consequently, litigants caught in the crossfire of jurisdictional conflict once again looked to the House of Lords for remedy when Parliament reconvened in 1640. Predictably, the complaints took a variety of forms and involved a variety of courts. The case of *Walker* v. *Lambe*, brought to the house in January 1641, provides a classic example of the general problem.[26] It involved a dispute over two administrative offices in the diocese of Lincoln, held by patent by the plaintiff, Walter Walker. Walker had been disturbed in the offices in January 1631 by Sir John Lambe and in response brought an action of trespass in the court of King's Bench. Initially, Lambe refused to answer the suit and instead applied to the court of Audience for an inhibition against Walker. Those proceedings were promptly quashed by a prohibition issued out of King's Bench. Undeterred, Lambe then brought a bill in Chancery, seeking an injunction to stay Walker's suit, but the justices there, Jones and Croke, dismissed the bill and ordered him to plead to the action in King's Bench the following term. Accordingly, a trial took place at the Leicester assizes in the summer of 1631 which resulted in a 'special verdict'[27] and the case was duly returned to King's Bench, where (after considerable delays engendered by Lambe) a judgment passed for Walker. Lambe then returned to Chancery claiming that he intended to bring a writ of error to reverse the judgment and requested an injunction awarding him quiet possession of the offices until it could be determined. The court obliged him. Deprived of remedy once again, Walker sued out a writ of *Novel Disseisin* in the summer of 1632, but without success. Lambe procured an order under the King's seal prohibiting all further action for the offices at common law. There the matter rested until Walker appealed to the House of Lords in January 1641.

In fact, this dispute had involved from the start a number of intrusive political considerations. The Crown had clearly wanted Sir John Lambe installed in those particular offices and was eventually persuaded to intervene in the proceedings to guarantee his success. Up to that point, however, the case had represented a fairly standard example of jurisdictional gamesmanship. The Lords clearly recognized it as such and roundly condemned Sir John Lambe for his 'violent oppressions' and 'unjust vexations' (language no doubt coloured to some extent by Lambe's growing notoriety as a defendant in other cases in their house).[28] In the event, they awarded Walter Walker £1,250 in damages. The award was based on the fact that he had unequivocally proved his right and title to the offices through trial at common law – 'where patents for life, being freehold, are only triable' – and was therefore entitled to compensation for lost profits.[29] This element of the decision is important because it reflects the house's general inclination to support actions at common law where they had been (or could be) used to resolve these disputes. They exercised that preference in a variety of ways while reviewing these conflicts.

They did so, for example, in the case of *Hampson* v. *Powney*.[30] This suit, brought before the Lords in December 1640, concerned the possession of 11 small islands (and associated rights of fishing and fowling) in the middle of the River Thames. The plaintiff, Thomas Hampson, claimed that the islands belonged to the manor and lands of Taplow, Buckinghamshire, while the defendant, Richard Powney, insisted that they were part and parcel of the manor of Cookham located directly across the river in Berkshire. The suit had originated in the equity side of the Exchequer in 1639 on Powney's bill for quiet possession. Hampson had duly answered the bill, setting forth his own title, and after a preliminary hearing the parties were directed to proceed to a trial for title in the plea side of the court. Powney subsequently brought an action of trespass and the matter was tried by a jury from the county of Berkshire, resulting in a verdict for Powney for 4 of the 11 islands. Hampson was then allowed to bring a similar action of trespass, and the matter was again tried, this time by a jury from Buckinghamshire. In this instance, however, Powney refused to cooperate and would only enter the appropriate plea for one of the islands concerned.[31] As a consequence, evidence could only be heard for that one parcel. A verdict again passed for Powney, as regarded that one island, but the jury made clear that the verdict was not to prejudice Hampson's title to the remaining parcels. Not content with that result, Hampson decided that a real action (as opposed to a personal or possessory one) would be more conclusive, and accordingly arraigned an assize of *Novel Disseisin* before the justices in Buckinghamshire. Informed of those proceedings, the Exchequer immediately issued an injunction to stay further action on the assize.[32] The barons then reheard the case in equity on the basis of Powney's original bill and awarded him possession of all of the islands, ordering at the same time that he be repaid the mean profits (presumably from the fishing) since the time of his occupation of the manor of Cookham. Hampson refused to perform the award, and an attachment had issued out against him. It was at that point that he appealed to the House of Lords.

In his complaint he argued that the barons should never have accepted the case in equity, since it clearly involved nothing other than the question of title. Having done so, however, they should not have further constrained the parties to sue only in the Exchequer. He complained that he should have been free to take whatever action he could, in whatever venue he might choose, to prove his title, 'it being against the liberty of the free-born subject to be denied such course'.[33] His efforts to do so had been abruptly curtailed and he asked that the injunction be removed to allow the assize of *Novel Disseisin* to proceed to conclusion.

The Lords initially referred his petition to the barons of the Exchequer with directions that they give 'all reasonable satisfaction to his requests therein', or failing that, Chief Baron Davenport and Baron Henden were to appear two days hence to 'show good cause to the contrary'.[34] There is no record of the judges' response, but both plaintiff and defendant appeared before the Committee for Courts of Justice the following week, when the Lords were more decisive. They ordered that Hampson be allowed to proceed with his action at the next Buckinghamshire assizes, 'notwithstanding the said injunction', and that in the meantime 'all proceedings and attachments' in the court of Exchequer were to be suspended pending a final outcome. Richard Powney was fined £20 as compensation to Hampson for the charges already expended in the assize proceedings which he had delayed 'in an undue way'.[35]

The Lords did on occasion support the use of injunctions to enforce jurisdictional prerogatives where it appeared to be appropriate. In the case of *Featly* v. *Kerwin*, for example, they sided with the barons of the Exchequer in their efforts to stay proceedings in the court of King's Bench.[36] This case involved a disputed tenancy in the manor of Kennington in Surrey, then belonging to Prince Charles. The tenancy was held by Dr Daniel Fealty by virtue of a surrender from his wife (for which he had paid a fine and been admitted to possession before her death).[37] His possession was challenged in 1639 by Andrew Kerwin, his nephew by marriage, who claimed that the property should have descended to him on his aunt's death, by custom of the manor, as next of kin and nominal heir. Kerwin initially presented his claim to the Royal Commission for the Prince's Revenue, who referred the matter to trial at the next session of the manor court. The deputy steward of the manor subsequently reported to the prince's board that they could find no custom to support Kerwin's claim of inheritance and as a result the board ordered that Dr Featly was to be secured in his possession until such time as Kerwin might prove his right at law. In due course, Kerwin brought an action of ejectment in the court of King's Bench, to which Dr Featly responded by bringing an action of trespass in the plea side of the Exchequer.[38] Kerwin opted to answer the suit in the Exchequer, and the matter came to a trial which resulted in a judgment for Dr Featly. Kerwin then returned to King's Bench and attempted to bring his earlier suit to trial. Informed that he had revived the matter in King's Bench, the barons immediately issued an injunction to stay the suit.[39]

Kerwin then appealed to the House of Lords, asking that the injunction be overruled on grounds that the issue did not immediately concern the prince's revenue and that the Exchequer should not be allowed 'to injoyne the King's Bench on that pretense'. The case was once again referred to the barons for a report. In their certificate the barons assured the house that the manor and accompanying tenements were 'parcel of the possessions of the Prince his Highness' and that any action concerning them automatically fell within 'the order and survey of the Court of Exchequer'. They argued further that Kerwin had fully acknowledged the jurisdiction of the court by pleading to Featly's suit, which had, in any event, conclusively proved his title. They felt therefore that their injunction was both legal and appropriate. The Lords agreed and dismissed Kerwin's petition from the house.[40]

The equity side of the Exchequer in fact figured largely in these proceedings, perhaps because debtors to the Crown were numerous and it was relatively easy to enlist the help of the court on grounds that the Crown's interests were directly involved.[41] The same was of course true of the court of Wards which had, if anything, an even greater survey and responsibility to the Crown. Its powers could be invoked in

118

a number of ways, for any number of reasons. Not surprisingly, it too became the focus of several complaints regarding jurisdictional conflict. The case of *Gell* v. *Chaworth* provides a good example.[42] The petitioner, John Gell, had acquired a lease in 1636 of the manors of Norton and Tythby in Nottinghamshire, which was due to commence the following year for six years. Gell had attempted to take possession of the manors in 1637, according to the terms of the lease, but had been prevented by the presumptive owner, George, Lord Chaworth. When Lord Chaworth died in the summer of 1639, Gell had still been unable to execute the lease and as a consequence initiated a suit in the court of Requests to have relief. In the meantime, however, an inquisition *post-mortem* had determined that the lands in question had been held by Lord Chaworth by knight service *in capite*. His son and heir subsequently informed the court of Wards that proceedings had been initiated in the court of Requests to recover the properties and they immediately intervened, ordering Gell to cease his prosecution in Requests until he had answered the information in the court of Wards.[43] Gell was then forced to bring a new bill in the court of Wards, to which both the new Lord Chaworth and his mother submitted answers. In their replies they confessed that the land in dispute had not in fact descended directly to the new Lord Chaworth – that instead Lady Chaworth retained a life interest in both manors. The 'confession' (undoubtedly motivated by the prospect of paying mean rates for primer seisin on the property) effectively removed the protective powers of the court, and the parties were instructed to proceed to trial at law on the matter of the lease before the judges the following Michaelmas term. In the interim, however, Lord and Lady Chaworth returned to the court and, in Gell's absence, obtained a new order countermanding that instruction and prohibiting any further legal proceedings until Lord Chaworth sued out his livery. Gell then appealed to the House of Lords.

In his petition to the house Gell asked that the Wards' injunction be overruled on grounds that Lady Chaworth – who by her own confession held the only legal interests in the manors – had no right to protection from the court. He complained that he had been 'locked up' for five terms by the injunction and was in danger of losing all benefit from his original lease. In response the house ordered Lord and Lady Chaworth to appear and answer the complaint. After an extended hearing they overruled the injunction and ordered Gell to bring an action of trespass in the court of King's Bench the following term. The defendants were given precise instructions as to how they were to plead to the action so that Gell's right to the lease could be speedily determined by the Grand Jury at the next Nottinghamshire assizes.[44] The 'equity' of Gell's cause was then reserved for further consideration by the house until after those proceedings had been concluded.

Another similar complaint was lodged by William Latham, Roger Nott and a large group of creditors of the recently deceased earl of Carlisle. These petitioners alleged that before his death the earl had conveyed several manors and assorted lands in England and Ireland in trust to James and Archibald Hay, on the understanding that the collective profits from those lands would be used to repay all of his outstanding debts after his demise. On his death, however, his widow had taken possession of the lands and had appropriated the profits to her own use. In response the creditors had proceeded in Chancery on a bill of discovery to gain an accounting of the entire estate and to compel the trustees to perform their obligations. Unfortunately, the new earl of Carlisle had not yet sued out his livery and as a consequence the court of Wards had issued an injunction commanding the creditors to 'surcease and stay' their suit until further notice.[45] Unable to gain satisfaction they turned to the House of Lords to have the injunction overturned.

The Lords' response to this complaint was swift and decisive. The new earl of Carlisle immediately demanded his right of parliamentary privilege to stay proceedings in the house, but was abruptly denied. The house then went on to order that

> the injunction in the Court of Wards shall be dissolved, and . . . the Lady Lucy, the relict of the late earl of Carlisle, and James the now earl of Carlisle, and the said James and Archibald Hay . . . shall forthwith, without standing on any privilege whatsoever, fully and presently answer to a bill . . . preferred against them in Chancery by the aforesaid William Latham and one Nott; which bill to be proceeded in with effect, to the end that the whole estate of the late earl may be discovered.

By late February 1641 the Lords had in fact received a great many petitions asking for assistance in bringing the earl's executors to account. For that reason the house allowed in the same order that

> the rest of the creditors and any servants who have been now Petrs and also such others who have served the said earl, and were now present to demand their wages by their Counsel . . . for their ease of charge, may affix their several demands unto the [same] bill and so proceed to the proving of them . . . [so] that upon hearing of this cause, equal justice may be done for all of the said creditors and servants who were now petitioners. And for that purpose and to avoid further expense, their Lopps do recommend the consideration thereof . . . to the Right Honorable the Lord Keeper to expedite and settle the same with all possible speed, so that by his Lopp's directions, the charge on both sides may be avoided, and by proceedings upon one bill, put an end to the business.[46]

The order is worth quoting at length, not simply because it demonstrates the Lords' ability to intervene quickly and effectively to settle these conflicts (even when the interests of one of their own members were at stake), but because it demonstrates their understanding of and sensitivity to the other general administrative issue raised by this litigation – the matter of escalating costs. The remedy provided here was deliberately designed to 'avoyde further expense' and to 'allow ease of charge' for the parties involved. The point is made three times in the direction to the Lord Keeper and it testifies to the Lords' growing concern about the matter. The issue of cost was, to some extent, central to all the proceedings under review. It was arguably the 'mainspring' of all other judicial abuses,[47] but like the other problems mentioned, it had remained consistently immune to reform. The failure in this case was all the more conspicuous because the efforts to effect change had been so persistent and varied.[48]

Attempts to control extortionate judicial fees had been initiated on countless occasions in the decades before 1640, both from within and outside the courts. Both Bacon and Ellesmere, as Lord Chancellors, had made efforts to regulate the taking of fees during their respective tenures in Chancery – the most notorious offender among the courts – but had had little success. Ellesmere himself had led two separate investigations into his and other courts' fees in 1608 and 1610, and on one occasion strongly recommended that all court charges be restored to the levels existing in the 1570s.[49] The suggestion was wholly impractical and fell on deaf ears.

The question of fees was, again, of paramount importance in the discussions on legal reform in the Parliament of 1621 (though not always for the right reasons – the interest in Chancery fees at this stage was at least partly motivated by need to gather evidence against Lord Chancellor Bacon).[50] No less than five separate bills were introduced in that Parliament to regulate fees in various courts.[51] Only one measure, however, was debated at any length: the bill 'for avoydeing exactions of undue fees in Courts of Justice'.[52] This bill, authored by Coke and six others, attacked two central abuses thought to be common to all courts – 'the increasing of fees ... beyond that which anciently has been used and allowed' and the 'erecting of new offices in Courts of Justice', which had served to expand the number of fees taken. The measure would have voided all grants of offices made after the accession of James I, prohibited the granting of new offices and barred the taking of any fees greater than those allowed in 1598. The bill was eventually committed for minor amendments, but was never reported back to the Commons. Nor was it revived by Coke or anyone else in either house.[53]

The matter of fees had, of course, consistently attracted the attention of the Crown, which had begun appointing Royal Commissions on Fees

as early as the mid-sixteenth century. Both James I and Charles I had continued that tradition throughout the 1620s and 1630s, but the commissions
were, with few exceptions, notoriously ineffective. They produced vast
quantities of evidence and innumerable complaints of abusive practices,
but they suffered from a lack of serious commitment to the task of
reform. All too often they were appointed as a half-hearted political
concession to parliamentary and public protests.[54] The commission of
1630 did actually produce a set of concrete proposals for reform, authored
by Sir Henry Spelman, but they were never implemented with any effect.
During the 1630s, in fact, the commissions' activities dwindled markedly
and when they did meet their authority was often used solely to negotiate
composition fines with errant court officers to the financial advantage of
the Crown.[55] As Professor Aylmer has suggested, 'the commission's work
exacerbated instead of alleviating a grievance'.[56] On the whole, no one
appears to have taken very seriously Sir Thomas Wentworth's admonition
that 'it were a kind of injustice to make justice too dear'.[57]

The importance of cost as an element in the proceedings in the House
of Lords can be seen in a number of ways. Whether stated or not, it was
often a primary motivating factor behind the appeal. This was particularly
true, for instance, in the cases just discussed where litigants sought a final
resolution in the house, at least in part, to avoid the expense of maintaining
a continuing interest in multiple suits at law. Other litigants had simply
found themselves unable to continue litigation through normal channels
because their resources had been exhausted by proceedings up to that
point. Inevitably, the dispute remained unresolved and the petitioner
looked to the house to settle the matter without reference to expensive
proceedings elsewhere. Ralph Wingate, for example, petitioned the house
in November 1641 claiming to have spent £120 in fees in the courts of
Requests and Chancery attempting to recover a debt of £1,000 owed to
his brother.[58] On three occasions the court of Requests had ordered the
debt to be paid, but each of those decrees had been successfully evaded
by the defendant and a subsequent 'extra-judicial' order of the court had
directed Wingate to settle the debt for 500 marks. He claimed, correctly,
that the order was illegal because it reversed the earlier decrees without
the required Bill of Review being sued, but he was powerless to challenge
the order due to his resulting poverty. He therefore asked the house of
Lords to do it for him.

The problem could, of course, affect defendants as well. A number of
petitioners to the house claimed that they had been financially unable to
defend themselves against vexatious litigation brought by troublesome
plaintiffs. One, John Cooke, complained that he had been forced to spend
the preceding three years defending his possession of the rectory of West
Thorney, Sussex, from the repeated attempts of Benjamin Blaxton to oust
him at law.[59] In addition to having secured a fraudulent superinstitution

from the archbishop of Canterbury, Blaxton had brought a suit of *quare impedit* in the court of Common Pleas, three separate indictments at the Sussex assizes and, finally, an action of trespass in the court of King's Bench. Cooke claimed to have spent £350 in the process, and understandably asked that the house settle his rightful possession once and for all.

Predictably, there were numerous petitions as well from those who had been shut out of the legal system altogether by poverty. Complainants here were most often debtors, or women who had been abandoned by their husbands and left without any means of support – 'yor petitioner's husband having the purse and yor petr the penurie'.[60] As they had in the 1620s, the Lords either referred these cases to another venue, with instructions that the plaintiff or defendant be admitted to proceed *in forma pauperis*, or (more often) simply took responsibility for settling the dispute themselves, waiving the nominal fees associated with proceedings in the house. Even where those fees were not waived, the total cost of initiating a case in the house was insignificant, certainly by comparison with any other contemporary court. The level of expense depended, as it did in most courts, on the complexity of the cause and on the number of orders – to defendants, witnesses, or other courts – required to bring it to resolution, but the available evidence would suggest that few of these cases would have cost the petitioner more than £2 all in.[61] For that they would presumably have achieved a final settlement, which precluded (or severely restricted) proceedings elsewhere and thereby limited the potential for additional legal expenses in the future. The attraction was obvious.

SPECIAL PROBLEMS:
CHANCERY, WARDS AND THE EXCHEQUER

The other large group of cases brought before the house in this Parliament concerned specific problems in individual courts, rather than defects affecting the system as a whole. Complaints here focused on three courts in particular: Chancery, the Court of Wards and the Exchequer. Again, all of the problems presented here were familiar (or, indeed, notorious) and each of them had been considered extensively, either by Parliament or the Privy Council, at some point in the previous two decades. Specific proposals had been put forward to deal with each of them, but as so often, those measures proved to be flawed either in concept or execution.

Court of Chancery

The central complaint with regard to the court of Chancery (already mentioned) concerned the unwarranted expansion of its jurisdiction.

Time and again, petitioners complained that the court had exceeded the presumptive bounds of equity jurisdiction by deciding matters properly relievable at common law. Nor were these cases in which Chancery had attempted to hear a suit after judgment at law – the most controversial complaint about the court's proceedings. They were instead cases in which the court had acted in the first instance to settle issues which were properly determinable elsewhere. This had been a persistent complaint about the court for the better part of the century. The Chancery Clerk, George Norbury, for example, had drawn attention to the problem with considerable clarity in his well-known tract 'The Abuses and Remedies of the High Court of Chancery', which he composed in the 1620s as an advisory letter to the incoming Lord Keeper Coventry.[62] In Norbury's view the principal cause of the then considerable 'clamours against the court' was the 'Straininge of the Authority of the Court beyond its limits in matters of Judicature'.[63] Norbury maintained that the court had failed to exercise sufficient care in keeping to its appointed mandate and had increasingly accepted litigation over which it had little if any proper authority. He argued for a return to clearer lines of demarcation between the traditional responsibilities of Chancery and those of common law – between 'matters of fraud, trust, extremity, or casualty', on the one hand, and matters 'wherein the common law or civil law afford apt remedy', as in disputes over title, on the other. His divisions were perhaps too restrictive to accommodate the myriad legal complications which often arose in contemporary litigation, but they represented the expression of a general principle which found favour within the legal profession and, more emphatically, among litigants. Norbury's treatise had in fact emerged, at least in part, as a consequence of debates over the court's jurisdiction in the 1621 Parliament and his concerns mirror directly those voiced repeatedly by Coke and others about the growing tendency of the court to 'meddle' in matters determinable at common law.[64] As before, however, those concerns were never translated into constructive legislative reform and the court was left to proceed on course.

For the most part, the complaints subsequently presented to the House of Lords concerned Chancery's interference in disputes over title to real property.[65] The case of *Bourlacy* v. *Berry* was fairly typical. Nicholas Bourlacy and his wife Katherine had been defendants in a Chancery suit in 1638, brought by her uncle, Richard Berry. Berry had sued to recover possession of a property called Combmartin Park, then held by the defendants. He claimed right to the property by virtue of a deed from his brother Humphrey Berry (Katherine's father). He maintained that he had been granted the property as income to repay his brother's debts after his death. The defendants claimed, alternatively, that the property had descended to Katherine by a precedent grant, initially made from her father to her brother, and then to her as her brother's administratix.

As in Darcy's case, the court had referred the defendant's deed to justices Bramston, Jones and Berkeley to 'determine whether it be good in law or not'.[66] The judges apparently concluded that it was not, and the Lord Keeper accordingly found for the plaintiff Berry. He declared 'that the plaintiff hath good title both in lawe and equity' to the disputed lands and in consequence awarded him possession. The defendants were directed to surrender all deeds and records on the property and were ordered to make restitution of lost profits.[67]

In the course of the hearing both Bourlacy and his counsel had objected to the court's consideration of the question of title and had requested that the Lord Keeper dismiss the plaintiff's case 'to the Lawe'. He refused and the resulting decision led Bourlacy to petition the Lords. He based his case on the simple premise that 'all titles for land that depend on a point of law ought to receive a tryall at the Common Law, as not decreeable in a court of Equity, unless by consent of the parties'.[68]

Thomas Leveson prefaced his appeal to the upper House with a similar argument:[69]

> Whereas by the ancient and fundamental Lawes of this Kingdom, Courts of Equity were established for the mitigation of the rigour of the Common Law, and for the redress of frauds, trusts, and matters not relievable by the rules of ordinary judicature . . . For matters of Fact triable by jury and matters determinable in law by the judges, the same are properlie tryable in the Ordinary Courts of Justice according to the common law.

Leveson's father had been a defendant in a suit in Chancery in 1615 in which Joseph Hall (the future bishop of Exeter and Norwich) had attempted to gain possession of certain lands belonging to the prebends of Willenhall and Hatherton – part of the free chapel of Wolverhamton then held by the dean of Windsor. In his defence, Leveson's father had claimed title to the lands by virtue of a deed of enfeoffment, dating from 1550, which had been executed by the two prebendaries concerned and subsequently confirmed by the dean and chapter of Windsor. In this case Lord Chancellor Ellesmere had declined even to refer the deeds and records of confirmation to the attendant common law justices. On the basis of his own examination (and for reasons he failed to specify) he concluded that the original transaction in 1550 had been illegal and the subsequent confirmation by the dean and chapter 'suspicious' and of no legal bearing. He therefore declared that Leveson's title to the prebends was 'wrongful' and awarded absolute possession to Hall and his successors, until the defendant might recover possession at law.[70] Understandably, Leveson felt that his chances of proving his father's title had been severely compromised by the court's formal declaration on the validity of his father's claim, and he therefore requested that Ellesmere's decree be set aside and his own possession reconfirmed.

The argument presented by these two petitioners (and by Sir Conyers Darcy earlier) was a simple one. The responsibility for determining title fell exclusively within the jurisdiction of the common law and, whatever mitigating circumstances might otherwise be involved, Chancery was obligated to defer, if only as an interim measure, to proceedings at law – to a formal trial by judge and jury – to resolve the matter properly. The house clearly agreed. Both of these decrees were in fact 'set aside' (as Darcy's had been). In the former case, the Lord Keeper was directed to rehear the entire suit on its merits, and in the latter the parties were directed to proceed expeditiously to a trial in the King's Bench (on an action of trespass) for a determination on the question of title.[71]

Court of Wards

The complaints arising from proceedings in the court of Wards were also somewhat predictable. Petitioners raised two central issues which had been of immediate concern to MPs in the 1620s.[72] The first (already alluded to) concerned unwarranted protections granted by the court to wards and their sureties against actions of debt. The court had issued just such a protection to the new earl of Carlisle, in the case cited above and had done so in at least three other cases heard by the house. Had the earl's creditors not sought relief from the upper house, the prohibition would doubtless have continued to operate until he had sued out his livery. The earl was some 28 years old in 1641 and in theory should have sued out his livery five years earlier on the death of his father.[73] His case in fact points to another related complaint frequently made against the court: that it failed properly to enforce its rules requiring wards to sue livery within six months. The new earl of Carlisle had presumably been granted successive 'continuances' in exchange for the payment of a nominal fee – a process (increasingly sanctioned by the court) which allowed the ward both the benefits of his property and full protection at law.[74]

The abuse of granting protection to debtors had been repeatedly singled out for attack in the Parliament of 1621.[75] The great Coke was himself at the forefront of the assault and at one stage moved that a bill be drafted to remedy the grievance, even volunteering to serve on the committee responsible. Nothing came of the proposal and, as a result, litigants like Francis Paule had to look elsewhere for remedy.[76] Paule had initiated a suit to recover a debt owed to him by his recently deceased uncle, Sir George Paule. His suit (which in fact cited his uncle's executor, John Oldbury, as defendant) had been abruptly stayed by an injunction from the court of Wards. Sir George Paule had left a 10-year-old son as heir and the court had assumed custody of him as a ward. Paule accordingly exhibited his bill in the court of Wards to have relief, but the court refused to grant his request and enjoined him from seeking any remedy at law as long as the heir remained in wardship. Paule then appealed to the House of Lords to have the protection overruled, on the very sensible grounds that to allow the heir to gain his majority seriously risked the loss of important witnesses to his claim, and the potential depletion of his uncle's estate.[77]

The other grievance emerging from the court of Wards concerned abuse of procedures in inquisitions *post-mortem*. This too had been the subject of extended parliamentary discussions in the early 1620s, and those debates had actually produced a concrete proposal for reform, the 'Act against secret offices and inquisitions taken on His Majesties behalf'.[78] This measure was principally designed to protect new heirs from secret inquisitions – which inevitably found the land in question to have been held in chief, and therefore subject to reversion to the Crown – first, by requiring that they be given full and adequate notice of any pending proceedings touching their properties and, second, by allowing them to challenge or 'traverse' any office found, without the previously required 'special license' of the court. Despite considerable and very vocal support, this bill, like so many others, was recommitted in 1621 for consideration of amendments and never resurfaced during the Parliament. It was apparently revived in 1624, and again in 1626, but in the end failed to secure passage.[79] Perhaps, as Professor Russell has suggested, 'secret offices were like sin; everyone was against them, and few were excited enough to take effective action about them'.[80] The matter was left to be raised in the Grand Remonstrance.[81]

In the meantime, the House of Lords would hear at least a half dozen complaints touching the abuse,[82] of which the proceedings in *Browne* v. *Peacock* were fairly typical.[83] John Browne died in March 1634, leaving a son, Christopher, aged 15, as heir. He died seized of the manor of Basom Hill, Lincolnshire, and, as was customary, an inquisition was undertaken to determine the nature of his tenure. The manor was duly found to have been held by common socage. Sometime after that inquisition, one John Peacock exhibited information in the court of Wards claiming that the land had in fact been held by knight's service. On the basis of that allegation alone the court awarded a new writ of *mandamus* to authorize a second inquisition on the property. The proceedings went forward, but the jury failed to be convinced by Peacock's evidence and refused to find for the king's title. When their finding was reported to the court, Lord Cottington, then master, ordered the commission adjourned for four months. He then directed that if they remained uncooperative at their next meeting, they were to be adjourned again to be brought before the court in London to hear 'evidence' at the bar. In due course the jurors were summoned before the court and were given precise instructions to meet again the following Hilary term and find for the king. No evidence to the contrary was to be admitted. Under pressure, the jury complied. As a consequence, the petitioner, Christopher Browne had been forced to compound with John Peacock for his wardship at a cost of £1,000. He complained to the Lords that the proceedings had been collusive from the start; that John Peacock had undertaken the cost of the second inquisition on the basis of a prior agreement with the court that he would be granted the wardship if the tenure of knight's service could be established. He requested, first, that the illicit finding of the jury be vacated in order that his tenure might not be irrevocably prejudiced and, second, that he be awarded compensation for the illegal and unnecessary composition.[84]

Court of Exchequer

All five complaints levelled against the plea side of the Exchequer likewise involved the abuse of established legal procedures. They focused on the indiscriminate use of *quominus* procedure to recover debts in the name of the Crown. The privilege of suing to recover debts in the Exchequer had traditionally been limited to two groups; court officers and revenue agents (receivers general, customs farmers, sheriffs, and the like) who were obliged to render accounts of one form or another at the Exchequer; and the rather more general class of Crown debtors. The notion behind the *quominus* writ was a simple one; the plaintiff needed the special process of the court to levy the debt against the defendant in order better to satisfy his own liability to the king. In theory, his debtor's debt then concerned the royal revenue more or less directly, and it was therefore logical that the king's privilege and prerogative should be extended in this way for what was in the end his own personal gain.[85] However, the definitions of 'obligations' to the Crown were inherently flexible and such claims were rarely, if ever, challenged. As a consequence, the privilege was increasingly abused, most often by court officials. The most common complaint was that these notional 'officers' had availed themselves of the court's special powers to collect their own personal debts when they in fact had no corresponding obligation to the Crown. The individual would simply 'assign' his debt to the king on the pretence of a liability to the Crown and the debt would be collected in the king's name. The same process had frequently been taken a step further. Individuals outside the court's protection wishing to collect their own debts would enter into fraudulent bonds alleging a fictitious debt to a particular court official (usually with the official's cooperation) and on that basis the court's special powers would be engaged. Theoretically, the process could be extended downward indefinitely and contemporaries clearly recognized that as a danger – not least because a debtor's lands were often seized into the king's hands as a result.

This matter too was raised in the parliamentary debates in 1621 and a bill was in fact drafted to limit the Crown's ability to sue for debts not demonstrably related to its own revenue. The measure actually passed the House of Commons, but was dropped in the upper house – presumably because Solicitor General Heath had already suggested to the Lords that the problem would be better addressed through a royal Bill of Grace.[86] In the event, no such bill was forthcoming and the abuse went unchecked. Complaints proliferated to the extent that by 1640 the Crown itself was forced to intervene. On 30 March 1640 King Charles issued a proclamation condemning the 'divers indirect and unjustifiable courses' by which those not entitled to do so had 'sued for the debts in Our Name, to the abuse of Our Subjects'. The king claimed that these 'crafty and indirect courses' had 'abused Our said Just Prerogative … contrary to Our Gracious Pleasure and Royal Intention'. Accordingly, the proclamation prohibited all 'unwarrantable' practices of this kind in the future and commanded the barons of the Exchequer to 'take notice' of that prohibition. The king then allowed that any subject who had already been 'troubled, molested, oppressed, or damnified by reason of such or any like abuses' should 'freely addresse their Complaints to Our Privie Counsell, where they shall be heard and such order therein taken for their relief as shall be agreeable to Justice and Equity'.[87]

The proclamation clearly provided something of a lead, but by this stage petitioners apparently felt more comfortable (or found the prospects of success more promising) addressing their complaints to the 'King's Council in Parliament'. At least one of them actually referred to the proclamation as his authority for appeal.[88] The nature of the complaint and the Lords' response to it are clearly illustrated in the case of Lady Catherine Dyer.[89] In 1631 Lady Dyer had loaned £400 to Sir Richard Tichborne. The loan was due to be repaid within six months, but Tichborne defaulted and, having waited two years for repayment, Lady Dyer finally sued out the bonds and had judgment against him. Unfortunately, other claimants with greater privileges had preceded her. Sir Robert Pye, a senior auditor in the Exchequer, and other creditors had already put their own bonds against Tichborne into execution in that court and had procured extents on his lands in the king's name. Lady Dyer was therefore unable to have any benefit of her judgment. She eventually petitioned the House of Lords, protesting that her debt was of greater value and of longer standing than Sir Robert Pye's, and that her claim ought to have taken precedence. She maintained as well that Pye and his colleagues had abused the Exchequer privilege. They had 'made use of the King's Prerogative for their own private ends' by suing in the court in the absence of any genuine debt to the Crown. To that extent, she too appears to have clearly understood the message of the king's proclamation. Finally, she claimed that the lands which had been extended in the king's name had been deliberately undervalued so as to leave Sir Richard Tichborne a substantial income on which to live – they had been rated at only £362 per annum, when in fact they produced an annual income of over £1,000. She requested that the Exchequer proceedings be reviewed and that one or other of the parties concerned (Tichborne or Pye) be compelled to satisfy her debt.

After hearing from all the parties, the Lords ordered that Sir Robert Pye's interests in the extents – which had been 'gained by color of usurping the King's Prerogative' – should be immediately assigned to Lady Dyer. She in turn was to give assurances to Pye and the other creditors guaranteeing them payment of their respective debts out of the £362 rated against the property. Having done that, she was then to have full benefit 'of the surplusage of the true value of the lands . . . to satisfy herself . . . with costs and damages'. The form of the assurances between the parties was left to the discretion of 'counsel indifferent on both sides'.[90]

There was a curious irony about all of these proceedings. Technically, the only appellate jurisdiction generally recognized as belonging to the upper house was that confirmed by statute – the right to hear appeals from King's Bench and Exchequer Chamber by writ of error. And yet writs of error represented only a very small proportion of the cases brought before the Lords in the first three years of the Parliament. Less than twenty such writs were presented and few of those were actually serious complaints about legitimate errors in the law.[91] The vast majority of these cases were brought with the sole purpose of delaying execution of judgment in court of King's Bench. A number of the plaintiffs confessed under examination that they had no grounds on which to base an appeal under the rules of writ of error procedure, but hoped, as one plaintiff put it, 'to gain time to show the true state of their cause in equity'.[92] That was usually not revealed, however, until the hearing, by which point the case had already cost the house considerable time and effort with procedural and scheduling requirements.[93] In order to discourage the practice, in June 1641 the house began taxing costs against any plaintiff who sued out a writ of error 'without just cause' in order to delay execution.[94] The rule proved ineffective and the procedure had to be amended again in February 1642. On this occasion the house ordered that henceforth no writ of error was to be accepted unless and until the plaintiff had presented an accompanying petition which outlined 'some just and true ground of material error'.[95] In the event, only two plaintiffs made genuine efforts to assign errors as required and both of them were dismissed and their cases remitted to King's Bench when the Lords and attendant judges determined after hearings that the alleged errors were 'frivolous and insufficient'.[96]

Far more frequently the Lords heard complaints alleging judicial malfeasance of one kind or another against individual judges. Certainly, the atmosphere in Parliament in the early months of the session was conducive to this sort of protest. The initial (and imprecisely defined) charges of 'crimes and misdemeanors' levelled against the six common law judges in December 1640 and the subsequent attack on Lord Keeper Finch no doubt encouraged some of these petitioners to attempt the proverbial 'try on'. But in fact many of their complaints were entirely legitimate. One of the most common charges was that a judge in King's Bench or Common Pleas had failed to set adequate bail for defendants arrested in actions of debt. William Dudley, for example, had arrested Thomas, Lord Wentworth in early 1640 on a bill of Middlesex to recover debt of £400 which Wentworth had owed him for the previous five years. At the time of the arrest he had entered a formal caution with Justice Robert Berkeley requesting that sufficient security be taken to cover the debt before Wentworth was bailed. Berkeley, however, ignored the request and released Wentworth into his father's custody without taking any security whatsoever. Dudley had lost his chance to secure payment – Wentworth and his father, the earl of Cleveland, were now protected by parliamentary privilege – and he therefore asked for redress against Justice Berkeley.[97] The Committee for Petitions recommended that the errant judge pay Dudley £400 (the sum of his original debt) plus costs and damages, and the house promptly ordered Berkeley to do so.[98]

Petitioners complained about a variety of matters. One petitioner charged Justice Crawley with returning a false report of proceedings at the Winchester assizes, which led, he claimed, to an unwarranted prosecution in Star Chamber for cheating at dice.[99] Another accused her local JP, Dr Owen (later bishop of Llandaff), of releasing two prisoners without bail who had been charged and arrested for theft of her goods in Caermarthen.[100] Charges were levelled at Justice Malet for refusing bail to a defendant at the Southwark assizes,[101] and against Lord Keeper Finch and Justice Crawley for misappropriating funds brought into the court of Chancery.[102] The Lords also heard at least four separate complaints against Sir Henry Marten, judge of the Admiralty court, each of which raised serious questions about his integrity.[103] In two of those cases, Marten was reprimanded by the house and heavily fined.[104]

Predictably, the court of Star Chamber engendered a number of complaints as well. Petitioners here tended to claim either that they had been unjustly imprisoned – usually for failure to comply with the court's rules – or that they had been assessed extortionate fines which were wholly disproportionate to their alleged offence.[105] Perhaps the most notorious case here was that of Sir Richard Wiseman, who had been prosecuted in Star Chamber in 1638 on a charge of slandering Lord Keeper Coventry.[106] Wiseman had accused the Lord Keeper of taking bribes – a charge he made with some certainty since he himself had offered the bribe – but had been unable to prove his allegation to the satisfaction of the court.[107] His subsequent conviction had carried a heavy price. In addition to being fined £18,000, Wiseman had been deprived of his knighthood, had had both ears cropped, had been pilloried and then imprisoned 'at the King's pleasure' – for a total of almost two years by the time he appealed to the House of Lords. Though the Lords ordered Wiseman released from the Fleet so that he could prosecute his appeal in the house, the case had not gone forward by the time Wiseman was killed in the London riots in late December 1641.[108] His case was notable, however, because the special committee appointed to hear it was also given power to 'examine the Institution and Power of the court of Star Chamber' and its proceedings and the evidence it gathered helped pave the way for the court's ultimate demise.[109]

ARBITRATION

Of course, not all litigation presented to the Long Parliament was appellate. As in the 1620s, a great many cases were brought to the house in the first instance. Those who petitioned the house directly did so, in the main, because they had been unable to proceed elsewhere. In some cases they had simply been handicapped by poverty. In others the particulars of the dispute had in some way disqualified them from conventional legal proceedings; in still others there had been no remedy available at all. Generally, what they needed from the House of Lords was a forum for officially sanctioned arbitration. The most common cases of this type were those involving debt. As before, petitioners here were often creditors who had simply exhausted all of their available means attempting to collect outstanding obligations and who needed to enlist the power of the house to bring a recalcitrant debtor to account. More often, the cases involved complex commercial transactions, with multilayered credit relationships (secured by a variety of interlocking penal bonds) which made straightforward litigation enormously complicated, if not impossible – situations like the case of the Muscovy Company (see pp. 51–3). Interestingly, that case made a brief return to the house in 1641, when John Goodwyn, the executor of Sir Richard Deane, complained that he had been unable to collect the debt which the company still owed the estate of the former London alderman. He asked that he might have benefit of the Lords' order of June 1628 to bring the company to account.[110] The house immediately ordered the company to pay Goodwyn £250 in satisfaction of all demands.[111]

The Lords handled at least a dozen such conflicts in the early years of the Long Parliament.[112] The case of *Beaumont* v. *Abbott*, though not the most complicated, provides a good illustration of both the problems and their solutions. John Beaumont petitioned the House in early May 1641 on behalf of himself and dozens of other creditors of Sir

Edward Abbott. Abbott was a London merchant of some note who had become seriously indebted to a variety of investors, including his own father and brothers, to the tune of nearly £120,000. Beaumont and his fellow traders held bonds against Abbott worth some £30,000 for goods they had provided for his overseas ventures. Unfortunately, Abbott had attempted to avoid repayment by surreptitiously conveying his entire estate – goods, merchandise and property, both abroad and in England – to his father and brothers, and they had proceeded to sell parts of it to compensate themselves for their investment. Beaumont and his fellow creditors only had security against Edward Abbott himself, so their bonds were of no use at law against his family. For that reason they looked to the Lords to intervene.

In reviewing the case, the Lords determined that Edward Abbott was, for all practical purposes, bankrupt. However, rather than attempt to handle all the separate claims against Abbott's estate themselves, as they had in the case of the Muscovy Company, they decided that the most appropriate course of action was to invoke the provisions of the Elizabethan statute of bankrupts.[113] The Lord Keeper was therefore requested to issue a Commission of Bankrupts 'to some judicious and honest men' and they were to take responsibility for reviewing the accounts and apportioning payment among the creditors.[114] In anticipation of their work, the Lords ordered that the remainder of Edward Abbott's estate, as well as the goods and portions of his estate assigned to his father and brothers, should be sequestered into some safe hands to ensure that the assets remained intact.[115] Thereafter, they kept a careful watch on the Commission's proceedings in order to guarantee that the demands of all creditors were met.[116]

The Lords' intervention in these cases reflects not just their concern that right be done to deserving creditors, but a broader concern with the health of English commerce. Cases of this kind – and there were clearly many – hampered commercial expansion by undermining the confidence of potential new investors. By taking steps to ensure that creditors would be protected against dishonest tradesmen (or legitimate bankrupts) where the law had failed, the Lords provided a greater sense of security for London merchants – something which may have played a role in the development of political alliances on the eve of civil war.

The other type of case which required arbitration in the first instance also involved broader social concerns, albeit of less immediate importance. These were domestic disputes; quarrels between family members – most often husband and wife – which really required the enforcement of moral obligations, rather than the application of any existing law. Indeed, most of these petitioners applied to the House of Lords because there were few, if any, appropriate or effective remedies available. The plaintiffs in the vast majority of cases were women who had been deserted by or were in other ways estranged from their husbands and who had, typically, been left without adequate means of support. Women in such situations were extremely vulnerable. Legally they were still regarded as *femmes couvertes* and therefore had no recourse at common law and, though they could apply to the church courts or to High Commission for alimony, the effectiveness of such an order really depended on the husband's willingness to cooperate. If he chose to stand out against a decree, the church courts had few weapons, other than excommunication, to bring him to account, and even that was not very effective and was generally resisted on account of its severity. They had no means of attaching property or sequestering rents to ensure that payments were made.

There is considerable evidence that the court of Chancery was beginning, if only just, to take steps to offer more protection to women, but at this stage the court had not yet evolved anything like a coherent doctrine regarding the equitable rights of married women. That would only come in the latter half of the century.[117] The Privy Council had regularly (if rather reluctantly) involved itself in such disputes in the Elizabethan and early Stuart periods, if only because they found such quarrels embarrassing when they occurred among the gentry or aristocracy. They acted to avoid, as they said in one case, 'such unnatural suites in Law as might arise on this occasion, to the scandal of the family'.[118] Such matters were, in their view, 'more proper for a friendly composicion than a legal prosecucion'.[119] Where reconciliation proved impossible, however, the council had acted vigorously to protect the rights of married women and to ensure that they were supported commensurate with their position and their contributions to the marriage.

Petitioners to the House of Lords clearly hoped to find a similar reception there and they were not disappointed. The Lords proved to be more than willing to entertain cases of this kind, despite the seemingly inconsequential nature of the complaints. Almost all of these cases received attention, and most of them achieved final resolution, brokered either by the house itself or by specially appointed arbiters. In fact, if anything the Lords proved to be even more sympathetic to the plight of abandoned women and even less tolerant of their negligent husbands than the council had traditionally been. The case of *Walter* v. *Walter* provides a good example. Elizabeth Walter petitioned the house in late May 1641, complaining that her husband had forced her to leave their home and had subsequently refused support for her and her children.[120] She asked that he be ordered to provide her proper maintenance. Mr Walter was summoned to appear and the Lords heard the case in late June.[121] Initially, they requested that the parties attempt a reconciliation. Mrs Walter was told to 'repair unto him, and offer to cohabit once more', while Mr Walter was admonished 'not in any ways to wrong or abuse her'. They provided, however, that if he refused to live with her or 'to maintain and use her as was fitting', he was to provide her with an income of £60 per annum, payable half-yearly, according to assurances drawn up by her counsel.[122] A week later, Mrs Walter returned to the house claiming that her efforts at reconciliation had been in vain, that her husband was nowhere to be found and that he had told others that he intended to 'sell all his estate and withdraw to France'.[123] Recognizing now that the marriage had collapsed entirely, the Lords moved quickly to protect her interests. William Walter was ordered immediately to settle lands and tenements, cleared of all encumbrances, to the value of £60 a year, on trustees nominated by his wife for her use during her lifetime. Justices Heath and Foster were directed to advise Mrs Walter's counsel on how best to execute the necessary conveyances. Interestingly, the Lords also provided that if Mr Walter's estate should increase in the future, through inheritance or any other means, half of that increase was to be settled and paid to the trustees for the use of Mrs Walter and her children. Walter was then given one month to execute the settlement and, in the event that he refused, a writ of sequestration was to issue out against the named properties – something which was in fact done in May 1642.[124]

Similar settlements were made in a number of other cases.[125] On at least two occasions, the Lords imposed such settlements on members of their own house. The bishop of Worcester was commanded to settle a jointure and present maintenance on his daughter-in-law, Dame Helen Thorborough, according to promises he had made years earlier when she agreed to sell her own substantial inheritance to cover her husband's debts.[126] The earl of Chesterfield was likewise ordered to make good his promise to provide his daughter-in-law, Mary Stanhope, with an annuity of £40 during her widowhood. The earl was, according to the house, 'bound in Honour and Conscience' to provide appropriate support for his family.[127]

Given the magnitude of their other responsibilities, the close attention given these domestic cases may seem somewhat surprising. But in fact the Lords, like the council, saw them in a wider social context. Family quarrels of this type not only created scandal, embarrassing the parties involved and their social peers, but, more seriously, set a poor example and tended to undermine traditional social values. The Lords clearly felt that it was part of their general responsibility, both as political leaders in the house and as leaders in society, to guard against that process.

The Lords' approach to all these cases was in fact fundamentally conservative. There was nothing particularly adventurous about any of the remedies they provided. There were no attempts to blaze new trails in the law – save perhaps in providing greater security for the rights of married women – and, aside from the occasional requests that equity courts bend their rules to allow appeals in worthy cases, they made no attempt to compromise the integrity of inferior court procedures or personnel. Certainly, their conservatism was at least in part a consequence of the pervasive influence of the assisting judges. Their very evident inclination to defer to actions (or to support past proceedings) at common law, particularly in jurisdictional disputes, strongly suggests this. But the Lords were no doubt more comfortable themselves with the certainty provided by common law decrees and, moreover, knew that in the long run they provided greater security for their clients. Their insistence that long-standing rules and regulations be strictly enforced and that infractions be properly punished was no more than good law, necessary in all events to reinforce the notion that the law continued to work to the advantage of the honest litigant.

There was, in short, no hidden agenda here. The growing problems and complexities of the legal system and failure of law reform – for which the Lords had been at least partially responsible – plainly required intervention. Real inequities existed in the system and regardless of whether they were the result of inherent structural limitations or of deliberate abuse of existing rules and procedures, they needed to be addressed. Simple justice required as much. The Lords clearly understood that – there is, in fact, something distinctly paternal about their abiding concern with the welfare of individual litigants. Furthermore, they recognized that irregularities of any kind, if left unchecked, damaged the credibility of the system as a whole. Their response to these cases was largely determined by that broader concern, by a sense of responsibility for maintaining the integrity of the law.

NOTES

1 Denzil, Lord Holles, *The Grand Question Concerning the Judicature of the House of Peers* (London, 1669), p. 91.
2 For a full discussion of these proposals, see S.D. White, *Sir Edward Coke and the Grievances of the Commonwealth* (Chapel Hill, NC, 1979), pp. 46–85, and Robert Zaller, *The Parliament of 1621* (Berkeley, Calif., 1971), pp. 90–7.
3 HLRO, Main Papers, H.L., 19 April 1621. This is a draft of the act. See also Zaller, *The Parliament of 1621*, p. 97.
4 *CJ*, ii, p. 582. S.R. Gardiner, *The History of England*, Vol. 4 (London, 1883–4), p. 109.
5 Coke's position on the matter was curious. It seems unlikely that at this stage he would have felt compelled to rise to the defence either of the court itself or the royal prerogative by killing the bill through recommittal. His objection to the error may have been genuine (and was not untypical of his concern for detail), but the bill's failure to reappear would suggest otherwise. Perhaps it was simply a casualty of his rather ambivalent attitude toward parliamentary legal reform. See White, *Sir Edward Coke*, p. 49.
6 HLRO, Main Papers, H.L., 23 June 1541.
7 ibid.
8 PRO, C33/176, fol. 656.

9   HLRO, Main Papers, H.L., 16 May 1642.
10 PRO, C33/179, fol. 159.
11 D.E.C. Yale (ed.), *Lord Nottingham's Manual of Chancery Practice* (Cambridge, 1965), Introduction, p. lxv.
12 ibid, p. lxiv.
13 HLRO, Main Papers, H.L., 22 January 1640/1.
14 This was not an uncommon complaint in the Long Parliament. William Emott, another petitioner to the house, made an identical charge, alleging that his case had been accepted by Coventry, only to be subsequently dismissed by Finch on grounds of insufficiency (HLRO, Main Papers, H.L., 25 January 1640–1).
15 *LJ*, iv, p. 284.
16 PRO, C33/175, fol. 656.
17 HLRO, Main Papers, H.L., 17 May 1642.
18 ibid., 8 July 1641.
19 See, for example, HLRO, Main Papers, H.L., 10 July 1641 (*Harrison* v. *Falconbridge*); 8 June 1641 (*Hamilton* v. *Haggerston*); 12 June 1641 (Hawkins's case).
20 See, for example, PRO, C33/181, fol. 38 (*Darcy* v. *Savile*) C33/179, fol. 643 (*Hamilton* v. *Haggerston*); C33/180, fol. 547 (*Martin* v. *Libb*); C33/180 fol. 549 (*Pallavicine* v. *Meade*); C33/179, fol. 540 (*Digby* v. *Peterborough*).
21 As late as February 1642, Littleton, with the concurrence of Justices Reeve and Crawley, can be found referring a case over which he was presiding in Chancery to trial in the House of Lords. The case was referred because the 'variance' between the plaintiff and defendant was 'of great weight and consequence' and because it 'concerned an Office of Public Administration of Justice'. The office was the Fine Office in Chancery. PRO, C33/182, fol. 329 (*Blake* v. *Rolfe*).
22 For a discussion of this case, see Zaller, *The Parliament of 1621*, pp. 91–2.
23 *CD, 1621*, 6: 273; 5: 48–9.
24 ibid., 5:12.
25 White, *Sir Edward Coke*, p. 63.
26 HLRO, Main Papers, H.L., 15 January and 12 April 1641.
27 The 'special verdict' was one in which the jury did no more that state the facts of the case, as they appeared to them, and then 'prayed the discretion of the court' as to the results; that is, they referred the case back to the justices at Westminster to resolve the legal issues involved (J.H. Baker, *An Introduction to English Legal History* (London, 1979), p. 71.
28 HLRO, Main Papers, H.L., 12 April 1641.
29 *LJ*, iv, p. 183.
30 HLRO, Main Papers, H.L., 10 December 1640.
31 The specific procedure used in this case was the action of ejectment. Originally, the action worked as follows: the plaintiff, claiming title to property then in another's possession, would grant a lease of the property to a third party. He would then attempt to put his lessee in possession, with the intention that he would be ejected by the party then holding the property. The lessee could then bring an action of ejectment against the defendant, and the issue would be joined on the title; that is, the court would determine which of the real disputants had the better claim to the freehold. By this stage, however, the whole process had been replaced by an elaborate series of fictions, whereby the lease, entry and ejectment were simply alleged to have occurred, and the matter went directly to a trial on the title. In order for the process to work, however, the defendant then in possession had to 'confess', i.e. accept the fictions and enter the plea of not guilty. It was this that Richard Powney refused to do. For a discussion of this process and the legal fictions involved, see Baker, *Introduction to English Legal History*, pp. 252–5 and A.W.P. Simpson, *An Introduction to the History of Land Law* (Oxford, 1961), pp. 135ff.
32 PRO, E126/5, fol. 32–3.
33 HLRO, Main Papers, H.L., 10 December 1640.
34 ibid.
35 ibid., 23 December 1640, 'Orders on Private Petitions'.
36 ibid., 10 December 1640.

37 Dr Featly was the same activist Puritan minister who took part in the extensive debates over Arminianism in the 1620s and 1630s. See N. Tyacke, *The Anti-Calvinists: The Rise of English Arminianism c.1590–1640* (Oxford 1987), p. 73.

38 This represents an interesting variation on the proceedings mentioned above (n. 31). Kerwin appears actually to have granted a lease to try the matter, and his lessee attempted to enter the property and take possession. Instead of pleading to the ensuing action of ejectment, Dr Featly used his entry as the premise for instituting his own action of trespass in the Exchequer.

39 PRO, E126/1, fol. 333.

40 HLRO, Main Papers, H.L., 10 November 1641.

41 See, for example, HLRO, Main Papers, H.L., 10 February 1640–1 (*Coghill* v. *Potter*); 6 July 1641 (*Walsingham* v. *Baker*); 10 July 1641 (*Crompton* v. *Van Lors*); and 15 December 1640 and 21 January 1640–1 (*Ramsey* v. *Walsingham*).

42 ibid., 18 January 1640–1.

43 PRO, Wards 9/301 (23 October 1639).

44 HLRO, Main Papers, H.L., 23 December 1640, 'Orders on Private Petitions'. The instructions were that Lord and Lady Chaworth were to 'confess the lease, entry, and ejectment and outer, and such like circumstances as are necessary to bring the tytle to a tryall'. They were then to plead not guilty so that the action could go forward. These instructions, or variations of them, were issued repeatedly by the house in appropriate cases, suggesting perhaps the degree to which the fictions involved in the ejectment action had become institutionalized. The reference to the Grand Jury was deliberate. The Lords insisted that 'the jury to be retourned be such as are the Grand Jury' and instructed the sheriff to supplement the Grand Jury with 'the most sufficient men of the county of Notts' in the event that any regular members of the jury were unavailable. The Lords had in fact ordered a trial at the Nottinghamshire assizes four months earlier and it was the report of that trial that led them to make this decision, though for what reasons it is not clear. In all likelihood the earlier trial had been unfairly compromised in some way.

45 PRO Wards, 9/302 (6 July 1639).

46 HLRO, Main Papers, H.L., 11 February 1640–1.

47 Zaller, *The Parliament of 1621*, p. 94.

48 For a particularly insightful discussion of the matter of costs and legal fees, see C.W. Brooks, *Pettyfoggers and Vipers of the Commonwealth* (Cambridge, 1986), pp. 126–7, 146–50.

49 L.A. Knafla, *Law and Politics in Jacobean England, The Tracts of Lord Chancellor Ellesmere* (Cambridge, 1977), pp. 109–11.

50 Zaller, *The Parliament of 1621*, p. 97.

51 ibid., p. 94, n. 39.

52 White, *Sir Edward Coke*, p. 58; *CD, 1621*, 5:317; *CJ*, i, p. 569.

53 White, *Sir Edward Coke*, p. 58; *CD, 1621*, 7:22.

54 Brooks, *Pettyfoggers and Vipers*, p. 149.

55 The classic case here was that of the Six Clerks in Chancery (see Ch. 2 above).

56 G.E. Aylmer, 'Charles I's commission on fees', *BIHR*, 31 (1958) p. 67. In addition to this article there is a full discussion of the matter of fees in W.J. Jones, *Politics and the Bench* (London, 1971), pp. 108–20.

57 Cited in Jean S. Wilson, 'Sir Henry Spelman and the Royal Commission on Fees, 1622–1640', in J. Conway Davies (ed.), *Studies Presented to Sir Hilary Jenkinson* (London, 1957), p. 457.

58 HLRO, Main Papers, H.L., 30 November 1641.

59 ibid., 30 August 1641.

60 ibid., 29 December 1640 (*Weely* v. *Weely*).

61 Unfortunately, the fee structure in the house is not very well documented. The most comprehensive list of fees available suggests that litigants were charged a flat fee of £1 to the Clerk of Parliament 'for a Private Petition, read in the House, reported by the Committee, and adjudged' (HLRO, Braye MSS, 52/5). That wording would seem to suggest that the fee covered the petitioner's expense from the beginning of the process to the end, at least where formal actions by the Clerk himself were

concerned. In addition, petitioners appear to have been charged 14s 6d for each one-page order which emerged from the proceedings (with a surcharge of 5s for each subsequent page). That schedule also lists fees to be paid to the clerk's clerk of 2s 'upon reading and entering a petition' and 2s 6d for 'an order upon a petition', though these appear to be the fees paid by the clerk to his deputy, rather than fees paid by the petitioner directly. For a comparison of fees charged elsewhere, see Brooks, *Pettyfoggers and Vipers*, pp. 101–6.

62 F. Hargrave (ed.), *A Collection of Tracts Relative to the Laws of England* (London, 1787).

63 ibid., p. 430.

64 White, *Sir Edward Coke*, p. 60; Zaller, *The Parliament of 1621*, pp. 92–4.

65 This complaint accounts for at least ten separate petitions to the house in 1641 and 1642. See also J.S. Hart, 'The House of Lords and the appellate jurisdiction in equity', *Parliamentary History*, vol. 2 (1983), pp. 49–70. Other complaints frequently made against the court included claims that the party and his counsel had been denied a hearing, that the decree had been issued prematurely without examination of witnesses, that the Lord Keeper had signed the decree without hearing the suit himself, that is, only on the basis of a report from the Masters in Chancery. Petitioners complained as well about injunctions awarding possession of property solely on the basis of the plaintiff's petition. Interestingly, the State Papers collection in the Public Record Office contains a list of grievances about the court of Chancery that appears to have been presented to the Lords' Committee for Imprisonments and Courts of Justice in December 1640. The document outlines each of these complaints (including that regarding Chancery's interference with title) in detail. (It should be said, however, that neither the date nor the destination of the document are necessarily proved by internal evidence. The archivist's assumption makes perfect sense, but the possibility remains that the list was presented to an earlier Parliament; PRO, SP/16/473, fol. 106).

66 PRO, C33/ 175, fol. 656.

67 ibid., fol. 266.

68 HLRO, Main Papers, H.L., 27 November 1640.

69 ibid., 10 February 1641.

70 ibid. (transcript of Chancery decree).

71 ibid., 13 July 1641. *LJ*, iv, p. 158.

72 In addition to those discussed below, the house received three complaints against specific grants of wardship, four against Wards who failed to sue livery, two against injunctions awarding possession of property, and one about a decree voiding a recognizance bond. Three other petitioners requested that the house assist in the enforcement of an earlier Wards' decree.

73 Crummett, 'Lay peers in Parliament', p. 121.

74 H.E. Bell, *An Introduction to the History and Records of the Court of Wards and Liveries* (Cambridge, 1953), pp. 62, 76–7.

75 White, *Sir Edward Coke*, p. 64. *CD, 1621*, 2:100, 5:473.

76 HLRO, Main Papers, H.L., 8 December 1640.

77 There is no record of the Lords' response to the case, but given their decisive support of the creditors of the earl of Carlisle in similar circumstances, it seems fair to assume that Paule would have been granted his request to have the Wards' injunction overruled.

78 *CD, 1621*, 7:193–7.

79 White, *Sir Edward Coke*, pp. 64–5.

80 C. Russell, *Parliaments and English Politics, 1621–29* (Oxford, 1979), p. 44.

81 See Articles 44 and 46. John Rushworth, Historical Collections, 8 vols (London, 1721), Vol. 4, pp. 437–51.

82 See, for example, the case of *Andrews* v. *Coope* (HLRO, Main Papers, H.L., 8 June 1641).

83 ibid., 27 May 1641.

84 The case proceeded toward hearing in June and July 1641. Witnesses were examined, depositions were taken and preliminary hearings appear to have been held, but the

final resolution of the house was left unrecorded (HLRO, Main Papers, H.L., 23 December 1640, 'Orders on Private Petitions').

85 W.H. Bryson, *The Equity Side of the Exchequer* (Cambridge, 1975), p. 18.

86 *CD, 1621*, 5:16; White, *Sir Edward Coke*, p. 63; W.Holdsworth, *The History of English Law*, Vol. 1 (7 vols; London, 1903–24), p. 240.

87 J.F. Larkin and P. Hughes (eds), *Stuart Royal Procalamations*, Vol. 2 (Oxford, 1983), pp. 706–7.

88 HLRO, Main Papers, H.L., 21 June 1641 (*Bett v. Grosvenor*).

89 ibid., 7 January 1641.

90 ibid., 6 April and 25 May 1641 (see also the case of *Oliver, Lord St John* v. *George Benyon*; 14 August 1641); *LJ*, iv, pp. 607, 716; v, pp. 79, 99–100, 139, 338; and the case of *John Pynsent* v. *Gabriel Ludlow* (HLRO, Main Papers, H.L., 16 March 1641).

91 The plaintiff had to be able to prove that there were errors in law (rather than of fact) in the record. He might claim, for instance, that the final verdict did not agree with or went beyond the specifications of the original writ.

92 HLRO, Main Papers, H.L., 29 December 1640 (Hyde v. Lloyd). See also above, chapter 2, pp. 95–6 for a similar plea made by the London soapboilers, John Overman and Thomas Doughty.

93 The procedure required that the writ and the record of the lower court proceedings had to be brought into the house by the Chief Justice and received by the Lords in a formal ceremony. The original record and a transcript of it had to be compared before the record could be returned to the court. All further hearings on the writ had to be conducted at the bar of the house rather than in committee.

94 *LJ*, iv, p. 270.

95 ibid., v, p. 569.

96 ibid., iv, p. 259 (*Nash v. Kynaston*); v, p. 131 (*Lenthal v. Bruton*).

97 HLRO, Main Papers, H.L., 18 December 1640.

98 *LJ*, iv, p. 116. Berkeley agreed and put up his house and lands in nearby Barnet as security. See also the similar complaint of Ralph Bradley (HLRO, Main Papers, H.L., 24 December 1640).

99 HLRO, Main Papers, H.L., 10 February 1640–1 (*Wells v. Westropp*).

100 ibid., 6 February 1641 (*Webb v. Llandaff*).

101 *LJ*, iv, p. 672 (*Kiffin v. Malet*).

102 HLRO, Main Papers, H.L., 12 December 1640 (Gerrard Wright's case).

103 ibid., 19 January 1640–1 (*Rookes v. Marten*); 21 January 1640–1 (*Plisher v. Marten*); 26 January 1640–1 (*Peele v. Marten*); 26 August 1641 (*Warwick v. Marten*).

104 *LJ*, iv, p. 266 (*Rookes v. Marten*); p. 378 (*Warwick v. Marten*).

105 HLRO, Main Papers, H.L., 9 January 1640–1 (*Marshall v. Pennyman*); 21 January 1640–1 (William Hull's case) 20 January 1640–1 (John Smith's case); 22 January 1641 (*Stoning v. Bridges*); 2 July 1641 (*Hanger v. Kilvert*).

106 ibid., 10 January 1640–1.

107 Wiseman had made the allegation in an earlier petition to the king. He was clearly piqued because, he claimed, Coventry had accepted the bribe and then decreed for his opponent, John Stone, in a case in Chancery.

108 Anthony Fletcher, *The Outbreak of the English Civil War* (London, 1981), p. 172.

109 The committee conducted the initial hearings in the house on the court's jurisdiction, entertaining arguments from various attorneys and from the Attorney General (*LJ*, iv, pp. 167, 248). The bill itself was considered by a committee of the whole house.

110 HLRO, Main Papers, H.L., 1 July 1641. For the Lords' previous orders in the case, see Chapter 1 above.

111 ibid., 12 July 1641.

112 See, for example, HLRO, Main Papers, H.L., 13 January 1640–1, 5, 9 February 1640–1 and 29 March 1642 (*Vernatti v. Latch*); 30 September and 6 October 1642, 4 January 1643 (*Legrand v. Beverly*).

113 13 Elizabeth I, c.7

114　*LJ*, iv, p. 242. The Lords appear to have been informed at some stage that Abbott was also indebted to the king for £12,000. They therefore directed that the king's debt should be paid before all others. Holdsworth, *History of English Law*, Vol. 1, p. 470, claims that the first application to the Lord Keeper for such a commission under the provisions of the statute was in 1676. This appears to belie that assertion.

115　*LJ*, iv, pp. 242, 248.

116　ibid., pp. 292, 300, 388.

117　Chancery's primary concern in the late Elizabethan and early Stuart periods was with the rights and needs of widows, rather than with 'divorced' or abandoned women. Importantly, the court had begun to articulate the general principle that a woman was entitled to a portion – or security as a widow – commensurate with her contributions to a marriage. That idea would come to be known as the doctrine of 'a wife's equity to a settlement', but as yet it had not been extended to offer protection to a woman while her husband still lived. For a discussion of Chancery's treatment of women's rights in the Elizabethan period, see Maria Cioni, *Women and Law in Elizabethan England* (New York, 1985); also Holdsworth, *History of English Law*, vol. 5, pp. 313–14.

118　*APC*, 1621–3, p. 368.

119　ibid., 1628–9, p. 334. For a discussion of the council's work in this area, see J.P. Dawson, 'The Privy Council and private law, in the Tudor and early Stuart periods', *Michigan Law Review*, Vol. 48 (1950), p. 421.

120　HLRO, Main Papers, H.L., 26 May 1641.

121　It is not altogether clear whether Mr Walter made an appearance at the hearings before the committee. He responded to the Lords' summons by petitioning the house protesting his wife's appeal and claiming that she had been unfaithful – a fairly standard response – but he apparently failed to make his case (HLRO, Main Papers, H.L., 21 June 1641).

122　*LJ*, iv, p. 283.

123　HLRO, Main Papers, H.L., 1 July 1641.

124　*LJ*, iv, pp. 309, 693.

125　See for example, HLRO, Main Papers H.L., 4 March 1640–1; *LJ*, iv, pp. 277, 304 (*Dutton* v. *Dutton*); HLRO, Main Papers, H.L., 10 February 1641; *LJ*, iv, 654 (*Slingsby* v. *Fortescue*).

126　ibid., 15 January 1640–1; *LJ*, iv, pp. 174, 220.

127　ibid., iv, p. 114.

4

The Long Parliament (iii):
the King's Council in Parliament

The judicial responsibilities of the House of Lords really developed during the Long Parliament in response to three distinct sets of problems. The first two have already been discussed: those arising from the careless disregard for legal propriety shown by the Crown in its drive for administrative efficiency in the 1630s, and those arising from Parliament's failure to follow through with its legislative proposals for law reform in the 1620s. Paradoxically, the third set of problems facing the house emerged, after 1640, for precisely the opposite reasons: because of the precipitate collapse of the Privy Council as an effective governing body in late 1640 and as a side effect of Parliament's subsequent success in legislating legal reform – specifically, in abolishing the courts of Star Chamber and High Commission and in curtailing the judicial authority of the council itself. They developed, in short, from the wholesale collapse of the machinery of conciliar government.

The king's government was in serious disarray long before Parliament assembled. The events of the previous summer had left the Privy Council hopelessly divided and demoralized, unable either to resolve the crisis in the north or to reconcile an inconsolable and immovable king to political reality. Parliament then exacerbated the crisis in December by removing from office, either directly or by threat, many of the council's leading members (and in the process, the senior officers of both Star Chamber and High Commission) – Archbishop Laud, the earl of Strafford, Lord Keeper Finch, Secretary Windebank, Lord Chief Justice Bramston and five of his colleagues on the common law bench. The purge (however predictable) immobilized the board and emasculated the prerogative courts. The council, deprived of its former leading lights, ceased to meet with any regularity after the late autumn; the court of Star Chamber met only rarely and with little effect; and the court of High Commission appears not to have met at all.[1] By February, as Parliament began to examine ways of regulating the 'power and institution' of all three bodies, it was clear that their authority would be seriously curtailed, and by July the fatal legislation had been enacted. The collapse had occurred with inordinate speed.

These developments inevitably created a vacuum at the centre, as no doubt some members of both houses intended that it should, if only to allow for the emergence of new leadership and a fresh start. But in the rush to destroy the instruments of Personal Rule, the parliamentary reformers had overlooked a number of important considerations. First, they failed to appreciate that by abolishing Star Chamber and High Commission, and restricting the judicial prerogatives of the Council, they were at the same time (and with very little warning) removing three institutions which had been responsible in various ways for the arbitration of private legal disputes. Public outcry in Parliament and their own personal perceptions led MPs to overlook the fact that each of these institutions had traditionally served a useful and important function in judicial administration and had been, moreover, until very recently immensely popular tribunals. Rather more ominously, they failed to take into account the fact that all three had played a major, indeed indispensable role in the maintenance of public order. Those responsibilities would necessarily have to be absorbed elsewhere. Likewise, parliamentary reformers failed to anticipate that by declaring in the enacting legislation that those institutions had acted illegally and without proper authority – over an unspecified period – they were creating a whole new set of secondary legal problems: casting doubt on untold numbers of court decrees and creating legal liabilities for the officers and employees of those courts. Those complications would also have to be addressed in the immediate future and with considerable care. On all counts, the repercussions would be felt in the House of Lords.

The specific responsibilities inherited by the upper house can be seen first in the area of litigation: in the appearance of private party cases previously heard before the Privy Council in 1639 and early 1640, but left unresolved; in the appearance of a number of more general legal disputes which, at least in theory, ought to have been handled by the council in 1641; and in the appearance of private civil and criminal cases which had been terminated *sub judice* by the abrupt demise of Star Chamber and High Commission. Beyond that, they can be seen in the extensive efforts made by the house to indemnify the officers and employees of all conciliar institutions against legal actions arising from their prior services to the Crown. And, finally, they can be seen in the increasing time and attention devoted to the suppression of public disorders – fen riots, enclosure riots, disturbances in local parish churches – and to the punishment of offenders and to the general maintenance of public peace.

Some of these responsibilities were assumed by simple default, others by virtue of specific directions from the Crown, but in either case they were largely unavoidable. The upper house remained the only institution at the centre equipped to act with equal authority in both a conciliar and a judicial capacity. It was able to undertake a full range of administrative duties because its membership included all but a handful of the king's privy councillors and all of the administrative officers of the realm. It was equally able to execute the various legal and judicial functions exercised by the council and its subsidiary courts because its own authority as High Court had been well established and because the necessary procedural machinery was by now operational. The transfer of authority, such as it was, could be easily accomplished. In the event, what changed during the course of 1641 was not so much the nature of conciliar government as the nature of the council itself. The king's Privy Council, in all its guises, gave way to the King's Council in Parliament.

THE DECLINE OF THE PRIVY COUNCIL

The collapse of the Privy Council as an effective governing body in 1641 can be measured in a number of ways. On the most basic level, it can be seen in the relative infrequency of its meetings. A comparison of the first twelve months of the Long Parliament with the preceding twelve-month period reveals a dramatic drop in the number of times the board met to conduct business.[2] Between November 1639 and October 1640 the council assembled on 126 occasions, an average of over ten times a month. By contrast, between November 1640 and October 1641 it met only 47 times, a two-thirds reduction from the year before, with an average of just under four meetings a month. A further breakdown of the figures for 1640 and 1641 reveals an even more significant pattern because the number of meetings was not spread evenly throughout the year and the ostensible average was maintained only rarely. The high point came in the first three months of the Parliament, when the council met on a total of 18 occasions; 5 times in November, 4 times in December and 9 times in January.[3] Thereafter, however, the number of meetings rapidly declined. Over the next six months, from February through July 1641, the council met on only 14 occasions, an average of just over twice a month, with a notable high in April (4 meetings) and lows in May and June (1 meeting a piece). The numbers increased to 5 in August, in preparation for the king's journey to Scotland, dropped to 1 in September and rose again to 4 in October.[4]

To some extent, the dearth of council meetings during this period can be attributed to the disruptive effects of Parliament itself. The focus of attention and activity quite naturally shifted into Parliament once a new session had convened and council members were bound to be somewhat preoccupied with new responsibilities there.[5] Nonetheless, practical difficulties do not adequately explain the decline. During the Parliament of 1628/9, by comparison, the council met on 34 occasions: 23 times in the first fourteen-week session and 11 times in the second seven-week session.[6] It had also met 7 times during the three weeks of the Short Parliament[7] and, the Scottish Campaign notwithstanding, it would be difficult to argue that the problems facing the government were any less urgent in autumn and winter of 1640/1 than they had been the previous spring. Paralysis had clearly set in. No doubt, the disintegration of the council's 'corporate morale' over the summer and the ensuing parliamentary attacks in the autumn had much to do with this,[8] but it is also hard to escape the conclusion that it was, to some extent, a matter of choice. Certainly, after February 1641 the infrequency of council meetings must have reflected the king's reservations about (not to say distaste for) the changing composition of the board. The addition of seven leading critics of the Crown in mid-February (and of an eighth, the earl of Warwick, in late April) drastically undermined the political homogeneity of the council, which had already been severely shaken by the loss of its leading lights – and the king's closest advisers – in November and December.[9] It is doubtful that the king ever fully appreciated the long-term advantages of the earl of Bedford's so-called 'undertaking', or that he had ever been willing to embrace the venture in the spirit in which it had been advanced. The failure of the initial concession to halt the flow of reform legislation, or, more importantly, to save the earl of Strafford, could only have confirmed his distrust, and the virtual dearth of council meetings between the beginning of April and 1 July (5) and the king's absence from all but one of them indicates the depth of his alienation.[10]

That impression is confirmed by a review of the business conducted at those few meetings actually held. The Privy Council registers do not necessarily offer a complete picture of the board's activities in each case, since they record only the final decisions made and not the discussion which may have preceded them. Even so those decisions do provide some sense of the general preoccupations of the board at any given moment, and by any measure those for the first twelve months of the Long Parliament are remarkably thin both in number and content. Rarely do more than three or four orders emerge from any one meeting, and they are on the whole extraordinarily mundane: warrants to the Treasury for various payments, grants of export licences, passes to travel abroad. There is no evidence whatever of any discussion of general matters of policy. The registers do not contain a single reference to religious issues or concerns, or to the enforcement of social policy (poor relief, regulation of alehouses and the like). Official contacts with local magistrates are in fact very limited and relate in most cases to specific problems, such as the prosecution of a Catholic priest in Lincolnshire, or proceedings against a citizen of Hull for the transportation of fuller's earth. Perhaps less surprisingly, there is little if any evidence of business being conducted in relation to proceedings in Parliament. Only once in the whole of 1641 did the council consider presenting legislation of its own – a bill to define the authority and powers of the Lords Lieutenant[11] – and no effort appears to have been made to confront the consequences of those measures Parliament had actually passed as, for instance, the obvious administrative and legal problems generated by Parliament's declarations on Ship Money.[12] What is missing from the board's proceedings is any sense of direction or purpose, any sense that the council was exercising control or guiding events.[13] On the contrary, they leave an abiding impression that the board was doing little more than serving time, and that its central purpose in the running of government had been abruptly and dramatically curtailed.[14]

The first evidence of the council's decline was the appearance in the upper house of private party disputes. By the end of January the Lords had already received numerous petitions from complainants whom the board had failed to satisfy. In most cases, the council had heard the dispute on one or more occasions and had issued directions for a settlement, but had then failed to ensure that its orders were carried out. A typical example here was the complaint presented by Rice Williams, a Surrey brewer.[15] Williams petitioned the house on behalf of his wife, whose first husband, William Widmore, had died with substantial assets owed to him by the East India Company. Neither she nor Williams had been able to obtain an accounting of Widmore's legacy from the company and, 'not being able to contest in lawe with so potent [an] adversarie', had petitioned the council in March 1640. The council reviewed the complaint and ordered that it be referred to the governor of the East India Company, who was then 'prayed and directed' to give the petitioner satisfaction, or certify to the council his reasons for not doing so. The council's order was subsequently presented to the company, but the governor and his committee chose to ignore it, suggesting instead that Williams proceed to law, his reservations about their potency notwithstanding. In his petition to the house on 26 January, Williams asserted

> that yor petr hath laboured theis last three monthes by his peticion to acquaint the said Lords [of the council] with the premises that thereby he might have further reliefe, but hath lately had his peticion redelivered him wth the answeare that their Lopps hath not answeared any peticions all theis last three monthes; wherefore yor petr being remedilesse, is inforced to seek reliefe from this honoble assembly.

There is no indication in Williams's petition as to whether the answer he received was an official one, say from the clerk of the council, or whether it was simply information gleaned by his attorney, but in either case it leaves a very strong impression that for all practical purposes the council had ceased to act as a forum for private litigation.

Numerous other cases convey the same impression. In October 1640 the board had considered the case of Elizabeth Manley who had petitioned the council for relief in a domestic dispute. Her father-in-law, Sir Richard Manley, had conveyed to her and her husband a house in Westminster, together with an annuity of £120 as part of her jointure on her marriage the previous spring. Subsequently, however, Sir Richard had himself remarried (at age 76) and under the influence of his new wife had reneged on the agreement. He refused to pay the promised annuity, reconveyed the property in Westminster to his second son (with a remainder to his new stepson) and then threatened to evict the parties from the house. The council had found her cause 'very considerable' and deserving 'all Just Favor and reliefe' and had accordingly ordered John Glynn and Serjeant Francis, the two responsible JPs, to secure Elizabeth Manley in her quiet possession 'until the same shall happen to be evicted . . . in an orderly and legal course'.[16] The council's orders were not effective either in settling the family dispute or in securing her in her possession. In May 1641, having failed to reenlist the council's support for her cause, she readdressed the same complaint to the House of Lords.[17]

Throughout the 1630s the council had also attempted to settle the long-standing dispute between the Dean of York, Dr John Scott, and his creditors.[18] Numerous hearings had been held and as late as October 1640 the council had commissioned new audits to settle the accounts. By September of 1641 the case had found its way into the House of Lords.[19] In December 1640 the council had undertaken the complaint of the creditors of Anthony Hooper and in response had appointed a special commission to investigate the accounts and report their recommendations for a settlement. In June 1641 the same creditors were applying to the House of Lords seeking settlement of precisely the same issues and requesting the appointment of a new commission to achieve their ends.[20] In late May 1640 the council had entertained a complaint from Sir Henry Worsley against a decree of the Commission of Sewers (later confirmed in the Exchequer Chamber) made on behalf of Sir Bevis Thelwall. The council had conducted a preliminary hearing on 21 May, during which the parties were directed to prepare briefs for consideration by a commission of referees. The king then promised to make a decision on the basis of their report.[21] The referees were Archbishop Laud, Lord Keeper Finch, Secretary Windebank and Lord Chief Justice Littleton. In late November 1640, Worsley complained to the upper house that 'no end had been made therein' and accordingly, 'with his Maties gracious favour', he was requesting that the Lords review his appeal.[22]

Perhaps the most striking case in this group was that of *Trelawny* v. *Babb*. At some stage during the 1630s a contract for goods had been negotiated in New England between Edward Trelawny and Thomas Babb. Differences appear to have arisen over the contract and Babb ultimately sued Trelawny successfully for recompense in the court of the Admiralty. Trelawny promptly brought an action for damages in King's Bench, citing the statute of 2 Henry IV, c. 11, which provided that double damages could be awarded where a suit had been wrongfully brought in the Admiralty court.[23] Babb then appealed to the council to stay the proceedings in King's Bench, arguing that his suit in the Admiralty had been perfectly jurisdictionally correct. The council agreed to hear the dispute on 3 July 1640, but was forced to delay the proceedings because the judges of King's Bench were then on circuit. The judges were ordered to attend the council on their return, and the King's Bench action was stayed in the meantime.[24] Despite those instructions, no further action was taken in council. On 1 February the case was brought before the House of Lords, not by the parties themselves, but by the Lord Admiral, the earl of Northumberland.[25]

Northumberland's action is, at the very least, suggestive of a lack of direction in council. The case clearly involved a major issue of court jurisdiction, such as had traditionally been resolved by recourse to king and council and, as Northumberland rightly pointed out, this particular dispute – between Admiralty and King's Bench – had been the subject of prolonged council debate in the early 1630s. Those discussions had led to what, in his mind at least, had been a definitive agreement between the respective courts executed in council in February 1632 granting the Admiralty court jurisdiction over all contractual disputes arising 'beyond the seas'.[26] Northumberland complained to the house that that agreement was being violated, not only by the King's Bench in this case, but by 'divers prohibitions and actions' which had recently been commenced 'to the infringeing of the Ancient Jurisdiction of that Court'. He requested that the Lords consider the articles of agreement and 'if they be just, afford them your authority or otherwise dismiss them'.

On the face of it, Northumberland's decision to bring this matter before the Lords made perfect sense. There would have been seemingly no better place to settle a jurisdictional conflict than in the High Court of the realm. But the matter was not that simple. This was an issue of considerable importance, over which the council had already assumed direct responsibility. The king himself had expressed a determination to settle the dispute only five months earlier. Removing the matter into the upper house might therefore have been seen as a direct affront to the council's authority and jurisdiction and under normal circumstances the king could have been expected to object. But there were no objections here. The king does not appear to have been concerned about (or perhaps even conscious of) such matters at this stage and Northumberland was allowed – by default or otherwise – to proceed with his appeal.[27]

There is some evidence to suggest that the king and council had made a collective decision in early January to divest themselves entirely of the responsibility of adjudicating private disputes – regardless of their content. On 10 January the board was informed by the clerk that numerous requests had been made by parliamentary committees for copies of council warrants and orders relating to such diverse matters as

Denzil Holles's imprisonment in 1628 and Alderman Abel's grant of the vintner's monopoly. Beecher requested some guidance on how to respond, and the king took the occasion to order that the clerk should 'from time to time give copies not only of the orders, petitions and warrants and complaints before mentioned, but also of any other warrants, orders, petitions, and complaints as concern any particular business between party and party'.[28] In principle, of course, the referral of private party suits to Parliament made sense. They were, as suggested earlier, generally considered a nuisance and a drain on the council's time and resources. Clearly, however, the issues raised by *Trelawny* v. *Babb* were out of the ordinary and the council's failure to address them suggests a rather striking level of distraction. Two subsequent references to the House of Lords, in April and June 1641, convey much the same impression. On 31 March the king received a petition from Samuel Cordwell, the Royal Gunpowder Maker, who asked to be relieved of his obligation to produce gunpowder for the Tower according to the terms of his annual contract. Cordwell explained that the House of Commons was then considering a petition attacking the royal gunpowder monopoly and he feared that 'if the manufacture of gunpowder not continue in his Maties hands' he in turn would lose his concession and, having produced the requisite gunpowder, would be bankrupted by the unusable stock. The king referred the matter to the council, who considered the matter at their next meeting.[29] In the end, however, 'after mature deliberation by his Matie with the advice of their Lopps' it was decided that the matter should be

> in his Maties name proposed and recommended unto the Lords of Parliament to the end that by conference with the House of Commons or otherwise, according to their Great wisdome, the said business may be settled for the service of his Matie and the safety of the Kingdom. And it is further ordered that in the meantime his Maties Attorney general and the rest of his Counsel learned should likewise consider the state of this business and the manufacture of Gunpowder as the same now pertains to the said Gunpowder maker, and prepare a certificate under their hands what they find touching his Maties right and legality of the said business, whereby to give the House of Lords a cleare satisfaction for the point of Law when the same by them shall be called for.[30]

Again, this reference seems somewhat surprising, at least in so far as the complaint directly involved the king's right to grant monopolies and, rather less directly, the defence of the realm. It is possible that the king sensed (or was convinced by members of the board) that he was still able to use the upper house to thwart the political ambitions of the lower and that some political advantage might be gained by being seen to defend his and his client's legal rights in Parliament, rather than through some direct action by the council. Significantly, perhaps, this meeting was attended by the earl of Bedford and Lords Say, Mandeville and Savile, all new members of the council who might well have argued for just such action. Though the evidence is hardly conclusive, this referral might have been Charles's one grudging concession to the politics of Bedford's undertaking. On the other hand, it is equally possible that the king remained wholly preoccupied at this stage with the fate of the earl of Strafford, and simply dismissed the matter to the upper house to be rid of it. There is, interestingly, no evidence that the king's legal case was ever prepared for the Lords' consideration by his legal counsel. The matter was never raised in the house, and the Commons' bill abolishing the monopoly was eventually passed.[31] On 16 July the earl of Newport complained to the upper house that the king's contracts with the gunpowder makers had not been fulfilled and there was now a 'scarceness' of powder in the forts.[32]

The second reference to the Lords was, if anything, even more telling. In late June 1641 the council was asked to arbitrate a major conflict which had erupted over the London shrievalty elections. On the 24th, the annual meeting of the mayor, aldermen and commonality of London had been held to elect the principal officers of the city. The mayor had rightfully claimed that tradition ('continued for 300 years or thereabouts') dictated that the mayor and aldermen elect one sheriff and the commonality the other. On this occasion, however, the Common Hall had insisted not only on the right to elect both sheriffs, but on the right to nominate and elect the chamberlain, bridgemasters and Auditors of Account. The parties had failed to agree and as a consequence the mayor and aldermen petitioned the king seeking 'directions'. The petition was considered on the 26th, and promptly referred to the upper house – 'His Matie, with the advice of his Privy Counsel, was pleased to recommend it to the Lords' House of Parliament to take such further order therein as they shall find cause.'[33]

The council's decision in this case is in dramatic contrast to the elaborate measures undertaken the previous September to regulate the London mayoral elections, when opposition from Common Hall had similarly threatened to displace the Crown's favoured candidate (and the rightful successor) Sir William Acton. On that occasion Secretary Windebank had insisted that the council intervene, both to protect tradition and to ensure the election of a sympathetic candidate. The situation as it then stood, Windebank had said, 'falls out most unhappily now that the State has so much cause to use the City'.[34] That sort of reasoning ought to have been even more applicable in June. Events over the previous six months, and especially those surrounding Strafford's trial, should have amply demonstrated the need to maintain close ties with the centres of power in London, in particular with the mayor and aldermen, who had been for the most part politically and financially supportive of the Crown. The dispute at hand ought to have been seen as a compelling (if admittedly risky) opportunity to manage events, either to reinforce the Crown's alliance with the city government, or to effect a Crown sponsored compromise amenable to both sides which would reflect favourably on the king. Instead, either through bad advice or plain indifference the problem (and ultimately the credit) was passed to the House of Lords.[35]

THE ABOLITION OF THE PREROGATIVE COURTS

The upper house would also inherit a variety of problems and private cases as a consequence of the abrupt demise of the prerogative courts. Star Chamber would in fact pose the most immediate problems. It is not clear at what point the court ceased to function altogether – Professor Phillips suggests that it simply 'faded away' in the aftermath of the impeachments in the autumn of 1640 – but there is little doubt that its precipitate disappearance left a good deal of pending litigation unresolved. Again, dissatisfied litigants found their way to the House of Lords. The first such case arose in March 1641, brought by the earl of Lindsey, the Lord Great Chamberlain, against Sir Walter Norton, a former sheriff of Lincolnshire. The complaint involved Norton's administration of the Ship Money levy in the 1630s. As Lord Lieutenant of Lincolnshire, Lindsey had received numerous complaints, beginning in 1637, alleging that Norton had abused his authority and had used the Ship Money writ to extort great sums of money from the inhabitants of the county. He was alleged to have taxed certain towns and villages 'sundrie times' and was accused of lessening or abating the excess levies in exchange for various bribes and rewards. In all, he was said to have collected some £4,000 more than he had warrant for and was said to have used the surplus to fill his own purse.[36] Lindsey had in fact complained to the king about Norton in 1637 and had been commissioned to investigate the charges, but Norton managed to persuade the council to supersede Lindsey's commission in favour of proceedings by the justices on assize. According to Lindsey, they had eventually declared Norton a 'delinquent' and in February 1639, the Attorney General had brought an information against him in Star Chamber. A commission set out from the court in late February to examine witnesses and take depositions. A second commission followed in July and a third almost a year later, in June 1640. Witnesses were still being interrogated the following December.[37] By January, however, it had become clear that the prosecution would not be carried forward. (Attorney General Bankes, who had personally taken charge of the case, had by that stage been elevated to the post of Chief Justice of Common

Pleas.) The earl of Lindsey was determined, however, that Norton should be punished and accordingly appealed to the House of Lords to prosecute the case. A month earlier, on 2 February, the house had ordered the Lord Keeper to issue a writ of *ne exeat regnum* against Norton, to prevent his escape from the kingdom, but it is not clear who informed the house on this occasion of the 'divers misdemeanors' against him.[38] On receiving Lindsey's petition on 4 March the house ordered the Gentleman Usher to bring Norton to London to answer the charges. He appeared at the bar on 22 April, at which point he was required to put in bail of £5,000, and was remanded in custody until he had done so.[39] On 14 June he was ordered to put in his answer to Lindsey's petition and two weeks later, on 1 July, the house directed that all depositions and exhibits returned into Star Chamber on the Attorney General's information should now be delivered into the house for their use.[40] On 16 July a preliminary hearing was held, with counsel present on both sides, and Norton was granted a new commission to examine witnesses in which the earl was to be allowed to participate, and to which both parties would nominate members.[41] The new commission was to be returned the second week of Michaelmas term. By March 1642, however, the case had still not received a formal hearing and no further proceedings appear to have taken place, presumably because of the outbreak of hostilities and the earl's subsequent death at the battle of Edgehill.[42]

The earl of Lindsey was not the only complainant who turned to the upper house when Star Chamber failed to reconvene. In early June 1641 Sir Gilbert Gerrard petitioned the house complaining that his own Star Chamber action against George Pitt had been brought to a halt. At some stage in the previous year he had preferred a bill against Pitt for what he called 'an outrageous and barbarous Ryott'. (Pitt and others had apparently cut down, in the dead of night, a row of thirty-two trees adjoining Gerrard's manor house in Middlesex.) Gerrard's suit in Star Chamber had proceeded to examination and publication, but, as Gerrard complained, 'Yor Petr can have noe fruite of his said suite by reason there hath been noe sitting in the Cort of Star Chamber since the beginning of this present Parliament'.[43] As a prominent member of the House of Commons, Gerrard would have been aware that the court was unlikely to sit again – the Commons' committee had recommended the abolition of the court on 31 May – and he requested that the Lords take charge of his cause.[44] The case was accepted and scheduled for hearing on 29 June. The hearing was then postponed to 21 July, but on that day the defendant, Pitt, failed to appear. Having been given ample notice, he was fined £5 costs and the case was rescheduled to the 27th. On this occasion Pitt appeared and argued that as lord of the manor he was entitled to do what he liked with the property. He claimed, somewhat more cogently, that the case turned on a dispute over the customs of the manor and that issue, he insisted, was only triable at common law. He requested that it be dismissed accordingly. The Lords agreed that the matter ought to receive a trial at law, and with Gerrard's consent they directed that he bring an action to try the custom of the manor in King's Bench the following term. Pitt was then given strict instructions to plead to the action without delay and was required to provide Gerrard with copies of the manor court rolls for his use over the next month. Gerrard was then given permission to reapply to the house for consideration of damages if the outcome of the trial made that appropriate.[45]

Once the court had been abolished by statute, new problems arose. On 1 August the Lords received a petition similar to Gerrard's from Thomas Pococke. Pococke had been a defendant in an action of trespass and assault at the Berkshire assizes during Michaelmas term 1639. He had in fact been convicted of trespass, but he alleged that the witnesses had been bribed to perjure themselves in the plaintiff's behalf and, as a consequence, he had petitioned the king for permission to sue out a bill for subornation in Star Chamber. The bill had eventually been preferred but had been abated by the court's abolition. Pococke therefore requested that the Lords 'cast your eyes upon the bill, and convent the delinquents before you'.[46]

Far more serious was the problem presented to the house on 24 July by the judges of King's Bench. Earlier in the term one Wooten, a prisoner in the Fleet, had applied to the court for a writ of habeas corpus. The writ was granted and the return subsequently indicated that Wooten had been imprisoned by Star Chamber, after having been convicted on a charge of 'challenging for a duel'. (He had also been fined £500 to the king and £200 to the complainant.) His attorney argued for his release on the basis of Parliament's recent declarations in the act abolishing the court. As the judges pointed out to the Lords, his reasoning had been sound. The preamble to the act had condemned the judges of Star Chamber for failing to keep to the points limited by the statutes of 3 Henry VII and 21 Henry VIII, which were cited in the act as the statutory basis for the court's jurisdiction. The obvious inference from the wording was that the court had only had jurisdiction over offences mentioned in the Henrician statutes and since challenging for a duel was not one of them, Wooten's counsel had 'pressed it very strongly' that he be released.

The implication of his arguments was clear. As the judges suggested to the house in a classic piece of understatement, 'it might go far to look back to all Decrees of that Court which have been made in Cases not expressed in the Statute of 3 Henry VII, which are very many in several ages since that Time'.[47] They had accordingly taken time to advise before proceeding further and requested directions from the house. The Lords resolved to take the matter up with the House of Commons at their next conference, but no further action was taken. On 27 November the judges again reported that a writ of habeas corpus had been granted to Wooten and would be returned to court the following Monday. They again sought directions from the house and were instructed to 'forebear to deliver your opinions or to make any rule in the cause' until the house had debated the matter the following week.[48] No debate ever took place and the judges appear to have been left to their own devices. The Lords' failure to respond may have been deliberate. It was, to some extent, a 'no-win' situation. Any declaration would undoubtedly have drawn attention to the flaws in the statute and would just have surely generated a flood of requests for review of recent (and not so recent) Star Chamber decrees. The Lords would not have wanted to undertake that kind of wholesale review. What was needed, of course, was a clarifying amendment to the act, but that required cooperation from the Commons and it is unlikely that either house would have been inclined at this sensitive stage to tinker with one of their most recent and notable legislative accomplishments. If nothing else, doing so would have left the impression that they had acted recklessly and with too much haste. It may have been decided simply to ignore the problem in the hope that it would go away. It is also possible, of course, that the neglect simply reflected the Lords' preoccupation with other more urgent matters – not least the Irish rebellion – at this crucial juncture.[49]

They did not, on the other hand, hesitate to offer assistance and protection to officers and employees of either prerogative court. Beginning in mid-June, the Lords began to receive petitions from officers and attorneys of Star Chamber and High Commission asking to be considered for compensation once the courts had been 'vacated'. The clerk of the process of Star Chamber, Thomas Saunders, petitioned the house on 29 June complaining that the court's demise would deprive him of an office (which he had held by patent for the previous eight years) valued at over £5,000. He claimed that he had 'never offended (at least knowingly or willfully) in his place' and he asked the Lords to 'take pity' and make provision for his maintenance and that of his wife and ten children.[50] His petition was preceded by one from Barnabas Holloway, his underclerk, and followed by one from William Pennyman, one of the court attorneys.[51] A similar request was presented at roughly the same time by John Wragg, a pursuivant from the court of High Commission (who attempted to enhance his plea by enclosing a list of all the Catholics whom he claimed to have personally exposed during and since the Gunpowder Plot).[52]

The king himself intervened on their behalf in early July. Three days after the abolition bills had received the royal assent, he submitted a formal request via the earl of Essex that Parliament consider the plight of the officers and decide 'how they might have reparation for the loss of their several offices'.[53] In fact, the Lords had already established a committee to consider the problem and the king's request was forwarded to them for a report.[54] On 13 July the bishop of Lincoln reported to the house that the committee

> are of the Opinion, and do not conceive of any fitter Way of Reliefe for these poor Officers, the King's Servants, than to remit them to the King's mercy, that His Majesty would be graciously pleased to allow a proportionate Relief ... out of such fines as may accrue to his Majesty in the High Court of Parliament, to be apportioned by the Lords of the Committee, or otherwise, as their Lordships shall be pleased to approve of.[55]

Under the circumstances, the recommendation seemed appropriate enough.[56]

The abolition of the courts created one further problem in this regard, which derived, if inadvertently, from the legislation itself. Both of the pivotal acts passed on 2 July had declared that the courts had acted beyond the scope of their statutory authority. Star Chamber was said to have 'undertaken to punish where no Law doth warrant, and to make decrees for things having no such authority'. High Commission was likewise said, among other things, to have exercised authority 'not belonging to the ecclesiastical jurisdiction'. Neither act, however, had anticipated that those declarations would be seen as an open invitation to seek redress, on an individual basis, for the alleged wrongs perpetrated by the courts and their officers. No provision was made in the statutes to indemnify those officers from subsequent legal actions. The repercussions were felt almost immediately. On 6 August the house received a petition from Henry Hopkins, Warden of the Fleet.[57] Hopkins complained that he was then being sued for false imprisonment by two residents of the Fleet. The first, Sir Edmund Plowden, had been committed by High Commission for refusing to provide maintenance for his wife according to an earlier decree of the court. Plowden had in fact appealed for release on two previous occasions: once to the House of Lords during the Short Parliament, and subsequently to King's Bench on a writ of habeas corpus, both times without success. In November 1640 Plowden again petitioned the Lords and was eventually persuaded by the house to perform the High Commission decree. After paying the specified amount and giving security for the 'well-usage' of his wife, he had been released from the Fleet (without, as Hopkins complained, paying the £30 in fees he owed the warden).[58] Notwithstanding those proceedings, Plowden had then commenced a suit for false imprisonment against Hopkins and his officers, 'pretending illegality' on the basis of the declarations in the statute regarding the court's authority.

The other prisoner, Thomas Insley, had been committed by the council for refusing to distrain for Ship Money. He had finally been released by the board and had recently been awarded £50 damages against Hopkins in a similar action. Hopkins protested that he had been required to perform his duty as an officer, and 'not to dispute the jurisdiction of the courts'. He claimed as well that 'more of these vexations are threatened agst yor Petr since the suppressing of the Star Chamber, and the regulating of the Counsel Board, and questioning the Courts at White Hall'. He asked that he might not 'suffer for his discharging his duty to obedience and be questioned by every perverse spirit that now seeketh his disquiet upon the advantage of the suppression of those courts'.[59] The Lords immediately ordered that Hopkins be freed 'of and from all Suits or judgement that are, or shall, or may grow' in consequence of his performing his duty. They then directed that 'if there be any cause of complaint, they are to take their course or remedy against the prosecutors, and not against any officers that are merely ministerial'.[60]

The Lords appear to have clearly understood the implications of Hopkins's appeal. Three weeks later when the House of Commons requested the Lords' concurrence in its additional resolutions concerning the Council in the North, the upper house felt compelled to enter a caution. The first Commons' resolution had declared that the 'Commission and Instructions' issued to the President and Council in the North had been illegal 'both in creation and execution'.[61] The Lords, while concurring in the declaration, expressed their concern that 'in regard of the word "illegal" . . . there may be some Danger and Trouble accrue to the judgement, and judges that have been ministers of Justice there and have done and made those sentences and judgement which they thought in their consciences to be just'. They therefore declared their opinion that

> such Judgement, Decrees, and Sentences that have been Justly made by the Judges and Officers, and no matter of corruption appearing against such Judges, shall not be liable to any Trouble or Question hereafter; but the Judgement and Decrees are to stand good, unless there be some lawful cause to question the same, other than the Illegality of the Constitution of the said Court.[62]

The order made in August in answer to Hopkins's petition and this admonition were not apparently effective in pre-empting further suits against the officers. By February 1642 the problem appears to have escalated significantly, and the Lords resolved on a more decisive course of action. Serjeants Glanville and Whitfield were ordered to draw a bill

> for the preventing of suits commenced after the 10th day of February 1642 against any Sheriffs, Constables, Gaolers, and other Ministers and Officers, for executing or obeying any Warrant, Order, Decree, or Process from the High Commission, Star Chamber, Courte of York

and Stannaries; and for the staying of all Actions and Suits brought before the said 10th of February 1642, against any of the said Officers or Ministers, for executing any such Order, Decree, Warrant or Process, whereupon no judgement was had before the 10th day of February aforesaid.[63]

Other responsibilities outstanding in the wake of the court's abolition (and the council's decline) were assumed with equal alacrity. Late in July 1641 the inhabitants of Westminster and the surrounding London suburbs addressed a petition to the house claiming

that where several proclamations, decrees of the Cort of Star Chamber, and Orders of the Council, as well in time of the late Queen Elizabeth and King James, as of his now Matie, were made and published for the relief of the poor, suppression of Inmates, and the prevencion of the growing infection of the Plague; Since the dissolving of the Court of Star Chamber, some question hath arisen how far the same shall be put in execution, by reason whereof, the reliefe of the poor, restraint of inmates, and the usual means to prevent the spreading of the plague are like to be neglected.

The inhabitants requested that the upper house 'order the justices and ministers appointed and trusted to put the same into execucon, do carefully perform the same, or that some such orders may be speedilie set downe by yor Lopps.'[64] The Lords appear to have raised the matter with the House of Commons and orders were issued, though they remain unrecorded. On 21 October the Lord Keeper, reporting the business conducted by the Committee for the Recess, informed the house that on 5 October the committee had ensured that Parliament's previous orders to the burgesses of Westminster had been enforced. The burgesses and their assistants had been 'strictly required' to see the same orders 'duly executed and observed'.[65]

MAINTAINING THE PUBLIC PEACE

The reaction to the Westminster petition was hardly surprising. By this stage the Lords had amply demonstrated their abiding concern with the maintenance of public order. Their responsibilities in this area had begun almost from the opening of the first session, when the council seemingly abdicated its traditional role in directing law enforcement. In early November 1640 the council could still be seen taking charge of public disorders. On the 1st, for example, the board was informed of a major riot – described as a 'seditious tumult' – committed by some sixty people in St Paul's, London, and responded promptly and decisively, commanding the mayor the same day to convene a commission of oyer and terminer 'to proceed with all care and diligence for the discovery . . . and punishment of the present disorder'.[66] On the 29th a similar disorder in the parish church of Halstead, Essex, was reported to the council by the Lords Lieutenant, the earl of Warwick and Lord Maynard. This time, by contrast, the Lord Keeper was directed to inform the House of Lords of the matter and to recommend the 'examination and proceedings thereof' to the 'Justice and Wisdom of their Honorable House'.[67] In theory, there was nothing to prevent the board from directing the Attorney General to initiate proceedings against these delinquents in Star Chamber – no action had been taken against the court at this point.[68] Nor, for that matter, was there anything preventing the council from acting as it had before, to initiate proceedings locally, or indeed, to summon the delinquent parties before the board. But neither action was pursued and the referral to the upper house established a pattern. The evidence suggests that a decision – however informal and unofficial – had been made to transfer these responsibilities into the House of Lords.[69] Certainly, the Council's own activity in this area declined markedly from then on. Only three times in the subsequent twelve months did the board take measures to ensure public order. All three orders were directed exclusively to London, and each was general and precautionary: on 1 March the Lord Mayor was directed to muster the trained bands and establish careful watches in anticipation of Lent celebrations on Shrove Tuesday; on 21 March the same order was issued before the commencement of the earl of Strafford's trial; and on 26 April it was reissued in advance of May Day.[70] By contrast, the upper house was actively engaged, often at the direction of the Crown, in the suppression of numerous public disorders which arose at intervals during the first year of the Parliament.

Religious disorders

The riot in Halstead church was only the first of a number of serious disturbances in local parishes for which the house took responsibility. Their response to the king's request in this case was typical. When the Lord Keeper reported the incident on 30 November, the house took immediate steps to apprehend those involved with the aid of the Deputy Lieutenants and the local JPs.[71] Ten days later the delinquents, led by Jonathan Poole, were brought before the house to answer the charges. The charges were serious indeed. The defendants were accused of entering the church during divine service and assaulting the curate. They allegedly knocked the prayer book from his hands and kicked it up and down the church, calling it a 'popish' book. They then took the curate by the throat and forced him to surrender his surplice and hood, which they subsequently tore into pieces in the middle of the church. The defendants denied the charges and as a consequence the Lords directed that a formal hearing be held. Poole and his associates were committed to the Fleet to await trial. Witnesses were summoned and the hearing took place a week later on 19 December. Testimony from numerous witnesses ultimately proved the charges and the defendants were severely censured for their 'foul and contemptuous' behaviour. They were reminded that the *Book of Common Prayer* had been 'established and confirmed by Act of Parliament' and that their behaviour was therefore an 'Offence of a very high Nature'. The Lords then issued a general warning that 'if any Person whatsoever shall hereafter dare presume to commit the like Offence, he shall be severely and exemplarily punished'. The defendants, 'being poor and silly men', were released from the Fleet on condition that they make a formal submission and apology before the congregation of the parish in the presence of the two responsible JPs.[72]

Problems of a slightly different nature surfaced in January. On the 16th, at the request of the king, the Lord Privy Seal transmitted to the house a report on the activities of a group of sectaries from the London borough of Southwark.[73] They had been apprehended while holding a conventicle and had been brought before the local JP, Sir John Lenthall. During interrogation the leaders of the group had reportedly refused to return to their parish churches and, in the process had repudiated both the authority of the bishops and the king's authority in religious matters. Lenthall reported the incident to the house and was ordered to bring the group before the Lords the following Monday morning. The Lords then ordered that

> the Divine service be performed as it is appointed by the Acts of Parliament of this Realm; and all that shall disturb that wholesome order shall be severely punished according to Law. And that Parsons, Vicars, and Curates in [their] several parishes shall forbear to introduce any rites or ceremonies that may give offence otherwise than those that are established by the Laws of this Land.[74]

When the leading sectaries appeared two days later they denied the charges. Nonetheless, witnesses again provided sworn testimony and the Lords were satisfied of their guilt. Surprisingly, however, the Lords elected to free them with only an admonition. They were ordered to attend their parish churches to hear divine service and were 'to give obedience thereunto'. They were then read the Lords' order of 16 January and were warned that if they failed to heed its commands they would be 'severely punished according to the Law'.[75]

The impact of the Lords' general order was understandably undermined to some extent by a wholly contradictory declaration of intent issued by the House of Commons a week later.[76] On 23 January, the lower house had elected to appoint new county commissioners who were to be responsible for seeing that 'all images, altars or tables turned altarwise, crucifixes, superstitious pictures, ornaments, or relics of idolatry' were removed from the churches in their shire.[77] Curiously, the Commons' action failed to provoke any reaction or protest from the Lords. It did not apparently go unnoticed by others, however, and on at least three subsequent occasions the Lords were forced to carry out their promise to enforce the law.

In early June two parishes in the same London borough of Southwark erupted in violence and the Lords brought the full force of their authority to bear on the troublemakers. On 9 June the parishioners of the churches of St Saviour and St Olave petitioned the house complaining of 'great disorders' during the communion services. It was alleged that seven men of the parish of St Saviour had entered the church during the administration of the sacrament and had pulled down the rails around the communion table 'in a violent and tumultous manner'. Four other men were said to have interrupted the service in the church of St Olave by making a 'great tumult and disorder' and by abusing the minister with irreverent speeches. All of the troublemakers were named by the petitioners, and all were promptly summoned before the house on 17 June. A full hearing was held to consider both cases. The accused were allowed to speak for themselves, and extended testimony was taken from witnesses. Both groups were found guilty of the complaints made against them. Consequently, in the parish of St Saviour the Lords ordered that the rails were to be replaced 'about the communion table in the same manner as they have been for the space of fifty years last past, not as they have been for four or five years last past'.[78] The charges for the new rails were to be assessed against the troublemakers, who were in addition to make a full public submission for their faults before their congregation. They were then committed to the Fleet 'during the pleasure of the House' where they remained for the next month.[79] The miscreants of the parish of St Olave were treated rather more severely. Two of them were committed to the Fleet for six months and fined £20 to the king. On their release they were directed to make a full submission 'upon a high stool in Cheapside and Southwark for two hours on two market days', and were to enter into bonds for future good behaviour. The other two were likewise committed to the Fleet until they could provide sureties to guarantee their appearance at the next Surrey assizes, where they were to be proceeded against 'according to the Law'.[80]

Later in June the house entertained a petition lodged by the parishioners of St Thomas Apostle in London. They too complained that a group of men had entered their church 'in a violent manner' and removed the communion rails. Again the miscreants were summoned to the house, but in this case (for reasons that are not entirely clear) the dispute was referred to Lord Seymour. On 13 July Seymour reported to the house that the differences between the parishioners and the defendants had been settled and 'composed'. Nonetheless, the house insisted that the offenders be punished and accordingly fined them £10 apiece for their misdemeanors, which they were then directed to pay to the overseers of the poor of the parish.[81]

The punitive actions taken by the house in these cases (and the evident reasoning behind them) help to explain their angry response to the Commons' subsequent declarations on religious practice issued in early September, just prior to the parliamentary recess.[82] The published resolutions of the lower house – again endorsing a wholesale and largely indiscriminate attack on 'innovations' – not only seriously compromised the Lords' own efforts to combat iconoclasm, but publicly undermined the authority of the High Court itself, by suggesting (albeit indirectly) that the penalties already imposed by the Lords were unwarranted and unjust. That, as much as anything else, compelled the upper house to publish its earlier order of 16 January, reiterating the demand that the divine service be conducted according to statute law. Their position on the matter had remained consistent and it was vitally important that that be clearly understood.[83]

During the same period, of course, the Lords were equally diligent in rooting out clerical misconduct which appeared potentially disruptive. It should be stressed, however, that in following up these complaints the Lords were only attempting to fill the vacuum created by the collapse of the church courts and, ultimately, of High Commission. They were not, as Shaw has suggested, exercising 'dictatorial' powers in a coordinated campaign with the House of Commons to usurp clerical jurisdiction in the interests of initiating ecclesiastical reform.[84] In the first place, the number of petitions presented was insignificant, certainly by comparison with the hundreds presented to the lower house. The Lords entertained just over a dozen such complaints in the first two years of the Parliament and their response to them was anything but draconian or arbitrary.[85] For the most part the charges were quite mundane. In May 1641, for example, the inhabitants of the parish of Abbotisham, Devon, charged their vicar, Nicholas Honny, with drunkenness and absenteeism.[86] Similar complaints were made, also in May, against the vicar of the parish of Kensington,[87] and in August the inhabitants of Cropedy, Oxfordshire, complained that their minister, Mr Brounker, refused to reside in the parish and underpaid his curates.[88] All three of these petitions were referred to the Committee for Petitions and appear to have been settled through arbitration. In early February the house had also entertained a petition from the parishioners of the village of Pilton, Somerset, who complained that their vicar, Nathaniel Abbot, had failed to read the divine service or administer communion since Christmas. The house responded by ordering the errant minister to 'perform his Duty in discharging his said Cure, as formerly he hath done'. They then directed that the 'Peculiar of the said Hamlet doth take care that the Divine Prayers and sacraments be read and administered as they ought to be'.[89] The house does appear to have been rather more concerned about two additional clerics, Mr Knowles and Mr Grey, who were alleged to have preached 'seditious sermons' in the city of London in late December 1641. Their reaction here, however, was to order the Attorney General to proceed against them according to the law.[90]

In only three cases did the house take (or attempt to take) direct action to deprive a sitting cleric after a hearing. In two instances they were responding to allegations that the ministers involved were crypto-Catholics and in the third to claims that the cleric was a devout and practising Arminian. In early December 1640 the inhabitants of Banbury claimed that their vicar, John Howes, was a person 'ill-affected to the State' and had for two successive years refused to execute the prescribed ceremonies on 5 November – 'in memory of the Great Deliverance from the Powder Plot' – refusing in particular to utter the words 'whose religion is rebellion and whose faith is faction'. In addition he was alleged to have 'cast out aspersions' on the character of Lord Say and Sele.[91] The vicar was brought before the house and, rather surprisingly, was acquitted. The house decided, after a lengthy hearing, that 'there was not sufficient proof made whereby to censure Mr Howes on those particulars'. They did, not surprisingly, decide to proceed against him for maligning Lord Say and Sele. However, Lord Say himself declared (somewhat testily) that if the house did not see fit to censure Mr Howes, they ought not to bother to proceed against him at all, and he asked that the secondary charges be remitted. Howe was nonetheless committed to the Fleet overnight, and was released on making a formal apology to Say at the bar.[92]

The charges against Hugh Reeve, a clerk in the parish of Ampthill, Bedfordshire, were more convincing. In early February his parishioners, led by Benjamin Rhodes, alleged that Reeve had preached the doctrine of transubstantiation, that he had been confessed by a 'popish priest', that he had been reconciled to the church of Rome and that he had persuaded others to do the same. The parishioners' accusations were taken seriously (not least because Reeve had served as a bishop's surrogate) and the whole matter was heard by the Lords' Committee for Courts of Justice. In the event, Reeve confessed to the truth of most of the charges and agreed to make a recantation devised by the bishops of Durham and Salisbury. The committee subsequently reported to the house that Reeve 'hath not done these things out of Malice, which if they were would deserve a far greater Censure, but out of Ignorance,' and they therefore recommended that as a punishment he be deprived only of his ecclesiastical livings. Their recommendation was adopted and Reeve was disabled for life.[93]

The same fate awaited Dr John Pocklington of Cardington, Bedfordshire. One of his parishioners, a Mr Harvey, had petitioned the house in January 1641 claiming that Pocklington was superstitious and idolatrous and had published two pamphlets 'wherein he defends all of those unhappy innovations introduced into the church'.[94] Harvey's petition was referred to the Committee for Petitions, and Pocklington was summoned to answer the charges.[95] The committee reviewed the evidence and examined both pamphlets and concluded that he was in fact 'a great Instrument and Introducer of Innovations in the Church, and a Perverter of the People'. Pocklington does appear to have been a textbook Laudian cleric and the committee was careful to enumerate his errors in their report. His conduct of services had been 'very superstitious and full of Idolatry, as bowing to the Altar, and using many gestures and ceremonies in the church, not being established by the Laws of this Realm'. His doctrine, as outlined in the two pamphlets, they had found 'most seditious and Dangerous', from his claim that 'Altars are the Throne of the Great God on Earth, and we must bow to them', to his insistence that 'Canons and Constitutions of the Church are to be obeyed without examining or looking into them'. According to the committee, Pocklington had twice before recanted his 'unsound views' (and appears to have offered a third recantation to the Lords) but remained unreformed. He was guilty, they claimed, of 'things which, by the Common Law, he is to be deprived for'. The house endorsed their findings and Pocklington was deprived of all his ecclesiastical preferments.[96]

The committee's report in this case is notable for two reasons: for the severity of its condemnation and for the repeated references to the law. The former suggests, perhaps not surprisingly, that the Lords were as intolerant of 'popish' innovators as they were of radical or indeed revolutionary 'reformers'. The latter attests to their continuing and impartial reliance on the rule of law as the basis of their decisions. Their insistence that Pocklington's innovative ceremonial practices had never been 'established by the Laws of this Realm' reflected that strongly held view (clearly articulated in other contexts) that the Laudian innovations had never received proper legal sanction. Their claim that his transgressions warranted deprivation 'by the common law' arose ostensibly from a straightforward reading of the statute of 13 Elizabeth I, c. 12, which specifically required that a cleric be deprived when he was found to endorse (or maintain) doctrines contrary to those expressed in the Thirty-nine Articles.[97] The Lords in fact resorted to the law, both in these cases and in the ones just discussed, with a common aim. Simply put, what they were attempting to do – and what they felt senior clerical officials ought to have done, clearly did not do and now could not do

– was to protect the established church of Elizabeth and James from the various and disruptive forces of change.

Agrarian disorder

The Lords' fundamentally conservative approach to threats of disorder was evident as well in their response to agrarian riots. Again, the problems arose in the early months of the Parliament. The first request for assistance was presented on 26 February by the Royal Commissioners for the Prince's Revenue, who complained of numerous enclosure riots on the prince's lands at Berkhampsted, Hertfordshire.[98] The Lords responded in customary fashion. The Gentleman Usher was ordered to apprehend the named offenders and to keep them in his custody prior to a full hearing which took place on 6 April at the bar of the house with counsel heard on both sides. The defendants apparently attempted to justify their actions by claiming right of common on the properties and the evidence suggests that the Lords were, to some extent, sympathetic. In the event, the house ordered that the prince should be maintained in his quiet possession, but they stressed that he was entitled to protection by virtue of his parliamentary privilege, as a nominal member of the house, and not on the basis of any implied determination on the question of title, which they left 'to the determination of the Law, after the time of the Privilege of Parliament'. The charge against the defendants, having been fully proved, was then 'remitted' with a warning that any similar behaviour in the future would be 'severely punished'.[99]

Later in May the house was informed of further enclosure riots in the king's properties in Hounslow Heath, Middlesex.[100] Again, orders went out to the justices of the county to quiet the king's possessions and to apprehend those responsible, if necessary with the aid of the Lord Lieutenant and his deputies. On 2 June seven delinquents were presented and the house ordered that they be tried at the next Middlesex quarter sessions. In the meantime they were to put in sufficient bail to guarantee their appearance to answer the indictments.[101] The same instructions were issued in June to quiet the possessions of the earl of Hertford in Somerset[102] and those of the bishop of Lincoln at Buckden.[103] In the latter case the riot had been particularly severe with extensive damage to the properties. The 'principal actors' were therefore summoned before the house and imprisoned in the Fleet until they agreed to make a formal submission and apology at the bar, which they did roughly two weeks later.[104]

Beginning in April and May the house had also been preoccupied with various riots in the fens. On 2 April the queen's agents complained that certain improved lands in Somersham, part of the Great Level in Huntingdonshire, had been illegally occupied and that fences had been destroyed by certain 'disorderly persons', some of whom had also refused to pay their rents. On the 6th, the earl of Lindsey made an identical complaint to the house about riots in the Lincolnshire fens, and on the 22nd the earls of Bedford and Portland sought assistance in suppressing riots in Whittlesey, Isle of Ely.[105] Initially the Lords followed roughly the same procedure in each case. Order was given to establish quiet possession for the undertakers and their tenants, 'until proceedings in Parliament or other Courts of Justice determine otherwise', and directions were issued to local authorities – to sheriffs or JPs or both – to apprehend the offenders and bring them before the house.[106] However, as Keith Lindley has suggested, these measures were not always effective and disturbances continued throughout the spring and summer in all three areas, particularly in the Lindsey Level.[107] On at least one occasion the Lords were forced to order that the trained bands be mustered, and on two others were compelled to summon local magistrates to the house to answer for their failure to perform the directives of the upper house.[108] One of them, William Lockton, a Lincolnshire JP, was in fact dismissed from the Commission of the Peace for what appeared to be flagrant disobedience – though the Lord Keeper was allowed to reinstate him if and when he proved himself worthy.[109] The Lords' measures were rarely heavy handed. Imprisonment in the Fleet was regularly used, but rarely lasted for more than two weeks (if that) and was normally remitted sooner when the parties agreed to make a formal apology at the bar and a public submission in the locality. On one occasion in May the house did sentence the offenders to be pilloried for their spoken contempt of the Lords' orders, but the sentence was remitted when the earl of Lindsey, the original complainant, requested that they be spared.[110] In June the house began to require that the offenders enter into bonds for good behaviour, usually of £100, but in no case were other fines imposed.[111] Of course, the journey to London and an extended stay there could prove a considerable hardship in itself, but the house was careful to insist that any complainant who failed to prove the charges of misconduct should be liable to the defendant's costs.[112] Damages were awarded against two offenders in one incident, but only after a lengthy hearing and the charges proved; the damages amounted to only £30, far less than the £180 requested by the complainant, Sir William Killigrew.[113]

In so far as these disturbances represented a challenge to the authority of decrees of the Commissions of Sewers – and at least indirectly they all did – the responsibility for dealing with them did actually belong to the upper house. The king had reminded the Lords of that fact in early May when he presented them with a special paper on the subject of fen drainage. He complained to the house that the great benefits of the various drainage projects were being endangered by increasing public vandalism and by unwarranted attacks against commission decrees at common law.

He pointed out that the Commissions of Sewers were courts of record, whose orders and decrees were 'not subject to be repealed by any other jurisdiction but by Parliament . . . where the Legallety and Equitie thereof is examinable and is to receive the judgement of the Supreame Court'. He requested that they 'take cognisance of this Great and General Business . . . and so to settle ye undertakers in their peaceable possession in all places until the whole matter may be fully heard and determined in this High Court in such Just and Equitable Way as shall be thought fit'.[114] The king was clearly concerned that the projects and the undertakers be secured, but he was perfectly right to expect that they should be, until proper legal recourse had been exercised. The statute of 1531 (to which the king was clearly alluding) did in fact specify that any commission decrees properly certified, engrossed and assented to could not 'in any wise be reformed unless it be by authority of Parliament'.[115] The statute clearly only referred to formal legal appeals and not to 'challenges' made by more direct physical means, but the king's request that the Lords secure the undertakers' peaceable possession was perfectly in keeping with the authority conferred by statute and was in his view appropriate to the responsibilities of the 'Supreame Court'.[116]

The Lords' response to the fenland riots needs to be seen in that context. Keith Lindley has characterized their role in dealing with these riots as entirely partisan and motivated by self-interest – the Lords 'springing' to offer assistance to fellow members of the house whose complaints were always 'sympathetically' heard.[117] It is true, as he points out, that the undertakers' complaints generated a far more decisive response in the upper house than in the lower (where 'influential voices' instead made 'sympathetic noises' in support of the fenmen),[118] but that decisiveness was not motivated by the Lords' wish simply to protect the vested interests of the undertakers and their clients. It was motivated by their determination to maintain order and preserve the public peace. On at least three occasions the Lords entertained petitions from fenmen requesting a hearing on their legal right to common areas and, while the hearings were delayed (due in large measure to the press of other judicial business), the Lords scrupulously avoided taking any action which might later prejudice a determination on questions of common right or title. Their primary aim, clearly and repeatedly stated, was to restore order on a temporary basis until proper legal proceedings could be initiated.

In early July the house was forced, in response to continuing complaints both from the fens and elsewhere, to issue a general order for the suppression of riots and tumults. The wording of that order offers an appropriate summary of the Lords' central concerns:

> Whereas daily complaints are made unto this House, of violent breaking into possessions and Inclosures, in riotous and tumltuous

manner, in several Parts of this Kingdom, without any due Proceeding by Course of Law to warrant the same, which have been observed to have been done more frequently since this Parliament began than formerly; It is thought fit and so Ordered, by the Lords in Parliament, that no Inclosure or Possession shall be violently, or in a tumultuous manner, disturbed or taken away from any man which was in his possession on the first day of this Parliament or before, but by due Course and Form of Law; and that such possessions of all men shall continue and remain unto them as they were on the first day of this meeting of Parliament, unless it hath been or shall be by some legal Way of Proceeding in some of his Majesty's Courts of Law or Equity, or by some Act or Order of Parliament determined or ordered to the contrary.[119]

The Lords' response to the public disorders in London in November and December 1641 sheds further light on their attitude and methods (as well as on those of the Commons). The Lords were greatly alarmed by the riots in Westminster on 29 and 30 November, and on 1 December they ordered the judges in the house 'to consult amongst themselves what course is fit to be taken to prevent Riots, Routs, and unlawful assemblies, and having considered the Laws and Statutes in this case, to present their opinions to this House'.[120] The next day, Chief Justice Bramston reported their opinion that the best way to handle the problem was to invoke the provisions of the statute of 2 Henry V, c. 8. That statute had provided that where local JPs, sheriffs, or undersheriffs had failed to suppress riots according to their duty, the king could issue writs directly to the named magistrates, commanding them to fulfil their responsibilities according to the statute of 13 Henry IV, c. 7, which in turn imposed a penalty of £100 for dereliction of duty.[121] The statute was read in the house and the Lord Keeper was ordered to issue the appropriate writs to the sheriffs and JPs of the cities of London and Westminster, and to those of the counties of Middlesex and Surrey.[122]

It was on the basis of those writs that the Lords summoned the London and Middlesex sheriffs and the Westminster JPs on 29 December to answer for their failure to prevent the subsequent riots after Christmas.[123] Interestingly, the sheriffs explained that they had followed the specified procedures according to the writs and had dispatched guards to the Houses of Parliament. They had then been called before the House of Commons to explain why they had done so. Having presented their case, they were instructed by the lower house to dismiss the guards. The Lords were not impressed and ordered that the statute of 13 Henry IV be read to the assembled sheriffs and JPs. They were then commanded to do their duty 'at their perils' and were instructed that 'if they doubt of any Thing, then they are to resort to this House for Advice and Directions therein'.[124] The Lords were clearly concerned on this occasion with their own immediate safety and wellbeing, but there was a great deal more to their instructions than simple self-interest. They recognized that these particular riots were another attempt (clearly sanctioned by the Commons) to introduce public violence into the political process and it was that as much as anything else which they were attempting to resist.

Certainly by this stage their task had become markedly more difficult. The tide of radical reform was running strongly in December and the Lords increasingly found themselves in an adversarial position, not only here, in relation to the House of Commons, but more importantly in relation to other members of the peerage. Divisions within the house itself over major matters of policy – the orders on religious observance, the Bishops Exclusion Bill, the attempts to limit the king's powers of appointment and impressment – had became more evident after the September recess and the absence of a complete consensus undoubtedly undermined the force of their decisions in other areas. It did not, however, deter the prevailing majority of the house from pursuing their primary objectives.

What is striking is the consistency of the Lords' response to these problems – in the face of both external pressure and internal discord. The actions taken in London in December 1641 differed very little from those taken a year earlier in response to the first 'seditious tumult' in the parish church of Halstead. Both incidents represented a threat to order (albeit on very different scales) and both moved the house to resort to the law. Their determination to see the law properly and fairly enforced informed all of their activities during this period – their efforts to offer legal remedy (and legal protection) to the disadvantaged, to defend religious orthodoxy and to protect private property. Those responsibilities were undertaken not just with a view to preserving the public peace, but with the rather broader aim of preventing or at least minimizing social division and unrest.

Ultimately, of course, their assumption of this 'conciliar' role came to be seen by the Commons (and, in some measure, by the public) as part of a larger betrayal. But the view from the upper house was rather different. By tradition the Lords saw their role – as members of the King's Council in Parliament – as one of leadership, and that role had never been more important than in this particular Parliament. Members of both houses had been demanding – and had now been given – the opportunity to demonstrate by example, to king and public alike, the means and methods of responsible political leadership. Reform was clearly part of that assignment and the Lords had cooperated extensively with the Commons in all the major legislative programmes of the first session. But the privilege of reform – and the challenge of leadership – carried certain obligations. Change in their view could not be allowed to take place at the expense of order and stability and, least of all, at the expense of the proper and impartial application of the law.

NOTES

1 H.E.I. Phillips, 'The last years of the court of Star Chamber, 1603–41', *Transactions of the Royal Historical Society*, 4th series, Vol. 21 (1939), p. 129. Professor Phillips claims that the court simply 'faded away' in the absence of its leading members. This is substantiated by Professor Barnes's investigation of estreats of fines from the King's Remembrancer's Memoranda Rolls, which show no fines imposed by the court after Michaelmas 1640. PRO, E159/480, 481. The last sessions of the court of High Commission were likewise those of Michaelmas 1640. R. Usher, *The Rise and Fall of High Commission* (Oxford, 1968), p. 333.

2 The following information is taken from the Privy Council registers, PRO, PC2/51, 52 and 53, and from the notes of Secretary Nicholas in *CSPD*, 1640–1, p. 407.

3 *CSPD*, 1640–1, p. 407. January was the only month in which the council met, as it had done during the 1630s, on an average of twice a week. Kevin Sharpe, 'The personal rule of Charles I', in Howard Thomlinson (ed.), *Before the Civil War* (London, 1983), p. 64.

4 These numbers differ very slightly from those calculated by Professor Fletcher. See his *The Outbreak of the English Civil War* (London, 1981), p. 46.

5 James I had complained of the distractions of Parliament in 1621. He cited, as a reason for dissolving it, 'the interruption of government in the country ... by the attendance of His Majesty's Privy Council' (*CD, 1621*, 4:383). I am grateful to Peter Salt for bringing this reference to my attention.

6 PRO, PC2/37, 38, 39.

7 PRO, PC2/52, fols 214–32.

8 D. Hirst, *Authority and Conflict* (London, 1986), p. 197.

9 Edward Hyde clearly saw the addition of these new members – Bedford, Essex, Saye and St John – as a serious mistake. W.D. Macray (ed.), *The History of the Civil Wars and Rebellion in England ... by Edward Earl of Clarendon*, Vol. 1 (Oxford, 1958) pp. 256–61. See also Fletcher, *The Outbreak of the English Civil War*, p. 46.

10 The king attended just over half (24) of all council meetings in the first year of the Parliament.

11 PRO, PC2/53, fol. 32.

12 This responsibility was assumed by the House of Lords as well. From February the Lords received petitions from county sheriffs seeking directions for the disposal of surplus Ship Money and Coat and Conduct Money. See, for example, HLRO, Main Papers, H.L., 19 February 1640–1 (John Bellott); 27 July 1641 (George Warner). A committee was appointed to handle the matter on 4 June and on 6 August the house issued a general order to all sheriffs to repay the money to the justices of their counties. It was then to be redistributed at the next general sessions as the bench should dictate (*LJ*, iv, pp. 167, 191, 223, 265, 345).

13 That assessment was made by Secretary Nicholas himself. See Fletcher, *The Outbreak of the English Civil War*, p. 46.

14 The legislation which ultimately restrained the powers of the council only limited its judicial authority. King and council were prohibited from exercising 'any jurisdiction, power, or authority by English Bill, petition, articles, libel, or any other arbitrary way whatsoever, to examine or draw into question, determine or dispose of the lands, tenements, hereditament, goods or chattels of any subject of this Kingdom'. 17 Charles I, c. 10.

15 HLRO, Main Papers, H.L., 26 January 1640–1.

16 PRO, PC2/53, fol. 2.

17 HLRO, Main Papers, H.L., 12 May 1641. See also the case of Mary, Abigail and

Judith Stoddard which had a similar history (PRO, PC2/51 fols 82, 94, 109; PC2/53, fol. 4; HLRO, Main Papers, H.L., 28 January 1640–1).

18 PRO, PC2/51, fols 21–2; *CSPD*, 1640–1, p. 353.

19 HLRO, Main Papers, H.L., 8 September 1641.

20 PRO, PC2/53, fol. 27; *LJ*, iv, p. 329.

21 PRO, PC2/52, fols. 237, 280.

22 HLRO, Main Papers, H.L., 26 November 1640. Worsley had appealed the decree to the upper house in the Short Parliament, but the hearings had been terminated by the dissolution.

23 *Statutes of the Realm*, ii, p. 124. The statute was originally intended to restrict the jurisdiction of the Admiralty court, albeit in a roundabout way.

24 PRO, PC2/52, fol. 313.

25 HLRO, Main Papers. H.L., 1 February 1641.

26 ibid. See also A.K.R. Kiralfy, *Potter's Historical Introduction to English Law*, 4th edn (London, 1958), p. 201.

27 The Lords initially stayed proceedings in the King's Bench action to allow time to consider Northumberlands's complaint. A week later the parties were heard at the bar of the house and the King's Bench plaintiff was allowed to proceed with his case, on the understanding that the defendant would be allowed to appeal any ensuing decision by writ of error if he were unsatisfied. The Lords were also careful to specify that the decision was being made 'without any prejudice to the Jurisdiction of the Court of Admiralty in General' (*LJ*, iv, pp. 149, 155). In June 1641 a bill was drafted and presented to the House which would have defined the Admiralty jurisdiction by statute (HLRO, Main Papers, H.L., 10 June 1641). The bill was read once, but went no further, no doubt because of ensuing events. Both houses were still attempting to define the court's jurisdiction at the end of the decade.

28 PRO, PC2/53, fol. 32.

29 *CSPD*, 1640–1, p. 521.

30 ibid. PRO, PC2/53, fol. 56.

31 *CJ*, ii, pp. 217, 219, 224–5.

32 *LJ*, iv, p. 316.

33 HLRO, Main Papers, H.L., 28 June 1641. (The reference is penned to the mayor's original petition to the council.)

34 Valerie Pearl, *London and the Outbreak of the Puritan Revolution* (Oxford, 1961), p. 112.

35 It is possible that the king was deliberately attempting to compromise the house by placing the Lords in the middle of a difficult and potentially embarrassing political problem. The evidence does not suggest that, however. Secretary Nicholas's subsequent report of the Lords' proceedings on the matter is communicated to the king quite straightforwardly, and elicits no interest or response from Charles. Nicholas's continuing admonitions to the king about the importance of the City over the summer and autumn of 1641 appear to have fallen on deaf ears. The king remained steadfastly uninterested in the City and its workings.

The Lords did have some difficulty in effecting a compromise. They initially ordered that six citizens of the commonality be appointed to treat with the mayor and aldermen to try and reach a settlement. That proved ineffective and the Lords then appointed a committee of their own to bring about an agreement. They too were unsuccessful and on 21 August they reported to the house that they had been unable to settle differences. The house then ordered Lord Saye and Sele and the bishop of Lincoln to devise a settlement that would simply be imposed on the parties for this particular occasion. Bishop Williams subsequently reported their recommendation to the house that the commonality be allowed to elect both sheriffs 'for this time' with the hope that they would elect the party nominated by the mayor and aldermen (which they in fact did). The house supported the recommendation, declaring at the same time that their order should be considered 'no way prejudicial to the Right and Prerogative' claimed by either side. It was only meant to be an interim solution. Even so, the mayor and aldermen were wholly unsatisfied and protested that the order threatened 'the Ancient government of the City'. Their protest was rejected and the order was left to stand (HLRO, Main Papers, H.L., 26 August 1641; *LJ*, iv, pp. 242–3, 373). See also Pearl, *London and the Outbreak of the Puritan Revolution*, pp. 120–3, and W. Bray, *The Diary and Correspondence of John Evelyn*, Vol. IV (London, 1906), p. 74.

36 HLRO, Main Papers, H.L., 4 March 1641; *LJ*, iv, p. 244.
37 ibid., 30 June 1640, 23 January 1640–1, 22 April 1641
38 *LJ*, iv, p. 158.
39 ibid., p. 175
40 ibid., p. 297.
41 HLRO, Main Papers, H.L., 16 July 1641.
42 *LJ*, iv, p. 629.
43 HLRO, Main Papers, H.L., 21 July 1641.
44 Fletcher, *Outbreak of the English Civil War*, p. 30.
45 HLRO, Main Papers, H.L., 23 December 1640, 'Orders on private petitions'.
46 ibid., 1 August 1641. As late as November 1643 the Lords were being asked to enforce previous Star Chamber orders and decrees. See, for example, Main Papers, H.L., 15 November 1643 (*Parker* v. *Norcott*).
47 *LJ*, iv, p. 327.
48 ibid., p. 454.
49 It is perhaps significant in this context that the Lords did not, at this stage, take up the cases of Bastwick, Burton, Prynne and Lilburne. The four addressed their complaints instead to the House of Commons, which pardoned all four of them and declared the Star Chamber and High Commission proceedings against them illegal (*CJ*, ii, pp. 90, 102, 123, 124). Those declarations proved ineffective, however, and all four men were forced to readdress themselves to the upper house in 1644. See Chapter 5 below.
50 HLRO, Main Papers, H.L., 29 June 1641.
51 ibid., 22 June 1641; *LJ*, iv, 278.
52 ibid., '1641'.
53 *LJ*, iv, p. 302.
54 ibid., p. 298. The committee was composed of the earls of Bath, Bedford and Salisbury; the bishops of Lincoln and Coventry and Lichfield; and Lords Mohun, Robartes and Howard of Charleton.
55 Ibid., p. 312. The House of Commons had also appointed a committee to consider the problem, but it failed to meet or produce any recommendation. *CJ*, ii, pp. 201–3.
56 The solution had been proposed by Thomas Saunders, the Star Chamber Clerk, in his initial petition to the House.
57 HLRO, Main Papers, H.L., 6 August 1641.
58 ibid., 10 November 1640. There is no extant record of the Lords' decision to settle the conflict between Plowden and his wife. The information comes from Hopkins.
59 ibid., 6 August 1641.
60 *LJ*, iv, p. 345.
61 *CJ*, ii, p. 127; *LJ*, iv, pp. 311–12.
62 ibid., p. 381.
63 The bill was drawn and had a first reading on 18 February. It was read a second time and committed on 23 March and was then brought in for a third reading on 20 May. However, it was rejected and a new bill was ordered to be drawn 'leaving out the Council table' as one of the courts whose officers were to be protected (*LJ*, iv, pp. 593, 664; v, p. 76). The instructions for the new bill were seemingly a consequence of the increasingly partisan political complexion of the house. By this point, desertions had reduced the membership to roughly one-quarter its normal size and sympathy with past and present members of the King's Council (not still members of the house) was in short supply. The new bill was presented for a first reading on 6 June and for a second on 9 June, but went no further.
64 HLRO, Main Papers, H.L., 21 July 1641.
65 *LJ*, iv, p. 397
66 PRO, PC2/53, fol. 11.
67 *LJ*, iv, p. 102.

68 The case had arisen very near the close of Michaelmas term, but actions brought by the Attorney General under *ore tenus* procedure took priority over all other cases in the cause list and could be expedited very quickly (T.G. Barnes, 'Due process and slow process in the late Elizabethan and early Stuart Star Chamber', *American Journal of Legal History*, Vol. 6 (1962), p. 230).

69 The impression is also supported by the referral of two other criminal cases to the house in November. The first was ostensibly one of treason and involved a 'romish priest' named O'Connor who had allegedly threatened the king's life (*LJ*, iv, p. 89). The second involved the stabbing of Justice Heywood, a Westminster JP, by one John James, also said to be a Catholic (*LJ*, iv, p. 93).

70 PRO, PC2/53, fols 46, 47, 58.

71 *LJ*, iv, p. 107

72 ibid., pp. 109, 113. The earl of Warwick later confirmed to the house on 13 March that the offenders had made their submission according to the order of the house. (*LJ*., iv, p. 183).

73 ibid., p. 134.

74 ibid.

75 ibid.

76 For a full discussion of the Commons' response to religious issues see J.S. Morrill, 'The attack on the church of England in the Long Parliament, 1640–42', in Derek Beales and Geoffrey Best (eds), *History, Society and the Churches, Essays in Honour of Owen Chadwick* (Cambridge, 1985), pp. 105–24. See also, Fletcher, *Outbreak of the English Civil War*, pp. 91–125.

77 *CJ*, ii, p. 72.

78 The distinction here is an important one and it reflects the Lords' general position (shared by many traditional Anglicans who chose the 'middle-way') regarding communion rails. The rails, in and of themselves, did not represent an innovation. They were customary in many churches in the land. What was innovatory was moving the table from the nave or chancel and railing it in at the east end of the church – the practice of 'the four or five years last past' referred to in the Lords' order. That was seen as objectionable by Lords and traditionalists alike. For an interesting contemporary discussion of the controversy which takes this same position, see Ephraim Udall, *Communion Comelinesse* (London, 1641), p. 20. I am very grateful to Judith Maltby for this reference.

79 *LJ*, iv, p. 277. The costs were later remitted when the defendants pleaded poverty (ibid., p. 378).

80 ibid.

81 ibid., p. 312.

82 For a full discussion of this episode, see Fletcher, *Outbreak of the English Civil War*, pp. 115–19, and Morrill, 'The attack on the church of England'.

83 The Commons, of course, responded to the Lords' action by publishing a statement of the proceedings in both houses, stressing the fact that the Lords' order of September had passed by only eleven votes to nine. See Sheila Lambert, 'The beginning of Printing for the House of Commons, 1640–42', *Library*, 6th series, Vol. 3 (1981), p. 50. The nature of the vote is significant for at least two reasons. First, it testifies to the existence of important divisions within the house on the question of religious practice. Second, however, it also suggests that those peers who supported the actions taken by the Commons were unable – despite a radically reduced house – to prevail on the upper house to concur with the lower. The nine members who voted against publishing the order of 16 January were the earls of Bedford, Warwick, Clare, Newport and Manchester, and Lords Wharton, Mandeville, Littleton and Hunsden. Six of those nine (Bedford, Warwick, Clare, Newport, Wharton and Mandeville) then entered a formal protest against the refusal of the Lords to confer with the House of Commons (and to gain their assent) before publishing the order (C.H. Firth, *The House of Lords during the Civil War* (London, 1910), p. 96.

84 W.A. Shaw, *The History of the English Church during the Civil Wars and under the Commonwealth*, Vol. II (London, 1900), pp. 175–6. Shaw's assertions are based on a list of 'superstitious, innovating, scandalous or malignant clergymen' who were 'dealt

with' by the Long Parliament in the first two years. He cites 23 cases in the House of Lords, but fails to distinguish those brought by way of formal impeachment proceedings from the House of Commons (of which there were four in the list) from those brought by way of petition from local parishioners. He also includes five cases in which the Lords took action as a consequence of formal appeals against High Commission proceedings in the 1630s (which had themselves resulted in an illegal deprivation; see Chapter two above). The cases are listed in ibid., pp. 295–300.

85 In five of the cases cited by Shaw, the Lords took no action at all.
86 HLRO, Main Papers, H.L., 17 May 1641; *LJ*, iv, p. 251.
87 HLRO, Main Papers, H.L., 13 May 1641; *LJ*, iv, p. 248.
88 HLRO, Main Papers, H.L., 14 August 1641; *LJ*, iv, p. 364.
89 *LJ*, iv, pp. 155–6
90 ibid., p. 494.
91 ibid., pp. 108–9.
92 ibid.
93 ibid., p. 170.
94 HLRO, Main Papers, H.L., 13 January 1641.
95 *LJ*, iv, p. 131.
96 ibid., pp. 160–1.
97 *Statutes of the Realm*, iv, pp. 546–7.
98 *LJ*, iv, p. 187.
99 ibid., p. 209. The order was not entirely successful. The Commissioners applied for assistance again in May 1641 (HLRO, Main papers, H.L., 25 May 1641).
100 *LJ*, iv, p. 247.
101 ibid., p. 263.
102 ibid., p. 281.
103 ibid., p. 262.
104 ibid., pp. 289, 304.
105 HLRO, Main Papers, H.L., 2, 6, 22 April 1641.
106 *LJ*, iv, pp. 204, 208, 224.
107 Keith Lindley, *Fenland Riots and the English Revolution* (London, 1982), pp. 108, 139.
108 *LJ*, iv, pp. 252, 297, 375.
109 ibid., p. 390.
110 ibid., pp. 247, 251.
111 ibid., pp. 264, 393.
112 ibid., pp. 299, 375, 393. Lindley cites one complaint from a fenman who claimed to have expended £80 as a consequence of the Lords' proceedings (Lindley, *Fenland Riots*, p. 125).
113 ibid., p. 428.
114 HLRO, Main Papers, H.L., 13 May 1641; *LJ*, iv, p. 247.
115 23 Henry VIII, c. 5. The issue of the Lords' statutory authority had already been raised in the house, apparently by counsel for the earl of Lincoln. The earl petitioned the house in November 1640, protesting the decrees of the Commission of Sewers in the Lindsey Level (and the activities of the undertakers which followed from them). The Lords referred the matter to two of the judicial assistants, who were to consider 'the points of Law arising from the statute of 23 Hen. VIII' (HLRO, Main Papers, H.L., 19 and 24 November and 15 December 1640). No report was ever made.
116 It is perhaps significant that the king delivered his paper in person, when appearing in the house to give his assent to two bills recently passed (and that he waited to make the presentation until after the Commons had been dismissed). The king's action is somewhat curious, given that the house had been actively engaged in this business, in various contexts, for a number of months. His behaviour may have been motivated, once again, by his wish to use the upper house to thwart the plans of the lower. It cannot have been entirely coincidental that a week earlier a bill had been introduced into the Commons designed to restore the earl of Bedford as principal undertaker in the Great Level (a fact which in itself, suggests that Bedford's

relationship with the king had deteriorated significantly some time before his death) (Lindley, *Fenland Riots*, p. 115).

117 ibid., pp. 113, 115.
118 ibid., p. 138.
119 *LJ*, iv, p. 312. After 13 July complainants had to ask to have the 'benefit' of the Lords' public order and on that basis were given authority to engage local JPs, or, where necessary, the sheriff, to restore possession. The house allowed that if names could be supplied and sworn affidavits provided, the offenders would be sent for and ('if they shall be found guilty') would receive appropriate punishment. The order was put into effect on numerous occasions in 1641 and 1642. See for example, *LJ*, iv, p. 483 (Endimion Porter); p. 629 (Edward Syndenham and Sir William Killigrew); p. 699 (earl of Sussex); p. 704 (John Van haesdanke). In late April 1643 the earl of Suffolk sought to use the order to suppress 'divers disorderly inhabitants' of Newport in Essex. They had apparently broken down fences and destroyed crops on a parcel of land which he held by virtue of a Chancery decree issued 30 years earlier. The offenders were said to have claimed that 'if they took not advantage of the times, they would never have the like opportunity again'. The Lords ordered that the earl was to have benefit of the order and, in the event of any further disturbances, 'the Deputy Lieutenants, Sheriffs, Justices of the Peace, and all other his Majesty's Officers shall . . . use all their power to prevent any Disorders or Tumults that may arise to the Disturbance of the said Quiet Possession,' (*LJ*, vi, p. 21).
120 ibid., p. 458.
121 *Statutes of the Realm*, ii, pp. 169, 184.
122 *LJ*, iv, p. 460.
123 ibid., p. 494.
124 ibid., p. 496.

5

The Long Parliament (iv):
the war years

The history of House of Lords' judicature after 1642 is clearly different from that which had gone before. As it did all things, the Civil War severely disrupted the judicial proceedings of the upper house. In simple practical terms, the radical depletion of its membership and the desertion of the greater part of its judicial personnel drastically impaired efficiency. It was difficult to delegate judicial responsibilities when the referees (both inside and outside the house) had disappeared. The committee structure, on which judicature largely depended, had collapsed and with it went the procedural mechanisms which had defined and ordered proceedings. Hearings in individual cases had to be conducted by the assembled house, which was understandably disinclined to devote the time and attention needed for private causes when the public ones had become so overwhelmingly important. By the same token, the credibility of the High Court had also been seriously undermined. The house could no longer claim to be a large and widely representative tribunal committed to mediating without prejudice between the legal interests of subject and subject, and between subject and sovereign. Nor, despite its protestations to the contrary, could the House be said to be exercising legal authority in the name of the Crown. The king's success in establishing his government in exile, in holding Parliaments in Oxford and in convening courts of law had made that abundantly clear and cast a very long shadow over all the concurrent proceedings at Westminster.

The Lords continued to insist, of course, that Parliament alone retained control over the administration of justice. It had become imperative to do so, if only to demonstrate that the centre of government remained in London. But the pretence became increasingly difficult to sustain. It was obviously difficult to provide genuinely effective legal remedy when the weight of judicial authority and the principal instruments of judicial process lay in Oxford. The Lord Keeper, the Master of the Rolls and seven of twelve common law justices (including both chief justices and the chief baron) had settled and set up business in Oxford by January 1643 and, more importantly, were in possession of the Great Seal – the linchpin of all judicial process – and the individual seals of all three central courts. However earnestly the Lords might attempt to solve private party legal conflicts, they were forced (or at any rate had forced themselves) to operate

175

for the most part in a vacuum. They could only be really effective when they acknowledged (however indirectly) the authority of the personnel and operations at Oxford – and that ran directly counter to their own public position and proclamations which had comprehensively disavowed those proceedings. Their efforts, however well intentioned, were therefore beset with limitations and inescapable contradictions.

On balance, most of the judicial undertakings of the house after 1642 were severely compromised by the inherent incompatibility of their aims. Even in this limited sphere, it proved impossible simultaneously to uphold the king's government and to challenge it. The Lords appear to have understood this, albeit without acknowledging it, and the character as well as the content of House of Lords' judicature was inevitably altered. Where their responses to legal issues and concerns had previously been positive, forthright and responsible, they now became inconsistent, uncertain and unconvincing. The Lords remaining in London found themselves caught in a trap of their own making. Instinctively, they wanted to insist – indeed, they had to insist – that nothing had changed in 1642, that no real division had taken place and that their own authority remained firmly wedded to the king's. Practical reality and political necessity, however, required that they continually betray that posture. They were, to a large extent, working at cross-purposes or, at the very least, in response to contrary impulses and their endeavours suffered as a consequence. In the end justice itself suffered and inevitably – and fatally – so too did the authority of the High Court.

DIVISION AND DISRUPTION

The nature of judicial proceedings in the house altered in stages which generally reflected the escalating political divisions of the pre-Civil War period. The first sign of change came, quite naturally, with declining attendance in the spring of 1642. The problem was clearly apparent in April. The three calls of the house made on the 2nd, the 15th and the 21st show that the maximum number of peers present was 39, 37 and 40 respectively. Those figures correspond roughly with those of the earl of Dover, who took attendance on the 5th, 6th, 7th, 12th and 18th, and found 44, 45, 33, 26 and 36 members present.[1] On the 9th the house appointed a special committee to investigate absenteeism (with reference to specific members) and then directed that any member found away from the house, other than with formal leave, would be censured by the house. All future leaves were then cancelled.[2] By mid-June the problem had become critical. Crummett has estimated that by then political divisions were such that the House of Lords could count on no more than 36 members being present at any one time.[3] Only 22 of those 36 sat on the Committee for Petitions, of whom 3 were already disqualified by age or infirmity. Of the remaining 19, at least 7 members were too committed to the administration of the Militia Ordinance or other military preparations to attend on any meaningful basis.[4] At best, the committee would have had no more than a dozen members at its disposal, though that total was undoubtedly susceptible as well to the irregular daily attendance habits of individual members. It would seem fair, then, to conclude that after June 1642 the Committee for Petitions operated (when it did so at all) at, or very near, its operating quorum.

There is in fact evidence to suggest that the committee was unofficially dispensed with during the early summer of 1642. References to it disappear almost entirely after June. The one new case that was referred to the committee, on 6 August, was referred provisionally; that is, the house directed that 'if the Lords' committees have other business, so as they cannot meet, the Lord Chief Justice is to hear the business, by counsel on both sides, and report the same to the House'.[5] The case did actually go to Bramston, and he reported it in a certificate dated 18 August.[6] From late May the Lords had begun referring cases to smaller groups of two or three peers for their investigation and report and that practice had quickly become very much the rule rather than the exception. Nineteen of twenty-three new cases accepted by the house between May and December 1642 were handled in this way. The remaining fourteen were referred, as above, to one of the senior legal assistants of the house. In either case, any further hearings necessitated by the referees' reports would then be conducted by the assembled house in open court.

As a consequence, the legal assistants began to assume an even greater importance to the house, ironically at precisely the point when they came under intense pressure to abandon their parliamentary responsibilities altogether. The problem had developed initially in mid-May 1642, when the king attempted to adjourn the upcoming legal term to York. The king's intention, fully confessed by the Lord Keeper in the house, produced an immediate and unequivocal response from the Lords. They declared the move 'illegal' and ordered the Lord Keeper not to proceed.[7] The Lords objected primarily to the intended separation of the 'Court of Parliament' from the courts of Westminster and their personnel, a separation which was, in purely practical terms, wholly infeasible, given the judicial proceedings in the house. Their first line of defence (and in fact their only one) was the writ of assistance. They declared that the proposal to remove the term was 'contrary to the express writ which calls Assistants to this House'.[8] The judges, for their part, were instructed to abide by their primary obligation to Parliament. But the new writs for adjournment were never issued, and in the absence of any alternative command the judges were temporarily spared the necessity of openly choosing sides.

The dilemma was implicit in any case. Lord Keeper Littleton, who was in a marginally different position (to the extent that he was not summoned to the house by writ of Assistance), clearly recognized that a confrontation on the issue could not be avoided for much longer, and made his decision to join the king a week later.[9] He was followed shortly by Chief Justice Bankes of Common Pleas. Unlike Littleton, however, Bankes applied for and was given leave of the house. The request for leave appears to have been all important, at least at this stage. When Justice Heath removed himself to York in the first week of June – at the king's command – he failed (no doubt deliberately) to solicit the permission of the house and was consequently declared a 'delinquent'. An order was issued for his arrest, so 'that some example may be made' of him.[10] Heath's predicament is all too apparent from the letter which he wrote to the speaker of the house three days later. While he claimed that the king's command represented 'the double obligation of my duty and my Oath to his Majesty [which] compelled me to a ready obediance', he acknowledged at the same time 'the Tie that lyeth upon me, for my Attendance upon the Honorable House of Peers, where I am an Assistant'.[11] He asked the speaker to intercede on his behalf to prevent his being censured by the house, but the attempt was unsuccessful. The house declared that 'Mr Justice Heath's going from Parliament without Leave is against his oath, but his staying at the Parliament, being sent for from thence, is not against his oath'.[12] In truth, the matter was not nearly so clear cut, but the house plainly needed to make some kind of strong statement regarding the responsibilities of the judiciary during a parliamentary session. The pronouncement in Heath's case really reflects the fact that political considerations were fast becoming as important as practical ones.[13] The judge's presence in Parliament represented something of a strategic advantage, albeit a largely symbolic one, and the Lords undoubtedly had it in mind to discourage the other assistants from following Heath's example.

The warning was effective, at least temporarily, though the continuing loyalty of Justices Bramston and Crawley and Barons Davenport, Trevor and Weston needs to be qualified. Each was additionally constrained by a £10,000 recognizance bond entered into at the time of their impeachment in December 1640. Those bonds would almost certainly have been forfeited had they decided to absent themselves from Parliament. The house remained somewhat suspicious of the others, however. Six of the judges were given leave of absence in early July. Justices Reeve, Foster and Malet and Baron Henden were all discharged to go on circuit, but Reeve and Henden were both instructed to return home after the assizes and were to remain there until called by the house. Chief Baron Davenport and Baron Weston were, on the other hand, simply given leave to return to their homes until the beginning of Michaelmas term.[14] Justices Bramston and Crawley and Baron Trevor remained in attendance. Later in the month the Lords also granted leave to Sir Edward Leech, one of the masters in Chancery, and to Sir Charles Caesar, the Master of the Rolls. In the former case the house ordered the Clerk of the Crown to bring in a list of the available masters from which a replacement might be chosen, 'that this House may not want Attendants'. In the latter, Caesar himself was directed to appoint someone to stand in his place.[15]

As it turned out, the Lords' generosity proved rather misplaced. Only Justices Foster and Reeve returned to serve the house. Justice Malet and Baron Hendon refused to give legal sanction to the Militia Ordinance, or to Parliament's general political position at the assizes.[16] For their pains the former was committed to the Tower and the latter was impeached by the House of Commons. Henden, in consequence, fled to the king. He was followed by Weston and, when the close of his authorized 'vacation' forced his hand, by Baron Davenport. The Lords' order of 29 September, 'that all of the judges shall have notice, and be commanded to attend this House, according to their writs', did not produce the intended result. Over the next three months, the Lords would lose three more of their senior assistants. Chief Justice Bramston's career had in fact been marked since early August when he had refused the king's summons to York, choosing instead (with no little help from the house itself) to fulfil his parliamentary obligations. The king dismissed him on 17 October and his services to the house were immediately terminated.[17] Ironically, the king's action created another dilemma for the house. Bramston's dismissal left the court of King's Bench without a presiding judge and the Lords were forced to release Justice Berkeley from the Tower to sit in the upcoming sessions.[18] On 29 December Justice Foster received his own summons from the king. He duly presented the letter to the house and asked for their directions. In this case, curiously, the Lords decided that 'the integrity of Mr Justice Foster' was sufficient insurance and, on the assumption that 'he may do much good there', gave him leave to join the king. He did so almost immediately. The last judge to go was Justice Crawley, who appears to have absented himself without leave at some point between the beginning of Michaelmas term and the end of December 1642.[19]

By the close of 1642, then, the Lords' legal staff had been decimated. Only three senior members of the common law bench remained: Reeve of Common Pleas, Bacon of King's Bench (appointed in the wake of Bramston's dismissal and Heath's elevation to Chief Justice) and Trevor of the Exchequer. Of the remaining nine, two were in the Tower (Berkeley and Malet) and seven were with the king. The Lord Keeper had been with the king since May, and the Attorney General had been impeached, convicted and removed from office in April. The Master of the Rolls, Sir Charles Caesar died in December as well, leaving the king to appoint in his place one of his own privy councillors, Sir John Colepepper. Unlike Bacon, whom the king had also appointed, Colepepper not surprisingly

179

declined the invitation to attend the house in his capacity as an assistant. The house was therefore forced to fall back, as much as possible, on the services of the three remaining judges and on the remaining secondary assistants – the king's serjeants and the masters in Chancery. The reduction in these forces would not be corrected for almost two years.

The king's attempt to summon judicial personnel to attend the term in Oxford in January 1643 was also strenuously resisted. Justice Bacon was summoned twice, on 11 and 20 January, and was instructed on both occasions to attend the house according to his writ. The second letter from the king did, however, prompt the Lords to order that a letter be written to Oxford explaining their position.[20] Essentially the same answer was given to queries directed to the house by the Chancellor of the Duchy of Lancaster, the Master of the court of Wards (Lord Say and Sele) and various other lesser court officials, all of whom were responding to the king's proclamation adjourning the legal term to Oxford.[21] By this stage the process had become a formality; most public officials had already chosen sides.

The desertion of their judicial assistants created all manner of problems for the Lords. Their departure not only handicapped the Lords' own judicial operations, it obviously constrained normal proceedings in Chancery and the common law courts in London, which in turn created new pressures on the upper house. This was particularly true of Chancery, to which the house had referred numerous petitions over the previous year. Many of those cases came bounding back to the house when the Lord Keeper's absence halted proceedings in the court. In May 1641, for example, the Lords had considered the appeal of Sir Robert Hamilton against a former decree made in Chancery by Lord Keeper Finch, and had asked the new Lord Keeper to consider the complaint.[22] Littleton had done so on 13 July, electing to set aside the former proceedings. A new commission, returnable the following Michaelmas term, had then been awarded to examine witnesses.[23] The case was scheduled for several hearings during the Lent term (1642), but was repeatedly put off. On one occasion the hearing had been postponed because Littleton had 'gone to the Parliament' and Baron Henden, presiding in his absence, had refused to proceed on grounds that the Lords had ordered Littleton himself to hear the dispute.[24] In the event, Littleton's subsequent departure for the north left the matter permanently in abeyance and Hamilton readdressed his complaint to the house, requesting 'that some of the Judges now in Towne be ordered to hear the Cause and settle it'.[25]

In July 1641, the Lords had entertained a complaint from Edward Winstanley against William and Hugh Bullock and had likewise referred the matter to the Lord Keeper for 'speedy consideration'.[26] The case had been heard in Chancery the following Michaelmas term and the Lord Keeper had directed the defendants to submit a cross-bill which they duly did, and the suits were joined. The dispute was scheduled for hearing on numerous occasions but was repeatedly postponed. Winstanley later claimed that Littleton had finally scheduled the case to be heard on Ascension Day at his house, and that a hearing had actually taken place – or at least had proceeded to the opening of the two bills – when Littleton 'pretended an indisposition' and abruptly terminated the proceedings, rescheduling the case for 27 June. Winstanley soon realized that no such hearing would take place, and accordingly repetitioned the house.[27]

The Lord Keeper's absence also forced the house to assume responsibility for a number of cases which ought to have fallen first to Chancery (or the court of Requests). In February 1642, for example, Lady Mary Carr had petitioned the house complaining that her husband, Sir Robert Carr, had denied her maintenance.[28] (Having conveyed certain lands to appointed trustees to secure her an allowance out of the rents, he had then instructed his tenants to withhold payments.) The house accepted her petition and directed Chief Justice Bramston to call Sir Robert before him and take whatever measures were necessary to secure her support, until the Lords themselves could hear the case.[29] Bramston's efforts were apparently unsuccessful and in Easter term Lady Carr brought an action at common law, in the name of the trustees, against the principal tenant involved. The matter was tried at the Lincolnshire assizes in the summer of 1642, and Lady Carr obtained a successful verdict. The suit, however, had only confirmed the validity of the original conveyances. It was not effective in forcing Sir Robert or his tenants to fulfil their obligations. Lady Carr therefore reapplied to the upper house for assistance, claiming that 'at present, by reasone of the absence of the Lord Keeper, and the obstruction of the Great Seale, yor petr hath no remedy for the settling of the rents, according to the Course of Equity, as is usual in cases of this nature'. The Lords responded sympathetically and directed the tenants to pay all of the rents required by the original conveyances until the house should determine otherwise.[30]

The collapse of equity proceedings produced a similar complaint from one John Reade.[31] In April 1642 Reade had become bound for John Dingley to one Thomas Gunton, for a debt of £400. Dingley defaulted and both he and Reade were arrested on the bond. Reade, however, appears to have been deliberately set up by the other two men. After their arrest, Dingley quickly made a 'settlement' with Gunton and was released, but Gunton refused to allow Reade to be released until Dingley had given his permission. Dingley in turn refused his permission until Reade paid him £400 which Reade's brother had borrowed from him some time earlier. Reade had known nothing of his brother's debt to Dingley – for which he was not responsible – and he was unable (and no doubt unwilling) to pay it. He had clearly been the victim of a deliberate deception, but in the eyes of the common law the procedures appeared to be perfectly legitimate and above board, and he was left without recourse. By the time he petitioned the Lords in December 1642, he had been in prison for four months. He had in fact presented a bill for relief to the court of Requests, but had discovered that 'no proceedings could be had this term in any court of Equity', and had therefore sought help from the upper house. His petition was referred to the remaining justices of Common Pleas to examine and report.[32]

Reade's inability to gain equitable relief through normal channels testifies to the disorder and confusion which had crippled the legal system by December 1642. The general crisis had in fact been exacerbated from late November by the respective attempts of king and Parliament to control the legal term and the administration of the courts. On 18 November the king had fuelled the conflict by issuing a proclamation, together with accompanying writs to the judges, suspending the remainder of the Michaelmas term. The move was clumsy and ill considered. By that stage the term was nearly over and the proclamation, had it been observed, would only have created havoc by adjourning proceedings before the all-important return day. In the event, the proclamation and writs were intercepted by the House of Commons, and the lower house then requested that the Lords countermand the instructions to the judges to adjourn. The Commons argued that the adjournment of the term in mid-stream would be 'obstructive to the whole proceedings of the Law'. They reminded the Lords that the proceedings of the previous summer assizes would be lost because no judgment could be awarded. In addition no original writs – for instance habeas corpus – could be issued, and no fines or recoveries could be taken to finalize the sale or conveyance of property. More tellingly, they suggested that 'there being an Army in the field, and the King's Colours flying, it would be accounted *Tempus Belli*, when all laws sleep, and are silent and dissolved; and then there would be no property, nor violence counted an injury'.[33] The Commons appear to have recognized the importance of maintaining the semblance of legal order, as much for symbolic reasons as for practical ones. Not surprisingly, the Lords fully endorsed their arguments, and the writs remained unopened. The judges were instead directed to 'sit and proceed to dispatch the Public Justice of this Kingdom, according as is usual in their several Courts'.[34]

The battle was reengaged in December. On the 27th, the king issued another proclamation, this time suspending the upcoming Lent term and adjourning all equity courts to Oxford. The two houses responded by petitioning the king to revoke the order. The petition was not particularly well drawn, however. Of the five arguments supporting their request, priority was given to the matter of parliamentary privilege. The petition reminded the king that the 'Supreme Judges' of the courts of Chancery and Wards and Liveries, as well as the masters in Chancery, and the Chancellor of the Duchy of Lancaster were members of and/or assistants to the House of Lords, and that their absence without leave (which clearly would not be granted) would constitute a breach of privilege. The argument was not only tactless, it was largely irrelevant. With the notable exceptions of Lord Saye and Sele, the Master of Wards, and Lord Newburgh, the Chancellor of the Duchy of Lancaster, the principal figures involved were either dead or with the king.[35] The petition then argued against the transfer of equity proceedings on practical grounds, suggesting that the king's subjects would be endangered by having to pass through two armies on their way to Oxford; that the king's army in Oxford would inhibit the 'Freedom and Liberty' of the courts themselves; that the subjects' legal records and documents would be in great danger; and that the physical separation of courts of equity from those of common law would create 'much prejudice and inconvenience'. Again, they resisted the suspension of the upcoming term on grounds that it would 'much delay Your Majesty's subjects in their legal proceedings'.[36]

The parliamentary petition was wholly (and rather artfully) rejected by the king. His answer was carefully constructed to emphasize Parliament's own break with the traditions of the law. He insisted that it was customary for the upper house to grant leave to its members when requested to do so by the king; he claimed that they were 'bound in law' to attend the king when summoned and stated that it was within his rights to dispense with any peer's attendance on the house – without breach of privilege – when he felt it was necessary. This prerogative, he suggested, had 'not been denied by former Parliaments'.[37] In any event, as he rather ruefully pointed out, the Lord Keeper's presence in Oxford naturally presupposed that the court of Chancery should convene there 'so that his subjects may have their cause determined by the Supreme Judge of that Court'. To Parliament's suggestion that the subject would be endangered by the presence of the armies, the king replied that

> he doth not know that they are to pass through more armies to his city of Oxford, than they must to his City of London; or that the Courts of Justice cannot proceed with the same freedom and Liberty here, where his army is, as there where there is an army against him.

His subjects, he asserted, could expect 'little benefit by their legal proceedings whilst his Majesty and the Law are no better able to defend one another'.[38]

Predictably, his answer moved Parliament to pass a long and detailed ordinance on 21 January which rehearsed the whole dispute and reiterated their previous arguments against the proclamations – arguments advanced, it was said, 'in performance of their Duty and Trust reposed in them by the

Kingdom whom they represented'. As expected, the ordinance forbade any judge or officer of the courts involved, or any member or assistant of either house of Parliament, to go to Oxford without leave, and directed that court business was to be conducted 'in the Places usual for the doing and executing thereof'. It then declared that 'no person shall remove or cause to be removed any record or writings of any of the said Courts . . . to or toward the city of Oxon', and provided that those who disobeyed would be proceeded against as 'wilful condemners of the Authority of Parliament, and Disturbers of the Peace of the Kingdom'. Aware that the proceedings in Oxford would continue notwithstanding, Parliament then declared that no orders, decrees and judgments 'made out of the usual Places where the said Courts and Receipts have been accustomed to be held and kept' would bind any person or party involved 'without their voluntary consent'. As a final insurance, the ordinance indemnified all 'Judges, Officers, or other persons from any Danger or Inconvenience that may or can happen to them' if they obeyed.[39]

Despite appearances, neither the king's proclamation nor Parliament's ordinance was more than peripherally concerned with the legal interests of individual litigants. They were primarily concerned with asserting control over the courts themselves, and particularly over the English revenue courts, such as the court of Wards. Whatever their actual intent, the legal interests of litigants were profoundly affected. The combined impact of both measures was to create an impossible situation in which legal proceedings in one venue would inevitably be contradicted or contravened by proceedings in the other, and in which no final resolution, however arduously obtained, would carry indisputable authority.

The king clearly had the upper hand, if only because he possessed the Great Seal, and in due course the upper house was inundated with petitioners seeking exemptions from Parliament's prohibitions against proceedings in Oxford. At least initially, the Lords' response to these requests demonstrated a sympathetic understanding of the dilemma – or perhaps simply a lack of conviction in their own earlier declarations. In April 1643 Captain John Hardwicke complained to the house that he had obtained a writ of *Certiorari* which he had been unable to execute. The writ had been addressed to the Chief Justice of the King's Bench and procedure required that he alone break it open. That was not possible because he remained ensconced in Oxford and Hardwicke therefore requested that a pass be granted to some person whom he might appoint to travel to Oxford and back with the writ.[40] The pass was granted.[41] Later in April, the cursitors of the court of Chancery petitioned the house with a similar request:

Yor Petrs do make all originall writs out of the Chancery retournable in King's Bench, Common Pleas, and Exchequer Chamber, and dureing theis troublesome times have had libertie to send theire writts to Oxford to be sealed with the Great Seall and to retourne again, until now of late when yor peticioners writts are staied for want of Licence from this honourable House for the safe passage of their usual messanger.

The cursitors then outlined the consequences if approval were withheld:

No fines and recoveries can pass the Common Pleas, and suits cannot proceed for debt process, neither can there bee proceedings in the inferior Corts of any county of this Kingdom without the originall writts out of Chancery enablinge some to hold pleas and others to remove accons.

Asserting that these restrictions would 'tend to the Great Prejudice of the subject without spedy redresse', they requested that the house grant a pass to their messenger, Edmund Gardener, to carry writs to Oxford and back 'as often as need shall require'.[42] Gardener had his pass the same day.[43] Joseph de Silva was treated with equal alacrity. He petitioned the house in mid-May, claiming that he had been engaged in a suit in the court of Admiralty for the previous two years. In April he had gone to Oxford to defend his suit, but had been forced to return to London to obtain some earlier 'acts of court' and other writings. He now needed a pass to return to Oxford to complete the proceedings.[44] Despite the fact that the request directly contravened the terms of Parliament's ordinance of 21 January, he was granted the necessary pass.[45] So too were Thomas Smith and James Pickering. They had recently arrested the duke of Eperson for having seized their ship, the *Unitie*, some four years earlier. They had accepted bail in the form of sureties and had subsequently allowed his release. The sureties had then threatened to leave the country, so they had obtained a writ of *ne exeat regnum* against them. They claimed, however, that the sureties' agents were now on their way to Oxford to obtain a writ of *supersedeas* to defeat them, and that it was therefore necessary for them to travel to Oxford 'to prevent the malice of their adversaries'.[46] Permission was granted.[47]

On 12 May the Lords entertained a petition from one Dorothy Brograve against a decree issued by the Prerogative Court of Canterbury concerning the estate of her brother, Sir Thomas Leventhorpe. According to the petitioner, Dr William Merrick, the judge of the court, had granted letters of administration the previous July to executors 'of remote kyne to the deceased' in violation of the statute of 21 Henry VIII which provided for administration, where possible, by next of kin.[48] Brograve had attempted to appeal the award, but claimed that 'by reason of the distraction of theis times' she had been unable 'to prosecute with effect'.[49] In fact, Dr Merrick

had himself fled to Oxford only four days earlier, disavowing as he went
any future acts of the court executed in his absence.[50] In consequence,
the Lords agreed to hear the dispute on 1 June. After presentation by
counsel on both sides, however, they elected to 'remit the Cause to
Proceedings in the Proper Courts' – specifically, the plaintiff was to
be allowed a Commission of Adjuncts in order to proceed to appeal
in the court of Delegates (with the understanding that she would then
have the right to appeal any resulting decision to the house itself).[51] The
Lords' response was perfectly proper and in accordance with the appellate
procedures established by statute,[52] but the remedy presupposed, and
indeed required, the appointment of commissions (both original and
adjunct) under the Great Seal, and therefore anticipated proceedings by
the king and/or the Lord Keeper in Oxford.

All these decisions suggest that the upper house was as yet unwilling to
sacrifice the legal interests of their clientele to the political demands of the
moment; that they were not ready to countenance a complete break with
authority in Oxford. Increasingly, however, that position placed them at
odds with the House of Commons. On 19 May the lower house had itself
appointed a Committee for Obstructions in the Courts, which was given
authority to

> receive and examine all Informations concerning Obstructions in
> Courts of Justice by reason of the Absence of the Great Seal, or any
> of the judges, or any Seal of any Court; and to stay all Proceedings
> in such suits as they shall find cause, and to give such other redress
> to the Parties grieved as they find just, until they can make report to
> this House.[53]

This committee's mandate was distinctly combative and divisive, rather
than cooperative. They were clearly expected to stay any proceedings
which might require coordination with judicial process in Oxford and,
conversely, to limit as much as possible the effects of Oxford proceedings
on litigants in London – a course conspicuously at odds with that of the
upper house. Curiously, the Lords do not appear to have challenged this
committee, either on grounds that its activities were disadvantageous to
the long-term interests of litigants – which they clearly were – or on the
more obvious grounds that they represented an serious invasion of the
judicial prerogatives of the upper house. They appear either to have been
unaware of its existence (which seems rather unlikely), or to have been
of two minds about its ultimate value as a political weapon.

In fact this committee was probably intended to do little more than
gather evidence for use by the Commons in their long-running argument
with the upper house over the need to create a parliamentary Great Seal.
The two endeavours were directly related. The committee was appointed

on 19 May and on the 20th the Commons presented to the Lords the first of a series of resolutions on the Great Seal, in which they argued, among other things, that the obstructions in the courts created by the absence of the Great Seal represented 'a great Mischief' which it was their 'duty' to remedy.[54] Despite the practical logic of their argument, and the very real problems involved, the Commons faced an uphill battle. The Lords remained distinctly unenthusiastic about the prospect of commissioning a new seal. The Commons' resolutions were not even considered by the house for another week and when they were, the Lords firmly rejected the two central motions put forward by the Commons: that which maintained that the 'Great Seal ought to attend the commands of Parliament, according to the Laws of the Land', and that which proposed that 'a Great Seal be forthwith made to attend Parliament, for Dispatch of the Affairs of Parliament and the Kingdom'.[55] The Lords' own position was formulated over the next two weeks and, as it was presented in conference, differed markedly from that of the Commons. The lower house was informed that it was 'their Lordships' sense

> that the Parliament, having, in all its Resolutions and Actions, gone upon the Power of their Ordinances, their Lordships conceive that it will be proper to continue on that Ground; that the making of a new Great Seal will not hinder or prevent the Use or Power of the King's Great Seal; If we find that the sealing of Original Writs, and Writs of Error be denied, we shall join with them to take it into our care to do what shall be necessary and of Advantage to Parliament, and the free Course of Justice, and the Laws of the Kingdom.[56]

The Lords were determined, at this stage at least, to proceed with caution, realizing that the step being urged on them by the Commons would represent an irrevocable breach with the king's authority. Where they had to, they clearly preferred to confront the Crown's authority on a less direct, case by case basis, as they had done, for example, in the case of John Feriby.[57] Feriby had been indicted at the Oxford assizes the previous summer and had been bound to appear again at the forthcoming Lent sessions. He had declined to appear 'by reason of the forces lying there and the threatening speeches given out against him', and instead had sued out two writs of *Certiorari* to remove the cases into the King's Bench in London. The writs were eventually delivered to Justice Heath, then sitting as justice of assize, but he refused to recognize or return them, and issued a warrant for Feriby's arrest. As Chief Justice, he then sent instructions to the clerks of the court in London to issue a writ of *Procedendo*, superseding the *Certiorari* on grounds that the plaintiff's reasons for removal had not been sufficiently proved. Feriby accordingly appealed to the House of Lords to intervene to stay the clerks in London from issuing the writ. His request was granted and his case was then referred to Justice Bacon.[58]

The Commons, however, continued to apply pressure over the summer. In one notable case in July the lower house prevailed on the upper to provide judicial remedy by way of parliamentary ordinance, rather than allow proceedings in Oxford. In early July the Commons' new judicial committee had entertained a complaint from one Catherine Pettus relating to the execution of a previous decree in Chancery.[59] In 1631 Pettus had obtained a judgment against Thomas Bancroft (her father-in-law's executor) for £1,600 which had been left to her as a legacy. However, she had been unable to collect the award, either from Bancroft, or, after his death, from his widow, and had eventually returned to Chancery to obtain a commission of sequestration. In due course the commissioners had identified and sequestered properties in Norfolk belonging to Bancroft and for the previous year Pettus had received the profits. She complained that she had recently been expelled 'by violence and force' by others claiming title. She wanted and needed to return to Chancery to obtain an order securing her possession, but had been prohibited 'by reason of the Ordinance of Parliament restraining all proceedings in Oxford'.

Rather than allow her a pass, the Commons' committee ordered an ordinance be drawn 'to enable Mrs Pettus to prosecute her Decree and Suits in Chancery, and to receive the Fruit and benefit of the sequestration thereupon granted' – without resort to the Lord Keeper in Oxford.[60] The ordinance was drafted and eventually passed the lower house on 15 July, and was then forwarded to the Lords.[61] However, the upper house did not take up the ordinance until 8 August, some three weeks later, despite a reminder from the Commons on the 1st that it required an answer.[62] It is possible that consideration was simply deferred in order to pursue other more important business, but on balance the delay appears to have been intentional. Despite their earlier declaration that procedure by ordinance could be used in such cases, they may not have been entirely comfortable with it when the moment arrived. The ordinance was in fact rather innocuous. It simply commanded the appropriate officers in Chancery to execute the decree and sequestration. But it represented a direct usurpation of the Lord Keeper's authority and, more broadly, of the king's. The Lords' own judicial authority was, of course, being usurped by the Commons at the same time, and that may well have accounted in some measure for the delay.[63] In the end the Lords gave their assent to the ordinance,[64] but they may well have done so for tactical reasons – to deflect mounting pressure from the Commons over the issue of the Great Seal. In early July, just as this case was proceeding through the Commons' committee, the Lords had, once again, rejected the Commons' urgent proposals for the making of a new seal, declaring instead that they would 'adhere to their former Resolutions'.[65] They may have concluded that a sign of cooperation was now in order and that by demonstrating their willingness to proceed by ordinance (notwithstanding the issue of judicial privilege) they would diminish enthusiasm for the alternative course.

If that was their primary ambition, it was doomed to failure. The Commons were determined to pursue the commission of a new seal, with or without the sanction of the upper house. When the Lords rejected their proposals for a second time, on 4 July, the Commons simply ignored their opposition and proceeded without them. The next day they appointed a committee 'to give order for the Present Making of a Great Seal of England and to see it done'. Sir Robert Harley was appointed to 'take care of the speedy and effectual execution' of the assignment.[66] The project had proceeded far enough by 2 September for the Commons to authorize the payment of £400 'out of the Sequestration money' for the purchase of the necessary silver by the appointed artist, Thomas Symonds. The lower house ordered that the seal was to be delivered 'this day a month'.[67]

It was in fact just over a month later that the Commons made their final and successful assault on the upper house to gain their approval, arguing that 'new mischiefs had sprung up' which required the making of a new Great Seal 'more at this time than at others'. The 'new Mischiefs' primarily involved the uses being made of the Great Seal in Oxford: to grant new Commissions of Array, new commissions to county sheriffs, commissions of oyer and terminer to try those who had 'held with Parliament', and to issue proclamations seizing the estates of Parliament men. All of this had been true earlier, if perhaps on a somewhat smaller scale, and the Lords had already argued in June and July that the making of the new seal would not prevent the 'use and power' of the king's seal to continue these designs. For that reason, the Commons were also careful to stress that the king's seal itself was no longer in the hands of a sworn officer, but in those of George Radcliffe, whom Parliament had condemned for treason. He was said to have refused to permit its use for 'normal' purposes and as a consequence there had been, they claimed, 'a general Stop and Denial of Justice'.[68] There is no evidence that this alleged 'stop' of justice had actually occurred, but in combination with the other arguments, the suggestion was no doubt persuasive for those already inclined to listen. In fact, as the Commons no doubt understood, the upper house was more likely to be receptive now than at any time over the previous six months. The collapse of the so-called Peace Party in August and the desertion of six key members of the house – the earls of Portland, Bedford, Clare and Holland and Lords Lovelace and Conway – left it notably less able (and probably less inclined) to resist the pressure of the lower house.[69] Whatever the cause, the Lords finally capitulated on 11 October.[70] The ordinance 'annulling' the Great Seal at Oxford and creating a new parliamentary seal was read and committed in the upper house on 1 November and was finally given the Lords' assent ten days later.[71] The upper house had now committed itself to a decisive break with the Crown and the traditional vestiges of the law.

THE LAW BETRAYED: THE DEMANDS OF CIVIL WAR

To some extent, the Lords had already seriously damaged their credibility as an impartial tribunal. Their assent to the parliamentary Sequestration Ordinance the previous March,[72] and their subsequent participation with the Commons in the wholesale seizure of private property fatally compromised their position. The Lords had, of course, previously sequestered all manner of private property – land, ecclesiastical livings, administrative and judicial offices – in the course of adjudicating civil suits. But they had always done so as a temporary measure to allow the legal rights of the litigants to be properly and fairly determined. The proceedings undertaken in the spring of 1643 turned that procedure – and the legal premises behind it – on its head; by ignoring the rights of private property holders altogether (indeed, denying them as a presumption of the process itself) and by seizing property on a permanent basis. Having taken elaborate precautions to secure and protect property rights, in all manner of contexts, over the previous two years (and in previous Parliaments), the Lords now found themselves required to do the opposite. However much they might argue for the importance of the national objectives involved (or point to the fact that the king himself had freely indulged in the practice), there was no escaping the fact that the sequestration proceedings were arbitrary, unjust and illegal, and that they contravened every sacred legal principle previously articulated by the High Court. The volte-face must have been painfully obvious to even the most politically committed members of the house.

The resulting unease would seem to account for the Lords' attempt in mid-March 1643 to impose 'orthodox' judicial procedures on the sequestration proceedings, if only so the pretence of judicial fairness could be maintained. On 17 March, as an example, the lower house forwarded to the Lords two orders for the sequestration of church livings in Surrey. The Commons were subsequently informed, however, that the upper house had elected to 'hear the Proofs made against the persons mentioned' before proceeding further, and they were therefore requested to inform the parties involved of the forthcoming hearing.[73] On the 23rd the Commons again forwarded orders for the sequestration of a dozen church livings in London and Middlesex. These were agreed to, but only provisionally, on the understanding that the ministers involved would be allowed a subsequent hearing to offer 'what they could say touching the said orders'. The Lords also reserved the right to 'proceed to further judgement against them, or to make such Mitigation for their subsistence as they shall see Cause'.[74] At this stage, the Lords appear to have been reacting more or less instinctively, rather than in response to any predetermined policy. That soon changed, however. In late April, having received another series of sequestration orders from the Commons, the upper house decided to issue a protest:

> This House conceiving that these Orders of Sequestrations are an Invasion of the Privileges of this House in Point of Judicature, Resolved to have a conference with the House of Commons, to desire that Things of this nature may proceed in the same manner as in Ancient Times; and that Informations and Witnesses may be brought up together, and so that their Lordships may see the Grounds upon which they are to ground their Judgement.[75]

Their demands were perfectly reasonable. The Lords were well aware of the respective role of the two houses in what were ostensibly criminal proceedings, and they were jealously guarding their own prerogative as judges. But their insistence that a trial take place (however perfunctorily) in each case reflected a genuine concern about the summary nature of the proceedings and they held to the position with notable consistency, at least with regard to the sequestration of church livings. They insisted that a minister should be allowed to receive the profits of his living until such time as the appropriate orders had passed both Houses of Parliament.[76] Complaints from clerics that they had been ejected without trial were taken seriously and genuine efforts were made to afford the complainant the opportunity to make his defence.[77] In one case, in fact, the Lords determined that the notice of trial given the defendant had been 'too short' and accordingly rescheduled it for a week later.[78] Counsel was always granted where requested and efforts were made to ensure that testimony was taken from two witnesses before the house proceeded to judgment.[79] In the end, of course, the vast majority of these 'trials' resulted in the anticipated sequestration. Nonetheless, the Lords did alter the terms of some orders and occasionally made allowances – limiting the period of sequestration, or allowing the minister a portion of the income from the living.[80] Significantly, however, in only one case was the order actually reversed.[81] On balance, the proceedings suggest only that there remained a strong residual sense of responsibility among the members of the house to adhere to the form, if not the letter, of the law. In any event, they were undoubtedly fighting an uphill battle to restrain the excesses of the local sequestration committees and were only able to provide even this token legal recourse to a very small proportion of the ministers ejected during the period.

Where the sequestration applied to the estates of 'notorious delinquents' and members of the house itself, the pretence of a trial was clearly out of the question since the nominal defendants were unlikely to appear and no doubt would have challenged the legal propriety of the entire operation if they had. Once the sequestrations had been put into effect, however, the Lords were frequently asked to review individual cases in order to remedy a variety of secondary legal complications which had been overlooked by local sequestration committees. The most immediate complication arose in the form of complaints from wives and children of so-called 'delinquents' who suddenly found themselves without means of support. Their plight was fairly obvious and by June 1643 it had been made sufficiently clear for the upper house to feel compelled to act. On 3 June the Lords decided to 'give liberty to the Lords' Committee for Sequestrations to make such allowances to the maintenance of Wives and Children of persons whose estates are sequestered as they shall think fit', and on the 26th they communicated their wish to the lower house that their committee be given the same authority.[82]

All the problems were not equally straightforward. Quite often the properties sequestered by Parliament were encumbered with prior obligations – debts, mortgages, trusts and annuities – to parties sympathetic to the parliamentary cause. Lady Catherine Stanhope, for example, complained to the house in March 1643 that she had been deprived of an income of £1,000, due to be paid to her as part of her jointure, from the lands of her father-in-law, the earl of Chesterfield. His lands had been sequestered. She protested that, unlike the earl, she was and had always been 'a devout Honorer of the proceedings of Parliament' and requested their assistance in remedying the injustice. She requested that either the tenants involved or the local sequestrators be ordered to pay her her annuity.[83] Similarly, John Viscount Purbeck complained to the house that he had had rents of £900 a year assured to his use by 'lawful conveyance' from the estate of Sir Edward Coke in Cambridgeshire and Suffolk. The properties had since descended to Coke's son, Sir Robert Coke, whom the local sequestration committee had declared a 'delinquent'. The lands had accordingly been seized and Purbeck had lost what he claimed was his only source of income. He too requested that the Lords intercede with the local committee.[84] William Wombell, on the other hand, sought help from the house in collecting a debt of £50 from the sequestered estate of Arthur Fry, 'one of the plotters of the late horride conspiracy agst the City',[85] while Cornelius Burgess, a vicar of Watford, requested assistance in recovering tithes amounting to £30 from the sequestered estate of Lord Capel.[86]

In most of these cases, the injustice was obvious and the Lords were willing and able to correct the problem simply by issuing an order to the local committee to pay the amount due from the sequestered assets. But in other cases the complainants challenged the sequestration proceedings themselves and forced the house to review the local committee's decision in its entirety. Though the Lords were willing to entertain these petitions, their responses were often rather indecisive and betrayed an unease about engaging in direct conflict with local authorities on their own. In October 1643, for example, Edward White appealed to the house against the proceedings of the Essex Sequestration Committee, on behalf of the Catholic-born Lord Petre, then a minor and ward of the Crown. At some earlier stage Lord Petre had been committed to the care of the earl of Northampton, who had in fact placed him in the hands of a Protestant tutor in Oxford. Despite his Protestant upbringing, and his obvious neutrality in the conflict, his steward claimed that the local committee had seized his estates 'as if he were a papist and a delinquent, when he is neither' and now threatened to sell his goods and cattle and waste his woods. He asked that the sequestration be lifted and the committee be prohibited from proceeding as planned.[87] The Lords temporarily stayed the sale of goods and timber, but referred the case to the Grand Committee for Sequestrations.[88]

Earlier in March, Henry Noel, the second son of Viscount Camden, presented a similar protest, claiming that goods and livestock had been seized by the Lincolnshire committee, despite his own clearly expressed and demonstrated neutrality.[89] In response to the petition, the Lords asked for assurances that the sequestration had been authorized by Parliament. They then provided that, if it had not been, Noel was to be granted a protection from the house, his goods were to be redelivered, and his woods preserved from further cutting.[90] Their directions were not very effective. Two weeks later, Noel petitioned the house again, claiming that their order had been openly flouted by the Lincolnshire committee (chaired by Lord Willoughby) and that large quantities of livestock had already been stolen and trees cut down with their permission.[91] The Lords reissued their earlier directive and admonished the committee and all others 'to obey the order in all points'.[92] This order was apparently equally ineffective. Noel was again forced to petition the house in June to complain that his estate remained sequestered.[93] On this occasion, the Lords elected to refer the matter to the House of Commons, with a request that the case be referred to the Committee for the Advance of Monies at Haberdasher's Hall, providing only that it should be returned to the house if the committee were unable to conclude the matter.[94]

Beginning in 1644 the Declaration of Both Kingdoms established the principle of compounding for delinquency, and the Lords' activities with regard to sequestered estates began to diminish in favour of proceedings before the Committee at Goldsmith's Hall – later referred to as the Committee for Compounding.[95] Those with problems or complaints about sequestration proceedings in the localities began to apply directly to that committee for relief, and the upper house accordingly began to refer petitions to the committee rather than hear the cases themselves.[96] The Lords' involvement in the process of compounding was essentially peripheral; their primary responsibility was to pass the ordinances granting the pardons and confirming the established fines.[97] However, on at least two occasions in 1645 and 1646 the Lords did intervene with the committee to order that they admit individuals to compound where special circumstances (financial hardship, loss of documents) had prevented the process from going forward.[98] In three other cases in 1647 and 1648 they accepted appeals against the Committee's proceedings, acting in one instance to allow a party to compound where the committee had refused to consider the case, and in another to mitigate the fine they had imposed.[99]

On the whole, though, none of the Lords' activities with regard to the sequestration proceedings (and those that followed from them) was particularly edifying. Their attempts to mitigate the legal side effects of Parliament's actions perhaps demonstrated some residual commitment to notions of fairness and equity, but their willing complicity in the programme from the start seriously undermined their credibility, at least in royalist circles, and made a mockery of their previous efforts to uphold the law at all costs.

The Lords, of course, refused to acknowledge their compromise. They appear to have viewed their use of the court for political advantage as somehow divorced from and unrelated to their traditional responsibilities as a court for private litigation – an entirely understandable position, but an intellectually dishonest one all the same – and they continued to behave as though the authority of the High Court remained sovereign and untarnished. Certainly, those subjects who resided within the compass of parliamentary authority (and/or were sympathetic to Parliament's position) appear not to have regarded the Lords' power and authority as in any way diminished, and continued to appeal for legal assistance throughout the later 1640s. The operations of the court for private litigation therefore continued more or less unabated, albeit on a significantly smaller scale and with consistently diminishing returns. The Lords had little choice but to maintain those operations. First, there was a considerable backlog of unresolved cases when war broke out – perhaps as many as 100 – and the parties involved saw little reason to withdraw them. Indeed, they continually pressed the house (largely without success) to proceed to hearing and determination. Second, there was also a steady flow of new petitions to the house – some two to three dozen cases a year – right up to the close of 1648. Certainly, during the early years of the war that was largely because litigants had nowhere else to go. Until the parliamentary Great Seal had been approved and made operational, no legal process of any kind could be undertaken in the courts at Westminster. And even when that situation had been rectified, problems remained. The eighteen-month absence of a seal, from May 1642 to December 1643, had created an extraordinary backlog of demand. Bulestrode Whitelock claimed that when the new Commissioners of the Parliamentary Great Seal were sworn in, in December 1643, they sealed over 500 new writs, 'so desirous were people to have the course of Justice to proceed'.[100] Assuming that his estimates were accurate (and not merely political hyperbole) the courts in London – which were by then hopelessly understaffed, with only one justice each in residence – must have been almost immediately overwhelmed. A petition to the upper house no doubt seemed a more expedient option. However, the Lords continued to receive new petitions long after the central courts and Chancery had become operational again. The litigation was, for the most part, little different from that which had gone before: property disputes, debt cases (usually involving London merchants), disputed wills and trusts, domestic conflicts, plus a variety of conventional appeals from the courts of Admiralty and Chancery (including two appeals against the proceedings of the Parliamentary Commissioners of the Great Seal).[101]

Much of the Lords' time and attention was also taken up with writs of error. In fact, the house faced something of a crisis with regard to them in the later 1640s. The problems really began in early 1644 when it became clear that it was no longer possible to initiate new writs of error according to traditional practice. Litigants wishing to bring a writ of error had always been required first to petition the king for permission to appeal. The king would then authorize a writ, sealed by the Lord Chancellor, to be directed to the Chief Justice of King's Bench, granting him license to remove the record into Parliament. Seeking the king's permission was no longer practical, so the Lords had to direct that litigants first apply to their house for permission to sue out the writ. That clearly did not solve the problem because the writ still had to be sealed by the Lord Chancellor and delivered to the house by the Chief Justice of the King's Bench. Since neither officer was (or was likely to be) available to carry out their task, the two houses were forced to draft an ordinance to amend the procedure. Passed in May 1644, it allowed new writs of error to be sealed by any three Commissioners of the Great Seal (providing that at least one of them was one of the Lords' Commissioners). It then gave permission for the record to be brought into Parliament by any sitting justice of King's Bench.[102]

Two new writs of error were then brought before the house in 1644, followed by a half dozen more in 1645. Thereafter, however, the house was flooded with new writs: 86 in 1646, 99 in 1647, 123 in 1648. Certainly, the revival of operations in the central common law courts in 1644 (however reduced in scale) would account for the appearance of at least a few of these appeals by 1646. But the Lords rarely, if ever, received more than a dozen writs of error a year, under normal circumstances in the pre-Civil

War Parliaments, so these numbers must be considered highly unusual. It is possible that the increase was due in part to the absence of the so-called court of Exchequer Chamber, created by statute in 1585 to handle appeals from the court of King's Bench. That court had simply ceased to function by late 1643 when it became impossible to assemble the required complement of judges.[103] Those wishing to appeal a King's Bench decree would then have had to go directly to the House of Lords, thereby adding to the caseload. In all likelihood, however, the bulk of the increase was the result of deliberate abuse of the procedure by vexatious litigants. Writs of error were often brought simply to delay the execution of judgment in the original court, and no doubt the confusion and disorder of the times and the general uncertainty surrounding legal proceedings in Westminster tempted even the most scrupulous litigant to seek temporary advantage through the writ. The Lords clearly recognized the game, and as early as May 1646 issued new procedural regulations to force the hand of these litigants. Those bringing such writs were required to assign errors on the record within eight days of the writ's submission, or risk automatic default and remission of the case to an appropriate court for judgment.[104] Complaints that this did not allow plaintiffs sufficient time to secure their evidence convinced the house to increase the time to fourteen days, but in either case the rule made little appreciable difference. Litigants ignored it at will. They quickly realized that the house could not possibly keep track of all of the writs in process and, even when they made efforts to do so, parties often waited up to twelve months before the case was scheduled for hearing. In the end less than 10 per cent of these cases ever reached a hearing. Even during its most productive period in 1647, the house only managed to complete proceedings on 22 writs – 21 of which failed and were remitted – and they were able summarily to dismiss half of those when the plaintiff failed to appear. The remainder – a backlog of nearly 250 cases by the close of 1648 – were ostensibly *sub judice*, but would never see the light of day; these plaintiffs had secured a very long-term strategic advantage.

The Lords' failure to complete proceedings on more of these writs was in fact typical of their overall rate of success during the later 1640s. The problem was principally one of diminished resources. The House of Lords' ability to proceed to hearing and judgment on large numbers of cases in the past had depended on two things: its ability to delegate responsibility to independent committees who reviewed petitions for merit, heard arguments of counsel on both sides and recommended final solutions; and on its easy access to judicial expertise. Neither of those resources could be fully drawn upon after 1642. The membership had been drastically reduced to some thirty voting members and daily attendance levels rarely rose above twenty during the war years, and after the summer of 1647 rarely above half that number. Many of the peers who did attend were also fully committed to other official (and time-consuming) responsibilities. Seven members, for instance, sat on the Committee for Both Kingdoms, and two others served for a time as Commissioners of the Great Seal. It was simply not possible to delegate responsibility as before and the vast majority of cases had to be scheduled for full hearing at the bar. Interestingly, in March 1647 the Lords revived the Committee for Petitions, ordering that it sit regularly on Monday afternoons, but the committee had to be recomposed to include all sitting members of the house – thus the house as whole would devote itself to the preliminary hearing of private business on Monday afternoons.[105]

The loss of judicial expertise was potentially more debilitating, since the house, reduced as it was, was increasingly disinclined to proceed to judgment without input from the bench, particularly in complex or difficult appeals. Parliament was in fact remarkably slow in appointing new justices to replace those who had been disqualified for joining the king. Perhaps the lack of qualified personnel was to blame, but new judges were not appointed until the end of September 1645, and then only three positions were filled: Henry Rolle was made justice of King's Bench, Peter Phesant justice of Common Pleas and Edward Atkins, baron of the Exchequer.[106] The three men did not in fact begin duties in the upper house until the end of October when the necessary writs of assistance were finally issued.[107] Up to that point the Lords had only been able to call on the services of three senior judges and even with six now at hand the workload was too large to be handled efficiently, especially given the other demands on the judges' time. The result was that references to the bench took months to be reported. In one case in 1645, for example, the Lords waited almost three months for the judges to issue a simple ruling on the applicability of the statute of limitations to a case of debt.[108] In 1647, they waited almost five months for the judges to assess the viability of errors assigned by a plaintiff in a writ of error.[109] These delays, while entirely understandable, were a fatal impediment to productivity.

It also proved difficult to make much progress on pending litigation when the house failed to keep to a consistent schedule of sittings. The normal pattern of sitting six days a week was periodically abandoned for weeks at a time during the war years. In July 1644, for example, the Lords elected (together with the Commons) to forego Tuesday and Thursday meetings – a practice which lasted some six weeks.[110] In May 1645 they again announced their intention not to sit on Tuesdays and Thursdays, but appear to have been convinced (no doubt by the Commons) to abandon the idea because of the press of business.[111] However, the following August they again decided to restrict their meetings to two a week (on Tuesdays and Fridays) and kept to the policy with some measure of consistency for nearly a month.[112] None of these breaks was in itself dramatic, but given the extensive (and perpetual) backlog of cases and the fact that the house normally only conducted hearings on private causes in the afternoons when they did sit, the reduced workload seemingly represented a luxury the court could ill afford.

The fact was the adjudication of private causes had increasingly taken a back seat to the more urgent matters of state. That was only to be expected in a time of civil war, and perhaps even more so during the protracted negotiations for peace and resettlement which followed. The by now standard orders of the house to 'put off' private causes were issued, during the later 1640s, for periods of up to six months, though, inevitably, they were little more effective than those issued in the past.[113] All the same, the Lords clearly found it increasingly difficult to commit the necessary time to private litigation. The vast majority of cases brought between the beginning of 1643 and the close of 1648 never reached the hearing stage at all, and those that did often had their hearings abruptly cancelled or interrupted because of other business. Cases were often rescheduled dozens of times, stretching over periods of two and three years.[114] Over the period as a whole, the Lords completed hearings and reached some kind of final judgment or resolution in only fifteen cases. Another seventeen were heard and subsequently dismissed, but the combined total represents substantially less than 10 per cent of all of the cases ostensibly under consideration. Not surprisingly, litigants began to lose patience, and as early as 1644, to request permission to withdraw their cases from the house. The refrain was generally the same in each instance – 'Your Petitioners have attended your Lordships many days, with their counsel, at great charge, but cannot obtain a hearing by reason of the weighty affairs of State'.[115] Most of these petitioners opted instead to seek other outside arbitration, or to submit their suit to Chancery, or (once they were fully operational) to the courts of common law. In most of these cases the house was more than willing to oblige them.[116]

In certain notable cases the house was willing to act expeditiously. Predictably, Dr John Bastwick, Henry Burton and William Prynne found a receptive audience when they petitioned in 1644 to have their notorious 1637 Star Chamber convictions overturned. A response in these cases was in fact long overdue. The House of Commons had considered their cases three years earlier, in the spring of 1641, had declared their respective sentences illegal and unjust and had recommended that they be freed from all fines and penalties.[117] But the cases had never been transmitted into the upper house and the Lords had never voted on the Commons' resolutions. As a result the sentences had never been formally vacated and, more seriously, the fines in the Exchequer had never been discharged. The court was still trying to collect them when the three men appealed to the upper house in the autumn of 1644.[118] The House considered their cases together in two (rather brief) hearings in October 1644 and March 1645, and then issued a comprehensive judgment in May, which vacated all sentences in all courts and discharged the three men of their respective fines.[119]

The following January John Lilburne also appealed to the house to have his Star Chamber sentence set aside and he was treated with even greater alacrity.[120] On 13 February the upper house declared the sentence null and void, and ordered it removed from the records.[121] At the urging of his counsel, the Lords also elected to award Lilburne damages and 'reparations' of £2,000 – an act of generosity all too quickly (and conveniently) forgotten by the recipient.[122]

However, political notoriety was not necessarily a prerequisite to success in the upper house. The Lords did actually work hard to settle a number of other, comparatively mundane cases during the war years. In 1645, for example, they were able to award judgment in the long-standing appeal of Ann Hawes, setting aside a former decree in the court of Wards and restoring to the plaintiff (and, in remainder, to Christ's Hospital in London) long overdue bequests from the will of Thomas Hawes.[123] In 1646 they finally settled the complex, multiparty dispute over the commercial debts of Abraham and Thomas Dawes,[124] and in 1647 they overturned two former Chancery decrees, issued by Lord Keeper Coventry in the 1630s, and awarded costs and damages to London Alderman John Fowkes in a suit against the East India Company.[125]

Interestingly, the Lords also showed a continuing concern to protect the rights of married women who had been abandoned without support. Their petitions were always considered promptly and (with one curious exception discussed below) the house rarely failed to take immediate action to secure them support.[126] In January 1646 the Lords actually established a committee to examine the 'defects' of the ecclesiastical courts and their lack of 'coercive power to execute judgement' in cases of alimony – precisely the problem raised by most of the cases brought before them.[127] The committee never reported and in any event the matter became a dead issue the following October when the Lords joined the Commons in abolishing the courts altogether. But the Lords' concern about the welfare of these women was genuine and they did not hesitate to use their own coercive powers to enforce orders for support. In one case, in August 1645, the Lords imprisoned Arthur Stavely, a recent parliamentary appointee as High Sheriff of Leicestershire, for refusing to maintain his wife according to a former order of the house. Stavely remained in prison until February 1647 when he was given a six-week conditional release to settle his estate and provide for his wife's future. He was to be returned to the Fleet if he failed to do so.[128]

For all of that, there were often troubling inconsistencies in the Lords' decisions and frequently during the war years a sense of disorganization and inattentiveness about the proceedings as a whole. A number of cases were accepted for hearing on their merits only to be dismissed subsequently for insufficiency.[129] Others were rejected at the initial hearing only to be accepted when resubmitted by the plaintiff.[130] And in at least two cases the Lords actually reversed their own earlier decisions. In 1641, for example, the house had settled a domestic dispute between Elizabeth Walter and her husband, William. Mrs Walter had been deserted and left without maintenance and the Lords had awarded her an annuity of £60 which was to be paid from her husband's estates. The property had later been sequestered for that purpose.[131] In 1646 Mrs Walter petitioned the house claiming that her husband had evaded the sequestration and was receiving the rents earmarked for her and her children.[132] Twice, in November 1646 and January 1647, the house ordered Walter to pay his wife's alimony according to their original settlement.[133] Then a month later, the Lords suddenly reconsidered the case at the request of Mr Walter. On this occasion his counsel argued that there was no ground in either statute or common law to allow the award of alimony. The Lords, seemingly confused, asked the judges to rehear the arguments of counsel on the question of whether 'by the Law, there may be Alimony given to a Wife', and when the judges reported that Mrs Walter's counsel could find no statute or authority at common law which allowed grants of alimony, the Lords lifted the sequestration on Mr Walter's property and dismissed her petition from the house.[134]

The question referred to the judges and the decision which followed from it made little, if any, sense. The question of alimony was not a matter of law but of equity and neither the church courts nor indeed the house itself had ever been constrained by common law doctrine from granting alimony in deserving cases. As mentioned above, only a year earlier the house had been concerned to strengthen the ability of the church courts to enforce such awards. And, more strikingly still, the Lords had rather emphatically enforced their own decree for alimony in a nearly identical case – *Stavely* v. *Stavely* mentioned above – only ten days before. This decision may have been an aberration, but it is telling all the same. It points to a degree of confusion and inconsistency not seen before. No doubt the problem stemmed from the fact that individual cases were being heard at different times by different groups of members – something virtually unavoidable given the irregular attendance habits of the peers remaining in London. As a consequence, there was little sense of collective memory, even with regard to particular cases, and without it the Lords were increasingly susceptible to the arguments of counsel presented on any given day. No doubt the press of other business at this critical stage of events also made them generally more receptive to arguments which allowed for dismissal.

The other case in which the house reversed itself suggests something even more disturbing – the intrusion of simple political expediency. In 1641 the house had considered the complaint of William Latham and other creditors of the late earl of Carlisle that their attempts to collect their debts in the court of Chancery had been stalled by the new earl's claim of privilege; they asked that his parliamentary protection be suspended so that they could proceed. On that occasion the house had voted to deny privilege and instead insisted that the earl answer the suit in Chancery with all convenient speed. The Lords had been demonstrably concerned at the time that justice be done to all of the creditors.[135] The earl had complied and a decree was eventually issued, in 1644, by the Commissioners of the Great Seal, on behalf of the creditors. At that point, however, the earl insisted on his privilege, claiming that, while he had been willing to plead to the suit in Chancery, he was not now willing to forego his personal protection and allow himself to be attached for the debts. The creditors then repetitioned the upper house in May 1645 protesting that to allow him protection now was contrary to the spirit of the Lords' earlier decision.[136] Unfortunately for the creditors, the earl, a former royalist, had compounded for his delinquency only three months before (agreeing to a fine of £800 as composition) and the Lords no doubt wanted to ensure that his assets would remain unencumbered.[137] They did nothing with the case for nearly nine months and then, in January 1646, lamely declared that it had never been their intention 'to take off the Privilege of the Person of the earl of Carlisle'. They then ordered that a declaration be drawn to proclaim the privileges of peers generally and to restate that their persons were to remain free of any and all legal attachments.[138]

Political considerations also seem to have played a role in the Lords' very curious proceedings in *Langham* v. *Lymbrey*. This case proceeded through the house from October 1643 to August 1647 and in many ways is illustrative of the confusion and disorder that frequently beset the house during this period. The case had arisen in the late 1630s over a maritime contract between London Aldermen John Langham and Sir John Cordell and a group of merchants led by Captain John Lymbrey. In 1638, Langham and his partners had leased a ship, *Royal Merchant*, to Lymbrey and his fellow merchants for a trading expedition that was to last some fifteen months. Lymbrey and his partners kept the ship for forty-four months, at which point it was lost at sea on its return voyage to London. Langham and his partners subsequently sued Lymbrey in Common Pleas to recover damages for the lost ship, but later abandoned the suit when they realized it would only be heard by one judge. Lymbrey then sued Langham in King's Bench to recover the cost of their lost freight, alleging that the ship had not been seaworthy. At that point, Langham petitioned the House of Lords, requesting that the King's Bench proceedings be stayed on grounds that the case was too complex and technical to be heard by an ordinary jury at common law.[139] He asked that the Lords either refer the case to a group of indifferent merchants to settle or, failing that, order that a special jury of merchants be selected to hear the case in

King's Bench. He reminded the house (none too subtly) that he and his partners were, and had long been, 'employed in the Great Public Business of the Kingdom, and by reason thereof, could not heretofore, nor yet can, attend the said private Law Suits, without neglecting the Public Occasions'. The Lords initially agreed to refer the matter to a group of London merchants, but had to retract when Captain Lymbrey petitioned in protest.[140] Instead, the case was referred to a select committee of the house. They subsequently heard arguments of counsel on both sides and reported to the house two weeks later on 15 November. On their recommendation, the Lords elected to allow the proceedings in King's Bench to go forward, but reserved to themselves further consideration of any matters in equity. They therefore warned Captain Lymbrey that if he were successful, he was to stay execution of any judgment until the house had reviewed the matter.[141]

Captain Lymbrey did in fact secure a judgement for £18,000 damages at the close of that Michaelmas term, but was stayed from execution by the Lords' earlier order. Shortly thereafter the court of Chancery reopened under the authority of the new parliamentary commissioners and, sensing a possible strategic advantage, Alderman Langham once again petitioned the Lords, in May 1644, asking that they dismiss his earlier petition and allow him to take whatever equitable remedy he could find in that court.[142] Captain Lymbrey objected, but the Lords agreed to Langham's request and subsequently dismissed the case from the house.[143]

Nothing more was heard from either party until October 1646. In the meantime, Alderman Langham and his partners had applied to the court of Chancery and (in what appears to have been a highly arbitrary proceeding) secured a decree for a new trial at common law. No doubt disinclined to risk another trial, Alderman Langham once again petitioned the House of Lords, requesting that they rehear the entire case on its merits.[144]

Despite their earlier dismissal of the cause, the Lords agreed. On this occasion, however, Captain Lymbrey's counsel challenged their right to do so.[145] In a carefully presented argument they claimed, *inter alia,* that both Langham's appeal to Chancery and this subsequent appeal to the House of Lords violated statute law, and they cited in point the statute of 4 Henry IV, c. 23, which specifically prohibited further appeal to the king, his council, or Parliament (except by attaint or error) after judgment had been secured at common law.[146] The statute had in fact been designed to prevent precisely this type of vexatious litigation and it had already been cited by two other defendants in earlier cases (with notably inconclusive results).[147] Appropriately, the Lords referred the matter to the judges to determine whether or not the case fell within the limits of the statute.[148] Three weeks later, the judges reported their unanimous opinion that it did and though they said nothing further, the obvious conclusion was that the case ought to be dismissed.[149] Nothing was resolved at that point, but the matter was taken up again three days later. This time the house adjourned into a Committee of the Whole to debate the defendants' demurrer and the judges' report. Having resumed, they then put the matter to a vote and by a substantial majority elected to retain the cause in the house, despite the clear implication from the judges that to do so was a violation of statute law. Significantly, two members of the house, the earl of Lincoln and Lord Hunsdon, insisted on registering their dissent.[150]

The decision represents a significant departure from past practice. Up to this point the Lords had always scrupulously followed the recommendations of their judicial assistants on complex points of law and had almost always deferred to prior judgments at common law where they appeared to have settled the central issues in the case. To do so in this instance, however, would have been to incur the wrath of two powerful London aldermen at a time when relations with the City were of critical importance. It was not apparently a risk the house was willing to take. As it was, the subsequent hearings on the case did little to enhance the Lords' reputation as a deliberative body. The case was heard repeatedly through the winter and spring of 1647, but Captain Lymbrey's counsel continued to insist that the case had been properly settled at common law and that the subsequent Chancery decree (if not now the Lords' own hearings) violated statute law. Finally, in March 1647, the Lords once again referred the case to the judges, asking them to consider precisely the same issue they had reported on four months before – the applicability of the statute of 4 Henry IV, c. 23.[151] No doubt confused by the order, and perhaps somewhat hesitant to challenge the authority of the house again, the judges took some time to respond, but they finally delivered a written opinion in early June. Their answer was the same: Alderman Langham's proceedings in Chancery after judgment in King's Bench were against the statute and so, by implication, were his appeals to the House of Lords.[152] After hearing oral presentations from the judges in July, the case was finally dismissed from the house on 26 August. In fact even this final decision was evasive (and perhaps deliberately) ambiguous. The Lords simply declared that the house would 'retain the said Appeal [against the Chancery decree] no longer, but leaves it in the same State and Condition as it was when it was brought into this House'.[153] They conspicuously failed (or refused) to rule on the central issue of Chancery's right to rehear cases after judgment at common law.[154] In the event their decision left the Chancery decree standing, which neither party wanted – Lymbrey because he felt Chancery had not had authority to rule in the case in the first place and Langham because it required a new trial at law which he was destined to lose. There were no winners here.

THE COURT UNDER SEIGE

Though they were clearly exceptional, the arbitrary (or, at best, careless) proceedings in these cases were symptomatic of a declining standard of performance – and a loss of judicial integrity – that progressively undermined the Lords' authority within the legal community and, indeed, outside it. There were ominous signs of this as early as 1645. Litigants routinely complained to the house that the Lords' orders were being openly defied or, worse, treated with contempt and ridicule. On one occasion in June 1645 Christopher Cable, a plaintiff in the upper house, attempted to serve the Lords' order of summons on John Ramsay, a defendant in his case, and was told by Ramsay that 'he had nothing to do with the Lords nor the Plaintiff, and the Plaintiff might take up the said order and wipe his arse with it, for it was good for nothing else' – this from a former soldier in Parliament's army.[155] On another occasion in the autumn of 1645 sheriffs' officers in London met with armed resistance when they attempted to seize goods in execution of a judgment of debt. When the officers explained that they were carrying out the judgment of the House of Lords, the resisters countered that 'we are not to obey any Order of the Lords, for they are private men for themselves, and it is illegal and contrary to the Laws of the Realm'. 'The Lords,' declared another, 'are against the Liberty of the Subject'.[156]

That perception, a clear reflection of growing Leveller influence in London, would of course gain much wider currency, particularly after the Lords' proceedings against John Lilburne the following summer. Lilburne's case, heard in June and July 1646, was the stuff of high drama and gained instant and widespread notoriety.[157] Initially arrested and brought before the house to answer for his published attack on the earl of Manchester, he obstinately refused to speak at the bar of the house and in a written protest which he handed in (and later published) adamantly denied their authority to pass judgment on any commoner in criminal cases.[158] Appealing to the supremacy of the House of Commons and citing Magna Carta, he demanded the right to a trial by his own peers.[159] Understandably, he was committed to Newgate prison for his contempt, and there exacerbated the situation ten-fold by publishing another pamphlet, *The Free Man's Freedom Vindicated*, in which he once again denounced the earl of Manchester and attacked the authority of the upper house. Brought to the bar in July to answer formal charges, he once again behaved with undisguised contempt, refusing either to hear or respond to the allegations.[160]

The Lords were clearly incensed by Lilburne's attack on Manchester, but they were equally disturbed by his refusal to acknowledge their jurisdiction. Both Houses of Parliament had always (and routinely) exercised the right to punish those who had attacked the authority of their institutions or the integrity of their members. The continued viability of Parliament as a governing body demanded that they do so. Indeed, Lilburne had already spent three months in Newgate prison, on the orders of the House of Commons, for refusing to acknowledge their right to punish him for slandering *their* Speaker, William Lenthal, the year before – Lilburne was nothing if not consistent.[161] However, the issue of jurisdiction was perhaps more keenly felt in the House of Lords, not only because of their self-conscious appreciation of their own history as a court, but because of other recent acts of defiance of the kind mentioned above. Lilburne's protest and subsequent behaviour must have been particularly galling, given that only three months before he had enthusiastically enlisted the judicial authority of the upper house to reverse his 1637 Star Chamber conviction and gain reparations. All the same, the Lords played into Lilburne's hands by overreacting. The sentence they eventually imposed was inordinately severe: a £2,000 fine ('to the King'), seven years' imprisonment and perpetual disqualification from any military, civil, or ecclesiastical appointment.[162]

The sentence was a clear reflection of the intense anger which Lilburne had aroused in the house, but it no doubt reflected as well the Lords' wish to make an example of a central figure in the Leveller movement. Instead, it only succeeded in creating a martyr. In the immediate aftermath pamphlets poured forth from clandestine Leveller presses in London roundly condemning the Lords' actions and denouncing their court as hopelessly corrupt and arbitrary.[163] The Lords' subsequent arrest and imprisonment of the leading Leveller pamphleteer, Richard Overton, in August 1646, while equally justifiable, only perpetuated the growing hostility toward the house among the London populace.[164] By mid-summer 1646 the house had come to be seen, certainly within Leveller ranks, as entirely self-serving, tyrannical and oppressive. All sense of proportion had been lost. Overton himself denounced the Lords with bitter sarcasm, in the infamous pamphlet *A Pearl in a Dunghill*, for failing to remedy the excesses of the Personal Rule:

> What fearful enemies you were to Ship Money and to the proceedings of the High Commission, Star Chamber, and Council Board – indeed your goodness was inexpressible and undiscernible before this Parliament . . . What have they ever been but a mere clog to the House of Commons, in all their proceedings? How many necessary things have they obstructed? How many evil things promoted?[165]

The same sentiments were expressed even more graphically in the Levellers' so-called 'large petition' presented to the House of Commons in March 1647. The activities of the house ('the pretended Negative voice') were seen as every bit as arbitrary as those of Charles's Privy Council in the 1630s – 'than which nothing can be more repugnant and destructive to the Commons just liberty'.[166] Memories had grown very short in the white heat of social and political combat.

In due course, as Leveller ideas were progressively taken up by the army rank and file in the spring and summer of 1647, condemnation of the upper house became part and parcel of the emerging popular manifesto. There was some irony here as well. The upper house had repeatedly acted both during and after the Civil War to safeguard the interests of Parliament's soldiers – at their request – by issuing parliamentary protections against arrest and imprisonment for debt. The policy extended to the rank and file as well as to senior officers and often involved securing the release of those already imprisoned – to the very evident annoyance of both creditors and the wardens of London prisons who were invariably sued by creditors for an illegal release.[167] The policy was clearly a matter of military necessity for a time and after the war was only fair, given Parliament's persistent failure to meet the army's payroll. But the fact remained that a number of soldiers in 1647 owed their freedom to the authority of the House of Lords – something all too quickly forgotten in the ensuing months.

What would, of course, matter in the long run was the success of Leveller ideology, and of Lilburne's own ceaseless propaganda, within the lower ranks of the army. After August 1647 the fate of the upper house, as with so much else, rested in the hands of the army or, more accurately, in the hands of the Grandees. Democratic forces within the rank and file were clearly committed to the abolition of the House of Lords or, at the very least, to drastic reform of its powers, and during the course of the Putney debates in October and November 1647 their representatives on the Army Council made their intentions very clear. Lilburne had managed to keep his and Overton's cases very much to the fore – the unwillingness of the council to demand their immediate release earlier that summer still rankled – and efforts were made to bring other notable cases to light. During the previous May and June, for example, the upper house had prosecuted one John Poyntz (alias Morris), his wife and four other defendants for allegedly forging an act of Parliament for use in a property dispute at the Essex assizes. The charge was in fact brought by the Clerk of Parliament, John Browne, from whom the defendants claimed they had received a certified copy of the act. Browne insisted that no such act had ever existed and that he could not therefore have made one available. He had protested to the house that the forgery impugned his integrity and for that and other obvious reasons the house had doggedly pursued the case.[168] In the event, the defendants were convicted and severely punished. They were fined £2,000 (again, 'to the King') and £500 to Browne and imprisoned during the pleasure of the house.[169]

The case appears to have attracted considerable attention in London and was taken up by agents in the Leveller movement and subsequently in the army. Poyntz himself and his co-defendants appealed to Lord General Fairfax in early October, claiming that they had been denied a fair hearing (which was patently untrue). They asked that he prevail on the upper house to remit their fines and release them from prison.[170] A week later Fairfax received a letter purportedly from the officers from Colonel Edward Whaley's regiment and four others which likewise requested that he intercede with Parliament on behalf of Poyntz and his co-defendants.[171] The case was not in fact taken up by Fairfax or the council, but the threat seemed real enough. At one point in mid-October, John Rushworth wrote John Browne with some urgency, advising him to enlist the support of some officers whom he had 'an interest in' to attend a scheduled meeting on the matter.[172]

Despite the fact that the effort was unsuccessful, the attempt to introduce the case at Putney suggests just how committed the radical elements were to damning the House of Lords in the eyes of the Grandees. Holding them at bay required compromises, and Ireton's original *Heads of Proposals* as well as most of the constitutional settlements debated envisioned, at the very least, placing new restrictions on the Lords' judicial authority.[173] In fact the concern about that authority was one-dimensional. The representatives were concerned soley about the Lords' criminal jurisdiction – about the issues raised by Lilburne and Overton – and about that there seems to have been something of a consensus within the council. Ireton himself agreed that, whatever else might befall the upper house, the Lords should be denied the right to prosecute and punish any commoner without the consent of the House of Commons.[174] But beyond that the Lords' judicial authority was presumably to remain intact. Of course, none of these proposals ever saw the light of day. The army leaders retreated in the face of growing hostility and impending mutiny within the rank and file and the debates were suspended in the interests of restoring order. Events then overtook the process when the king's escape effectively redefined the situation. All the same, there were clear signs of trouble ahead.

The early months of 1648 did not alter the situation appreciably, despite the apparent unanimity between Parliament and the army in the ensuing second civil war. The undercurrent of antipathy towards the Lords' judicial authority remained strong and surfaced from two notably different quarters in mid-April. On the 14th, the House of Commons conveyed to the Lords a draft ordinance (presumably written by members of the Independent majority) which was designed to severely constrain their legal jurisdiction in civil as well as criminal cases. The ordinance would have precluded either house from entertaining any petition or complaint between party and party, 'in matter of title, interest or trespass etc', unless it involved a matter of privilege, or defiance of some specific parliamentary order. All other cases, whether civil or criminal, were to be left to the ordinary courts of justice. The ordinance reserved to Parliament only the responsibility of correcting any 'maladministration' within those courts. Just how well supported the ordinance was in the lower house is unclear, but its appearance alone suggests that powerful forces in the Commons had taken up the cause of judicial reform raised in the Putney debates. That did not bode well for the upper house. Predictably, the Lords referred the ordinance to a committee where it was later 'laid by'.[175]

Four days later the Lords received a series of petitions from London Aldermen Sir John Gayre, Thomas Adams and James Bunce, all of whom had been impeached and imprisoned in the Tower in the wake of the City's counter-revolutionary uprisings the previous July. The three men – all moderate Presbyterians – challenged the right of the house to proceed against them, claiming (in words all too reminiscent of John Lilburne) that Magna Carta had guaranteed each his ancient birthright 'to be tried by God and his country in His Majesty's Court of Justice by sworn Judges of the law and by a jury of his equals'.[176] Their pleas fell on deaf ears. The petitions were answered with citations for contempt (for questioning the jurisdiction of the house) and with fines of £500.[177] That response no doubt fatally undermined whatever small reserve of good will may still have existed among moderates within the City toward the authority of the upper house. In the long run that would matter less than the alienation already growing among the radical elements of the populace, but it cannot have helped. By this stage there was precious little support in any quarter for maintaining the jurisdiction of the High Court in its traditional form.

The one lone voice in the wilderness was that of William Prynne. In March 1648 Prynne rose to the defence of the upper house and its judicial prerogatives in a published treatise entitled *A Plea for the Lords*. He was sufficiently attuned to the public mood to realize that the very survival of the House of Lords was now at stake and his treatise was an impassioned plea for retaining its power and authority. He insisted, first, that the English nobility possessed an 'undoubted, ancient, just privilege to sit and vote in all Parliaments of England without any election by, or commission from the people'.[178] Indeed, as he pointed out, their right had been established long before that of the Commons. However, in Prynne's view the presence of an independent peerage was not only justified by historical precedent; it was essential to maintaining an appropriate degree of constitutional equilibrium. Drawing directly from the *King's Answer to the Nineteen Propositions*, he argued that it was the Lords' 'right and honor to moderate the Excesses and Encroachments both of King and Commons, one upon the other, and keep them both within their just and ancient bounds' – a position he carefully supported with examples from pre-Civil War parliamentary proceedings.[179] In direct response to the assertions of Leveller pamphleteers, Prynne insisted that the Lords had always been 'most able and forward to preserve the laws and the people's liberties'. He reminded his readers that it was the Lords who were responsible for the calling of the Long Parliament and stressed the fact that they had been 'very active' in the suppression of Star Chamber, High Commission and the arbitrary powers of the Privy Council.[180]

Prynne's subsequent defence of the Lords' judicial authority focused almost entirely on the issues raised by John Lilburne and other recent defendants in the house. He appears to have been particularly offended by Lilburne's unprincipled behaviour before the Lords in 1646 – asserting the authority (and accepting the justice) of the house when it was to his advantage, denying it when it was not. This sort of expedient reasoning, Prynne suggested, was all too typical of Lilburne's ilk ('those Sectaries and Levellers') but it would not hold up. The by now oft-repeated premise that the Lords could not proceed judicially against a commoner in a criminal charge was dismissed out of hand:

> If the Lords be sole judges in all writs of error concerning the goods, estates, freeholds, inheritances, lives and attainders of commoners of England, notwithstanding Magna Carta, then by the self same reason they are and may lawfully proceed against them in all other civil and criminal cases.[181]

Throughout the essay Prynne characterized the Lords' judicial authority in the broadest possible terms – largely to emphasize his view that their services were indispensable. But he curiously failed to make anything more than veiled references to the Lords' important and successful proceedings in civil litigation. A discussion of those proceedings (still continuing) would have served as a useful reminder of the positive side of the Lords' authority and would undoubtedly have strengthened his general argument.

All the same, Prynne's efforts, however valiant and well reasoned, were ultimately quixotic – a case of too little too late. The house he described was the house of the past (and of the distant future), but certainly not of the present. The small conclave of members who remained active in London had become a minority within a minority, exercising power and influence out of all proportion to their numbers. However determined they may have been to maintain and protect the traditional vestiges of their authority (political and judicial) against all comers, the pretence of legitimacy could no longer be seriously sustained. Even if that had not been true, the threat to the institution would have remained. The ascendant radical minority objected as a matter of principle (or political ideology) to the presence and influence of the peerage in Parliament because it was the product of birth and privilege rather than the natural result of popular choice. That, of course, made it easier to object to the exercise of judicial powers by the same body – particularly when its decrees were being issued by an increasingly select group of peers who were seemingly as much (or as often) in pursuit of political objectives as of impartial justice.

By the summer of 1648, then, the credibility of the house – and of the High Court – had been irreparably damaged. 'This Court,' declared London radical William Pendred in August, 'was now made as badd as ever the Starr Chamber was, the High Commission, or the Spanish Inquisition'.[182] That characterization, while not universally accepted, was certainly orthodox opinion in the quarters that mattered – in the army and within the democratic ranks of the London populace. The subsequent triumph of the Army and its Independent allies in December guaranteed that the upper House would in due course fall victim to the forces of revolution.

When it came the demise of the House of Lords was sure and swift. In the wake of Pride's Purge the Lords continued to sit, though sporadically and in ever decreasing numbers. But after their refusal to concur in the ordinance for the king's trial, their proceedings and their periodic overtures to the lower house were contemptuously ignored.[183] Their fate had been largely (though not conclusively) decided.[184] Despite the efforts of conservative forces to save the upper house, albeit primarily as an advisory body, the Commons resolved on 6 February that 'The House of Peers is useless and dangerous and ought to be abolished'. Subsequent declarations justified the decision on grounds that both the legislative and the judicial powers of the upper house had been 'a great Inconvenience'. The former had allowed the Lords to exercise 'a negative voice over the people, whom they did not at all represent' and the latter 'a hereditary judicature over the people tending to their slavery and oppression'.[185]

Such a sweeping condemnation of the Lords' judicial authority was undoubtedly short-sighted. It was largely (if perhaps not entirely) the result of those few but very public criminal prosecutions undertaken by the house in the late 1640s. It took no account of the positive achievements of the past or of the potential benefits to be derived in the future from the Lords' proceedings in civil litigation. But it was also unavoidable. The fate of the court could not logically be separated from the fate of the house itself (any more than the fate of the house could be separated from that of the king). Larger forces were clearly at work. The damage, however, would be short term. The process would work just as surely in reverse; the inexorable drift back from revolution to Restoration would inevitably carry the High Court home in its wake.

NOTES

1 J.B. Crummett, 'Lay peers in Parliament, 1640–1644', unpublished PhD thesis, University of Cambridge (1986), p. 234.

2 *LJ*, iv, p. 708.

3 Crummett, 'Lay peers in Parliament', pp. 232–42.

4 The seven were the earls of Essex, Bolingbroke, Bedford and Stamford, and Lords Grey, St John and Brooke. The remaining twelve were the earls of Holland, Lincoln, Nottingham, Warwick and Salisbury, Viscount Saye and Sele, and Lords Howard of Escrick, Kimbolton, North, Robartes, Wharton and Lovelace.

5 *LJ*, v, p. 268.

6 ibid., p. 303.

7 ibid., p. 68.

8 ibid. The first two resolutions voted by the House on the issue claimed that the removal of the term was 'contrary to the Practice of Parliament, and inconsistent to the Sitting of Parliament, and the Act of Parliament lately passed for the continuance of Parliament'.

9 Littleton's true position in the crisis has never been entirely clear. Whitelock maintained that he had become the object of considerable suspicion in the king's eyes after his very visible support of the Militia Ordinance. Littleton later maintained, however, that his vote was simply an attempt to disarm the growing distrust of him in the House of Commons and to prevent the premature seizure of the Great Seal. That explanation is born out by his actions, since he did in fact secretly send the Seal to York two days before his own departure. Sir Simonds D'Ewes later reported the general view that Littleton had been in league with the king from the start:

> In the opinion of many, the King had left that spy here by agreement so that he might explore the final Counsels of the Lords and of the more fervid ... in our assembly. Whence, he moving all things against the King with highest ardour, obtained such trust amongst them, that I should easily believe they hid nothing from him. (BL, Harleian MSS, 377, fols 217–18).

I am grateful to Peter Salt for bringing this reference to my attention. See also E. Foss, *The Judges of England*, vol. 6 (London, 1884–64) pp. 348–9.

10 *LJ*, v, p. 122. The original warrants had gone out against both Heath and Justice Foster. The house had been led to believe that Foster had deserted to York as well. The mistake was corrected shortly afterwards and the warrant for Foster's arrest was vacated and the whole proceeding struck from the record.

11 *LJ*, v, p. 124.

12 ibid. The Lords' first declaration on this matter, entered in the journal the same day, was extraordinary. The house declared its opinion that 'The Judges are not tied by their oaths' (*LJ*, v, p. 123).

13 The house was primarily concerned at this point with the publication of the Nineteen Propositions and with securing declarations of support for the Propositions from the judges. On 10 June the house ordered that 'the assistants to this House are to be asked whether they will declare themselves in this business, and how far' (*LJ*, v, p. 123). It was not clear whether the order was ever carried out or, if it was, what the results were.

14 *LJ*, v, pp. 188, 190, 198, 199.

15 *ibid.*, pp. 212, 249.

16 For a full discussion of Malet's role in the Kentish Petitions and the subsequent events of the summer assizes see T.P.S. Woods, *Prelude to Civil War, 1642: Mr Justice Malet and the Kentish Petition* (London, 1980). This book offers a good perspective on the position in which the judiciary as a whole found themselves during this period.

17 *LJ*, v, p. 404. In October of 1645 a motion was put before the House of Lords suggesting that 'some course might be taken that the Lord Chief Justice Bramston might again supply his place as one of the assistants of this House'. A committee

was appointed to consider the proposal and to examine the journal entries for 12 and 15 January 1641, which concerned Charles I's agreement to a change in the judicial tenure from *durante bene placito* to *quamdiu se bene gesserint*. The Lords clearly felt that Bramston's dismissal had violated the spirit, if not the letter, of that agreement (*LJ*, vii, p. 626). In fact, Bramston might have been able to qualify for a post had the house been able legitimately to issue a writ of assistance in his name. Bramston had been made a king's serjeant by Charles I on 10 February 1643, ostensibly as a gesture of conciliation after his dismissal. Nothing apparently came of the proposal to reinstate him (Foss, *The Judges of England*, vol. 6, p. 262).

18 *LJ*, v, p. 405.
19 *DNB*; Foss, *The Judges of England*, Vol. 6, p. 286. Crawley was rewarded for his loyalty with a doctorate of civil law from Oxford in January 1643.
20 *LJ*, v, pp. 545, 564.
21 ibid., pp. 561, 562, 563.
22 HLRO, Main Papers, H.L., 23 December 1640, 'Orders on private petitions'.
23 PRO, C33/179, fol. 643.
24 ibid., fol. 480.
25 HLRO, Main Papers, H.L., 19 May 1641. The second petition is undated.
26 ibid., 23 December 1640, 'Orders on private petitions'. The original petition no longer exists.
27 ibid., 18 June 1642.
28 ibid., 8 February 1641–2.
29 *LJ*, iv, p. 569.
30 ibid., v, p. 540. The house later received a request from the tenants that they be indemnified against any punitive actions taken by Sir Robert Carr in consequence of their conformity with the Lords' order. The request was granted (*LJ*, v, p. 406).
31 HLRO, Main Papers, H.L., 5 December 1642.
32 *LJ*, v, p. 474.
33 ibid., p. 450.
34 ibid.
35 The Master of the Rolls, Sir Charles Caesar, had died on 6 December 1642, and the Lord Privy Seal, the first earl of Manchester, a month before that. Lord Newburgh did eventually apply for leave to join the king on 20 January 1643, but was denied. He then remained with Parliament.
36 *LJ*, v, pp. 547–8
37 The matter of the writ of summons and attendance in the house was nowhere near as clear cut as the king made out. Few if any members would have allowed the notion that the king could dispense with a peer's attendance at will, without breach of privilege. The issue had been raised time and again in the Parliaments of the 1620s, and indeed in both the Short and Long Parliaments in cases involving, among others, the earls of Bristol, Arundel, Hertford, Northumberland and, eventually, the former Lord Keeper, Bishop John Williams. For the king to suggest that his alleged right to control attendance had 'not been denied' by recent Parliaments was patently dishonest. The house may not always have been successful in withstanding the Crown's repeated attempts to manipulate attendance, but they were unquestionably seen as a serious breach of parliamentary privilege, and were strenuously resisted on each occasion. Charles I was certainly well aware of that history. For a further discussion of the issue and these cases, see, E.R. Foster, *The House of Lords, 1603–49* (Chapel Hill, NC, 1983), pp. 16–18, and C. Russell, *Parliaments and English Politics, 1621–29* (Oxford, 1979), p. 16
38 *LJ*, v, ibid., p. 562
39 ibid., p. 569.
40 HLRO, Main Papers, H.L., 10 April 1643.
41 *LJ*, v, p. 705.
42 HLRO, Main Papers, H.L., 25 April 1643.
43 *LJ*, vi, p. 18.
44 HLRO, Main Papers, H.L., 9 May 1643.
45 *LJ*, vi, p. 38.

46   HLRO, Main Papers, H.L., 17 June 1643.
47   *LJ*, vi, p. 100. The exercise may well have been in vain, since the duke himself had been granted safe passage to return to France in early April (*LJ*, v, pp. 712–13).
48   21 Henry VII, c.5. *Statutes of the Realm*, iii, pp. 285–6.
49   HLRO, Main Papers, H.L., 1 June 1643.
50   *LJ*, vi, p. 51.
51   ibid., p. 75.
52   25 Henry VIII, c. 19 (repealed 1–2 Philip and Mary; revived 1 Elizabeth I c.1). *Statutes of the Realm*, iii, p. 460 and iv, p. 530.
53   *CJ*, iii, p. 92.
54   *LJ*, vi, p. 55.
55   ibid., p. 65.
56   ibid., p. 96.
57   HLRO, Main Papers, H.L., 3 June 1643.
58   *LJ*, vi, p. 70.
59   ibid., p. 173. The original petition does not survive.
60   *CJ*, iii, p. 154.
61   ibid., p. 168.
62   ibid., p. 191.
63   It is perhaps significant here that all further proceedings in the case were conducted in the upper house (*LJ*, vi, pp. 193, 213, 223, 321).
64   ibid., p. 173.
65   *CJ*, iii, p. 154; *LJ*, vi, pp. 117–19.
66   *CJ*, iii, p. 155.
67   ibid., p. 226.
68   *LJ*, vi, p. 253.
69   C.H. Firth, *The House of Lords during the Civil War* (London, 1910), pp. 135–7.
70   ibid. Within a few weeks, the Cursitors of Chancery were again petitioning Parliament – this time the House of Commons – complaining that the passage of the ordinance on the new Great Seal had created further problems for them. They claimed that they had a number of writs ready for sealing which had to bear dates before the passage of the ordinance and they requested permission to send them to Oxford to be sealed 'as formerly'. Their request would suggest that they had not experienced, up to that point, any difficulties in executing their business in Oxford, despite the Commons' claims about Radcliffe's failure to cooperate (HLRO, Main Papers, H.L., 27 November 1643). The Commons refused to grant permission and instead referred their petition to the House of Lords 'as a motive for the new Great Seal' (*CJ*, iii, p. 300).
71   *LJ*, vi, pp. 287–8, 300–2.
72   C.H. Firth and R.S. Rait (eds), *Acts and Ordinances of the Interregnum 1642–1660*, Vol. 1 (London, 1917), p. 106.
73   *LJ*, v, p. 652.
74   ibid., p. 662.
75   ibid., vi, p. 12.
76   ibid., p. 48 (Drs Meredith and Reade).
77   HLRO, Main Papers, H.L., 8 May 1643; *LJ*, vi, p. 35 (John Reade).
78   ibid., p. 48 (Nehemiah Rogers).
79   ibid., p. 25 (Soame); p. 54 (Barrell).
80   ibid, p. 48 (Reade); p. 42 (Soame).
81   ibid., pp. 48, 59, 97 (Newstead).
82   ibid., p. 79, 104.
83   ibid., v, p. 686.
84   ibid., vi, p. 173. See also, HLRO, Main Papers, H.L., 7 November 1644.
85   ibid., 18 August 1643; *LJ*, vi, p. 186.
86   HLRO, Main Papers, H.L., 17 August 1643; *LJ*, vi, p. 183.
87   HLRO, Main Papers, H.L., 24 October 1643.
88   *LJ*, vi, p. 271.
89   HLRO, Main Papers, H.L., 14 March 1643.

90 *LJ*, v, p. 650.
91 HLRO, Main Papers, H.L., 1 April 1643.
92 *LJ*, v, p. 686.
93 HLRO, Main Papers, H.L., 19 June 1643.
94 *LJ*, vi, p. 101.
95 For a full discussion of the development of the committee's responsibilities see M.A.E. Green (ed.), *Calendar of the Committee for Compounding*, 5 vols (London, 1889–93) Vol. 1, pp. i–xxiv; vol. 5, pp. i–xlii.
96 See for example, *LJ*, vii, p. 707 (petition of Grace Belais, on behalf of Lord Falconbridge). This petitioner was directed to 'apply herself to a proper way where compositions are made for delinquents'. See also, Green, *Calendar*, Vol. 5, p. ix.
97 Green, *Calendar*, Vol. 5, p. x, describes the Lords' role in these proceedings as 'nugatory'. The Lords would not have entirely agreed. In early 1647 they protested that the compositions made by the committee were not being presented to Parliament for approval. They instructed the county commissions to ignore the orders of the committee (ibid., Vol. 1, p. 55).
98 HLRO, Main Papers, H.L, 22 October 1645; *LJ*, vii, p. 655 (John, earl Rivers). Main Papers, H.L., 14 November 1646; *LJ*, viii, p. 565 (James, earl of Northampton).
99 HLRO, Main Papers, H.L., 16 March 1647; *LJ*, ix, pp. 103–4 (Sir Thomas Windebank); HLRO, Main Papers, H.L., 3 April 1648; *LJ*, x, p. 168 (Lord Molineux), p. 365 (Lord Dunesmore).
100 Foss, *The Judges of England*, Vol. 6, p. 218.
101 HLRO, Main Papers, H.L., 'January' 1645–6; *LJ*, viii, pp. 112, 177, 202, 226, 338, 503 (*Chamberlain* v. *Nichols*). HLRO, Main Papers, H.L., 18 May, 3 November 1647; *LJ*, ix, pp. 192, 196, 510 (*Corbet* v. *Hunt*). Neither appeal was successful.
102 *LJ*, vi, pp. 423, 440, 554.
103 27 Elizabeth I, c.8. The statute required that King's Bench decrees be reviewed by all of the justices of Common Pleas and the barons of the Exchequer.
104 *LJ*, viii, pp. 324, 336. The regulation was ordered to be printed and published. Late in 1647 the Lords began to levy heavy fines on plaintiffs who failed to prosecute their writs. See, for example, *LJ*, ix, p. 511 (*Alford* v. *Smith*), p. 565 (*Clarke* v. *Cole*).
105 *LJ*, ix, pp. 81, 93.
106 ibid., vii, pp. 571, 614, 624.
107 ibid., pp. 663–4.
108 The case was referred to the judges on 24 October 1645 and was reported on 17 January 1645–6, though the report was not taken up by the house until 2 March (*LJ*, vii, p. 658; viii, p. 192 (*Balmerino* v. *Heath*)).
109 *LJ*, ix, p. 495 (*Hoste* v. *Lynnen*).
110 ibid., vi, p. 611.
111 ibid, vii, p. 386.
112 ibid., p. 537.
113 ibid., p. 476.
114 For that reason the house imposed heavy fines on litigants who failed to appear on appointed hearing dates. In one case they fined a 'delinquent' plaintiff £40. See *LJ*, vi, p. 377 (Thomas Dawes); vii, p. 92 (*Hitchum* v. *earl of Suffolk*); vii, p. 313 (*Mansell* v. *Harris*).
115 HLRO, Main Papers, H.L., 11 April 1646 (William Allen).
116 See, for instance, HLRO, Main Papers, H.L., 16 February 1644; *LJ*, vi, p. 429 (*Middleton* v. *Clotworthies*); HLRO, Main Papers, H.L., 13 October 1645; *LJ*, vii, pp. 633, 653.
117 *CJ*, ii, pp. 90, 102, 123, 124, 134.
118 HLRO, Main Papers, H.L., 20 August 1644 (Prynne), 7 October (Bastwick), 12 October (Burton). Bastwick's request was in fact presented in a petition from his wife, Susan. The Lords stayed proceedings in the Exchequer in response to Prynne's petition (*LJ*, vi, p. 681).
119 ibid., vii, pp. 26, 282, 352. The Star Chamber sentences and the Exchequer estreats were brought into the house and vacated the following December (*LJ*, viii, pp. 39, 61).

120 HLRO, Main Papers, H.L., 2 February 1645–6. The House of Commons also made
a separate request that the Lords concur in their earlier votes on Lilburne (*LJ*,
viii, p. 127).
121 ibid., vii i, pp. 130, 165.
122 ibid., viii, pp. 201, 217. Lilburne's award was to be paid from the sequestered estates
of Lords Cottington and Windebank and the warden of the Fleet. Both Bastwick
and Prynne subsequently applied to the house for reparation. (HLRO, Main Papers,
H.L., 16 March 1645–6 (Burton), 1 June 1646 (Prynne)). Bastwick was eventually
awarded £4,000, to be paid from the estates of the duke of Richmond, the earl of
Dorset and Lords Cottington and Windebank.
123 *LJ*, vii, p. 706.
124 ibid., viii, pp. 159.
125 ibid., ix, pp. 178–9.
126 See, for example, *LJ*, viii, p. 107 (Lady Berkeley); p. 189 (*Dutton* v. *Dutton*); p. 575
(*Walter* v. *Walter*).
127 ibid., p. 107.
128 ibid., vii, pp. 193, 217, 406, 555; ix, p. 14.
129 See, for example, HLRO, Main Papers, H.L., 24 October 1645, 1 January 1645–6;
LJ, vii, p. 658; viii, pp. 78–9, 194 (*Cromwell* v. *Tracy*).
130 See, for example, *LJ*, vi, p. 440; vii, p. 148 (*Lecuer* v. *Hooper*).
131 For a discussion of this case, see above, p.135.
132 HLRO, Main Papers, H.L., 1 June 1646, 29 January 1646–7.
133 *LJ*, viii, pp. 575, 693–4, 696.
134 ibid., ix, pp. 25, 32.
135 For a discussion of this case, see above, Chapter 3, pp. 119–20.
136 HLRO, Main Papers, H.L., 12 May 1645; *LJ*, vii, pp. 366–8.
137 ibid., p. 192.
138 ibid, viii, p. 86.
139 The petition is not preserved in the Main Papers collection, but is reprinted in full
in *LJ*, viii, pp. 605–6.
140 HLRO, Main Papers, H.L., 31 October 1643.
141 *LJ*, vi, p. 306.
142 ibid., p. 543.
143 ibid., pp. 553, 568.
144 ibid., viii, p. 529.
145 Lymbrey's counsel were Bulstrode Whitelock and Oliver St John.
146 *LJ*, viii, pp. 556–7, 604–7; *Statutes of the Realm*, ii, p. 142.
147 *LJ*, iv, p. 307 (*earl of March* v. *earl of Pembroke*); vii, p. 358 (*Hitchum* v. *Suffolk*).
When the statute was raised by counsel for the earl of March in 1641, the house
took great offence and referred the matter to the Committee for Privileges to examine
what were 'the due and right Privileges of this House in Matters of Judicature'. The
committee never reported its findings. Its first and only meeting on the matter
apparently erupted into a minor brawl when the principals began hurling insults
(and then objects) at one another. The episode caused a minor scandal in the house
and the parties were severely censured (HLRO, Braye MSS 2, ff. 177–8). The incident
is summarized in HMC reports, xi, Addenda, pp. 275–7. In the second case, in May
1645, the matter of the statute was also referred to a committee of the house to
consider, but it never resurfaced (*LJ*, viii, p. 104).
148 ibid., p. 557.
149 ibid., p. 573.
150 ibid., p. 576.
151 ibid., pp. 680, 683, 697; ix, pp. 25–6, 49, 57.
152 ibid., p. 247.
153 ibid., p. 407.
154 Ironically, the case quickly came to be seen as a more definitive statement on the
limits of equity jurisdiction than the Lords intended. Their proceedings were in fact
cited in 1655 in a suit in the equity side of the Exchequer. The plaintiff here sought
relief against a judgment for debt issued by the plea side of the court. The defendant

215

entered a demurrer, similar to Captain Lymbrey's, citing the statute of 4 Henry IV, c. 23. It was ruled in his favour and 'Langham v. Lymbrey was cited in point, which was ruled in the House of Lords by the advice of all of the Judges in the last Long parliament' (*Reports of Cases in the Exchequer, 1655–1669*, ed. Thomas Hardres, 2nd edn, (Dublin, 1792), p. 23 (*Morel* v. *Douglas*).

155 *LJ*, vii, p. 465. Ramsay was subsequently arrested and imprisoned, but when he petitioned the house two weeks later, claiming that he had failed to appear at the scheduled hearing 'out of mere ignorance', the house released him (HLRO, Main Papers, H.L., 12 July 1645; *LJ*, vii, p. 495).

156 HLRO, Main Papers, H.L., 11 November 1645 (*Jhannes* v. *Legay and Fairfax*); *LJ*, vii, p. 699 (affidavits of John Norlord and William Harrison). Norlord claimed that the men refused to obey the Lords' orders because 'the Lords were against the Liberty of the Subject'.

157 For a concise summary of the Lords' proceedings against Lilburne, see Firth, *House of Lords*, pp. 156–9, and Pauline Gregg, *Free-Born John* (London, 1961), pp. 141–3.

158 *LJ*, viii, pp. 370, 387–8.

159 Lilburne subsequently restated his views on the jurisdiction of the house in an unsolicited address to both Houses of Parliament in October 1647. He was now willing to recognize the appellate authority of the House of Lords (based on his reading of the statute of 14 Edward III, c. 23) providing, as he put it, 'they have the King's particular Commission therefore'. He acknowledged as well that that authority had been confirmed by the Elizabethan statutes which created writ of error procedure. However, he continued to deny that the Lords had 'any original jurisdiction over any commoner whatsoever, for life, limb, liberty or estate' and he offered to debate the matter before the houses 'with any forty lawyers in England' ('The proposition of Lieutenant-Colonel John Lilburne, prerogative prisoner in the Tower of London, made unto the Lords and Commons assembled in Westminster and to the whole kingdom of England, October 2, 1647', cited in M.Hale, *The Jurisdiction of the Lords' House* (London, 1796), p. lxxiii).

160 *LJ*, viii p. 432.

161 Howard Shaw, *The Levellers* (London, 1968), pp. 40–1.

162 *LJ*, viii, p. 432.

163 See Firth, *The House of Lords*, pp.159–66.

164 *LJ*, viii, p. 457.

165 'A pearl in a dunghill, or Lieut-Colonel John Lilburne in Newgate' (June 1646) Thomason Tracts, E 345 (5), pp. 3–4.

166 Cited in G.E. Aylmer, *The Levellers in the English Revolution* (New York, 1975), pp. 75–7.

167 See, for example, *LJ*, vii, p. 201 (Peter Alston), p. 360 (*John James* v. *Jervas Blackwall*); p. 430 (*Lindsey* v. *Jackson*); p. 638 (*Wyndis* v. *Holt*); ix, p. 56 (Colonel Thomas Home); p. 77 (Captains Swain and Griffin); p. 547 (John Grover).

168 HLRO, Main Papers, H.L., 23–5 June, 3 July 1647; *LJ*, ix, pp. 182, 198, 207, 229–30, 244, 266, 293–4, 332–3, 346, 441.

169 ibid., pp. 437, 441.

170 HLRO, Main Papers, H.L., 7 October 1647.

171 ibid. Colonel Whaley later wrote Fairfax disclaiming any part in the letter. He insisted that it was the work of 'private agitators' in his regiment.

172 ibid. The case was later appealed to Lord Protector Cromwell (HLRO, Main Papers, H.L., 10 March 1655–6).

173 Firth, *The House of Lords*, pp. 172–87.

174 ibid., p. 186. The house was to be allowed the right to imprison an offender until he could be tried by the House of Commons.

175 HLRO, Main Papers, H.L., 14 April 1648; *LJ*, x, p. 193.

176 HLRO, Main Papers, H.L., 18 April 1648.

177 *LJ*, x, pp. 207–8; HLRO, Main Papers, H.L., 22 April 1648. The charges against the aldermen were later dropped and the men were finally released in June as part of a general political settlement with the City. See Robert Ashton, *The English Civil War, Conservatism and Revolution 1603–1649* (London, 1979), pp. 325–6.

178   William Prynne, *A Plea for the Lords*, 1st edn (London, 1648), p. iv.
179   ibid., p. 22.
180   ibid., p. 25.
181   ibid., p. 31.
182   HLRO, Main Papers, H.L., 26 August 1648. Pendred was a witness in the behalf of the defendants John Poyntz (alias Morris) and his wife in the aforementioned case involving the forged act of Parliament. He made the statement at the doors of the upper house – to its guards – and was subsequently arrested and imprisoned on orders of the Clerk of Parliament, John Browne, for 'stirring the people to sedition' against the House of Lords.
183   Firth, *The House of Lords*, pp. 210–15.
184   For a detailed and illuminating discussion of the final stages of the process which led to abolition, see J.S.A. Adamson, 'The peers and politics, 1642–1649', unpublished PhD thesis, University of Cambridge (1986).
185   *Parliamentary History*, iii, p. 1,300.

6

The court restored

Your Lordships will easily recover that Estimation and Reverence
that is due to your high Condition, by the Exercise and Practice of
that Virtue from whence your honours first sprang; the example of
your Justice and Piety will inflame the Hearts of the People towards
you, and from your practice they will make a Judgement of the King
himself. They have looked upon your Lordships, and will look upon
you again, as . . . their greatest security and protection from injury
and injustice, and for their enjoying whatsoever is due unto them
by the law.[1]

The restoration of the House of Lords was accomplished in April 1660
with remarkable ease and with surprisingly little protest. Only two
months earlier the political climate for such a restoration had seemed
distinctly unpromising. Opposition to a revived upper house remained
strong and vocal within the army. Indeed, General Monck had felt
compelled to bar even loyal Presbyterian lords from taking their seats
with the Secluded Members in the newly restored Long Parliament.
'The state of these nations be such,' Monck had claimed, 'as cannot
bear their [the Lords] sitting in a distinct House.'[2] Even as restoration in
the forthcoming Convention Parliament appeared increasingly likely, after
supportive votes in the House of Commons in mid-March, predictions
were made that their sitting would be the cause of considerable discord.[3]
And the peerage itself remained divided over the composition of any
future assembly. Those lords who had remained sitting in 1648 – the
so-called 'Presbyterian Knot' led by the earls of Northumberland and
Manchester – were determined to exclude all former royalist lords, as well
as new lords who had succeeded to their titles during the Interregnum.
That in fact remained the position of Monck himself and the majority of
the Council of State as late as mid-April.

And yet within two days of the opening of the Convention Parliament,
the so-called 'young Lords' had taken their seats, the Presbyterian cabal
had been overwhelmed and the way had been cleared for the return of the
former royalist peers, most of whom drifted back – some by invitation,
others on their own initiative – over the next two weeks. By the end of May
the house had even agreed to seat those peers created by Charles I after
1642. And, despite all of the rhetoric of the recent past, no serious attempt
was made (nor would be made) to circumscribe the Lords' traditional

218

rights and privileges. Restoration simply brought restitution, without challenge, or comment, or conditions, of the long-standing legislative and judicial prerogatives of the upper house – and of the High Court.

What had, of course, happened in the interim was that the views of the general public had been canvassed on the nature of a future political settlement – in the form of elections to the Convention Parliament – and the result had been the return of an overwhelmingly royalist House of Commons. The election had clearly been a referendum on the issue of monarchy,[4] but the result had been less a vote of confidence in Charles II and the house of Stuart than an endorsement of the ancient constitution. In voting to restore the monarchy, the public had implicitly voted to restore all that went with it – a government of and by king, lords and commons, in which each component had (or so it seemed in retrospect) a well-defined role and specific responsibilities. Once that decision had become clear any resistance to the restoration of the upper house became pointless. The fact that that restoration took place unconditionally, without restrictions being imposed on the authority of the house, reflected the consensus view (certainly of royalist MPs and their constituents) that the traditional powers exercised by the lords in Parliament – both legislative and judicial – had been, despite the aberrations of the later 1640s, of considerable value and importance to the good government of the realm.

In fact that conclusion had been reached much earlier by Oliver Cromwell himself and by members of the second Protectorate Parliament. The repeated failure of single-chamber Parliaments during the Interregnum, with their narrow agendas and even narrower constituent support, had led inexorably to the drafting of a new constitution in 1657, the most important feature of which – apart from the offer of a crown to Cromwell – was the restoration of a second house of Parliament. The Lord Protector and numerous others had finally come to see the wisdom of having a second chamber – 'an excellent screen and bank' – to mediate between the respective interests and opinions of the Supreme Magistrate and the Commons, and they set about rebuilding the tripartite government of pre-Civil War England in *The Humble Petition and Advice*.

The authors of the *Petition and Advice* plainly assumed that the new house would take up the role and responsibility of the old House of Lords and therefore took little care to define its powers and privileges with any precision. It was simply taken for granted that the new house would exercise a coordinate power with the House of Commons in legislation and that in due course it would resume operations as a high court of justice. In the latter case the authors did in fact attempt to spell out, in pre-emptive terms, the future legal jurisdiction of the new body. The 'other House' was not to proceed in any civil causes, *except* in writs of error, in cases adjourned from inferior courts into the Parliament for difficulty, in cases of petitions against proceedings in Courts of Equity, and in cases of privileges of their own House. [Nor] . . . in any criminal causes whatsoever against any person criminally, but upon an impeachment of the Commons assembled in Parliament, and by their consent (emphasis added).

The new house was further admonished not to proceed in any civil or criminal cause 'but according to the known laws of the land, and the due course and custom of Parliament'.[5]

The jurisdiction was plainly defined in negative terms, but it is misleading to place too much emphasis on its proscriptive nature. In fact, the exceptions to the rules are more revealing than the rules themselves. Read carefully, the new house was left with essentially the same jurisdiction in civil causes which the House of Lords had exercised since the 1620s – writs of error, cases adjourned from inferior courts for difficulty, appeals from equity courts, and cases of privilege. Only cases brought by petition in the first instance were not specifically mentioned. That omission may have been deliberate, but it seems unlikely. There was nothing particularly contentious about that aspect of the Lords' civil jurisdiction and it was certainly no more potentially threatening than their appellate jurisdiction over both common law and equity courts, which the new proposals clearly recognized. The new definition had in fact been drawn up by a committee headed by Bulstrode Whitelock who, as a sometime practising lawyer at the bar of the House of Lords and a long-standing Commissioner of the Great Seal, would have been entirely conversant not only with the recent operations of the High Court, but with the kind of troublesome jurisdictional issues which might arise in the future – not least where they involved his own court of Chancery.[6] The broadly defined civil jurisdiction was therefore telling.

The only substantive alterations in the Lords' traditional jurisdiction in this proposal involved criminal proceedings undertaken independently of impeachments in the House of Commons. Such proceedings were expressly prohibited under the new constitution. This limitation was obviously a by-product of the lingering unease over the Lords' notorious proceedings against Lilburne, Overton and others in the late 1640s and to that extent was entirely predictable. Cooler heads might have recognized that the Lords had, for the most part, exercised their criminal jurisdiction relatively rarely and usually in the broader interest of preserving law and order. But, given the prevailing sensitivities in republican circles and in the army, restricting the powers of the new house in this way made sense. It was a small concession to make for the larger gain.

The subsequent debates over the 'other House' in January 1658, and in Richard Cromwell's Parliament the following year, reveal that there had been considerable discussion of the matter during the drafting of the new constitution. Those in favour of reviving the powers of the High Court had apparently argued their case as much on grounds of practical necessity as of constitutional propriety. Certainly, the doubts raised (both inside and outside the house) about the Commons' own right to proceed judicially against the notorious James Nayler the previous year contributed to the decision.[7] But MPs had also expressed concern that if they failed to revive the judicial authority of the upper house, they themselves would be forced to hear petitions for judicial remedy (as, indeed, they had already done). 'Judgments,' claimed Walter Waller, 'will necessarily fall upon us.'[8] Colonel Joachim Matthews recalled that MPs had argued in favour of giving the new house these judicial powers because 'Complaints from Courts of Justice and Equity . . . would take up too much of your time'. 'Here,' he suggested (rather disingenuously), 'was your ground for another House.'[9]

Those suggestions were also taken up almost immediately by the seemingly indefatigable William Prynne, who revised and expanded his earlier treatise, *A Plea for the Lords*, for republication in 1658, under the new title *A Plea For the Lords and the House of Peers*.[10] The principal difference between Prynne's earlier essay and the new edition was in fact the inclusion of a much more detailed account of the history of House of Lords' judicature. As before, Prynne was primarily concerned to prove that the right of judicature lay exclusively in the upper house. But he was also at pains to demonstrate both the breadth of the Lords' jurisdiction and the inherent advantages which that jurisdiction had traditionally offered to litigants. Not surprisingly, he placed great emphasis on what he called 'modern precedents' – cases drawn from the 1620s and from the Long Parliament, which he no doubt hoped would be more immediately familiar to his readers. His citations were carefully chosen to include cases brought both in the first instance and on appeal from courts such as Chancery, the High Commission, the court of Admiralty and, of course, Star Chamber. His own and his co-defendants' successful appeals against their Star Chamber convictions in the 1630s featured largely in the discussion, ostensibly as proof of the Lords' continuing willingness (and ability) to protect the legal rights and interests of the subject.[11]

The new essay appears to have had a far better reception than the old. With Selden's *Privileges of the Baronage of England* it was cited as an authoritative guide to the rights of the old house at least once in the debates on the second chamber in March 1659.[12] By that stage, however, Prynne would have been preaching to the converted. A majority of MPs had already concluded that the second chamber provided for in the new constitution was both necessary and beneficial. Unfortunately, this crucial first session of Richard Cromwell's Parliament was poorly managed (as indeed his father's final session had been) and a more vocal and tactically superior republican minority was allowed to control the debates and ultimately obstruct any further progress toward a definitive political settlement. The inevitable result was the fall of the Protectorate and the return of the Rump.

But the republican triumph was only a temporary setback. The *Petition and Advice* and the discussions on the second chamber which followed in early 1658 and again in 1659 make clear that the revolution of 1649 had done little permanent damage to the traditional standing and reputation of the House of Lords as an institution. In its absence, MPs had developed a far greater appreciation of its legislative function – as a tempering influence on the House of Commons – and of its remedial role as a high court. Regardless of whether MPs supported the new 'other House', as composed by Cromwell, or a return of the ancient House of Lords, the arguments in favour of a second chamber in 1659 were essentially the same. The Lords were, as the Presbyterian Arthur Annesley put it in 1659, 'good to be a balance between the Supreme Magistrate and the people, and to supervise and protect the laws'.[13]

The public clearly shared that perception. That was, in some measure, evident in the elections to the Convention Parliament the following spring which, at least indirectly, suggested strong support for a restored House of Lords. But the real measure of public faith in the upper house came when the Lords finally took their seats in April 1660. Almost immediately private suitors began once again to flood the upper house with petitions for legal redress, seeking relief against a variety of alleged injustices perpetrated by the parliamentary government of the late 1640s and the Cromwellian governments of the 1650s. The numbers were impressive. In the eight short months of this Parliament, the Lords received nearly 800 individual petitions. They came from clergymen who had been deprived of (or sequestered from) their ecclesiastical livings; from public office holders who had been ousted from their 'freehold'; from masters and fellows of Oxford and Cambridge colleges who had been removed from their university posts. There were appeals as well from former royalists seeking restoration of property taken or sequestered during the Civil War and Interregnum and from families seeking restitution for the 'crimes' of the Cromwellian High Courts.

On the face of it, the situation in 1660 was more than a little reminiscent of the crisis which had faced the Long Parliament House of Lords 20 years earlier. The specific complaints were of course different, but the general expectations were much the same. As in 1640, petitioners to the Convention Parliament looked to the authority of the upper house to settle differences which had arisen between the subject and the central government over the previous 15 years or more. In their headlong pursuit of 'public' policy, the governments of the late 1640s and 1650s had often been every bit as cavalier (or 'Cavalier') about traditional legal guarantees as Charles I's government had been during the Personal Rule, and just as their counterparts in 1640, these complainants were simply unwilling to accept the abrogation of those rights – perhaps even less willing in this case because of the questionable authority of the governments themselves. They appealed to the upper house to 'protect the law' by restoring (and affirming) their individual legal interests against the potential threat of arbitrary rule.

However, the challenge facing the Restoration House of Lords was infinitely more complex and difficult than that which faced the Lords in the Long Parliament. In 1640 the Lords had been asked to enforce the rule of law against the Crown – to correct the patently irregular and arbitrary proceedings sanctioned by the king and his government during the 1630s. In a sense that was Parliament's job and the legal issues had been, for the most part, perfectly straightforward. Now in 1660 they were being asked to enforce the rule of law against Parliament itself – or at least against those members who had presumed to govern in Parliament's name in the late 1640s – and against the Cromwellian governments of the 1650s, both of which had acted in response to the special conditions and demands of civil war and revolution. The legal issues were anything but clear. Nor could these ostensibly private complaints be treated in isolation from the broader course of public events. The plaintiffs in the House of Lords in 1660 represented, as a group, the losing side in the political battles of the previous two decades. They were undeniably victims, but they were royalist victims and any attempt by the upper house to redress their grievances would, inescapably, be seen in political terms. Their decisions therefore had to be very carefully considered and even more carefully made. They had to be (and be seen to be) solidly grounded in the law. The appearance of anything resembling partisanship would have done irreparable damage, both to the credibility of the High Court itself and, perhaps more importantly, to the essential process of national reconciliation. Both clearly hung in the balance in the spring of 1660.

THE CONVENTION PARLIAMENT: LAW AND THE POLITICS OF RECONCILIATION

All things considered, the resumption of judicial business in the Convention Parliament occurred with remarkable speed and efficiency. Despite the 11-year intermission, the Lords simply picked up where they had left off, with little if any sign of uncertainty. A Committee for Petitions was duly appointed on 2 May, just five working days into the session.[14] Initially, it included only 15 members, and not surprisingly, given the composition of the house at that early stage, it was dominated (numerically

223

at least) by the so-called 'New Lords' – men who had succeeded to their titles in the late 1640s or 1650s and who had had little direct involvement in the political divisions of the Civil War period.[15] They represented 10 of the 15 members. The other 5 included 4 Presbyterians (the earls of Lincoln and Nottingham and Lords Grey de Wark and Howard of Escrick) and one royalist, William Lord Craven, who had actually taken his seat on 27 April.[16] However, there is no real evidence to suggest that the composition of this committee, or any other, was engineered along the party lines of the past in an attempt to favour one group over another. The committee was gradually expanded over the next two weeks as the house began to fill up and new appointees were drawn from the ranks of former royalists and parliamentarians alike, in roughly equal proportions. A handful of Catholic peers were included as well.[17] At least initially, the committee appears to have been chaired by the new earl of Pembroke.[18] Over the summer additional members were added, in part to accommodate members of the king's Privy Council, and the total eventually reached 63, the largest such committee ever appointed.[19]

As in the past, the committee was empowered to receive and consider petitions and report the result to the house as a whole with the proviso, issued to all such committees in previous parliaments, that they were to dismiss all petitions 'which have any relief in any other court of Law or Equity'.[20] In late June objections appear to have been raised about the wide discretionary powers given the committee to hear and dismiss petitions on its own accord. This was in all likelihood the result of complaints made by rejected suitors to individual members. It had happened in the 1620s and in the Long Parliament and the result was the same. The house reversed its earlier directions and now insisted that every petition be first read in the house itself, rather than being taken directly to the committee.[21] By early July, as the number of petitions began to escalate dramatically, the house was forced to revise the procedure once again. A special subcommittee of the Committee for Petitions was appointed to act in the capacity of the old medieval receivers and triers. New petitions initially referred to the Committee for Petitions were to be vetted by this subcommittee, who were to determine whether the cases should be heard at all and if so, whether they should be heard by the Committee for Petitions or by the house itself.[22]

Following standard practice, the house attempted to provide the committee with expert legal advice drawn from the ranks of its judicial assistants. In this case, however, the effort was complicated by the uncertain status of some of the judges. In addition to the Clerk of the Crown and the Master of the Rolls, the Lords initially summoned the then Chief Baron of the Exchequer, John Wilde, and the Chief Justice of the 'Upper' Bench, Richard Newdigate, both of whom had been reappointed (having been previously dismissed by the Lord Protector) by the restored Long Parliament in January 1660. Perhaps as a gesture of reconciliation, they also summoned former judge, and now serjeant, Thomas Malet, who had been disqualified as a justice of King's Bench in 1645.[23] Newdigate presented an immediate problem. He had apparently assumed that his appointment in 1660 had lapsed with the demise of the Long Parliament and as a consequence he had successfully stood for election to the Convention House of Commons. Summoning him as an assistant therefore created a complicated question of privilege. The matter was referred to the Lords' Committee for Privileges on 3 May, but was never reported. However, it appears to have been resolved in the Lords' favour, since Newdigate was summoned to appear as an assistant to the Committee for Petitions two days later.[24] Thereafter, the house declined to issue any further summons, no doubt anticipating (correctly) that the king would reconstruct the common law benches to his own liking as soon as he returned. A few key appointments were in fact made on 31 May – Wilde and Newdigate were both replaced – and on 4 June the Lords asked Lord Chancellor Hyde to move the king to grant the customary writs of assistance to his new judges.[25] They subsequently took their places, as did all those appointed over the next few months.

The Lords were therefore prepared more or less from the outset to handle a broad range of complaints. In the opening month of the first session they received just over three dozen petitions. The vast majority of those (28) came from two groups: public office holders and university officials. In both cases, the complainants sought to recover offices (or fellowships) from which they had been forcibly removed during the previous two decades. None of these offices was critical to the government of the state, aside perhaps from the university posts and political offices in borough corporations. They included such places as the office of Chief Register in Chancery, the Master of the Barges, Chief Customs Searcher in London, Comptroller of the King's Works and Clerk of the Irons in the Mint. But they were clearly of great importance to the previous holders and the Lords took their complaints very seriously. On the face of it, the questions before the Lords were fairly straightforward. Could the plaintiff prove precedent title (to that claimed by the incumbent) and if so, had he been illegally deprived of his office? If the answer to both questions was yes, it was only just that he should recover. However, the matter was not always that simple. The defendants in these cases claimed title by virtue of grants from Parliament itself in the 1640s, or from the Cromwellian Council of State in the 1650s, both of which had claimed to represent the sovereign political authority of the day. The defendants who had accepted appointment under their auspices felt that, under the circumstances, their grants were every bit as legal as those granted by the previous government. To deprive them of those offices was essentially to punish them for their complicity with the Revolution – something which may have seemed entirely justifiable, in broad political terms, but was not always reasonable or fair in individual cases. Many of these defendants had executed their offices in good faith and with considerable care and efficiency. There was also an inherent danger in deciding these cases too quickly. Denying the validity of the incumbents' grants implicitly, but unmistakably, denied the legitimacy and authority of the governments which had issued them and at this very delicate stage of events, before the king's return, there was a persuasive political argument to be made for avoiding sweeping condemnations of the previous administrations, parliamentarian and Cromwellian alike. More importantly perhaps, the Lords did not want to pre-empt Charles II's right to fill these offices with candidates of his own choosing. On all counts, the proceedings called for a measure of restraint.

The very first case handled by the house provides a good example of the problems involved and of the Lords' response to them. This was a dispute over the office of chief register in the court of Chancery. In 1638 Charles I had granted a patent to the office to Henry and Thomas Jermyn in trust for their father, Sir Thomas Jermyn (at the time, the king's Vice Chamberlain and one of his Privy Councillors). Sir Thomas had directed that the profits of the office should be settled on the wife and children of Henry (later Lord) Jermyn.[26] They had received the profits until December 1643. At that point Lord Jermyn was declared 'delinquent' and Parliament awarded the office and all profits to Walter Long, a member of the House of Commons.[27] Long held the office until April 1645, when he was removed under the terms of the Self-Denying Ordinance. Parliament later restored him to the post in April 1647,[28] but he was removed again in 1654 when the Lord Protector awarded the office by patent to Jasper Edwards and William Goldsborough. Long sued to recover in 1658 but was unsuccessful. He then took the case to the second Protectorate Parliament which heard the case (apparently with some reluctance) in March 1659, together with the newly submitted claim of Lady Mary Jermyn.[29] Nothing was resolved and the case then reappeared in the restored Long Parliament a year later, at which point it was referred to arbitration by Denzil Holles and Sir Harbottle Grimstone.[30] With the dispute still unresolved two months later, Long took it upon himself to seize all of the records and papers of the office, no doubt as material evidence to his claim, and then petitioned the newly restored House of Lords on 1 May to have his title confirmed. Lady Jermyn petitioned the following day to similar purpose and the case was referred to the newly appointed Committee for Petitions.[31]

The committee considered the case over the next 10 days, hearing council on both sides. Initially they recommended that Long be ordered to restore all of the books and records belonging to the office to Edwards and Goldsborough – the Cromwellian appointees who still held the office

– in whose hands the profits of the office were also to be sequestered (subject to an accounting by the house) until the title to the office was fully determined.[32] That was ordered accordingly, though Long proved rather uncooperative. In the end, the house did issue judgment in favour of Lady Jermyn's title. However, a compromise appears to have been worked out with the incumbents. Perhaps by prearrangement with Lady Jermyn, Edwards and Goldsborough were allowed to remain in office, serving now as deputy registers. The profits of the office were then reserved for the benefit of Lady Jermyn and her children.[33] Walter Long appears to have lost all claim to the office.

As a rule, the Lords were inclined to reinstate dispossessed office-holders more or less automatically in those cases where the plaintiff could support his or her claim to title with solid evidence of a prior royal grant. They did so, for instance, in the case of Edward Watkins, who had been ousted from the post of Head Customs Searcher of London in 1648 and who claimed title by virtue of a patent granted by Charles I in 1633.[34] They did so as well in the cases of Nowell Warner, former Master of the Barges,[35] Francis Wetherid, former Comptroller of the King's Works,[36] and George Clarke, former Clerk of the Deliveries in office of King's Ordnance.[37] In all three of the latter cases the Lords restored the individual conditionally – 'until the King's pleasure be further known'.

On occasion, however, compromises had to be made. In mid-May the Lords restored to office Richard March, Keeper of the King's Stores, and Edward Sherbourne, Clerk of the King's Ordnance, both of whom had been ousted in 1643.[38] They too claimed their right under patent from Charles I. Three days later the Lords heard from the incumbents of both offices, Francis Nichols and John Falkener.[39] The former claimed to have been appointed to his office by the then Council of State, and the latter by Parliament under the Great Seal, and both asked to be allowed to continue in service. Ordinarily, the Lords would not have honoured this request, especially since they had already recognized the validity of prior titles. But in this case, outside intervention appears to have carried the day. On 7 May General Monck had written to Secretary Nicholas specifically requesting that Nichols and Falkener be retained in office, claiming that they had assisted him in his efforts and that they were loyal subscribers to the Restoration.[40] That request was undoubtedly communicated to the upper house and the Lords accordingly suspended their previous order restoring March and Sherbourne and allowed Nichols and Falkener to continue in office until the king should determine otherwise.[41]

The Lords also moved somewhat cautiously in dealing with the ticklish problem of city and borough corporations. During the summer of 1660 three separate groups of aldermen (and/or common councillors) who had been removed from office in the purges of the late 1640s petitioned the house for redress. The three corporations involved were Winchester,

Bristol and Great Yarmouth. The Lords accepted all three cases, but apparently took action only in the first two. In mid-June the 'ancient citizens' of Winchester appealed to the upper house against the 'intruded' corporation officers installed by the Rump Parliament in 1649.[42] In this case the petitioners did not ask for immediate restoration, but instead for a proviso to be inserted in the Act of Indemnity, saving their right to prosecute suits against the intruders. The dispute was referred to the Committee for Petitions which conducted a preliminary hearing with both parties in late June. In the event, both sides agreed to arbitration and the matter was referred to the marquis of Winchester and the earl of Southampton to resolve.[43] Unfortunately, the marquis reported to the house in late August that they had been unable to settle differences because 'certain persons' of that city had been 'refractory'. Only then did the house decide that the best way to bring 'peace' was simply to exclude the recalcitrant parties from the city corporation and they directed that their names should be left out of Winchester's charter when it was next renewed by the king.[44]

The case involving the city of Bristol arose in early July. Former members of the Common Council petitioned the upper house claiming that they had been 'illegally' put out of their places by parliamentary ordinance in October 1645. They requested that their city be restored to its former privileges and that a 'writ of restoration' be granted to as many of the 'ancient senators' as were still living in order to 'displace those that were illegally chosen'. They asked as well to have discretion to fill the remaining seats on the council with 'such persons as will prove loyal subjects to his Majesty, lovers of the protestant religion and free from faction'.[45] The city leaders were clearly divided. Another group of aldermen and councillors subsequently petitioned the upper house and attempted to disown the earlier protest.[46] As before, the case was initially referred to the Committee for Petitions to hear both sides and report its findings, but the dispute was not scheduled for hearing until the first week of September.[47] In the event, the Lords refrained from making any final determination. Instead, they adopted the eventual recommendation of the Committee for Petitions that, 'for the preventing of any disturbance in the government of the said city for the future', the whole business ought to be referred to the king, 'to give such directions therein as to His Majesty shall seem meet'.[48] The Lords' decision may simply have reflected an unwillingness to become further embroiled in what was a highly contentious dispute, but given the earlier actions taken with regard to Winchester, that seems unlikely. It is more probable that by September the king had made known to them his wish to deal personally and directly with the composition of borough corporations and the Lords were simply honouring that request.[49] The king did in fact take a direct interest in the Bristol case, writing repeatedly to the mayor to order that the excluded aldermen be reinstated – orders which were largely ignored.[50] The Lords' decision to defer to the king in these cases probably explains the absence of any further proceedings on the case of Great Yarmouth, also accepted in early July and initially referred to the Committee for Petitions.[51]

University posts

The Lords were far more direct and forceful with regard to appeals from university officials. During May the Lords received a number of petitions from heads of colleges and fellows who had been ejected during the parliamentary visitation of 1648. The first to apply were the fellows of New College, Oxford, on the 14th.[52] They were followed by the president of Magdalene College, Oxford on the 18th,[53] and by the fellows of Magdalene on the 22nd.[54] Three days later, the Lords heard from Dr Thomas Walker, the Master of University College, Oxford, and from Humphrey Babington, a fellow at Trinity College, Cambridge.[55] All of the petitioners, save Humphrey Babington, had been ejected for refusing to submit to the authority of the parliamentary visitors. They had refused because, as the fellows of both Magdalene and New Colleges put it, they 'could not submit to visitors who were actual members of the University without manifest breach of their college oaths and statutes'.[56] Humphrey Babington had been ejected in 1650 for his refusal to take the Oath of Engagement.

The first two cases were handled expeditiously. As was customary, the petition of the fellows of New College was initially referred to the Committee for Petitions, who reported back to the house three days later recommending that the plaintiffs be immediately restored to their places and those installed by the former visitors be put out. An order was issued accordingly to the warden of the college.[57] In their rush, however, the Lords had drafted the order rather carelessly, offering no legal justification for their actions. It was therefore amended two days later. It now provided that the ten fellows who had been 'unjustly' ejected should forthwith be restored to their respective fellowships, 'by the Warden and Fellows, according to the Statutes of the said College'. It provided further that all such fellows who had been admitted into fellowships 'contrary to the Statutes' should be forthwith ejected and that no fellow should be admitted in the future in any way contrary to the statutes of the college.[58] Dr John Oliver was also restored to the presidency of Magdalene College the same day he petitioned the house. In this case the decision was made easier by the fact that the incumbent president, Dr Thomas Goodwin, had 'voluntarily receded' to the new claimant. All the same, the Lords added the standard proviso that Oliver should hold the office only 'until the King's pleasure be known'.[59]

In the other three cases the Lords proceeded more slowly. The

Committee for Petitions initially ordered that the incumbents appear and show cause why the petitioners should not be restored.[60] In the meantime, however, the house itself had moved to reinstate the chancellors of both universities; the marquis of Hertford at Oxford, and the earl of Manchester at Cambridge.[61] Having done that, the house then transferred to them the responsibility for determining these remaining cases and any future disputes. The chancellors were directed to

> take care that the several Colleges in the said Universities shall be governed according to their respective Statutes; and such persons who have been unjustly put out of their Headships, Fellowships, or other Offices relating to the said several Colleges or Universities, may be restored, according to the said Statutes of the Universities, and Founders of Colleges therein.[62]

Over the summer both chancellors proceeded to carry out the directive, issuing letters ordering the restoration of excluded members of their respective university's colleges. Manchester encountered little resistance, but Hertford's actions in Oxford created considerable opposition and some of the newly ejected officers looked to the Commons to intercede. In response the Lords prevailed upon the king in mid-July to appoint a special commission to undertake a visitation of the university. That commission – which again violated university statutes by including active members of the university – completed the task of removing the alleged intruders and restoring the royalist claimants.[63]

Church livings

The transfer of this business relieved the upper house of a major and potentially distracting responsibility – at a particularly opportune time. By the first week of June the Lords had come under increasing pressure to deal with the far more widespread problem of disputed church livings. This was one of the most difficult and potentially divisive issues before the Parliament in 1660, but one that was all but unavoidable. The dislocation of parish clergy during the previous two decades had been too pervasive and the issues raised by that dislocation – both religious and legal – were too central to a peaceful settlement of the kingdom for the matter not to take centre stage from the outset. In his Breda Declaration of 4 April the king did not specifically mention the matter of church livings, but he strongly implied that Parliament should play a central role in the settlement of religion and it was therefore natural that both houses should feel the need to address the issue directly.[64] However, their perspectives on the matter – and to some extent their religious sympathies – were different and, at least initially, their efforts were not well coordinated. Presbyterian leaders in the Commons were less concerned with legal rights than with right religion and were determined to protect incumbent Puritan ministers against the future claims of sequestered royalist clergy. They began work almost immediately on a bill that would have done just that, by confirming the titles of ministers already 'settled' in ecclesiastical livings. The bill was reported on 9 May, but its plainly one-sided aims were unacceptable to the king and it was allowed to go no further.[65]

With the issue unsettled, there was a clear danger that previously ejected office-holders, both lay and clerical, would take matters into their own hands and attempt to recover by force. Reports of such activities had already reached both houses. The Commons therefore drafted a proclamation in late May to prevent forcible dispossession; it was approved by the Lords on 29 May and issued by the king on 1 June. It declared, very simply, that incumbent office-holders should not be disturbed 'til our Parliament shall take order therein, or an eviction be had by due course of Law'.[66] The wording was important, emphasizing as it did the need for proper proceedings at law, and a good many ministers took the obvious lead and initiated suits at common law to recover their livings.[67] But the proclamation also underscored the fact that Parliament itself had been given authority to 'take order therein' and, given the threat that the Commons might again attempt to legislate away the rights of ejected clergy, many ministers clearly felt it would be more expedient to proceed directly to the House of Lords to secure a legal judgment from the High Court.

Appeals from ejected clergy were to constitute the largest single category of complaints brought to the Convention House of Lords – 632 separate petitions were presented over the summer and autumn of 1660. Initially the pace was relatively slow. The house received just 20 petitions in the first three weeks after the king's proclamation. However, there were ominous signs that a far greater number would follow. Many of these early petitions contained requests from multiple complainants, each of whom demanded either to be restored to his particular living or to have the profits sequestered until title had been determined. There were actually 65 individual benefices to be settled in these early cases. Moreover, the petitions containing multiple requests suggest very clearly that the royalist clergy were well organized, not only within particular counties, but across the country. The petition presented, for example, on 20 June by Dr James Dugdale included the requests of 14 other clerics in Somerset. More strikingly, the petition presented the same day by Dr Henry Ferne of Leceistershire, contained the pleas of 19 other clergymen from counties as diverse as Dorset, Hampshire, Essex, Wiltshire, Hertfordshire, Cambridgeshire, Oxfordshire, Yorkshire, and Rutland.[68] Precisely how this campaign had been coordinated is not clear, but a campaign it plainly was – a further testament, perhaps, to what has recently been called 'the passive strength of Anglican survivalism' – and it should have made clear to the Lords that large numbers of dispossessed clergymen would ultimately seek redress in their house.[69]

At least in the beginning, the Lords were determined that the clerics should seek redress in their house. That they would have welcomed these appeals was hardly surprising. The upper house was every bit as anxious as the lower to have a direct hand in the resettlement of religion and this issue – the composition of parish livings – was clearly central to that process. In all probability, partisan politics played a role as well. Certainly, there were those in the upper house who saw the potential of these proceedings to ensure the return of large numbers of mainstream Anglican clergy. But there was also genuine concern that simple justice be done. The Lords had a natural empathy with the dispossessed and in all but a few cases the complaints of these petitioners were entirely legitimate. Most had been unfairly deprived of their right and title to private property and the Lords clearly felt a sense of responsibility (as, indeed, they had in 1640) to redress that grievance. On a more practical level the Lords must also have sensed that, given its scale and significance, this litigation would give them an important opportunity to renew the reputation and public profile of the High Court.

In the event, however, the house proceeded with considerable caution. Typically, the cases were referred directly to the Committee for Petitions where, after an initial hearing, the incumbent minister was summoned to 'show cause' why the petitioner's plea for restoration should not be granted.[70] In most cases the petitioner asked as well that the profits of the living be sequestered in the hands of responsible parties until right and title had been established and that was normally granted as a matter of course.[71] For sequestered clergy the Lords usually provided that four-fifths of the profits should be secured in the hands of churchwardens, while the remaining fifth (which in many cases had been withheld for years) should be paid to the complainant.[72] By the last week in June the Lords had begun to realize just how widespread the problem was and, rather than treating each request separately, they issued a general order on behalf of all sequestered and ejected clergy. They ordered that

> all the Tithes, Glebes, and other Profits of or belonging to the several Rectories and other Ecclesiastical Livings and Benefices, of such of the Clergy as have been sequestered or ejected, without due Course of Law, in or since the Time of the late Wars, be, by Authority hereof, stayed and secured in the Hands of the Churchwardens or Overseer of the Poor of the said several Parishes, until the Titles of the said sequestered Clergy, and of the present Possessors thereof, shall be determined by further order of Parliament, or Eviction by due Course of Law.[73]

The following day the Lords authorized the clerk of Parliament to insert into the general order the names of any minister who petitioned the house for relief.[74] This may well have been done simply to expedite the process, but it amounted to an open invitation and it may well have been a deliberate attempt to attract business with a view to ensuring that the interests of all deprived or sequestered clergy were protected in the short term. Whatever the primary motivation, the orders produced a veritable flood of new petitions. During the next two months just over 600 ministers applied for and were given benefit of the sequestration order.[75] A number of them were also pluralists seeking sequestration of two or more livings, so the actual number of benefices involved was close to 620.

The sequestration order was not intended to prejudice the legal rights of any incumbent and was carefully worded to allay any impression to the contrary. All the same, the fact that ministers were able to obtain benefit of the order simply by applying to the clerk, rather than having to make their case before the Committee for Petitions or the house itself, left the system open to considerable abuse and, not surprisingly, a number of clerics attempted to gain unfair advantage. As a consequence the Lords were treated to a second wave of petitions from incumbent ministers appealing against the execution of their order. Their protests, though comparatively few in number (less than two dozen), indicate just how carefully the situation needed to be monitored. A number of clerics had used the Lords' order to reclaim livings from which they had actually resigned during the 1640s or 1650s.[76] Many had resigned under pressure, but they had resigned all the same and the provisions of the order did not apply. In other cases, ministers had used the Lords' order to lay claim to livings which they themselves had never possessed, or which had never actually been sequestered.[77] Still others had attempted to regain livings from which they had been ejected on perfectly legitimate grounds of 'scandalous' behaviour.[78] No doubt these individuals assumed that the Lords' order would not be challenged by the incumbent, or if it was, would never be heard and that the resulting sequestration could then be used as evidence to substantiate their claim in litigation. That may well have happened in some instances, but those who took the trouble to appeal to the upper house found a very receptive audience. In fact, all 18 appeals of this kind were eventually heard and the order of sequestration was revoked in every case.[79]

Predictably, the Lords' efforts to intercede in parish disputes were not always readily accepted. In at least a dozen cases ministers attempting to enforce the Lords' sequestration order encountered resistance. Some of the claims subsequently made to the upper house were no doubt exaggerated, but it is clear that the order provoked considerable discord within some parish communities and in some instances violence. In late August one Thomas Porter reported that the incumbent minister and his supporters in the parish of St Mabyn, Cornwall, had set upon the churchwarden's servant 'striking and drawing blood' as he attempted to execute the Lords' order.[80] John Cooke, rector of West Thorney, in Sussex (and a former petitioner to the house in 1641) claimed that the incumbent of his parish continued to detain the glebe in defiance of the Lords' order with the help of others in the parish and 'by force of arms'.[81] Uncooperative incumbents often fell back on the king's proclamation of June 1 as their first line of defence, claiming that it protected them from being 'molested'.[82] In other cases, it was the churchwardens themselves who refused to recognize the Lords' directives. Many of them had been responsible for prosecuting the ejected clergyman before the county committee in the first place and were therefore unlikely to be very sympathetic toward his efforts to recover. John Halke of Upminster, Essex, asked the Lords to appoint a special group of independent sequestrators for that reason.[83] On occasion residual hostility toward the upper house appears to have come into play as well. Walter Powell of Standish in Gloucestershire failed to get satisfaction from his parish churchwardens because, as he was informed by a friend, 'the [Lords'] order is not valued a pin, because it has no seal nor the hands of any of the Parliament men to it'.[84]

For the most part the Lords responded to these challenges with considerable restraint. It only made sense to do so, under the circumstances. It was arguably less important at this stage to protect the honour and authority of the house than to ensure a peaceable transition. The more recalcitrant were in fact cited as 'delinquents' and were summoned to answer for their contempt,[85] but the Lords declined to impose any punishments. Instead, they pursued diplomatic solutions. In most cases all parties were given a chance to be heard and new arrangements were worked out. Either new sequestrators were appointed, or the ejected cleric was required to give security, in the form of a bond, to be responsible for any tithes he received, in the event his claim was defeated at law.[86] In at least one case appeal to the House of Lords backfired. The subsequent hearing revealed that the complaining minister had not in fact been ejected for loyalty to the king, as he had claimed in his original petition, but had voluntarily resigned the living many years before and the Lords promptly revoked the sequestration.[87]

The evidence suggests that the Lords initially intended to hear and settle at least some of the disputes over title themselves. They had certainly begun the process in the early part of June. By the first week in July, however, they had changed their minds. On the 4th they ordered that all of the sequestered clergy who had previously petitioned the house for relief as to their titles should be dismissed and referred to a trial at law.[88] The decision was probably the result of a combination of factors. By early July the Lords had already received hundreds of petitions requesting sequestration orders and no doubt concluded that, given the obvious size of the problem and the uncertain future of this Parliament, it would be unwise to commit to further proceedings. More to the point, perhaps, progress was being made in the Commons on legislation to resolve the problem comprehensively. The Lords may have felt that further unilateral proceedings on their part risked angering the Commons, and they plainly did not want to endanger the progress of the bill. It is not clear whether, by this stage, agreement had actually been reached on the blanket reinstatement of sequestered clergy – the bill was not presented till 27 July – but given the king's clearly stated preferences, it must have seemed a distinct possibility that they would regain their livings without further litigation. In any event, the Lords had secured their legal interests for the time being. Permanent security would in fact come with the Act for the Confirming and Restoring of Ministers, which received the royal assent on 13 September.[89]

Land settlements

By contrast, there was little prospect that general legislation would be able to solve the complex issue of land settlements. The real problem here was not the public lands confiscated from the Crown and the church, but private estates confiscated from royalist and Catholic 'delinquents'. The restoration of the former was conceded early on. The Commons defeated two early legislative proposals to confirm the sales of public property during the Civil War and Interregnum and raised no objections when the Lords voted on 12 July to restore the king to possession of all of his former estates.[90] Though discussion continued throughout the first session on the issue of church lands, no legislative initiative emerged to settle the matter and the church was simply allowed to repossess its former estates, subject, where necessary, to arbitration by a special royal commission which the king appointed in early October.[91] The matter of private lands was far more complicated, simply because there was no real consensus on the rights of former royalist landowners and because circumstances varied too dramatically from case to case to allow the application of uniform rules and procedures.

Parliament's inability to legislate a comprehensive solution forced many royalists to pursue recovery through the courts and, not surprisingly, a number of them turned first to the House of Lords. The upper house had provided something of a lead here by taking swift and decisive action to recover the estates of its own members. In some cases they did so by simple order, in others by an act of Parliament, but in either case their actions were based on the premise that the lands in question had been confiscated, sequestered and/or sold illegally, 'without either Hearing or Summons, or Charge . . . or any Proof of that which is pretended to be the Offence, and without Trial by Peers (which is contrary to the fundamental Laws of this Kingdom)'.[92] The same principle was applied to Catholic lords whose estates had been sequestered on pretence of recusancy. The Lords discharged the sequestrations in all cases, except where the individual had been convicted of the charge 'by due Course of Law'.[93]

Private petitioners found the Lords equally receptive. Sir James Bunce, the former London alderman (who had been impeached and imprisoned by the upper house in 1647), applied to the Lords in late June 1660 to recover his former estates, which had been sequestered and later sold on order of the House of Commons in December 1649. Bunce insisted that the Commons had acted illegally, discharging him from office and seizing his property 'without any legal summons, hearing, charge, trial or conviction, contrary to the Great Charter and the fundamentals laws of the realm'.[94] (The wording of his plea was surely no accident. He had clearly been paying close attention to the Lords' own declarations a week earlier in the cases cited above.) His case was referred to the Committee for Petitions, who reported back to the house a month later, recommending that all of the 'dispositions, alienations, and Sales' of Sir James's lands be declared null and void and that he be fully restored to his estate, 'both real and personal', together with all of the arrears of rents and profits which had been 'unjustly' kept from him. The recommendation was adopted.[95]

In some of these cases the Lords worked closely with the Crown. In July 1660 Sir William Morice wrote directly to the Committee for Petitions to communicate the king's wish that they treat the complaint of Robert Long with special care. Long had been Clerk of the Chapel under Charles I and had served the present king, when he was prince, as 'Keeper of his balloons and paumes, and of tennis shoes and ancle socks'.[96] Long's estate in Yorkshire had been seized in July 1651 and had later been sold to the regicide William Say, and then to Slingsby Bethell, a former member of the Council of State. Long wanted to be restored to the estate and the king requested that the Lords accommodate him, notwithstanding any interest which might accrue to the king by the forfeiture of Say's or Bethell's estates.[97] The Committee for Petitions accordingly reviewed the case and found for Long, declaring that those in possession could show no title to the property. As in the case above, the house declared that the seizure and sale of Long's estate had been 'illegal' and 'contrary to the fundamental laws of the land' and ordered him restored to the property by the sheriff of the county.[98]

The process worked in reverse in the case of Mary Musgrave. In December 1648, Musgrave had been settled in a substantial property in East Greenwich by her father, Sir Andrew Cogan. Cogan subsequently left England and was assumed to have joined the king. As a consequence he was declared a 'delinquent', and the property in question was seized and later sold to the regicide Gregory Clement. Musgrave petitioned the Lords in June 1660, complaining that Clement had obstructed all of her subsequent efforts to reclaim the property at law. She asked that she be granted some reparations out of Clement's estate.[99] By this stage the estate had been forfeited to the Crown and the Lords therefore declared that Musgrave should be specially recommended to the king, 'as a person fit to partake of His Grace and Favor'.[100]

All in all, there were surprisingly few cases of this kind – just under two dozen – presented to the upper house during the Convention Parliament. That would seem to reflect the fact that the majority of royalists had managed to regain their estates before 1660 or, if not, did so thereafter on their own initiative, either through suits at common law, or through arbitration, or direct repurchase agreements.[101]

Appeals from Interregnum High Courts

The final set of complaints arising from the Civil War and revolution was in some ways the most compelling but the most difficult to resolve fairly. These were appeals from families of royalists who had been tried, condemned and executed by the Interregnum High Courts for various acts of treason. The Lords received just under a dozen of these appeals during June 1660. They came from well-known widows such as Arundel Penruddock, whose husband John had led the infamous rising against Cromwell in 1655, and from more obscure figures like Elizabeth Burley, whose husband John had attempted to raise the inhabitants of the Isle of Wight in the king's defence in December 1647.[102] In all of the cases the families complained about the unjust and illegal nature of the courts and their proceedings – notably the absence of a jury trial – and all sought to have those responsible punished, the proceedings condemned and the judgments officially reversed. What they wanted as well were reparations or, at the very least, leave to proceed at law against the officials who had conducted the trials. Accordingly, each offered a proviso to be attached to the forthcoming Act of Indemnity and Oblivion excepting the named individuals from its protections.

Initially, the Lords appear to have taken these complaints to heart. All of the petitions were referred to the Committee for Petitions and over the next six weeks the committee assigned counsel to the plaintiffs, summoned witnesses and held hearings.[103] By early August, however, the pressures building over the indemnity bill appear to have forced a change of policy. The king was clearly pressing both houses to complete the bill as quickly as possible and there was simply not enough time to complete the necessary hearings on all of the private amendments being proposed. The king was undoubtedly concerned as well that the proliferation of these amendments threatened to undermine the very purpose of the legislation. Accordingly, on 6 August the decision was made to drop from the bill all provisos 'whose matter was of Private Concernment'.[104] In fact, the issue of the Interregnum High Court personnel had already become the subject of negotiations between the two houses, the result of which was an agreement, reached on 9 August, that the judges of the assorted high courts should be spared capital punishment. The Lords agreed instead that they should be punished with permanent disqualification from public office. They insisted, however, that they should remain liable to any further penalties which Parliament might elect to impose by way of legislation.[105] Since no such legislation was ever forthcoming, the punishment stood and the judges had the general benefit of the Act of Indemnity. The above mentioned petitioners, on the other hand, were left without remedy. In this case, private interests had to be sacrificed to the broader public demands of national reconciliation.

The Lords' traditional clientele

There were, of course, a number of complaints presented to the Convention Parliament which had nothing whatever to do with the national crisis of the preceding two decades. The Lords' 'traditional' clientele – private litigants without recourse to ordinary remedies at law – appealed to the restored upper house in 1660 as readily (and as confidently) as they had ever done. For these petitioners, the reappearance of the High Court signalled – despite the Lords' obvious preoccupation with the demands of resettlement – the resumption of business as usual and they lost little time presenting their multifarious requests for relief. In terms of subject matter, their complaints represented familiar territory. (Indeed, at least two petitioners asked the Lords to reconsider cases which had been left unsettled by the Long Parliament.)[106] Disputes over property took their place alongside those involving debt, inheritance, commercial accounts, domestic quarrels and local community disputes. As before, the cases were brought both in the first instance and on appeal. The appellate cases – all but one of which challenged Chancery decrees from the 1650s – had to be handled with some care. During the summer, when most of these cases were presented, the Lords were involved in negotiations with the Commons over the Act for Confirmation of Judicial Proceedings, the principal purpose of which was to prevent mass appeals against Interregnum legal proceedings. The bill was designed to preclude challenges which were based solely on the uncertain legal authority of Interregnum judicial personnel. The Lords, therefore, had to be sure (both before and after the passage of the act) that the appeals they undertook complained of defects in the judgment, rather than 'defects' in the judges. All but one of the appellants did so.[107] There were, of course, a number of other disgruntled litigants who took the simpler, alternative route of submitting private amendments to the Act for Confirmation of Judicial Proceedings, hoping to have errant decrees exempted from its provisions.[108] Since their accompanying petitions do not survive, it is impossible to evaluate the merit of their complaints, but following this course – rather than a straightforward appeal to the house – proved a mistake. As it had with the Act of Indemnity, Parliament ultimately decided to 'lay aside' all private provisos before the act was passed.[109] As a consequence these complainants were left without remedy.[110]

Not surprisingly, given their other commitments in this session, the Lords were not able to resolve more than a handful of these conventional disputes in the time allowed. They did successfully hear at least three Chancery appeals to conclusion, setting aside all three earlier decrees and ordering a rehearing of two of the cases before the new Lord Chancellor.[111] They intervened with some success in a particularly troublesome domestic dispute involving the family of Sir Robert Carr, and were able to negotiate a temporary settlement in a trade dispute between Daniel Skinner and the East India Company.[112] But for the most part, petitioners had a long wait. Sarah Rodney, for example, petitioned the house in late July seeking a review of legal proceedings in case of debt. The Lords repeatedly scheduled hearings, but by the third week in December the case had not proceeded and Rodney finally had to request that the Lords refer her case to the Lord Chancellor.[113] By that point the dissolution of the Convention Parliament was clearly in view, and the house had already begun to reschedule cases for the early days of the next Parliament.[114]

On balance, the proceedings of the Convention Parliament must, therefore, be counted only a partial success. A significant number of litigants failed to gain satisfactory remedy. In fact, the Lords had never been able totally to satisfy the demands of private litigants. But in this case, their effectiveness had been more than usually constrained by the need to deal effectively with demands of national reconciliation which limited both their time and, ultimately, the responses which they could offer. All the same, they had accomplished a great deal. Those assisted or relieved directly by the house in 1660 far outnumbered those who had petitioned in vain. And, in truth, at this critical stage what really mattered was more the effort itself. The Lords clearly needed to demonstrate from the outset – and to a variety of audiences – not only that they remained fully committed to the provision of private justice, but that they were still capable of fulfilling those responsibilities with their traditional prerogatives intact and unimpaired. That had certainly been done. By the close of the Convention Parliament there could have been little doubt that the High Court was back in business to stay.

THE CAVALIER PARLIAMENT: AT WORK
AND UNDER FIRE

During the multiple sessions of the Cavalier Parliament which followed, the judicial proceedings of the upper house continued along established lines and achieved a kind of regularity that would, for the most part, render them quite unremarkable. Public interest in (and pressure on) the upper house remained constant, if somewhat less insistent than it had been previously. The first session of 1661/2 attracted a large number of petitioners (over five dozen), but thereafter the number of cases presented declined to less than a dozen each session, with notable exceptions in the sessions of 1667/8 (29) and 1670/1 (49). Of course, much depended on the length of the individual session. All told, just over 200 private suits were brought to the Cavalier Parliament.

The profile of the litigation itself remained essentially unchanged from the earlier Parliaments of the century. That was hardly surprising, however, since the fundamental problems which typically fostered petitions to the upper house had never been effectively redressed – despite much hard work and a great deal of thoughtful discussion from the Hale Commission on law reform in the early 1650s, and from William Sheppard and others during the Protectorate.[115] Litigants had traditionally petitioned the House of Lords in the first instance in order to avoid problems of congestion and delay (and the associated fees) or because the strict regulations (and/or complexities) of the law prevented them from proceeding through normal channels. Interregnum law reformers had clearly recognized those problems and had offered concrete proposals to remedy them. Both the Hale Commission and Sheppard proposed to relieve pressure on and congestion in the central courts by establishing a network of semi-independent local county courts with a wide jurisdiction to hear cases in the first instance.[116] Proposals were offered (notably by Sheppard) to place strict time limits on litigation, to streamline writ procedure and to standardize fees. Measures were also introduced to reform the law itself – to simplify conveyancing (and to mandate land registration at the local level), to offer better assistance to creditors and poor debtors and to improve and reorganize probate administration.[117] Unfortunately, just as in the 1620s, good intentions were never translated into lasting reform. Time and again these measures were sacrificed to other more immediate political concerns, or were simply defeated in Parliament by pressure from special interest groups in the legal community. The result was that the upper house would again be forced to entertain petitions in the first instance (roughly 40 per cent of the whole) because litigants could legitimately claim, for a variety of reasons, to be without expeditious remedy elsewhere. Not surprisingly, perhaps, a disproportionate number of these cases involved (as they had always done) disputes over real property, debt and inheritance.

The Lords would also be required to maintain their traditional appellate jurisdiction, again, at least in part, because of the failure of Interregnum reform proposals. The Hale Commission had roundly condemned the existing appellate mechanisms of both common law (the writ of error) and equity (the Bill of Review) as inefficient and inadequate. They recommended that both be abolished, and that in their place litigants be given ready access, by way of petition, to a permanent court of appeal established to hear both common law and equity cases.[118] The court would have been composed of twenty laymen and two common law judges, appointed by Parliament for one-year terms. But the proposal was never taken up, no doubt because lawyers and judges alike objected to the unprofessional nature of the tribunal. William Sheppard's proposed restructuring of the legal system also envisioned a superior appellate court in Westminster (in addition to local courts of appeal) staffed in this case by the combined common law and Chancery benches. But the second Protectorate Parliament refused even to consider the county court system, to which Sheppard's appellate system was tied, and the idea never saw the light of day.[119] Litigants in the 1660s were therefore left to pursue the traditional methods of appeal and that guaranteed continued litigation in the upper house. Common law writs of error were, in any event, returnable in the House of Lords and, as demonstrated earlier, the unsatisfactory nature of Bill of Review procedure in equity inevitably led litigants to pursue the same path by way of petition. The problems associated with appellate review in equity were particularly important, in light of the fact that the court of Chancery had successfully withstood all attempts to reform its procedure and jurisdiction during the 1650s. The wholly admirable reforms imposed by Cromwellian ordinance in 1654 had been allowed to lapse in the second Protectorate Parliament and the myriad problems which had plagued the court's proceedings since the turn of the century were therefore allowed to grow more serious and debilitating. As a consequence, the Lords would be asked to hear over six dozen Chancery appeals during the multiple sessions of the Cavalier Parliament. A dozen assorted appeals would also be brought from the equity side of the Exchequer, the court of Requests and the palatine courts of Durham and Lancaster. The remainder of the appellate litigation would be made up of just under four dozen writs of error.

None of this was new, of course, and the house was fully prepared to handle all of the litigation according to well-established rules and procedures. Occasionally, uncertainties arose over specific procedural matters and the house (or the Committee for Petitions) had to seek special guidance. In 1662, for instance, the Committee for Privileges was asked to determine (on the basis of past practice) the precise method for collecting costs and fines awarded against vexatious litigants.[120] (The house had continued to assess fines ranging from £10 to £20 against petitioners who brought frivolous suits.) In 1673 they sought clarification from the judges as to whether unfinished appeals could be carried over in status quo from session to session.[121] But such questions were rare. The house settled quickly and easily into a process which had become largely routine. If the proceedings of the Cavalier Parliament differed at all from those of the past, it was in their greater efficiency and productivity. The house exercised markedly better discipline in maintaining hearing schedules and in seeing cases to conclusion – something reflected in the relatively high percentage (22 per cent) of cases dismissed for lack of substance or merit after an initial hearing. The simple fact was that, in the absence of any pressing national crises, the house was able to concentrate more fully on the demands of private litigation.

By a curious irony, the responsibilities of private litigation would themselves engender two national crises, beginning in 1668 and again in 1675, when the jurisdiction and authority of the upper house were challenged by the lower. Both crises appear to have been, at least in part, the by-product of extraneous political gamesmanship, but the challenges were nonetheless serious in substance and intent, and the Lords' response to them reveals a great deal about their own perceptions of the role and functions of the High Court. The first crisis was triggered by the case of *Thomas Skinner* v. *the East India Company*.[122] In early 1657, Skinner had taken advantage of the then open trade policies of the Protectorate and furnished a ship, the *Thomas*, for an extended trading voyage to the East Indies. He arrived in 1658, bought an island home, Barella, rented a warehouse and opened for business. Unfortunately, shortly after his departure from London the East India Company prevailed on the Lord Protector to issue a new charter granting them exclusive trading rights to the East. Accordingly, in May of 1658 the company had issued instructions to its agents to seize all ships and goods of any Englishman then trading in the East Indies; in due course Thomas Skinner's ship was taken, the goods in his warehouse were confiscated and he himself dispossessed of his island home.[123]

Skinner eventually returned to England in 1661 and began what would be a long and unsuccessful campaign to gain redress against the company. He repeatedly petitioned the king asking that a court Constable and Marshal be convened to consider the matter.[124] The king, who was clearly sympathetic, instead referred the matter to a special committee of his Privy Council, who attempted on several occasions to mediate. The company, however, proved to be wholly uncooperative. Skinner's counsel established their liability at just over £17,000, but the company would offer no more than £1,500. The referees considered that wholly inadequate, but were unable to persuade the company to increase its offer and finally reported to the king in December 1666 that their efforts had failed. At Skinner's request, the king then referred the dispute to the House of Lords in mid-January 1667.[125]

The Lords proceeded with the case in standard fashion. After receiving Skinner's petition on 21 January, the Lord's ordered the East India Company to answer his complaint by the 28th. The company responded the following week. Their plea was a demurrer to the jurisdiction of the house. They challenged the Lords' right to hear the case, because Skinner's petition was 'in the nature of an original complaint, not brought by way of appeal, bill of review, writ of error, nor intermixed with privilege of Parliament'. They suggested, in addition, that if the house should hear the cause, they should consider the fact that the company's ancient charters had entitled them to take whatever action was necessary to exclude other traders (an argument which clearly ignored the fact that they had had no charter when Skinner established his trade). They admitted that injuries had been done to Skinner, but they claimed (in a grossly distorted reading of the statute) that they had been absolved of all responsibility by the Act of Indemnity and Oblivion.[126]

The Lords dismissed the plea and ordered the case to be heard. At the company's request, the hearings were postponed on four separate occasions in early February and Parliament itself was then prorogued for eight months on the 8th. Skinner promptly revived the case in the next session, repetitioning the house on 30 October 1667. Again the company was commanded to answer and again they pleaded a demurrer to jurisdiction. Counsel was heard on both sides in early December. The company's case was argued by Solicitor General Heneage Finch. He claimed that the Lords ought not to hear the case because they had no authority to grant relief in the first instance, except in those cases where remedy was unavailable elsewhere in the courts below. He maintained that relief was available to Skinner either in Chancery or in the Court of Constable and Marshal. He claimed as well that the 'liberty of the subject' would be 'injured' if the Lords assumed jurisdiction over cases relievable in lower courts. To do so would be to deny the subject the right of jury trial and, more importantly, the right to subsequent appeal. Finally, he reminded the house that they would be unable to execute any judgment against the defendants because the chief company officers were members of the House of Commons and were protected by parliamentary privilege. Skinner's case was handled by Serjeant Ayliffe, who countered that his client could not receive redress in any other court of law because the injuries had been inflicted beyond the seas. Citing precedent, he claimed as well that the house had previously provided relief in the first instance, even where the parties were relievable in lower courts, and always when other courts would not or could not provide appropriate remedy.[127]

As was usual in such cases, the Lords referred the matter to the judges to determine 'whether the petitioner be relievable upon the matters therein mentioned [in Skinner's petition] in law or equity, and if so, in what manner'.[128] Two days later the judges reported that Skinner was relievable in the courts at Westminster with regard to the seizure of his ship and goods and the assault on his person, notwithstanding the fact that these actions had taken place abroad. However, they argued that he would be unable to gain remedy in any ordinary court of law for the dispossession of his house and island.[129] After considering the judges report, the Lords elected to retain the whole cause, ostensibly on grounds that the two issues were part and parcel of the same complaint and that to divide them would prejudice Skinner's cause. The interpretation was perhaps somewhat self-serving, but not unusual. The court of Chancery, for example, customarily retained a cause when there was equity in any part of it.

Hearings were then scheduled for mid-December 1667, but were again postponed, and the house adjourned on the 19th. Proceedings resumed when the house reassembled in February 1668, and after several hearings in late February, the house finally resolved on 12 March that Skinner should be relieved against the company. A committee was appointed to consider the judgment and award damages.

In an attempt to head off that judgment, the East India Company petitioned the House of Commons in mid-April 1668, asking that they 'interpose' with the upper house on their behalf. Their petition was decidedly inflammatory. They claimed that the Lords' proceedings in the case had been 'unusual', 'extraordinary' and 'highly detrimental' to their interests. The Lords' actions had, in their view, violated 'the laws and statutes of this nation and the custom of Parliament' and therefore had not only done 'grievous' harm to the petitioners, but had 'set a precedent of ill consequence to all the Commons of England hereafter'. The Commons accepted the petition and referred it to a committee which had recently been established to consider the Lords' jurisdiction.[130] On 24 April the committee reported their view that the Lords' proceedings represented, first, a breach of the privileges of the House of Commons and, second, had been 'contrary to the law of the land', tending to the 'depriving of the subject of the benefit of the known law' and 'the introducing of an arbitrary way of proceeding'.[131] After debating the committee's report, the lower house passed a set of resolutions on 2 May condemning the Lords' actions out of hand and claiming that the Lords' cognizance of 'a common plea' in the first instance was 'not agreeable to the laws of the land, and tending [sic] to deprive the subject of his right, ease, and benefit, due to him by the said laws.'[132] Skinner himself was likewise condemned for bringing his appeal in the first place, thereby committing a breach of the Commons' privilege.

In the meantime, the Lords had reached a final decision. On 29 April they awarded Skinner £5,000 in damages against the company – a modest sum, all things considered, and especially given that their own committee had recommended that he be compensated in excess of £28,000! On the same day, however, the house was apprised of the company's petition to the Commons, which had apparently been published and circulated widely about Westminster. The Lords considered the petition 'scandalous' in both tone and content and were particularly offended by the company's assertion that they had been denied sufficient time to make their case – a charge that was patently untrue. The house immediately ordered the author of the petition, Robert Blackborne, the company secretary, as well as a number of the company's officers to appear and explain themselves. As a result, Blackborne, Sir Samuel Barnardiston, Sir Andrew Riccard, Roland Wynne and Christopher Boone were all committed to the custody of Black Rod in lieu of £2,000 bail.

The Lords were even less impressed with the Commons' behaviour in the matter. They were angered, first, that the lower house would have entertained a petition which had so clearly impugned the impartiality of their court and the integrity of its members. Second, the Commons had accepted the charges in the petition at face value, and had condemned the Lords' proceedings without conferring with, or seeking information from, the upper house. Indeed, their investigation of the company's complaint had been completed before the Lords had even reached a final decision. Their proceedings were clearly precipitous and they suggest that the Commons may have deliberately set out to provoke a confrontation. Why they chose to do so at this particular point is unclear. Indeed, the timing of this challenge to the Lords' judicial authority seems singularly ill advised. Only a week before the Commons had impeached Sir William Penn, and the success of his trial clearly would depend on cooperation between the two houses,[133] as would that of their bill to renew the Coventicle Act, which they had transmitted to the upper house only four days before.[134] Their willingness to risk both of those projects seems to suggest that the Commons were genuinely concerned about the issues involved – most particularly those of privilege – and, perhaps, that there were more widespread misgivings in the lower house about the extent of the Lords' judicial authority than had been made apparent at the Restoration.

On 5 May the lower house asked for and was granted a conference to discuss the case. Their arguments in conference differed little from those presented by the East India Company's counsel in earlier hearings at the bar of the House of Lords. John Vaughan, Serjeant Maynard and Solicitor General Finch reiterated the Commons' objection to the Lords accepting a case in the first instance, without an original writ. Again, they argued that to do so was to deny the defendants both the right to jury trial (guaranteed by Magna Carta) and further opportunity to appeal. Both Serjeant Maynard and Solicitor Finch went on to imply that the Lords, proceedings were somehow disloyal or disrespectful of the king's supremacy in the law. 'The reason of original writs,' said Maynard, 'is the respect and acknowledgement that all justice flows from his Majesty'. Finch followed that with the suggestion that 'proceedings without originals made, tended to make the laws independent of the Crown'. The argument was, to say the least, curious. The Lords' authority, like that of the court of Chancery, derived directly from the king. The fact that neither employed common law writ procedure did not diminish that relationship or the authority it created to exercise remedial justice in the king's name. The suggestion was particularly inappropriate in this case because the king himself had specifically requested that the Lords take up Skinner's case.

The report of the conference provoked a spirited debate in the upper house the following day, and the Committee for Privileges was commanded to prepare a response to the Commons' arguments. The committee reported to the house on 7 May. They had clearly done their homework. Having searched the records, they produced literally dozens of precedents, dating from the Parliaments of Henry IV to those of Charles I, which demonstrated unequivocally that the upper house had previously entertained and adjudicated all manner of cases in the first instance – including a number in which the defendants had been members of the House of Commons. The committee's report was then interrupted by a petition from Skinner himself, complaining that the deputy governor of the East India Company had refused to acknowledge or obey the Lords' judgment of 29 April. He asked leave to attend the house to prove his allegation, notwithstanding the fact that the Commons had just issued a warrant for his arrest. The house promptly issued him a protection.

When debate resumed, the house considered the heads prepared by the Committee for Privileges for a forthcoming conference with the Commons. Their protests were to concentrate on three separate issues: the East India Company's petition, the conduct of the House of Commons in response to it and the arguments against the Lords' jurisdiction presented by the lower house in conference. The company's petition was to be condemned both for the 'falsities' it contained and for the aspersions it cast on the 'honour and justice' of the house. The Lords were particularly concerned with the allegations that they had dealt unfairly with the company – by denying them sufficient time to present witnesses. This was to be strenuously denied. They were also concerned to refute the company's suggestion that their actions had somehow endangered the interests of 'all commoners' of England; the company, it was to be pointed out, did not represent the interests of all commoners – Skinner was a commoner as well and his welfare was every bit as important as theirs.

The lower house was also to be reprimanded for its 'unsuitable and unwarrantable' proceedings on the case. In particular, the managers of the conference were to object to the Commons' taking action on a case depending in the upper house before judgment had been given, and to their presuming to censure by vote the proceedings of the upper house, 'which the Commons cannot do, because they are not a Court of Judicature in any case, but less of the House of Peers [who are] the highest Judicature'. Indeed, the Commons had 'no power to give an oath, and so they have not the means to come to the knowledge of the truth, especially when they hear but one side, and not the party concerned, Mr Skynner, nor could they know the grounds and reasons upon which the Lords proceeded'.

The Commons' arguments regarding the Lords' jurisdiction were to be refuted largely on the basis of the precedents amassed by the Committee for Privileges. But the practical considerations raised by the Commons were to be addressed as well. As to the matter of jury trial, the managers were to point out that the upper house was empowered to try a man for his life and liberty on the basis of accusations presented by the House of Commons. It was logical to ask, therefore, 'how comes it to be a greater prejudice to be tried without a jury for a man's estate than for his life and liberty?' Nor, it was to be argued, did the Lords' proceedings violate the intent of Magna Carta. The charter required that a man be tried by his peers or 'by the law of the land'. The judicature of the House of Lords, it was to be stressed, was as much a part of ancient custom and the law of the land as that of any court in the realm. Had it been a breach, the Lords would suggest, it was 'a wonder that so many discerning eyes as have been in all ages and are now in the House of Commons, never discerned it until upon this occasion'.

At the close of the debate, the house approved two resolutions drafted by the Committee for Privileges. The first condemned the Commons' proceedings on the case as a breach of the privileges of the house of peers and as 'contrary to the fair correspondency which ought to be between the two Houses of Parliament, and unexampled in former times'. The second reaffirmed that their own proceedings had been 'agreeable to the laws of the land and well warrantable by the law and custom of parliament, and justified by many parliamentary precedents ancient and modern'. The resolutions were to be presented to the Commons in conference, together with an opening statement suggesting that the Commons' proceedings had shaken 'the very foundations and constitution of Parliament, and the ancient government of this kingdom'.[135]

The battle lines were clearly drawn. The Lords were determined not to yield any measure of their authority. The Commons were equally determined that they should, and not surprisingly, the ensuing conference on 8 May did little to repair relations between the houses. Indeed, the Commons' only response was to demand that the Lords suspend their sentence and judgment against the East India Company and free its officers.[136] Predictably, the Lords unanimously rejected the demand and immediately began proceedings against the officers responsible for the company's petition. The result was fairly innocuous. Christopher Boone was absolved altogether, Sir Andrew Riccard and Rowland Wynne were formally reprimanded, but were discharged after acknowledging their offence, and Sir Samuel Barnardiston, the deputy governor, was fined only £300. The following day, however, the Commons passed a resolution declaring that anyone 'aiding or assisting' in executing the Lords' order in Skinner's case would be deemed 'a betrayer of the liberties of the Commons of England, and an infringer of the privileges of this House'.[137] The crisis had now escalated beyond the point where any further business could reasonably be conducted between the two houses and the king requested that they adjourn until the second week of August in the hope that some compromise might be reached in the meantime. It was not. Parliament was twice adjourned until finally, on 1 March, the king prorogued it until October 1669.[138]

The king's hopes that the extended recess would cool tempers and allow good relations between the houses to be restored were quickly dashed. Hostilities were immediately renewed by the Commons. On the opening day of the session they appointed a committee to peruse the records of the upper house and determine precisely where the case stood.[139] Their investigation revealed that the Lords had fined and imprisoned Sir Samuel Barnardiston (their last act of business before adjournment) and they reported that he had submitted and paid the fine to gain his freedom. Barnardiston was immediately summoned to answer for his breach of the Commons' resolutions. However, when it was discovered that he had not in fact paid his fine and had gained his release without submission, the lower house commended him for being 'a good Commoner of England'.[140] The Commons also took immediate action against the publisher of a treatise on Skinner's case, which had been written by Lord Holles during the prorogation. Holles's treatise was a detailed examination of the parliamentary proceedings on the case and, not surprisingly, it took the form of an impassioned defence of the Lords' jurisdiction.[141] Unable to proceed against Holles, the Commons summoned his publisher and indicted him under the provisions of the Licensing Act.[142]

On 22 October the Commons also ordered a bill drafted 'for settling the difference in point of Judicature between the Lords and this House'. The bill was predictably one-sided, designed to 'settle differences' entirely in the Commons' favour. It would have prohibited any judicial proceedings involving the life, liberty, or property of any commoner of England, which had been brought before Parliament as an original complaint – other than those brought by the Commons themselves in impeachments. It would have protected all petitioners to the House of Commons from subsequent prosecution, fine or penalty by the House of Lords for the content of those appeals. And, finally, it would have vacated – and obliterated from the records – all of the Lords' proceedings in Skinner's case and their judgment against Sir Samuel Barnardiston.[143] After considerable debate and at least one division (on the clause vacating the Lords' proceedings) the bill was passed on 3 November.[144]

The Lords rejected the bill on its first reading on 10 November.[145] They then ordered their own bill to be drafted to clarify both the nature of parliamentary privilege and their own jurisdiction. The bill which emerged from the Committee for Privileges the following week gave nothing away, but was judiciously worded in the form of a compromise. It began by declaring that the upper house found the trying of civil cases brought as original complaints – where remedy could be had in inferior courts – to be 'burdensome and troublesome' and a distraction. The bill would therefore have enacted that

> no trial or judgement in any civil cause shall in the future be had or given in Parliament upon any original complaint, other than breach of privilege of Parliament or breach of privilege of peerage, and other than in cases where no relief can be had in inferior courts.

The Lords had never claimed more than that. The bill then went on to reserve to the House of Lords its 'ancient right and usage' to 'try, judge, and determine criminal cases, complaints of delay of justice, cases of difficulty upon resort to them, writs of error, and appeals from any inferior court'.

The most striking and controversial provisions of the bill had to do with parliamentary privilege. It argued that the duration of recent Parliaments – notably the Cavalier – had inflicted a grievance on the king's subjects by protecting members of Parliament and Convocation, their assistants, attendants, servants and families from suits at law. The bill therefore proposed to limit parliamentary privilege by guaranteeing only freedom from arrest and seizure of residences and goods. Members and assistants of both houses and Convocation and their assistants and servants would now be liable, even in time of Parliament, 'to be impleaded, sued and proceeded with according to the due and ordinary course of law'.[146] These provisions may have arisen as a consequence of the claims of privilege made by the defendants in Skinner's case. But they may also have been born of a genuine desire to correct what was in fact a long-standing and serious public grievance. In either event, the provisions would undoubtedly have doomed the bill to defeat, even if the Commons had been satisfied by the bill's statement on judicature. They were not, and the bill, which passed the upper house on 22 November, was rejected by the Commons on the 27th.[147]

Relations between the houses were now so soured that, again, communication came to a standstill, and on 11 December the king was finally compelled to prorogue the Parliament until mid-February 1670. When the new session opened on 14 February the king 'earnestly recommended' that the houses put their differences behind them, but his plea was ignored in the lower house. The Commons began almost immediately to reconsider the matter of the Lords' jurisdiction. The king – now desperate for supply – finally lost patience and intervened more forcefully. He ordered that all record of the dispute, in the journals of both houses, be erased and the dispute put permanently to rest. Both houses promptly agreed. The Commons had everything to gain and nothing to lose; their strongest wish, expressed in their final resolutions to the upper house in December, was that the Lords' two judgments (for Skinner and against Sir Samuel Barnardiston) be vacated.[148] That was now done. Undeniably, that represented a retrenchment of sorts for the Lords; but the long-term damage was more implicit than real. Only the record of this particular case had been removed and that without comment. Technically, the Lords' jurisdiction stood precisely where it had in 1667. Nothing of record had been done to alter their claims. All the same, the failure to defend their judgments left the impression that they had conceded the point. Few members at the time would probably have accepted that interpretation, but in practice it fell out that way. The house would hear only two more cases brought as original complaints during the remaining sessions of the Cavalier Parliament – one of which, interestingly, was a marital dispute, referred to the house by the king, in which the defendant, Sir John Reade, was a member of the House of Commons.[149] This was not, however, a consequence of the Lords' refusal to hear such cases. The fact was, no other first instance cases were brought before the house. Undoubtedly, the crisis over Skinner served to warn off those litigants who had not first exhausted all other avenues of redress.

The end result of the crisis (aside from the failure of Thomas Skinner to gain proper redress) was a *de facto* narrowing of the Lords' jurisdiction to appellate cases. That undoubtedly eased their burden to some extent, but it did not necessarily serve the best interests of litigants, some of whom, like Skinner, had genuine need of their services in the first instance. Nor did it prevent the issue of House of Lords' judicature remaining a source of political confrontation. Only six years later, in the spring of 1675, the Commons would launch another hostile challenge to the Lords' judicial proceedings. The issues involved here were no less serious than those in Skinner's case and, indeed, it would play out in similar fashion, leading to bitter standoffs and lengthy prorogations. But in this case, there was a clear political subtext to the proceedings. While the confrontations were genuine enough, they appear to have been deliberately exacerbated by certain members of the upper house (seemingly in collusion with members of the lower) who wished to bring parliamentary proceedings to a standstill with a view to forestalling or, indeed, destroying the king's legislative programmes. The principal target of these opposition members was a bill, introduced by the earl of Danby in the Lords on 15 April, which would have imposed a new loyalty test on all MPs. The bill would have required that all MPs swear not to undertake any alteration in the government of church or state, and that they take an oath of non-resistance to royal authority. It was self-evidently designed to silence opposition in Parliament and it provoked a long and bitter debate in the upper house.[150] The new quarrel with the Commons over the Lords' judicial proceedings arose, coincidentally, in the midst of that debate and provided opposition peers led by the earl of Shaftesbury with precisely the kind of diversion needed to paralyze parliamentary proceedings and ultimately defeat the bill. It is not entirely clear just how influential these opposition peers were in perpetuating the quarrel – it rapidly attained a life and momentum all its own – but it seems clear that they tried. Shaftesbury himself was the most outspoken and eloquent – and unyielding – defender of the judicial prerogatives of the upper house and he was plainly influential at crucial moments in defeating attempts at compromise with the Commons.

The dispute in this case was triggered by the appeal of Dr Thomas Shirley, one of the king's Physicians in Ordinary.[151] Shirley had sued in Chancery in the early 1660s to recover deeds belonging to the manor of Wiston, Sussex, of which he claimed to have been defrauded by Sir John Fagg and others during the Interregnum. Lord Chancellor Clarendon, however, had accepted Fagg's claim of purchase and had dismissed the doctor's suit. Shirley simply asked the Lords to reconsider the chancellor's decision and, if appropriate, cause the deeds to be produced. In fact, this was Shirley's second attempt to overturn the chancellor's decree. He had originally petitioned the house in early December 1669 in the midst of the crisis over Skinner, but the case had been lost in the ensuing prorogation.[152] Why he waited six years to renew the appeal is not clear. It is possible that he was 'invited' to reappeal at this stage, but there is no concrete evidence to suggest that and it seems unlikely, given the other developments in the crisis.

The Lords received Shirley's petition on 30 April and responded, as they had to countless other Chancery appeals, by ordering the defendant, Sir John Fagg, to submit an answer in writing within seven days.[153] However, Sir John was a member of the House of Commons and the order quickly touched off a dispute with the lower house. On learning of the Lords' order, on 5 May, the Commons sent a simple message requesting that the upper house 'have regard for their Privileges'.[154] They were going to insist, from the outset, that Fagg could not be required to answer the suit because of his parliamentary privilege. The Lords referred the matter to their own Committee for Privileges who reported that this

251

situation had arisen on any number of previous occasions – without incident.[155] However, they reminded the house that the Commons had issued a similar protest, in 1670, when the Lords began proceedings on Sir Henry Slingsby's Chancery appeal against William Hale, MP. On that occasion the upper house had also examined past practice and ultimately resolved that

> their proceedings had been according to the Course of Parliament and former Precedents; The Lords do assert it to be their undoubted Right in Judicature to receive and determine in Time of Parliament Appeals from Inferior Courts, though a Member of either House be concerned, that there may be no Failure of Justice in the Land.[156]

However, that resolution had never been communicated to the House of Commons. The Lords' initial and only response to the Commons' protest in 1670 had been to assure them (albeit in a rather hostile tone) that 'they need not doubt but that their Lordships will have a regard of the Privileges of their House, as they have of their own' – the wounds from the confrontation over Skinner had clearly not healed.[157] Parliament had then adjourned for six months before the Lords could inform the Commons of their further resolution and Slingsby eventually withdrew his appeal, so the incident went no further. But the Committee for Privileges now recommended that the house adopt the same position with regard to this new protest over *Shirley* v. *Fagg*. The house concurred and the 1670 resolution was ordered to be entered in the journal. A dispute then arose as to precisely what message should be sent to the lower house. It was generally agreed that the house should return the same answer that they had in 1670 with respect to privilege, but Shaftesbury and a number of opposition peers wanted to include the 1670 declaration on judicature. They protested that, as it stood, the message was too weak and ambiguous. The majority, however, opted for a more diplomatic approach and the motion was defeated.[158]

Diplomacy paid few dividends. The Commons failed to respond to the message for more than a week and when they did their answer took the form of a warrant, issued on 14 May, for the arrest of Dr Shirley for his alleged breach of Commons' privilege. The action was unduly provocative, particularly since Sir John Fagg had already entered a plea to the suit two days before, presumably waiving his privilege in the process.[159] Sir James Norfolk, the Commons' Serjeant at Arms, attempted to arrest Dr Shirley in Westminster Hall later that day, but was foiled by Lord Mohun, who snatched the good doctor and the Commons' warrant from his hands and delivered both to the upper house. The Lords, having considered the matter, concluded that the attempted arrest was a breach of their privileges and asked the Commons to verify the authenticity of the warrant. For their part, the Commons protested Lord Mohun's attempt to interfere with their instructions. The Lords rejected their protest and answered that Lord Mohun had 'done nothing . . . but what was according to his duty'.[160] They then issued a protection for Dr Shirley.

The crisis then escalated rapidly when the Commons discovered, on 15 May, that Dr Shirley's appeal was only one of three pending in the upper house in which the defendants were sitting members of the lower. On 19 April, Sir Nicholas Crispe had brought an appeal against a Chancery decree issued in favour of the Viscountess Cranborne and Thomas Dalmahoy, MP, and four days later, Sir Nicholas Stoughton had petitioned against a decree in the equity side of the Exchequer in a case against Arthur Onslow.[161] The Commons attempted to prevent both Dalmahoy and Onslow from answering the suits, but their instructions came too late. Both had already done so the first week of May.[162] They then issued warrants for the arrest of Crispe and Stoughton, both of whom immediately applied for and were granted protections from the upper house.[163] A series of conferences between the two houses reopened communication but did little to resolve the crisis. All three focused on the earlier conflicts of Shirley's case – the Commons protesting that Shirley's appeal represented 'a Breach of the undoubted Rights and Privileges of the House of Commons' and demanding that the proceedings be suspended; the Lords now conveying their earlier resolution of 1670, reaffirming their 'undoubted right in judicature' to hear appeals involving members of either house.[164]

On 31 May the Commons requested a further conference to discuss the appeal of Sir Nicholas Stoughton. By this stage, however, the upper house was rapidly losing patience. They agreed to the conference (over the protests of a handful of peers) so long as the discussion centred solely on the privileges of the House of Commons. The Lords resolved not to enter into debate about any aspect of their judicature and the managers of the conference were instructed to withdraw themselves if the matter was raised.[165] Not surprisingly, the conference never took place.

In the meantime, the Commons took steps which would exacerbate the crisis still further. On 27 May, Sir Nicholas Crispe petitioned the Lords complaining that the counsel which they had assigned him now refused to plead his case; they had apparently been informed by members of the Commons that if they assisted him, they would be imprisoned in the Tower.[166] Notwithstanding the threat, the Lords insisted that they appear and plead for the plaintiff or answer to the contrary; they did so. In the event, the Lords sided with the defendants and the plaintiff's appeal was dismissed – over the conspicuous protests of the earls of Shaftesbury and Strafford.[167] The dismissal of one of the three contentious cases should have gone some way toward easing tensions (as Shaftesbury clearly feared it would), but it did nothing of the kind. On 1 June the lower house made good its earlier threat and ordered Sir John Churchill, Serjeants Peck and Pemberton, and Mr Porter taken into custody for 'having subverted and betrayed the Liberty of the Subject and the Privilege of Parliament' in pleading for Sir Nicholas Crispe.[168]

The four men now became unwitting pawns in a high-stakes power struggle between the two houses. The Lords were outraged by their arrest and immediately ordered Black Rod to secure their release from the Commons' Serjeant at Arms and return them to the protection of the upper house. Once that was done, the Lords offered them a blanket protection from further arrest. The upper house then demanded a conference with the Commons to discuss what they called matters 'of high importance concerning the Dignity of the King and the Safety of the Government'.[169] The heads for this conference were prepared by the earls of Anglesey (the Lord Privy Seal), Bridgewater and Shaftesbury and Lord Holles. Not surprisingly, the resolutions which emerged condemned the Commons' actions in the most uncompromising and inflammatory language. Their arrest of the Lords' appellate counsel had been

> illegal and arbitrary . . . and a great Indignity to the King's Majesty in this His highest Court of Judicature in the Kingdom, the Lords in Parliament; where His Majesty is Highest in His Royal Estate, and where the last Resort of judging upon Writs of Error and Appeals in Equity, in all Causes, and over all Persons, is undoubtedly fixed and permanently lodged.

Quite apart from the fact that the arrest had been an 'unexampled usurpation' and breach of the privileges of the upper house, it had also represented a 'transcendant Invasion on the Right and Liberty of the Subject' because the Commons had ignored the guarantees of due process. They had overreached themselves because they had 'no Authority nor Power of Judicature over Inferior Subjects (much less over the King and Lords)'. All of which tended 'to the subversion of the Government of this Kingdom, and the introducing of Arbitrariness and Disorder'.[170]

These were plainly not resolutions designed to make peace with the lower house, but despite the strong language they were approved without protest or dissent. At least with regard to the defence of their judicial prerogatives the upper house was now willing to unite behind Shaftesbury's leadership. The resolutions were presented in conference on 3 June, but the Commons remained unimpressed. Predictably, they were offended by the Lords' assertion that the king was highest in his royal estate in their court, rather than in the full Parliament, something they claimed diminished the king's dignity and their own. They defended their actions as a legitimate defence of their own privileges and reminded the house that they had imprisoned others for similar infractions. Finally, and for the first time, they specifically challenged the Lords' jurisdiction to hear appeals from courts of equity – something which they claimed could not be supported 'by Magna Charta or any other law or ancient custom of Parliament'. As a further gesture of contempt, they proceeded the following day to rearrest the beleaguered attorneys (while they were pleading another case in Chancery) and imprison them in the Tower.

This was, for the Lords, the final straw. They resolved to conduct no further business with the House of Commons until their rights had been vindicated.[171] Their decision finally prompted the king to intervene with a speech to both houses on 5 June. However, the speech did little good, largely because the king attempted to paint the crisis as the handiwork of a few malcontents – 'Contrivers for a Dissolution', as he called them. There was clearly some truth in his accusation, but a majority in both houses had by now embraced the confrontation – the Lords would unanimously reject the king's supposition two days later – and neither was willing to concede any ground.[172] Matters had been allowed to go too far and the king was finally forced to prorogue Parliament on 9 June.

Unfortunately for the king, the prorogation failed to resolve the crisis. Less than a week after Parliament reconvened, on 13 October, Dr Shirley repetitioned the upper house, asking the Lords to set a date for hearing his appeal.[173] (The king had apparently tried to persuade Shirley to delay resubmission for a week or ten days, but he refused, explaining to the king that he was 'engaged to some persons of honor to bring it on speedily'.)[174] The petition triggered a long and difficult debate in the house. The prorogation had weakened the unified resolve of the spring and there was now significant opposition to reviving the case, chiefly on grounds that it would inevitably lead to a renewal of hostilities with the Commons. At this point Shaftesbury again seized the initiative. On 20 October he made a long and powerful speech in favour of proceeding.[175] Though he was clearly interested in perpetuating the conflict with the Commons for his own purposes, the speech is notable for its eloquent defence of House of Lords' judicature and for Shaftesbury's attempts to place the conflict in a broader political context. He first attempted to answer those who had suggested that matters of state – notably supply – ought to override the Lords' concern with their own privileges: 'Our all,' said Shaftesbury, 'is at stake.'

> This matter is no less than your whole judicature; and your judicature is the life and soul of the dignity of the Peerage of England. You will quickly grow burdensome if you grow useless. You have now the greatest and most useful end of Parliaments principally in you, which is not to make new laws, but to redress grievances and to maintain the old landmarks. The House of Commons' business is to complain, your Lordships to redress, not only the complaints from them that

are the eyes of the nation, but all other particular persons that address you.[176]

To put off private business for six weeks, as some had suggested, in deference to the king's need for supply, was simply too dangerous. Once he had achieved his own end, the king would surely not allow the house to take up Shirley's appeal – 'Time will be too short . . . to vindicate ourselves in the matter'.[177] Shaftesbury insisted that he intended no disloyalty to the king:

> My Lords, I have all the duty imaginable to his Majesty, and shall with all submission give way to any thing he should think of importance to his affairs: but in this point it is to alter the constitution of the government, if you are asked to lay this aside. And there can be no reason of state can be argument to turn yourselves out of that interest you have in the constitution of the government; it is not only your concern that you maintain yourselves in it, but it is the concern of the poorest man in England that you keep your station . . . for let the House of Commons and the gentry of England think what they please, there is no prince that ever governed without nobility or an army; if you will not have one, you must have the other, or the Monarchy cannot long support, or keep from tumbling into a democratical republic. Your Lordships and the people have the same cause, and the same enemies . . . . I therefore declare that I will serve my prince as a peer, but will not destroy the peerage to serve him.[178]

There were, Shaftesbury suggested, ominous signs of the potential threat of arbitrary government. He reminded the house of the recent history of the king's foreign policy and the fact that he had only been 'disengaged' from the 'French interest' under pressure from Parliament.[179] He pointed to the failure of the episcopal bench to join with lay Lords in the defence of 'essential' rights and to the dangerous resurgence of the Laudian doctrine of divine right monarchy – 'the root that produced the Bill of Test last session'.[180] He reminded the house as well that the king had recently declared against appeals in the Scottish Parliament, something about which the Scots had already begun to complain.[181] The real threat to their jurisdiction, he suggested, did not come so much from the 'interest' of the House of Commons as from the 'inclination' of the Court itself. He urged the house to recognize the dangers. The Lords' jurisdiction was 'essential' to the house, as the house was essential to the preservation of the constitution and the liberties of the subject. To give way on the former would be to risk the future of the latter and he therefore begged the house to defend their jurisdiction by proceeding with Dr Shirley's appeal.[182]

Shaftesbury's plea was not immediately successful, but it was clearly influential. Rather than defer the case (or, indeed, dismiss it), the house began an exhaustive review of all of the precedents and the arguments of the previous session. Finally, on 4 November they voted to retain the cause and scheduled it for hearing three weeks later.[183] That touched off a predictable response from the lower house. The Commons repeated their condemnation of the proceedings, again attempted to arrest both Dr Shirley and Sir Nicholas Stoughton (who had also renewed his appeal) and ultimately issued a public declaration condemning all those pleading to or participating in the proceedings as betrayers of the rights and liberties of the Commons of England. By 20 November the houses were again at a complete deadlock and Shaftesbury and the opposition peers made their move to gain a dissolution. The motion for dissolution was debated at length, but ultimately failed (albeit by only two votes). The message was clear, however. This Parliament was in deep trouble. The king sent them packing two days later under a prorogation that would last fifteen months.

That hiatus essentially ended the dispute. When Parliament reconvened in February 1677 neither house raised the matter – nor did Shirley or Stoughton attempt to revive their cases – and good relations were restored. The upper house resumed hearing Chancery appeals without protest, though the first new ones were not presented until February 1678 and in neither case did they involve members of Parliament.[184] In truth, the dispute had always been more about privilege than jurisdiction and once that was no longer an issue there was little point in pursuing the matter. In any event, by 1678 the judicial powers of the House of Lords had come to be seen as considerably less threatening than the policies and powers of the king and his ministers and the preoccupations of the lower house shifted accordingly.

That did not mean, however, that the matter had been put to rest. The debate continued for some time within the legal community. In the years following the controversy at least a half-dozen erstwhile legal scholars wrote, and in some cases published, learned treatises on the subject of House of Lords judicature. Lord Holles followed up his earlier defence of the Lords' original jurisdiction (written in the wake of Skinner's case) with a second defence, published in late 1675, of the Lords' appellate jurisdiction in equity.[185] As he had during the debates, Holles defended the jurisdiction on the basis of both precedent and practicality. A half-century of uninterrupted (and, until 1675, uncontested) practice seemed, in Holles's view, proof enough that the right lay with the upper house. It also made sense. Why, he asked, if the house had been given power to reverse erroneous judgments at common law by writ of error, should they not also have the responsibility of correcting errors in equity? As he pointed out, 'there is more danger from a court of Equity, where one's Doome depends on the will of one man, that is not tied to the strict rule of law, than where there are four judges who have the strict rule of law to go by'.[186] However, rather like Prynne in the late 1640s, Holles proved to be something of a lone voice. In fact his treatise became a kind of lightning rod, attracting a series of rebuttals from the likes of William Petyt,[187] Sir Matthew Hale,[188] Sir Robert Atkyns[189] and Francis, Lord Guilford.[190] With the exception of Petyt, who was something of a legal antiquarian, each of these men were (or had recently been) practising jurists and therefore approached the law with a healthy respect for technicalities and an acute sensitivity to the judicial prerogatives of their colleagues on the bench. They entered the fray, unavoidably, with some degree of bias. While each of them willingly acknowledged some measure of appellate jurisdiction in the upper house, they strenuously denied that the Lords had an inherent (or an acquired) right to hear appeals from courts of equity. The numerous mid-seventeenth century precedents cited by Holles were universally dismissed as being drawn from 'irregular' times. All of them insisted that the Lords could exercise this authority only by virtue of a special commission from the king, solicited in each case. Technically, they were probably correct. The law provided for appeal to the king and for the appointment of an independent review panel – though even Hale was forced to admit that this was both inefficient and impractical. Holles had insisted instead that there was no need to seek special permission; the Lords had a standing commission from the king. It was part and parcel of the authority anciently delegated to the upper house. The king, Holles claimed, was 'virtually always present' in their house and was implicitly part of their judgments.[191]

In fact that supposition was at the heart of both these disputes and the war of treatises that followed. All the authors questioned the legitimacy of the Lords' proceedings because, in varying degrees, they perceived them to be a usurpation of the king's authority. The Lords' failure to solicit the king's commission in Chancery appeals was only symptomatic of a larger problem. Hale and (rather more forcefully) Guilford implied that Holles and his colleagues were attempting to erect a judicial power which was somehow independent of the Crown – that the Lords were (as the Commons had suggested earlier) challenging the king's supremacy in the law.[192] But that seriously misrepresented the case. Whatever their political views, none of the Lords would ever have dared to question the premise that their authority derived directly from the king's. Indeed, that was its principal strength. They were (and saw themselves as) the king's judges, exercising the king's law, in the king's court, for the benefit of the king's subjects. That had always been both the duty and the honour of the peerage.

CONCLUSION

The half century between 1621 and 1675 forever changed the House of Lords and, to some extent, the peerage itself. Outside events – civil war and revolution, in particular – had an obvious and lasting impact. But in the long term they were really no more important than the transformation wrought by the revival of House of Lords judicature. That revival had seemed – to those who actually noticed it – innocuous enough in 1621. The odd private petition or the isolated writ of error hardly seemed the stuff of revolution. But within a very short time, the internal dynamics of the House of Lords had been irrevocably altered. So too had its public profile. What had been for at least the last three centuries primarily a legislative and advisory institution, now became (in almost equal parts) a judicial one. And that inevitably changed the way the upper house did business. On a purely practical level the changes were obvious. The steady influx of private litigation required new procedural mechanisms and, more importantly, major reallocation of both time and personnel. The business of the house had to be reorganized and managed more efficiently. New rules had to be established and basic responsibilities and priorities had to be redefined.

But there was a more important and subtle change at work in these proceedings which had to do with the Lords' relationship to the public. To some extent, the social position of the peerage and the hereditary nature of their assembly had always kept the Lords at one remove from the ordinary problems of their contemporaries. That is not to say they were ignorant of or even insensitive to the grievances of English commoners. They were not. But their role in rectifying them was generally more passive than active – in essence, responding to legislation normally offered by the king or the House of Commons. Private party litigation changed that by bringing the house into much closer contact with the public. It forced the Lords to take a direct, personal interest in the needs of individual litigants and, inevitably, to pay more immediate attention to the effect which particular problems – and major crises – had on their lives. Indeed, it required them to provide fast, effective and appropriate solutions to those problems – albeit largely on a case by case basis. As they did so, their role in parliamentary affairs became more obviously active, and, for their ever-growing number of clients at least, their house came to be seen as a more responsive, more meaningful institution. In a curious way the proceedings created for the upper house its own popular constituency. It was not, perhaps, a constituency that could be readily quantified in political terms, but it was real nonetheless. It existed as an increasingly widespread public perception that the upper house represented an indispensable last line of defence against the failure of justice and the rule of law. This was certainly true by 1640, when petitioners sought relief from the irregularities of the Personal Rule, but it was really true as well in the 1620s, when they looked to the house to rectify failings in the judicial system and again in the 1660s when they sought reassurance after the uncertainties of civil war and revolution. By 1675 the upper house really had become (as Lord Holles claimed it had always been) 'the Supreme Court of Judicature to which all persons aggrieved . . . did apply themselves for relief'.[193] It had assumed direct responsibility for protecting the legal rights and interest of all subjects and to that extent it too had become a 'representative' institution.

That change would not, of course, have taken place without the active support of the members. It needs to be stressed, however, that the Lords never made a conscious, premeditated decision to revive private party judicature for political reasons or any other. The revival in 1621 took place so unobtrusively and in such piecemeal fashion, that it was hardly noticeable. As time went on, of course, the dramatic increase in judicial business and the distractions it created made the members more fully aware that they were undertaking new responsibilities. But even then the proceedings generated little if any discussion. The Lords took charge of these complaints without any hesitation and without any visible signs of uncertainty either about what they were doing or about their obligation to do it. In part that reflected a common appreciation of their ancient history as the High Court – something certainly well understood before 1621. But it really reflected the much simpler fact that complaints presented by litigants were too serious and compelling to ignore.

The fact was that the Lords continued to see themselves (both as members of the peerage and as members of the house) as traditional guardians of the public welfare. Protecting the legal interests of individual subjects was perceived to be as much a part of that responsibility as passing legislation. Certainly, there was an element of old-fashioned paternalism about the proceedings – a wish to preserve order by ensuring that the law was properly enforced. The Lords were acutely aware of the disturbing (and ultimately destabilizing) effects of a breakdown in the legal system. But there was more involved here than a generalized sense of duty. There was a very evident and genuine concern to provide for the needs of individual complainants and to ensure (in so far as it was possible) that each received proper remedy and fair justice. That needs to be stressed in view of the traditional characterization of the seventeenth century House of Lords as somehow remote and indifferent and concerned only with the protection of their own – and the Crown's – vested interests. That was clearly not the case. Their extensive effort to enforce the law and offer redress against the king's government during the early years of the Long Parliament alone suggests just how broadly the Lords defined their constitutional role and how seriously they took the responsibilities of leadership.

Admittedly, some of the commitment and some of the standards of performance were lost during the years that followed. But that was not really surprising given the impact of civil war on the upper house. Some decline in performance was to be expected when the house itself was so much reduced by political division and when the attention of those who remained was so easily diverted to other more pressing concerns. If strict legal objectivity and fair justice were, on occasion, sacrificed to political expediency, that too was a temporary rather than a permanent failing – another consequence of the politics of war. In fact, such transgressions were comparatively rare. On balance, what is more surprising is that the Lords were willing and able to continue hearing private litigation at all during the war years. That they did so suggests that they had come to accept these proceedings as an inescapable part of the business of their house. They were plainly seen as a burden, but one which the house willingly acknowledged and, indeed, vigorously defended when their judicial authority came under fire at the close of the decade.

At the Restoration the Lords embraced their responsibility to private litigants even more strongly. In part, that was a natural reaction to the Revolution itself. The condemnation of their judicial authority had been a crucial factor in the decision to abolish their house and it therefore became imperative, as a matter of principle, to insist on the complete restoration of their powers. But there was more to it than that. The Lords, as much as anyone, had been moved by the careless disregard for legal rights (not least their own) engendered by revolution and by the policies of the various Interregnum governments. It had always been their responsibility (as in the early 1640s) to protect against such abuses and, given what had happened in their absence, that responsibility now seemed more important than ever. Undoubtedly, the Lords were also impressed by the flood of petitions to their house in the Convention Parliament, not just because of the problems they presented, but because of the testimony they offered to the public's continuing faith in the High Court. At a time when the Lords were bound to be rather sensitive to public perceptions of their role, that testimony made a difference. It made clear to the Lords (albeit indirectly) just how important their earlier assistance had been and how sorely it had been missed during the 1650s. As a consequence, what had often been seen in the past as an annoying if inescapable burden now became (in the wake of revolution) a kind of badge of honour – a prerogative to be defended with all the powers at hand.

The crises over *Skinner* v. the *East India Company* and *Shirley* v. *Fagg* in the Cavalier Parliament have to be seen in that context. Shaftesbury's attempt to use the latter case for political purposes was only possible because (as he recognized full well) the House of Lords remained extremely sensitive about their judicial authority. By that stage their judicial proceedings had not only become an integral part of the business of the house, they had become an essential part of its history. Over the course of the century the Lords had established a long and distinguished record of providing much needed remedy to an extraordinary range of litigants. The record had not been perfect. There had been failings along the way. But their accomplishments had been significant. Even Sir Edward Dering had had to admit, in the Common's debates over Shirley's case, that the precedents established in their earlier proceedings were 'too much to be blowne away with a breath in an hour's discourse'.[194] The Lords took justifiable pride in the services they had offered, but beyond that they saw them as fundamentally important to the good government of the realm. In some quarters the broad powers they had exercised were seen as a danger. But if their jurisdiction had been (as Hale would later assert) 'promiscuous', it had been so for a reason. There had been a demonstrable need – and a persistent demand – for a court which could operate generally to protect the law and guard against the failure of justice; a court which could provide, as Lord Holles's described it, 'ordinary remedy in extraordinary causes.'

As time went on and 'extraordinary causes' became far more the exception than the rule, there was less need for the Lords to exercise such an omnicompetent jurisdiction and their role was gradually confined to hearing appeals – from both equity and common law (by writ of error). Over the course of the eighteenth and nineteenth centuries the court continued to evolve. Its jurisdiction expanded in 1707 to include appeals from Scottish Court of Session, and again in 1800 to include those from Ireland. Throughout the early nineteenth century, efforts were also made to refine its procedures.[195] Congestion and delay had remained an ever present problem – a committee appointed in 1821 to investigate the matter reported a backlog of 296 appeals and forty-two writs of error – and proposals were put forward to rectify the problem by establishing a permanent quorum of appellate personnel and permanent meeting times.[196] Continuing criticism about the participation of unqualified members in appeal decisions led the house, in 1844, to restrict the right to hear and vote on appeals to members professionally qualified in the law.[197] By the 1850s the situation had improved dramatically. Delays were down significantly and there was general satisfaction with the quality of the Law Lords.[198]

The great law reform movement of the early 1870s inevitably turned its attention to the House of Lords and Gladstone's government actually saw through a bill, in 1873, which abolished the Lords' appellate jurisdiction altogether in favour of a newly created Supreme Court of Appeal. The abolition lasted less than three years. The fall of Gladstone and the return of the Conservatives under Disraeli ushered in a groundswell movement – led in part by the legal community – to overturn the bill. It was successful and in 1876 the Lords regained their status as the final court of appeal, though the structure of the court itself was significantly changed. The act created a permanent body of law lords and made the judicial sessions of the court independent from the legislative sessions of the house – both badly needed reforms which survive to the present.[199] Interestingly, the so-called Committee for Preserving the House of Lords, which spearheaded the drive to restore the Lords' jurisdiction, had written to Disraeli in 1875 to enlist his support. They argued that 'it would be wiser to attempt ... to secure for the suitors the moral weight and consideration which the present tribunal derives from its constitutional associations, from its antiquity, and from its long career of successful adjudication'. The jurisdiction, they claimed, 'is not a question of mere privilege which the peers can of themselves surrender; but a duty and a function cast upon them by the laws of the Realm'.[200] That legacy owed everything to the seventeenth-century House of Lords.

NOTES

1 Lord Chancellor Clarendon's speech closing the Convention Parliament, December 1660 (*LJ*, xi, p. 238).
2 *The Parliamentary History of England*, ed. W. Cobbett (36 vols; London, 1806–20), vol. 22, p. 142.
3 *The Diary of Samuel Pepys*, ed. Robert Latham and William Matthews (11 vols; Berkeley, 1983), Vol. 1, p. 113.
4 Ronald Hutton, *The Restoration* (London, 1985), p. 113.
5 S.R. Gardiner, *Constitutional Documents of the Puritan Revolution, 1625–1660*, (Oxford, 1889), p. 452. See also *The Diary of Thomas Burton Esq.*, ed. John Towill Rutt (4 vols; London, 1974), Vol. 1, pp. 387–8.
6 ibid., p. 387. Whitelock was also one of Cromwell's earliest nominees to the newly created 'other House'. The final wording of the jurisdictional clauses also strongly suggests a familiarity with the most recent treatises on the subject of the Lords' powers, Henry Elsyng's unpublished 'Of judicature', written in the 1630s, and John Selden's more familiar *Privileges of the Baronage of England*, commissioned by the House of Lords in 1621.
7 Burton, *Diary*, ii, p. 451.
8 ibid., ii, p. 398.
9 ibid., p. 451.
10 William Prynne, *A Plea for the Lords and the House of Peers* (London, 1658). Prynne claimed in his preface that

> this much augmented plea hath layed dormant ever since [his exclusion and arrest in Pride's Purge] and had never been allowed to walk abroad in Publicke, had not the late, loud, unexpected votes at Westminster of a new King and House of Lords under the Name and Notion of 'Another House' ... revived and raised it out of oblivion.

11 Prynne, *Plea*, pp. 401–504.
12 Burton, *Diary*, iv, p. 68. The editor of the diary assumes, mistakenly, that the speaker in question had reference to the 1648 edition of Prynne's treatise, rather than to the more recent version.
13 ibid., iv, p. 27.
14 *LJ*, xi, p. 9.

15 The exception here was Aubrey de Vere, twentieth earl of Oxford, who was born in 1627 and succeeded to his title in 1632, but refused to sit in 1648 and joined the king in exile during the 1650s.

16 *LJ*, xi, p. 5. Craven, who had been in exile with the king, appears to have been one of the earliest royalists to have taken his seat. Understandably, perhaps, there seems to have been some confusion about who was to be allowed to take their seats. On the 27th, the Committee for Privileges was ordered to consider 'the Cases of those Lords that have late come to sit in this House, and those as do not'. Presumably, this was meant to establish a policy with regard to both former royalists and Catholics. However, both Craven and the Catholic Lord Petre had just been appointed to that committee, so the point had been conceded for all intents and purposes. Officially, the house delayed the readmission of both royalists and Catholics until mid May, but representatives of both groups had taken their seats before that on their own initiative.

17 *LJ*, xi, pp. 14, 20, 27, 29, 30.

18 HLRO, Minutes of the Committee for Petitions, vol. 1, p. 4; C.H. Firth, *The House of Lords during the Civil War* (London, 1910), p. 224.

19 *LJ*, xi, pp. 52, 55, 59, 75, 81.

20 ibid., pp. 52, 57.

21 ibid., p. 69.

22 ibid., p. 81. In the second session the house appointed a new committee of fourteen members whom they specifically designated as 'Receivers and Triers of Petitions' and who were given responsibility for determining 'what Petitions are fit and Proper for this House to receive' (ibid., p. 184). With two exceptions all the members of this committee served as members of the original Committee for Petitions appointed the previous spring.

23 ibid., p. 5, 6, 9. The Clerk of the Crown, Valentine Willis, and his deputy, Henry Barker, were admitted as assistants on the basis of the former's patent to the office, granted by Charles I, which the house decided gave him undisputed title to the office.

24 *LJ*, xi, p. 15.

25 ibid., p. 52.

26 The sons of Sir Thomas Jermyn had held reversions to a number of administrative and judicial offices under Charles I (G.E. Aylmer, *The King's Servants* (New York, 1961), p. 339).

27 The order was agreed on 7 December, but was not confirmed by ordinance until 1 June 1644 (*LJ*, vi, pp. 329, 574–5).

28 ibid., ix, p. 162.

29 The case was heard by the Commons' Committee for Grievances. 'Divers' members apparently objected to hearing the matter on grounds that it was improper for the committee to intercede in a case that was remediable at law. Burton described it as 'an ill precedent' (Burton, *Diary*, iii, p. 595; iv, p. 244).

30 *CJ*, vii, p. 877.

31 HLRO, Main Papers, H.L., 1, 2, 4, 15 and 18 May 1660; *LJ*, xi, p. 9.

32 ibid., xi, p. 26.

33 HLRO, Main Papers, H.L., 18 May 1660.

34 ibid., 14 May 1660; *LJ*, xi, p. 27. Some of the Lords may have been familiar with Watkins. His right to the office had been challenged by Richard Ward and John Robinson in a case before the house in 1642. The dispute was never settled in the House, but appears to have been resolved between the parties (HLRO, Main papers, H.L., 15, 24 February and 28 June 1642; *LJ*, iv, p. 659; v, p. 177).

35 HLRO, Main Papers, H.L., 12 May 1660; *LJ*, xi, p. 25.

36 HLRO, Main Papers, H.L., 14 May 1660; *LJ*, xi, p. 27.

37 HLRO, Main Papers, H.L., 18 May 1660; *LJ*, xi, p. 32. See also the case of Dame Barbara Villiers concerning the Office of the Mint (HLRO, Main Papers, H.L., 18 May 1660; *LJ*, xi, p. 33); and the case of *Swallow* v. *Pight* concerning the Clerkship of the Coining Irons in the Mint (HLRO, Main Papers, H.L., 5 and 18 May, 5 June 1660; *LJ*, xi, pp. 15, 33, 53).

38 HLRO, Main Papers, H.L., 17 May 1660.
39 ibid., 19 May 1660.
40 *CSPD*, 1660–1, pp. 100–1.
41 *LJ*, xi. pp. 33–4. March and Sherbourne later petitioned the king to request reinstatement (*CSPD*, 1660–1, p. 101).
42 HLRO, Main Papers, H.L., 13 June 1660. The corporation had been remodelled in September 1649. A new mayor, three aldermen and seven common councillors were appointed by the Rump (David Underdown, *Pride's Purge* (London, 1971), p. 304; *CJ*, vi, p. 294).
43 *LJ*, xi, p. 60; HLRO, Minutes of the Committee for Petitions, vol. i, pp. 20, 21, 35.
44 *LJ*, xi, pp. 138–9.
45 HLRO, Main Papers, H.L., 11 July 1660.
46 ibid.
47 *LJ*, xi, p. 87; HLRO, Minutes of the Committee for Petitions, vol. 1, p. 52.
48 ibid., p. 82.
49 Hutton, *The Restoration*, p. 130.
50 *CSPD*, 1660–1, pp. 563, 569, 570.
51 HLRO, Main Papers, H.L., 3 July 1660 (petition of Thomas Johnson *et al.*). *LJ*, xi, p. 82.
52 HLRO, Main Papers, H.L., 14 May 1660.
53 ibid., 18 May 1660.
54 ibid., 22 May 1660.
55 ibid., 25 May 1660.
56 ibid., 14 and 22 May 1660.
57 *LJ*, xi, p. 31.
58 ibid., p. 34.
59 ibid., p. 33.
60 HLRO, Minutes of the Committee for Petitions, vol. 1, pp. 11, 13.
61 *LJ*, xi, p. 42.
62 ibid., p. 53. The order clearly developed in the Committee for Petitions during deliberation on the cases of Humphrey Babington and the fellows of Magdalene College (HLRO, Minutes of the Committee for Petitions, Vol. i, p. 13).
63 Hutton, *The Restoration*, p. 131; Pepys, *Diary*, Vol. 1, p. 227 and n.1.
64 I.M. Green, *The Reestablishment of the Church of England 1660–1663* (Oxford, 1978), p. 39.
65 ibid., pp. 39–40.
66 *LJ*, xi, pp. 45–6; *CJ*, viii, p. 47.
67 Green, *Reestablishment of the Church of England*, pp. 41–2.
68 HLRO, Main Papers, H.L., 20 June 1660.
69 John Morrill, 'The church in England, 1642–9', in John Morrill (ed.), *Reactions to the English Civil War* (London, 1982), pp. 89–114.
70 *LJ*, xi, p. 42; HLRO, Minutes of the Committee for Petitions, vol. 1. pp. 29, 31, 32.
71 See, for example, HLRO, Main Papers, H.L., 7 June 1660 (Dr Thomas Hurst *et al.*), 18 June 1660 (Andrew Sandeland); *LJ*, xi, p. 60 (Dr Hurst *et al.*), p. 70 (Richard Sharlocke).
72 *LJ*, xi, p. 60, 70.
73 ibid., p. 72.
74 ibid., p. 73.
75 HLRO, Main Papers, H.L., 23 June 1660. The petitions are contained in a single collection and are calendared alphabetically, by petitioner. The affected parishes are also listed by name and county. The clerk's office recorded the dates of submission in only a few cases, so it is not possible to determine exactly when the bulk of these petitions was presented. There are an additional 31 petitions presented in July and August which are calendared separately.
76 ibid., 23 August 1660 (Ralph Nevill), 6 September 1660 (Christopher Stone), 8 September 1660 (Richard Edwards).

77 ibid., 24 August 1660 (Joseph Hayhurst), 4 September 1660 (Samuel Coates), 27 July 1660 (Nicholas Dingley).

78 ibid., 24 August 1660 (Samuel Pepys), 8 September (Stephen Poole).

79 See, for example, *LJ*, xi, pp. 86, 98, 127, 141, 159, 163. In one case the Lords revoked their order, but required the incumbent to provide bond, to be sure that he would make good the tithes to his opponent if any future trial for title went against him (*LJ*, xi, p. 138 (*Nevill v. Keck*)).

80 HLRO, Main Papers, H.L., 23 August 1660.

81 ibid., 8 August 1660.

82 See, for example, HLRO, Main Papers, H.L., 17 July 1660 (Christopher Webb), 24 August 1660 (John Fish).

83 HLRO, Main Papers, H.L., 9 August 1660. The request was granted (*LJ*, xi, p. 122).

84 HLRO, Main Papers, H.L., 2 August 1660. See also, 18 August 1660 (William Ives).

85 See, for example, *LJ*, xi, pp. 138, 140.

86 See, for example, ibid., pp. 133–4 (William Ives), p. 148 (Dr Creighton).

87 HLRO, Main Papers, H.L., 1 September 1660 (Peter Withe); *LJ*, xi, p. 152.

88 HLRO, Minutes of the Committee for Petitions, Vol. 1, p. 42.

89 12 Charles II, c. 17; Act for Confirming and Restoring Ministers, *Statutes of the Realm*, v, pp. 242–6. For a detailed discussion of the evolution of the bill, see Green, *Reestablishment of the Church of England*, pp. 39–52.

90 *LJ*, xi, p. 93.

91 Hutton, *The Restoration*, pp. 139–41.

92 See, for example, *LJ* xi, p. 55 (Lord Craven), and p. 63 (Duke of Buckingham). The orders allowed the affected peers to recover arrears of rents and profits.

93 ibid., p. 67.

94 HLRO, Main Papers, H.L., 20 June 1660.

95 *LJ*, xi, p. 98.

96 *CSPD*, 1660–1, p. 18.

97 HLRO, Main Papers, H.L., 27 July 1660.

98 *LJ*, xi, pp. 114–15.

99 HLRO, Main Papers, H.L., 23 June 1660.

100 *LJ*, xi, p. 103.

101 H.J., Habakkuk, 'The land settlement and the restoration of Charles II', *Transactions of the Royal Historical Society*, 5th series, vol. 28 (1978), pp. 201–22.

102 HLRO, Main Papers, H.L., 8 and 26 June 1660.

103 See, for example, HLRO, Minutes of the Committee for Petitions, Vol. pp. 39, 42, 44, 55.

104 *LJ*, xi, p. 118.

105 ibid., p. 121.

106 HLRO, Main Papers H.L., 4 July 1660 (*Deicrow* v. *Edwards*) 20 July 1660 (*Calcott* v. *Smith*).

107 The exception was the appeal of David Jenkins (HLRO, Main Papers, H.L., 10 July 1660). Jenkins asked that he not be concluded by a Chancery decree, issued by the parliamentary Commissioners of the Great Seal in 1649, because he had not been heard in the case. In fact, he had not been heard because he had refused to appear, having been unwilling to submit to their authority. He asked for permission to submit a proviso to the Act for Confirmation of Judicial Proceedings and was granted the request (*LJ*, xi, p. 86).

108 For a list of these, see HMC, Seventh Report, Appendix, pp. 98–100.

109 *LJ*, xi, p. 126.

110 The one exception was the abovementioned case of David Jenkins. Over the summer the two parties involved had agreed that the case be reheard in Chancery. The Lords therefore suspended the earlier decree until that had been done (*LJ*, xi, p 126). Presumably, the other petitioners could have submitted a formal appeal to the house at a later date, had they had legitimate cause. However, none appears to have done so.

111 *LJ*, xi, pp. 72 (Edmund Veale), p. 103 (Benjamin Deicrow), pp. 199–200 (*Cary* v. *Cromwell*).

112 HLRO, Main Papers, 29 June, 2 July, 20 August 1660; *LJ*, xi, pp. 78, 80, 135 (*Carr* v. *Carr*). Main Papers H.L., 9 May 1660; Minutes of the Committee for Petitions, Vol. 1, pp. 3, 4, 6, 7. *LJ*, xi pp. 20, 29 (*Skinner* v. *East India Company*). (This last case is not to be confused with that of *Thomas Skinner* v. *the East India Company* which was brought to the upper house in 1667).

113 HLRO, Main Papers, H.L., 26 July, 20 December 1660; *LJ*, xi, pp. 140, 154, 183, 185, 200, 210, 219.

114 ibid., p. 207 (Sir Symon Fanshaw).

115 For a discussion of the Hale Commission, see Mary Cotterell, 'Interregnum law reform', *English Historical Review*, Vol. 82 (1968), pp. 689–704. See also, N. Matthews, *William Sheppard* (Cambridge, 1984) for an admirable discussion of law reform proposals generally.

116 Cotterell, 'Interregnum law reform,' p. 697; Matthews, *William Sheppard*, pp. 149.

117 For a discussion of the fate of these proposals in the second Protectorate Parliament, see Matthews, *William Sheppard*, pp. 186–230.

118 Cotterell, 'Interregnum law reform', pp. 699–700.

119 Matthews, *William Sheppard*, pp. 155, 201.

120 *LJ*, xi, p. 416.

121 ibid., xii, pp. 552, 581–3.

122 The record of the proceedings in this case was ordered to be expunged from the journals of both houses of Parliament as part of the compromise settlement imposed by the king. What follows is drawn from surviving documents and the MS journal or MS minutes in the Main Papers collection (calendared in HMC, Eighth Report, pp. 107–8, 165–74). A printed summary of the case (drawn largely from Denzil, Lord Holles's 1669 treatise, *The Grand Question Concerning the Judicature of the House of Peers*) is also available in *A Complete Collection of State Trials*, ed. W.Cobbett (33 vols; London, 1816–26), Vol. 6, pp. 710–70.

123 HLRO, Main Papers, H.L., 19 January 1666–7.

124 The court Constable and Marshall had jurisdiction to hear appeals of felonies committed overseas (J.H. Baker, *An Introduction to English Legal History*, 2nd edn (London, 1979) p. 107.

125 HLRO, Main Papers, H.L., 19 January 1666–7.

126 ibid.

127 HLRO, MS Minutes, 2 December 1667.

128 ibid.

129 ibid., Main Papers, H.L., 4 December 1667.

130 *State Trials*, vi, pp. 726–7. The committee appears to have been established in response to another earlier petition to the Commons from one Fitton, who had been fined and imprisoned by the upper house in 1663 for publishing a libel against Lord Gerard of Brandon. The committee was directed to investigate Fitton's case as well as the jurisdiction of the upper house. Fitton was heard at the bar of the Commons on one occasion, but the case was not apparently taken up again. The Commons no doubt recognized that the case involved parliamentary privilege. The presence of the committee suggests, however, that there was growing concern in the lower house prior to Skinner's case. See Francis Hargrave, introductory preface to M. Hale, *The Jurisdiction of the Lords' House* (London, 1796).

131 John Hatsell, *Precedents and Proceedings in the House of Commons* (4 vols; London, 1818), Vol. 3, p. 369.

132 ibid., pp. 372–3.

133 *LJ*, xi, pp. 232–3.

134 ibid., p. 236.

135 HLRO, MS Journal, 7 May 1668. An earlier draft of the introductory statement was rejected as too weak.

136 Hatsell, *Precedents*, Vol. 3, p. 376.

137 ibid, p. 377.

138 *LJ*, xii, pp. 247–9.

139 Hatsell, *Precedents*, Vol. 3, p. 377.
140 The exact circumstances of Barnardiston's release are not clear. The committee discovered that an entry had been made in the office of the Auditor of the Receipt in the Exchequer, dated 10 August, suggesting that he had submitted and paid his fine, but the fine appears to have been paid by someone else. The clerk involved claimed not to know who it was. Barnardiston was released by Sir John Eyton, Usher of the Black Rod, the same day (one of the subsequent adjournment days of the session), but was not told who had authorized his release. Eyton told him that 'there was a mystery in it' but assured him that he had 'sufficient authority' for what he was doing (Hatsell, *Precedents*, Vol. 3, pp. 377–80). The logical explanation would be that the king had arranged to have the fine paid (or seemingly paid) and Barnardiston released as a way of easing the crisis.
141 Holles, Baron Denzil, *The Grand Question Concerning the Judicature of the House of Peers* (London, 1669).
142 *State Trials*, vi, pp. 763–4.
143 HLRO, Main Papers, H.L., 19 January 1666–7.
144 Hatsell, *Precedents*, Vol. 3, pp. 380–384.
145 *LJ*, xii, p. 265.
146 HLRO, Main Papers, H.L., 19 January 1666–7.
147 Hatsell, *Precedents*, Vol. 3, p. 385.
148 ibid., p. 392.
149 HLRO, Main Papers, H.L., 18 March 1670–1; *LJ*, xii, pp. 462, 471–480, 604–6 (*Reade* v. *Reade*). See also, 19 April 1675; *LJ*, xii, pp. 662, 666 (*Leemkuel* v. *Throgmorton*).
150 J.R. Jones, *Country and Court, England 1658–1714* (London, 1978), pp. 185–6. For proceedings on the bill, see *LJ*, xii, pp. 666–712; HLRO, Main Papers, H.L., 19 April 1675.
151 ibid., 30 April 1675.
152 ibid., 10 December 1669.
153 *LJ*, xii, p. 673.
154 ibid., p. 679.
155 Typically, the committee had examined a number of precedents from medieval and early modern Parliaments (HLRO, Minutes of the Committee for Privileges, Vol. ii, pp. 116–17).
156 *LJ*, xii, p. 348.
157 ibid., p. 300.
158 ibid., pp. 680–1. Shaftesbury was joined by the earls of Bedford, Bristol, Bridgewater, Dorset, Denbigh and Newport, and Lords Howard of Escrick and Culpepper.
159 HLRO, Main Papers, 30 April 1675. Fagg claimed that the appeal was 'irregular' because relief was obtainable below, an argument that made little sense under the circumstances. The Commons' action does not suggest the presence of a conspiracy with opposition members in the upper house. The warrant was issued by the Speaker, Edward Seymour, who was a close ally of Danby's. It does suggest, however, that Danby was not paying close enough attention.
160 *LJ*, xii, p. 692.
161 HLRO, Main Papers, H.L., 19 and 23 April 1675.
162 ibid.
163 *LJ*, xii, pp. 695, 699.
164 ibid., pp. 694, 698, 700, 702. The second and third conferences focused on the Commons' objections to the Lords' request on 14 May, that they verify the authenticity of their arrest warrant against Dr Shirley. The Commons protested that this request was 'strange, and unusual' and 'unparliamentary', casting as it did an 'undue' reflection on the speaker of their house. The Lords attempted to assure them at the ensuing meeting that they were only trying to exercise restraint. They viewed the attempted arrest as a serious breach of their privileges and wanted to be sure that it was genuine before taking any further action.
165 ibid., p. 706.
166 HLRO, Main Papers, H.L., 19 April 1675.

167 *LJ*, xii, pp. 705–6, 709.
168 ibid., p. 715.
169 ibid., p. 716.
170 ibid., p. 718.
171 ibid., p. 723.
172 ibid., pp. 725–6. The Commons were more clearly divided on the issue than the Lords. The order to place the attorneys in the Tower went to a division and only passed by five votes. Over the next two days the Lords would attempt, without success, to free the attorneys from the Tower. The Lieutenant of the Tower, Sir John Robinson, refused to obey their orders and subsequently ignored the writs of habeas corpus which the house issued to secure their release. The Lords asked the king to dismiss him, but were refused (*LJ*, xii, pp. 726–8).
173 HLRO Main Papers, H.L., 30 April 1675; *LJ*, xiii, pp. 8–9.
174 HLRO, Mss Minutes, H.L., 20 October 1675.
175 BL Add. MS, 30294, folios 389–93. The speech is reprinted in full in *State Trials*, vi, pp. 1171–9.
176 ibid., fol. 390r.
177 ibid., fol. 390v.
178 ibid., fol. 391r–391v.
179 ibid., fol. 391v.
180 ibid., fol. 392r–392v.
181 ibid., fol. 389v.
182 ibid., fol. 393.
183 *LJ*, xiii, p. 12.
184 HLRO, Main Papers, H.L., 4 and 9 February 1677–8.
185 Holles, Baron Denzil, *The Case Stated Concerning the Judicature of the House of Peers in Point of Appeals* (London, 1675).
186 Holles, *The Case Stated*, p. 42.
187 William Petyt, 'A discourse on judicature in Parliament,' BL, Hargrave MSS, 115.
188 Hale, *Jurisdiction of the Lords House*. Hale's treatise was written at some point in late 1675 or early 1676, though not published until 1796.
189 Sir Robert Atkyns, *A Treatise on the True and Ancient Jurisdiction of the House of Peers* (London, 1699).
190 'A copy of an imperfect tract of the Lo Keeper Guilford relating to the jurisdiction of the House of Peers,' HLRO, Historical Collections, H.L., miscellaneous.
191 Holles, *The Case Stated*, p. 25.
192 Hale, *Jurisdiction of the Lords House*, p. 191; Guilford, 'Imperfect tract,' pp. 7–9.
193 Holles, *The Case Stated*, p. 45.
194 Maurice Bond (ed.), *The Diaries of Sir Edward Dering*, HLRO, Occasional Publications, 1 (London, 1976), p. 74.
195 A.S. Tuberville, 'The House of Lords as a court of law, 1734–1837', *Law Quarterly Review*, 52 (1936), pp.189–219.
196 ibid., p. 208.
197 W. Holdsworth, *The History of English Law*, Vol. 1, p. 377.
198 Robert Stevens, 'The final appeal: reform of the House of Lords and the Privy Council 1867–1876', *Law Quarterly Review*, 80 (1964), pp. 343–69.
199 Appellate Jurisdiction Act, 39 and 40 Victoria, c. 59.
200 Stevens, 'The final appeal', p. 363.

Select Bibliography

MANUSCRIPT SOURCES

Bodleian Library:

Carte MSS
Nalson Papers

British Library:

Hargrave MSS 115
Harleian MSS 337; 6686
Landsdowne 266

House of Lords Record Office:

Braye MSS 2
Braye MSS 8
Braye MSS 10
Braye MSS 16–44 (draft journals)
Braye MSS 52
Historical collections
Main Papers collection
Manuscript minutes
Minutes of the Committee for Petitions
Minutes of the Committee for Privileges
Parchment collection

Public Record Office:

C231	Crown Office Docket Book
C33	Entry Book of Decrees and Orders (Chancery)
C78	Chancery Decree Rolls
E126	Entry Book of Orders and Decrees
E159	King's Remembrancer's Memoranda Rolls (Exchequer)
PC2	Privy Council Registers
SP14	State Papers, Domestic Series (James I)
SP16	State Papers, Domestic Series (Charles I)
Wards 9	Book of Orders (Court of Wards and Liveries)

PRINTED SOURCES

Primary:

Atkyns, Sir Robert, *A Treatise on the True and Ancient Jurisdiction of the House of Peers*, London, 1669.

Bond, Maurice, *The Diaries of Sir Edward Dering*, House of Lords Occasional Papers, no. 1, London, 1976

Cobbett, William (ed.), *A Complete Collection of State Trials*, continued by T.J. Howell, 33 vols, London, 1816–26.

Coke, Sir Edward, *The Fourth Part of the Institutes of the Laws of England*, London, 1681.

Dassent, J.R. *et al.* (eds), *Acts of the Privy Council*, 32 vols, London, 1890–1907.

Finch, Sir Henry, *Nomotechnia*, London, 1613.

Firth, C.H., and Rait, R.S. (eds), *Acts and Ordinances of the Interregnum, 1642–1660*, 3 vols, London 1917.

Gardiner, S.R., *Notes of the Debates in the House of Lords taken by Henry Elsyng*, Camden Society, 1st series, vol. 103, London, 1870.

Gardiner, S.R., *Reports of Cases in Star Chamber and High Commission*, Camden Society, new series, vol. 39, London, 1876.

Gardiner, S.R., *Constitutional Documents of the Puritan Revolution, 1625–1660*, Oxford, 1889.

Green M.A.E., (ed.), *Calendar of the Committee for Compounding*, 5 vols, London, 1889–93.

Hale, Sir Matthew, *The Jurisdiction of the Lords' House*, ed. Francis Hargrave London, 1796.

Hardres, Thomas (ed.), *Reports of Cases in the Exchequer 1655–1669*, 2nd edn, Dublin, 1792.

Hargrave, Francis, *A Collection of Tracts Relative to the Laws of England*, London, 1787.

Hatsell, John, *Precedents and Proceedings in the House of Commons*, 4 vols, London, 1818.

Historical Manuscripts Commission, *Third Report*, App., House of Lords MSS.

Historical Manuscripts Commission, *Fourth Report*, App., House of Lords MSS.

Historical Manuscripts Commission, *Fifth Report*, App., House of Lords MSS.

Historical Manuscripts Commission, *Sixth Report*, App., House of Lords MSS.

Historical Manuscripts Commission, *Seventh Report*, App., House of Lords MSS.

Historical Manuscripts Commission, *Eighth Report*, App., House of Lords MSS.

Historical Manuscripts Commission, *Ninth Report*, App., House of Lords MSS.

Holles, Baron Denzil, *The Grand Question Concerning the Judicature of the House of Peers*, London, 1669.

Holles, Baron Denzil, *The Case Stated Concerning the Judicature of the House of Peers in Point of Appeals*, London, 1675.

Giles, Jacob, *A New Law Dictionary*, London, 1729.

Lambarde, William, *Archeion*, London (1635)

Larkin, J.F. and Hughes, Paul L. (eds) *Stuart Royal Proclamations*, 2 vols, Oxford, 1983.

Latham, Robert, and Matthews, William (eds), *The Diary of Samuel Pepys*, 11 vols, Berkeley, 1983.

MacQueen, J.F., *A Practical Treatise on the Appellate Jurisdiction of the House of Lords and the Privy Council*, London, 1842.

Macray, W. Dunn (ed.), *The History of the Civil Wars and Rebellion in England . . . by Edward, Earl of Clarendon*, 6 vols, Oxford, 1958.

Maitland, F.W., *Records of the Parliament Holden at Westminster in the thirty-third year of King Edward I*, Rolls Series, 1893.

Notestein, Wallace, Relf F.H., and Simpson, Hartley (eds), *Commons Debates 1621*, 7 vols, New Haven, Conn., 1935.

Notestein, Wallace, *The Journal of Sir Symonds D'Ewes*, New Haven, Conn., 1923.

Penry, John, *Th'Appellation of John Penri unto the highe court of Parliament, from the bad and injurious dealing of the Archb of Canterb and others his colleagues of the high commission*, London, 1589.

Petyt, William, *Jus Parliamentarium*, London, 1739.

Prynne, William, *A Plea for the Lords*, London, 1648.

Prynne, William, *A Plea for the Lords and the House of Peers*, London, 1658.

Relf, F.H., *Notes of the Debates in the House of Lords in 1621*, Camden Society, 3rd series, vol. 32, London, 1929.

Richardson, H.G., and Sayles, G.O. (eds), *Fleta*, London, 1973.

Rutt, J.T. (ed.), *The Diary of Thomas Burton*, 4 vols, London (1974).

Scott, Sir Walter (ed.), *A Collection of Scarce and Valuable Tracts . . . of the late Lord Somers*, 2nd edn, 13 vols, London, 1809–15.

Scott, W, and Bliss, J. (eds), *The Works of William Laud*, 7 vols, Oxford, 1847–60.

Selden, John, *The Privileges of the Baronage of England when they sit in Parliament*, London, 1642.

Smith, Thomas, *De Republica Anglorum*, ed. Mary Dewar, Cambridge, 1983.

Spedding, James *et al.* (eds), *The Works of Sir Francis Bacon*, 7 vols, London, 1870–6.

Udall, Ephraim, *Communion Comlinesse*, London, 1641.

West, William, *The Second Part of Symboleography*, London, 1594.

Yale, D.E.C. (ed.), *Lord Nottingham's Chancery Cases*, Selden Society, vol. 72, London, 1954.

Yale, D.E.C. (ed.), *Lord Nottingham's Manual of Chancery Practice and Prologomena of Chancery and Equity*, Cambridge, 1965.

Secondary:

Aylmer, G.E., 'Charles I's Commission on Fees', *Bulletin of the Institute of Historical Research*, vol. 31, 1958.

Aylmer, G.E., *The King's Servants, The Civil Service of Charles I*, New York, 1961.

Aylmer, G.E., *The Levellers in the English Revolution*, New York, 1975.

Baker, J.H. (ed.), *Legal Records and the Historian*, London, 1978.

Baker, J.H., *An Introduction to English Legal History*, 2nd edn, London 1979.

Baker, J.H., *The Legal Profession and the Common Law*, London, 1986.

Baldwin, J.F., *The King's Council in England in the Middle Ages*, Oxford, 1913.

Barnes, T.G., 'Due process and slow process in the late Elizabethan and early Stuart Star Chamber', *American Journal of Legal History*, vol. 6 (1962), 221–49, 315–46.

Barnes, T.G., 'Star Chamber litigants and their counsel, 1596–1641', in J.H. Baker (ed.), *Legal Records and the Historian*, London, 1978.

Bell, H.E., *An Introduction to the History and Records of the Court of Wards and Liveries*, Cambridge, 1953.

Bevan, Thomas, 'The appellate jurisdiction of the House of Lords', *Law Quarterly Review*, vol. 17 (1901), pp. 155–70, 357–71.

Bond, Maurice, *A Guide to the Records of Parliament*, London, 1971.

Brooks, C.W., *Pettyfoggers and Vipers of the Commonwealth, The 'Lower' Branch of the Legal Profession in Early Modern England*, Cambridge, 1986.

Bryson, W.H., *The Equity Side of the Exchequer*, Cambridge, 1975.

Cioni, Maria, *Women and Law in Elizabethan England*, New York, 1985.

Cockburn, J.S., *A History of the English Assizes, 1558–1714*, Cambridge, 1972.

Coleman, D.C., *The Economy of England, 1450–1750*, Oxford, 1977.

Collinson, Patrick, *The Religion of Protestants*, Oxford, 1982.

Cope, Ester, *Politics Without Parliaments*, London, 1987.

Cotterell, Mary, 'Interregnum law reform: the Hale Commission of 1652', *English Historical Review*, vol. 82 (1968), pp.689–704.

Dawson, J.P., 'The Privy Council and private law in the Tudor and early Stuart periods', *Michigan Law Review*, vol. 48 (1950), pp. 395–428, 627–56.

Duncan, G.I.O., *The High Court of Delegates*, Cambridge, 1971.

Elton, G.R., *Studies in Tudor and Stuart Politics and Government*, 3 vols, Cambridge, 1974–83.

Elton, G.R., *The Tudor Constitution*, 2nd edn, Cambridge, 1982.

Elton, G.R., *The Parliament of England 1559–1581*, Cambridge, 1986.

Firth, C.H., *The House of Lords during the Civil War*, London, 1910.

Flemion, J.S., 'Slow process, due process, and the High Court of Parliament: a reinterpretation of the revival of judicature in the House of Lords in the 1620s', *Historical Journal*, vol. 17 (1974), pp. 3–16.

Fletcher, Anthony, *The Outbreak of the English Civil War*, London, 1981.

Fletcher, Anthony, *The Reform of the Provinces*, New Haven, Conn., 1986.

Foss, Edward, *The Judges of England*, 9 vols, London, 1848–64.

Foster, E.R., 'The painful labour of Mr Elsyng', *Transactions of the American Philosophical Society*, vol. 62, pt 8 (1972).

Foster, E.R., 'The House of Lords and Ordinances, 1641–1649', *American Journal of Legal History*, vol. 21 (1977), pp. 157–73.

Foster, E.R., 'The journal of the House of Lords for the Long Parliament', in Barbara C. Malament (ed.), *After the Reformation*, Philadelphia, Pa, 1980.

Foster, E.R., *The House of Lords, 1603–49, Structure Procedure and the Nature of its Business*, Chapel Hill, NC, 1983.

Gardiner, S.R., *The History of England*, 10 vols, London, 1883–4.

Gray, C.M., 'The boundaries of equitable function', *American Journal of Legal History*, vol. 20, (1976), pp. 192–266.

Green, I.M., *The Reestablishment of the Church of England, 1660–1663*, Oxford, 1978.

Gregg, Pauline, *Free-born John*, London, 1961.

Guy, J.A., *The Cardinal's Court, The Impact of Thomas Wolsey on Star Chamber*, Totawa, NJ, 1977.

Guy, J.A., 'The origins of the Petition of Right reconsidered', *Historical Journal*, vol. 25 (1982), pp. 289–312.

Habakkuk, H.J., 'The land settlement and the restoration settlement of Charles II', *Transactions of the Royal Historical Society*, 5th series, vol. 28 (1978), pp. 201–22.

Hart, J.S., 'The House of Lords and the appellate jurisdiction in equity', *Parliamentary History*, vol. 2 (1983), pp. 49–70.

Hirst, Derek, 'The Privy Council and problems of enforcement in the 1620s', *Journal of British Studies*, vol. 27 (1977), pp. 46–66.

Hirst, Derek, *Authority and Conflict, England 1603–58*, London, 1986.

Holdsworth, William, *The History of English Law*, 7 vols, London, 1903–24.

Horstman, A.H., 'A new Curia Regis; the judicature of the House of Lords in the 1620s', *Historical Journal*, vol. 25 (1982), pp. 411–22.

Hutton, Ronald, *The Restoration*, London, 1985.

Jones, J.R., *Country and Court, England 1659–1714*, London, 1974.

Jones, W.J., *The Elizabethan Court of Chancery*, Oxford, 1967.

Jones, W.J., *Politics and the Bench*, London, 1971.

Jones, W.J., 'The Crown and the courts', in A.G.R. Smith (ed.), *The Reign of James I and VI*, London, 1973.

Kenyon, J.P., *The Stuart Constitution*, 2nd edn, Cambridge 1986.

Kirafly, A.K.R., *Potter's Historical Introduction to English Law*, 4th edn, London, 1958.

Knafla, L.A., *Law and Politics in Jacobean England, The Tracts of Lord Chancellor Ellesmere*, Cambridge, 1977.

Lambert, Sheila, 'The beginning of printing for the House of Commons', *Library*, 6th series, vol. 3 (1981), pp. 43–61.

Lamont, William, *Marginal Prynne*, London, 1963.

Lindley, Keith, *Fenland Riots and the English Revolution*, London, 1982.

Lockyer, Roger, *Buckingham*, London, 1981.

McIlwain, C.H., *The High Court of Parliament*, New Haven, Conn., 1910.

Maitland, F.W., *Historical Essays*, Cambridge, 1893.

Malament, Barbara (ed.), *After the Reformation*, Philadelphia, Pa, 1980.

Marchant, Ronald, *The Church under the Law*, Cambridge, 1969.

Matthews, Nancy, *William Sheppard, Cromwell's Law Reformer*, Cambridge, 1984.

Milsom, S.F.C, *Historical Foundations of the Common Law*, 2nd edn, London, 1981.

Morrill, J.S., *The Revolt of the Provinces*, 2nd edn, London, 1976.

Morrill, J.S., *Reactions to the English Civil War*, London, 1982.

Morrill, J.S., 'The attack on the church of England in the Long Parliament', in D.E.D Beales and Geoffrey Best (eds), *History Society and the Churches, Essays in Honour of Owen Chadwick*, Cambridge, 1985.

Ogg, David, *England in the Reign of Charles II*, 2nd edn, Oxford, 1984.

Pearl, Valerie, *London and the Outbreak of the Puritan Revolution*, Oxford, 1961.

Phillips, H.E.I., 'The last years of the court of Star Chamber, 1603–1641', *Transactions of the Royal Historical Society*, 4th series, vol. 21 (1939), pp.103–31.

Pike, L.O., *The Constitutional History of the House of Lords*, London, 1894.

Roberts, Clayton, *The Growth of Responsible Government*, Cambridge, 1966.

Russell, Conrad, 'The theory of treason in the trial of Strafford', *English Historical Review*, vol. 80 (1965), pp. 30–50.

Russell, Conrad (ed.), *The Origins of the English Civil War*, London, 1973.

Russell, Conrad, *Parliaments and English Politics, 1621–29*, Oxford, 1979.

Sayles, G.O., *The King's Parliament of England*, New York, 1974.

Scott, W.R., *The Constitution and Finance of English, Scottish and Irish Joint-Stock Companies to 1720*, 3 vols, Cambridge, 1912.

Seaver, Paul, *The Puritan Lectureships*, Stanford, Calif., 1970.

Sharpe, Kevin, 'The Personal Rule of Charles I', in Howard Thomlinson (ed.), *Before the Civil War*, London, 1983.

Shaw, Howard, *The Levellers*, London, 1968.

Shaw, W.A., *The History of the English Church during the Civil Wars and under the Commonwealth*, 2 vols, London, 1900.

Simpson, A.W.B., *An Introduction to the History of Land Law*, Oxford, 1961.

Stevens, Robert, 'The final appeal; reform of the House of Lords and the Privy Council, 1867–76', *Law Quarterly Review*, vol. 80 (1964), pp. 343–69.

Tanner, J.R., *English Constitutional Conflicts of the Seventeenth Century*, Cambridge, 1960.

Thomlinson, Howard, *Before the Civil War*, London, 1983.

Timmis, J.H., *'Thine is the Kingdom'*, *the Trial for Treason of the Earl of Strafford*, University, Alabama, 1974.

Tite, C.G.C., *Impeachment and Parliamentary Judicature in Early Stuart England*, London, 1974.

Trevor-Roper, Hugh, *Archbishop Laud*, Oxford, 1940.

Tuberville, A.S., 'The House of Lords as a court of law', *Law Quarterly Review*, vol. 52 (1936), pp. 189–219.

Turner, E.R., *The Privy Council of England in the Seventeenth and Eighteeenth Centuries, 1603–1784*, 2 vols, Baltimore, Md, 1927.

Tyacke, Nicholas, *The Anti-Calvinists: The Rise of English Arminianism c. 1590–1640*, Oxford, 1987.

Underdown, David, *Pride's Purge, Politics in the Puritan Revolution*, London, 1971.

Usher, Roland, *The Rise and Fall of High Commission*, 2nd edn., Oxford, 1968.

Veall, Donald, *The Popular Movement for Law Reform, 1640–1660*, Oxford, 1970.

Weston, C.C., *English Constitutional History and the House of Lords*, London, 1965.

White, S.D., *Sir Edward Coke and the Grievances of the Commonwealth, 1621–1628*, Chapel Hill, NC, 1979.

Wilson, J.S., 'Sir Henry Spelman and the Royal Commission on Fees, 1622–1640', in J. Conway Davies (ed.), *Studies Presented to Sir Hillary Jenkinson*, London, 1957.

Woods, T.P.S., *Prelude to Civil War, 1642: Mr Justice Malet and the Kentish Petition*, London, 1980.

Wrightson, Keith, *English Society 1580–1680*, London, 1982.

Zaller, Robert, *The Parliament of 1621*, Berkeley, Calif., 1971.

Unpublished Dissertations:

Adamson, J.S.A., 'The peers and politics, 1642–49', PhD thesis, University of Cambridge, 1986.

Crummett, J.B., 'Lay peers in Parliament, 1640–1644', PhD thesis, University of Manchester, 1970.

Hart, J.S., 'The House of Lords and the reformation of justice, 1640–1643', PhD thesis, University of Cambridge, 1985.

Horstman, A.H., 'Justice and the Peers: the judicial activities of the seventeenth-century House of Lords', PhD thesis, University of Berkeley, Calif., 1977.

Glossary of legal terms

Assumpsit An action at common law for breach of promise. Used when the defendant had 'undertaken' to do something, but had failed to perform as promised. It was eventually adapted to suits for debt.

Bill of Middlesex A petition to the court of King's Bench alleging a fictional trespass in the county of Middlesex which allowed the plaintiff to sue for debt in that court.

Bill of Review A petition to the court of Chancery alleging error in the law, which allowed a case to be reconsidered after decree.

Certiorari A writ granted to remove a case or documentation from another court of record.

Cross Bill A bill presented in Chancery which allowed a defendant to initiate a separate set of legal proceedings (usually for discovery of documents or evidence) in a suit commenced by his adversary, the original plaintiff.

Ejectment A trespass action at common law used by lessees to recover land from which they had been ejected, or by lessors to eject tenants whose terms had expired. It was later adapted to try freehold title.

Latitat A writ directed to a sheriff to arrest a defendant presumed to be a resident of Middlesex. Used in conjunction with the bill of Middlesex to allow civil proceedings in King's Bench.

Mandamus A writ directed to local authorities commanding them to undertake a specific task, usually a review of local government proceedings of some kind.

Ne admittas A writ of prohibition directed to a bishop commanding him not to admit a candidate to an ecclesiastical living.

Ne exeat regnum A writ prohibiting a person from leaving the kingdom.

Nisi prius The process of trying civil cases by jury at the local county assizes. The writ actually commanded the sheriff to empanel a jury for one of the central courts in London 'unless before' a specified date the king's justices should appear in the local county.

Novel Disseisin A real action at common law (one of the original petty assizes) which was used to determine freehold title to property. The jury was asked to determine whether the plaintiff had been 'recently dispossessed' of his property.

Quare impedit An action at common law designed to recover the right of presentation to an ecclesiastical benefice (advowson). The writ was directed to a bishop commanding him to present a clergyman to a benefice where there had been a previous obstruction.

Quominus A writ which initiated an action of debt in the court of Exchequer. The writ alleged (usually fictitiously) that the plaintiff was the Crown's debtor and was initiating the action against the defendant in order to make good his primary obligation to the king.

Procedendo A writ which commanded or allowed proceedings to continue in an inferior court, all other writs or process to the contrary notwithstanding.

Significavit A writ, issued on the basis of a bishop's certificate, ordering the imprisonment of an individual who had been excommunicate in excess of 40 days.

Superinstitution   An order granted by a church court which allowed the grantee to supersede an incumbent clergyman's presentation to a benefice, on the presumption that the incumbent's title to the living was suspect. The order anticipated further proceedings at common law to prove title.

Supersedeas   A writ ordering a stay of proceedings in another court.

Index

Notes: References to the notes (eg 101n) indicates that significant (further) information may be found there. The annotation nn means two or more notes refer.